Roppongi Crossing

Roppongi Crossing

THE DEMISE OF A TOKYO NIGHTCLUB DISTRICT AND THE RESHAPING OF A GLOBAL CITY

ROMAN ADRIAN CYBRIWSKY

THE UNIVERSITY OF GEORGIA PRESS

Athens & London

© 2011 by the University of Georgia Press
Athens, Georgia 30602
www.ugapress.org
All rights reserved
Designed by Walton Harris
Set in 10/13 Minion Pro

Printed digitally in the United States of America

Library of Congress Cataloging-in-Publication Data

Cybriwsky, Roman A.
   Roppongi crossing : the demise of a Tokyo nightclub district and the
reshaping of a global city / by Roman Adrian Cybriwsky.
      p.   cm. — (Geographies of justice and social transformation ; 7)
Includes bibliographical references and index.
ISBN-13: 978-0-8203-3831-6
ISBN-10: 0-8203-3831-1
ISBN-13: 978-0-8203-3832-3 (pbk.)
ISBN-10: 0-8203-3832-X (pbk.)
1. City planning—Japan—Tokyo. 2. Nightclubs—Roppongi (Tokyo,
Japan) 3. Roppongi (Tokyo, Japan) I. Title.
HT169.J32T645 2011
307.760952'135—dc22   2010043513

British Library Cataloging-in-Publication Data available

*To honest, hard-working immigrants
and foreign guests, I salute you!*

Believe me,
that was a happy age,
before the age of architects,
before the days of builders.

    —SENECA (4 BC–65 AD)

CONTENTS

FIGURES

TABLES

PREFACE

I did not set out to write a book about Roppongi; it just happened. I returned to Japan in 2001 soon after the death of my wife of nearly twenty-five years, looking for a change from my routines in hometown Philadelphia. I had considered moving to New York City or its doorstep in one of the gritty cities of northern New Jersey, but as I was apartment shopping in Jersey City, I received an unexpected call offering me a position in Tokyo. It would be my third time to live and work for a long period in Japan, and I accepted the job on the spot. An apartment was arranged for me near my work, which turned out to be a short walk from Roppongi, and that is how I began to know the neighborhood.

I had actually known Roppongi from earlier stays in the city because that was where my wife and I took the children to Mass every Sunday and then to lunch afterward. The children had two favorite restaurants, one Indian and the other with golden arches, and we alternated between them. We commuted a long way from the suburbs to pray and eat in Roppongi. Parishioners still come from far and wide for services, and I am happy to report that now, more than a quarter century after we first attended the Franciscan Chapel Center, it is still the rock of Roppongi—fully alive, full of children, and the best kind of international atmosphere.

The nightlife of Roppongi was never a part of my beat, and it entered my horizons only after I had settled nearby in 2001 and found myself coming to the neighborhood every now and then for dinner or relaxation after the day's work. Even in my youthful prime I was not a nightclub person, preferring the university's library or English department lounge as a place to scout around for interesting coeds, and I never would have predicted that by the time my hair had become substantially grey, I would be spending time in the clubs of one of the most famous entertainment districts of one of the greatest cities in the world. But so it happened. In addition to having some fun in Roppongi, I became interested intellectually in what was going on around me, and so the book was born.

It may have been an advantage to know little about such a place at the start, because I began fresh without preconceptions and could move forward by piecing sequential bits of new information together into a story. It did take a long time, however, because Roppongi is many kinds of complicated and is continually in flux. Moreover, it is filled with lies and misdirection, making truth hard to find. As best I could, I tried to package the neighborhood into a book, but it kept eluding me with constant motion and confounding me with contradictory information about what I had thought I already knew. Roppongi was no easy task, I learned again and again, but its many layers of interesting people, different activities, and intellectual challenges attracted me to the undertaking nonetheless. My other Tokyo books were more deliberately planned out; this project simply evolved.

I spend some time in chapter 1 discussing what the research process was like, so I need not go into detail here. However, let me just say that the work became extra challenging because, in the end, Roppongi turned out to be not my favorite place. There are different tastes for different folks, and for me, cruising a library is actually superior by far to what goes on in places like Roppongi. I generally try to be accepting of others' ways, but in Roppongi—that is, in the "bad" Roppongi that everyone now complains about—I truly had to bite my tongue. What is more, I also found myself to be no fan of "New Roppongi"—the upscale, redeveloped visage of the neighborhood that has taken prominence literally since my arrival. Not only are the changes "imperious," but they also do not necessarily produce anything better or even safer—only something different. Thus, I found myself writing about two versions of the neighborhood that, for me, had substantial minuses. I had to wonder about myself for committing such an enormous amount of time and energy to a place that ultimately disagreed with me, and I envied participant-observation researchers who were genuinely fond of their study areas and wrote about them with pride and joy. As I wrote up what I knew, I occasionally longed for other parts of Tokyo: what would have happened had I gotten to know, say, "intellectual" Ochanomizu or one of the several interesting historic neighborhoods along the lower reaches of the Sumida River instead of Roppongi? Certainly, I would have connected better with the "real" Japan and with the greatness of Tokyo.

I also had the problem of having to finish this book back in Philadelphia or on the road during my many travels. (The copyediting was done in Kyiv, Ukraine.) After about six years, my day job changed once more, and from mid-manuscript on, I was writing from thousands of miles away. However, that turned out to be a blessing of sorts in that it forced me to put limits to my data and made me work with what I had. On the other hand, I had developed some close personal relationships in Tokyo, including one in particular that has been very special, and I return again and again several times per year for visits. That, in turn, has led to episodes of what I call "Roppongi frustration"—the realization with each return to the neighborhood that important details have changed, and that I need to rewrite again what I had already written and rewritten to my satisfaction. But finally we have arrived; I have my story and can finish this book. I dot the i's, cross the t's, make final choices about photographs, and can now turn to the pleasurable task of writing acknowledgments.

This could be a long list. Let me start by expressing gratitude to three places that hosted me graciously despite my often minimal purchases for day after day after day of writing and Internet usage: Fishtown's Rocket Cat, the Getty Center near my daughter's home in Los Angeles, Elsewhere and the Foreign Correspondents' Club in Phnom Penh, and my favorite Starbucks in Roppongi, the one nearest Don Quixote. Next are the many kind individuals who showed me around Roppongi, opened doors to places and activities that I would otherwise not have known, and introduced me to key informants. I cannot name them all because of privacy concerns, but I can acknowledge K.K., who a long time ago, before I ever imagined writing a book about Tokyo, introduced me for the first time to Roppongi at night. I take pride that my current friends and acquaintances in Roppongi come from all continents (except Antarctica) and from multiple countries per continent. Some of them also read parts of my text and listened to my interpretations of the neighborhood, offering insider critiques. There were many Japanese among their numbers, of course, and other First-Worlders, many of whom were Roppongi consumers. Quite a few others came to the neighborhood as economic migrants from poor countries or economic chaos and form the backbone of what I call in chapter 4 the Roppongi proletariat. There are plenty of hard-working Japanese proletarians in the neighborhood as well. The bartenders, servers, kitchen staff, hostesses, dancers, musicians, street touts, and other workers all understand the neighborhood more intimately than do members of the Roppongi party crowd, and they were invaluable to me, particularly my dear friends from Belarus, Russia, and Ukraine, as well as those from West Africa. I thank them all and dedicate the book especially to the foreigners who work hard and honestly in Roppongi to better their lives and raise families.

Other people helped with the manuscript more directly by reading and criticizing my text, or by feeding me leads, readings, and explanations. In these regards, I gratefully acknowledge Eugene Aksenoff, Christopher Alexander, Tom Boardman, Kyle Cleveland, David Edgington, Stéphanie Feldman, Tom Gill, Chie Kato, Michi Koiso, Colleen Knapp, Aoi O'Brien, Nan Sato, David Slater, Neil Smith, Mami Suetsugu, Donald Richie, Barbara Thornbury, and most especially the incredible Mayu Ozawa, the world's nicest and most helpful person. I am also indebted to my editor Derek Krissoff for the many improvements to the book that he called for as we moved toward the final version, and for his patience in working with me; to the two excellent and insightful anonymous readers whom Derek had enlisted to review the original manuscript; to my super-sharp-eyed copyeditor Jane Curran for her significant improvements to my writing; to Erin McCann for drawing the maps; to George Baran, Sanjoy Chakravorty, and Richard Joslyn at Temple University, and David Ley and John Western at the University of British Columbia and Syracuse University, respectively, for their support and encouragement as my closest friends and professional colleagues; and to the amazing Rachel Wandless for putting up with me in three countries on three continents during days of writing. I also express heartfelt thanks to Elena Shpak, the principal of Fedotova Productions, for her insightful comments about *Roppongi Crossing* and for permission to reproduce a key photograph from one of her films. Her kind encouragement was instrumental in the birth of *Makarenko Sisters*, a next project for the both of us. Major parts of this film are to be set in Roppongi. My good friends Lera Alexandrova, Ilona Arkhangelska, and Uliana Milova were especially helpful on the scene in Roppongi, as was Viktoria Barysiuk and her staff in a very special restaurant where I had a favorite perch, a favorite singer, and the identification tag "#1" for my stored private bottles of the best vodka. Also very much a part of my world in Tokyo was the very talented Katya and her four-legged "children," Mika and Roka. Finally, I want to thank those who are closest to me because without their care and support I would not have been able to finish: my son Adrian and his beautiful Natalia, my other son, Alex, and my beautiful daughter, Mary Olga.

Roppongi Crossing

CHAPTER ONE

Roppongi and the New Tokyo

Ground Zero for Change

There are two interconnected stories in this book, one about the last years of Roppongi, a famous and controversial nightclub district in one of Tokyo's prestigious central neighborhoods, and the other about Tokyo itself as it changes in step with other great world cities in this time of globalized postindustrial economies and new fashions in urban living. The book's title, which has gone through seemingly 1,001 iterations during the writing process, refers both to the location in Tokyo of a specific place called Roppongi Crossing, the busy street intersection that is the center of the Roppongi playground, and to the fact that for so long and in so many ways what goes on in Roppongi has crossed Tokyo. Most particularly, the neighborhood has found its way to the wrong side of the city's most powerful business and political leaders who together represent the nexus of Japan's concrete-pouring construction state. Their patience with Roppongi's sins had vanished long ago, replaced by equal impatience to get at the hot real estate where Roppongi sits, and they have managed as a consequence to engineer a faster death for the nightclub district than its own rot would have brought. Now they are shaping a high-rise New Roppongi in its place and tout it as the future for Tokyo. Indeed, it seems from their own publicity that they have developed the answer for all urban civilization. Both stories, Roppongi at play and the construction state getting its way, are intriguing; the two together compelled this book.

For most of the second half of the twentieth century, Roppongi was one of the favorite places to play in Tokyo—quite hard after a hard day's work, and for many revelers, in an international atmosphere at that, at least as international as Tokyo had to offer. For most of the second half of the twentieth century as well, Tokyo itself was mostly about work: the center of Japan's economy, the main engine of postwar growth, and center stage for bubble-period wealth and excess. The national economy grew, Tokyo expanded, commuters commuted, and when there was still energy, or when the job called for after-hours, expense account entertainment, the commuters partied. There were many choices as to where, as the city was dotted with quite a few lively *sakariba* ("amusement quarters"; literally, "prosperous" or "flourishing places"). Some, like Ginza and Akasaka, thrived alongside the center of Japan's corporate world and the ministries of national government, while others, like Shinjuku, with its notorious Kabukichō district, were at other commercial nodes, closer to where commuters changed between the city's network of subways to the surface rail lines that, late at night, would finally take them home.

Roppongi was an especially popular choice for merrymaking, certainly from the 1970s through the headiest years of the economic bubble in the 1980s. During those years, the neighborhood was Tokyo's happy capital of disco, though that genre of dance music was but one of the many activities that drew consumers to its night. Roppongi was popular in the 1990s too, by which time clubs had changed to other music, but sometime around the turn of the new millennium, it started a steep slide. The result is that with respect to nightlife Roppongi is now but a shadow of what it once was. One task I've set out to achieve in this book is to explain this change of fortunes. To do so, I track the history of Roppongi beginning with its rise as nighttime playground in the "American" decades after World War II, with pauses at appropriate points to see the nightclub action at its height, and ending with tours of the neighborhood and observations of its routines during a time of decline in the first decade of the 2000s. Chapters 3 and 4 cover the latter portion of that journey, bringing us to the second half of this book in which the other story from Roppongi Crossing, that of its redevelopment, is told.

Regardless of whether one has been to the neighborhood, if one just says the word *Roppongi* in Tokyo, there will be instant name recognition. Everyone knows the place as having been one of the premier nightlife districts in a city that is itself replete with nightlife and as one of only a handful of places in Tokyo that was (and still is to a degree) active all night, as most of the metropolis sleeps during the wee hours and the transit system shuts down. Roppongi has also been one of the few truly international neighborhoods in Tokyo. Despite being Japan's main window to the world, Tokyo has only a small percentage of foreigners and few "ethnic" neighborhoods. In this context Roppongi has stood out as a gathering place for foreigners and as a place where party-minded "international" Japanese come to mix. Not entirely coincidentally, the district is also one of the few areas of the city with a bad reputation. While most of Tokyo is extraordinarily safe from crime and very clean, Roppongi is one of the more dangerous areas, known for being a center of drugs and having more than its share of petty crimes. There are also occasional murders. Parts of Roppongi have also come to be littered and graffitied. As a result, many Tokyoites, both foreigners and Japanese, don't or won't venture into the district, even as other Tokyoites crowd the area almost every evening to enjoy it. Indeed, in recent years the U.S. Department of State has issued warnings to U.S. citizens to stay away because of the crime.

Sadly, some strongly held opinions in Japan blame the ills of Roppongi on its long-standing international character. Roppongi had become, let us say, too international, with foreigners living, working, and profiting in the neighborhood not on Japan's terms but on their own. Moreover, such opinion holders say that the neighborhood was replete not only with foreigners but with "bad foreigners," who bring trouble and detrimental influences to the country. The New Roppongi, and the next incarnation of global Tokyo, for which New Roppongi is a testing ground, should be international too, the vision goes, but selectively so and within measure. Thus the New Roppongi is a primary stage where Japan's officialdom, represented by government, police, and corporate and construction interests, seeks to define and control the directions and pace of Japan's internationalization.

Many in Tokyo are thankful to see that Roppongi is being redeveloped, even if that change is being done in a quite imperious fashion. The same ground where the nightclub district once thrived and then turned dicey is now dotted with new buildings, new activities, and a new class of people. This is what I have referred to as the New Roppongi; a later chapter introduces its denizens and their proper new haunts. The neighborhood transformation is literally one from bare earth to ever taller skyscrapers, giving the neighborhood an entirely fresh look and feel, one not unlike that in the many other upscale and currently fashionable redevelopment zones in great cities around the world—for instance, the London Docklands and Canary Wharf, False Creek in Vancouver, SoMa (South of Market) in San Francisco, and the Docklands of Melbourne, as well as much of what Karen Till (2005) describes as "the New Berlin."

Readers who are familiar with the setting already know the outlines of what I mean by "New Roppongi." First, there is Roppongi Hills, a large, heavily promoted, and privately owned and operated redevelopment project that opened in 2003 to unabashed claims that it represents the future of urban life in Tokyo (or in Japan for that matter); and second is its neighbor, Tokyo Midtown, another ambitious development project, this one opened in March 2007. It is also large, heavily promoted, and privately owned and operated. Both projects are offspring of what I call Japan's construction state, the powerful and cozy alliance between politicians in the top echelons of Tokyo's (and Japan's) long-ruling Liberal Democratic Party (LDP) on the one hand and the country's biggest land development and construction companies on the other. Together, they hold great sway in the country, much like a "military-industrial complex" might rule another country, or generals and rich landowners rule a third. Roppongi Hills is the showpiece project of Mori Building Company, one of the largest and most aggressive real estate development and property management companies in the world, while Midtown is the domain of Mitsui Fudōsan, another of the giants of Japan's oversized construction and land development economy.

The two developments are business competitors located just blocks apart on either side of what is left of the nightclub district. Interestingly, neither acknowledges the other in any of its own promotions, and both have managed to succeed in photographing themselves without a hint of the other in the background. However, both are also tacit partners with common goals over and above just making money. First, they want to remake how Tokyo works and lives, particularly with respect to its form as a commuter city. They would fill the center of the urban donut with nighttime residents, bringing people closer to where they work, workers closer to their families, and everyone closer to a new world of improved recreation, higher cultural life, and green surroundings that are offered as part of a package. Nighttime Roppongi, which these developers say especially loudly has gone terribly bad, is in the way of their progress and needs to be cleaned up. Said cleanup is their second shared goal.

There are other notable new developments in the Roppongi area beyond Roppongi Hills and Midtown. Collectively, they more or less surround the neighborhood's heart, the famous street intersection known as Roppongi Crossing, and promise a complete makeover. It is easy to imagine that before long the last wildness of the night will be gone, and this key part of Tokyo—one located close to embassies for countries around the world, the center of Japanese national government, and the headquarters of a great many major Japanese corporations—will at last be tamed.

Yet, as New Roppongi rises, there is also conflict. Old habits die hard, and livelihoods are at stake in the waning nightclub district, so there are resistance to the changes and some noteworthy struggles to hold on. However, the resistance is mostly faint and fading. "There is nothing left here anymore," said a Nigerian who once had several clubs in the neighborhood, all but one now closed because of lost leases and redevelopment. There is also less than universal approval of what redevelopment brings, even as redevelopment's critics concede that the old Roppongi had gotten to be a bad Roppongi and that Tokyo as a whole, with its millions of lives oriented to harsh commuting, needs a serious fix and a fresh model. Some of what is new in the neighborhood is a disappointment to discerning observers and has brought Roppongi new controversies, new faults, and new rounds of dangers. One won't learn about those aspects of redevelopment from the Mori Building Company and Mitsui Fudōsan publicity machines, both of which are prolific and polished and exist only to advance their respective enterprises. Instead, as with the study of Roppongi's night, my closer look at the New Roppongi is independent, multisided, and based on evidence from fieldwork.

Although this case study focuses on one neighborhood in one city and could stand on its own as an interesting story, the larger scope of this book is about all of Tokyo and its soul, even about all of Japan. Roppongi is a lens through which one can view a myriad of contemporary social and political problems and controversies that come to the fore in Japan's capital city—for example, the delicate subject of the nation's internationalization, its debates about immigrants and immigration policy, and various other issues related to foreign affairs and foreigner affairs. Furthermore, the neighborhood allows one to look with some seriousness at the world of leisure and after-hours entertainment in urban Japan, most notably its characteristic nighttime pleasure zones, of which Roppongi has been a special variant. With respect to Tokyo specifically, powerful business and political leaders in the city have regarded nighttime Roppongi as extraordinarily problematic, as one of the worst neighborhoods in the city if not all of Japan, and envision as a remedy new ways of living, working, and enjoyment on that same space. For them, Roppongi is a blight to be removed and an opportunity for a clean-slate approach to urban living by trend-setting Japanese and their foreigner-peer neighbors—an opportunity not just for a New Roppongi, but also a New Tokyo, a New Japan.

It is an interesting story, this transition from nightlife rhythms to high-rise office towers, five-star hotels, and well-dressed consumers in high-priced shopping malls. This same story is told with different details in cities elsewhere, most notably in the remaking at the end of the twentieth century of Times Square, New York City (Berman 2009; Eliot 2001; Reichl 1999; Sagalyn 2001; Taylor 1991), and in the "bar wars" of London (Hadfield 2006), but the Tokyo context, and the context of Japan more generally, makes this story unique. The phrase "only in Japan" or "with a Tokyo twist" could be applied.

"Roppongi Crossing"

The "Roppongi Crossing" in the book's title refers to the main street intersection in Roppongi, the geographic center of the district.[1] Formed by the crossing of Roppongi-dōri (Roppongi Street) and Gaien Higashi-dōri (Outer Garden East Street), two of the major avenues that stretch through this generally upscale side of Tokyo, it has been the meeting place each evening for thousands of people, sometimes tens of thousands, who emerge there from subway exits and taxis to begin their nights out. The widened sidewalk outside Almond, a landmark coffee shop (*kissaten*) distinguished by bright pink and white striped awnings, had been an especially popular meeting place. "Meet you at Almond" is Tokyo vernacular that nearly everyone understands.[2] A low clock tower at the same corner adds to the "staging area" atmosphere. Up above, on the outside of sound walls encasing the Shuto Expressway, is an English-language sign reading "Roppongi High-Touch Town." Presumably, the slogan is meant to welcome visitors and set a happy tone for the neighborhood, but its exact meaning seems to be lost in translation.[3] It doesn't matter, because that sign is now gone, having been replaced with a stylized "Roppongi Roppongi" that was put in its place in connection with the ongoing reshaping of the neighborhood.[4]

I chose *Roppongi Crossing* as the title for this book because in addition to locating the place about which I am writing, the name also suggests a major theme: that Roppongi is one of the main gathering places in Tokyo and that its gatherings are worth studying. Specifically, Roppongi is one of the main intersections in Tokyo, and indeed in all of Japan, of Japanese people with foreigners. Even though nearly a century and a half has passed since Japan's "opening" to the foreign world near the end of the Tokugawa suzerainty, Japan has never allowed much immigration from abroad and has relatively few foreign residents. Japan has comparatively few foreign tourists as well, particularly when compared to the number of Japanese tourists traveling abroad.[5] While the shōgun's old capital is a more international place than other cities in the country, it too is overwhelmingly Japanese. In only a few places like Roppongi, close to foreign embassies and many of the office buildings of foreign companies doing business in Japan, do we see many foreigners and regular routines of foreigner-Japanese socializing.[6] As a result, Roppongi and a small number of other districts in Tokyo with disproportionate foreigner representation are major venues for Japan's ongoing internationalization, however slow. The history of the district indicates that Roppongi has had such a role for more than fifty years.

Thus, the word *Crossing* is meant to evoke an image of Roppongi as a crossroads of people from around the world. Each day, there are multitudes of interpersonal transactions in company offices, in bars, restaurants, and nightclubs, and even on the streets that reflect the global nature of contemporary Japan's economy. They include both social and business transactions and can take place between Japanese and foreigners, between foreigners of different nationalities, and among Japanese themselves but about foreign business or foreign people. While many of the transactions are between economic equals or peers, grow-

FIGURE 1.1 Street sign marking Roppongi Crossing. The bridge carries a major expressway above the length of Roppongi-dōri, as well as the words "Roppongi Roppongi" that recently replaced the "Roppongi High-Touch Town" slogan.

ing numbers of others involve people from poor countries who have come to Japan to earn a living in a broadly defined "services" sector of the economy. In this way, Roppongi is a crossroads of income transfer from more prosperous Japanese individuals and Japanese companies, as well as from well-heeled foreigners and their companies, to citizens of the Third World and other developing economies. There are many kinds of service jobs involved, both "formal" and "informal"—cooks, dishwashers and servers in restaurants, bar hostesses, bar security or bouncers, sidewalk touts (solicitors for bars, nightclubs and strip clips, and other businesses nearby who often pass out leaflets and offer to escort prospective clients to the door), performers (singers, musicians, dancers, strippers), masseuses/masseurs, prostitutes, and others. There are similar ethnic employment patterns emerging in other Tokyo neighborhoods and across Japan (Ballescas 1992; Komai 2001), although probably not to the same degree as in Roppongi. Studying Roppongi can illuminate this poorly understood side of Japan's economy.[7]

I expect that many Japanese people would be distressed to see that this book considers Roppongi as a place of cultural exchange between their country and the rest of the world. For them, the neighborhood is something of a dirty topic that should be talked about only as a social problem, if at all. It is not the good Japanese who go there, they would say, and those who do frequent the district do not represent the true Japanese in their activities. For such critics, "real" cultural exchanges are about "higher culture" like flower arranging, traditional cuisines, national costumes, business card etiquette, and useful idioms for effective international communication—not Roppongi's dance clubs, provocative fashions, sex talk, and drug and alcohol culture. Likewise, many Japanese would say there are good and bad foreigners who come to Japan and that Roppongi has too many of the latter who are interested in the wrong things. As their numbers grow, the bad foreigners are said to bring new problems and inappropriate lifestyles to Japan. If they are to be studied, it would be to document reasons why they should be arrested and deported. Yet, whatever judgments people make about what goes on in Roppongi, the goings-on do, in fact, go on. With few exceptions about specific topics such as Anne Allison's (1994) superb account of the culture of Roppongi's hostess clubs, this particular neighborhood or any place like it in Japan has not yet been looked at carefully as a subject of ethnographic interest.

As part of the book's subtitle, I settled on the words *and the Reshaping of a Global City*. Here, I call attention to Tokyo's great prominence in the world, hint at a popular buzzword of our times—globalization—that applies very centrally to our case study, and suggest that the city is somehow being reshaped in ways that connect with Roppongi. Together, the two parts of the title indicate that there are two stories in this book, one about the nightclub district centered on a street intersection named Roppongi Crossing and the other about a way of life new to Tokyo that is being shaped with accompanying conflict by Japan's construction state on ground where the club life is now in its last gasps.

Construction State

Imagine this. In the beginning, Tokyo was the shōgun's city, then called Edo, and its social geography was strictly prescribed by the highest authority. The center of the city was the castle and its soaring keep, or tower, the private domain of the shōgun and those closest to him, while outside the protective swirl of walls and moats lived the rest of the population, those with higher rank and connections mostly to one side of the castle on hilly ground called *yamanote*, and the masses of laborers, craftsmen, and merchants to the other side in a river flats area called *shitamachi*. Where Edo played was different still, from 1617 in a designated "licensed quarter" named Yoshiwara.

Several chapters of history later, New Tokyo is the domain of the construction state, the nexus of powerful government ministries and the rich and powerful construction companies with whom they sleep, and a new social geography is being shaped. There are multiple venues for the crossover, including a wholesale transformation of Tokyo's relationship with Tokyo Bay, perhaps the subject for a next book about the city, but Roppongi is indeed a central stage. It is where Mori Building has put up Roppongi Hills and Mitsui Fudōsan touts Tokyo Midtown, both castles of a sort with soaring keeps, and where authority as to who does what and where rests with corporate officials. They own the land and are acquiring more in the neighborhood.

The term *construction state* (sometimes capitalized) comes from the Japanese term *dokken kokka*. A workable definition of the term is provided by Jeffrey Broadbent in a short article for the German Asian Studies periodical *Asien:* "a government which puts much more public investment into the construction of public works than can be realistically justified by public need" (2002). His explication continues by describing an "iron triangle" at the heart of the construction state, consisting of three types of mutually supportive participants: government construction ministries and agencies; a "tribe" of construction-friendly politicians, mostly members of Japan's powerful Liberal Democratic Party (LDP); and construction and real estate development companies in the public sector. The three groups fatten from the large portion of public funds that is allocated for public works, and they engage in collusive practices that cement their positions of power and resist reform movements. Indeed, the term *dokken kokka* is commonly used hand in hand with the word *dango*, which refers to the common practice of rigged bidding for construction contracts. In Jeffrey Kingston's words, "dokken kokka is based on the three C's: cement, construction, and cash" (2004, 128). Some 10 percent of Japan's workforce is engaged in construction, much higher than other countries and more than that in Japan's celebrated automobile and electronics industries combined, and Japan has ranked far and away number one in the world in per capita consumption of cement (25).[8] At the end of the twentieth century, construction accounted for some 15 percent of Japan's GDP and was equivalent in size to the construction industries of the United States and West Europe combined (Westney 2002, 80–83).

There have been many critics of the construction state and its impact on Japan. From among the literature in English, Alex Kerr is probably the most frequently cited for his acclaimed commentary about Japan, *Dogs and Demons* (2001), in which he argues that because of an addiction to the pouring of concrete, Japan has squandered its natural beauty and turned itself into "arguably the world's ugliest country" (14). Kyoto and Tokyo are especially without soul, he writes. Equally damning is Gavan McCormack (1996), who has described a feeling of "emptiness" in a Japan that derives from the blend of corrupt political system and the squandering of hard-earned affluence on needless construction projects. Still another critic is André Sorensen, who has taken a different direction, one focusing on how a corrupt system of construction and allocation of public funds has interfered with sensible urban and environmental planning, resulting in the erection of dubious landmarks instead of projects that meet genuine local needs (2002).

There are many examples of what the construction state has brought to Roppongi, especially in recent years, which is explored in chapter 6 in a discussion of the remaking of the neighborhood. However, there is one older example, dating to 1964, that should be mentioned at this point because it became a Roppongi landmark, albeit a somewhat dubious one, at about the same time that the neighborhood was making its critical transition to becoming a nighttime entertainment district. That landmark, which has been viewed ever since as a local icon, is the Shuto Expressway Number 3, the super highway elevated on concrete pillars above Roppongi-dōri, which runs through the heart of the neighborhood. Built in a rush to prepare Tokyo for the 1964 Summer Olympics, the highway brings shadow and darkness to the street below, divides the neighborhood in half visually, and looms from above over Roppongi Crossing with, until recently, that silly sign: "Roppongi High-Touch Town." Were the highway not there, the intersection could bathe in the same neon glory that distinguishes other busy intersections in the city, such as Shibuya Crossing and Ginza Crossing.[9]

Thankfully, the environmental thugs who recklessly pour concrete to steady Japan's green hill slopes, drop untold thousands of oversized concrete tetrapods along the country's coastline to shore up its beaches, and cover historic rivers and bridges with sky-high highways on concrete piling are no longer visible in Roppongi. Instead, we have construction state developers with aesthetic sense. Their constructions generally have architectural interest and ingenuity and include some of the most pleasing urban landscaping anywhere. Perhaps this is an indication Kingston is right in his assessment that the marked erosion of the supply of the third *C*, cash, which has taken place over the time of Japan's prolonged postbubble economic malaise, combined with a simultaneous strengthening of Japanese civil society, will result in a smaller and weaker iron triangle (Kingston 2004, 122–56). It is also indication that at least in this small part of Japan there is a new generation of construction state at work, one no longer favoring "bridges everywhere to nowhere," as the faltering earlier generation of dokken kokka had done, but zealously advocating instead a neoliberal version of urban life and landscape, whether its recipients want it or not. This is a subject for chapters 5 and 6, as is the new round of faults and dangers that they have brought to the neighborhood.

"The Possible End of Japan"

As an alternative subtitle for this book I considered using the words "And the possible end of Japan." This opens an enormous subject that requires a thick book of its own, but I introduce it here and there as we move from Roppongi to the New Roppongi. I confess, though, that many aspects of this subject are really none of my business, as the future of Japan is something for Japanese to debate, not visitors. I have never felt comfortable with all the sermonizing that goes on in Japan by and among foreigners about what is right and what is wrong with the country, but such commentary is indeed a big business and a popular *gaijin* (foreigner) pastime. I hope that this book does not cross a line of propriety with respect to kibitzing about Japan, and that anything I do say along these lines will be interpreted as I mean it: I have sincere respect for Japan and profound gratitude that the country had welcomed me (and my family) for so many years as a visitor-tourist, resident with visa, and expatriate employee.

"The possible end of Japan" is my small caution about things that I think should concern my Japanese friends. You have a beautiful country and an enormously rich array of cultural traditions and distinctive customs, material culture, and ways of social interaction. Only the dullest of people could fail to appreciate the richness. But at the same time, there seems to be less and less of Japan in Japan, particularly so in Tokyo, where one finds in abundance everything that can be had in the world, but one is left with a sense of cultural confusion and a feeling of placelessness (Richie 1999). These thoughts fit my book not because I admire and hope to preserve the declining nightclub district that is Roppongi's yesterday (I don't), but because I am not impressed either with the New Roppongi that is being built in its place. It alarms me that the new landscape is being billed as Japan's future, or at least Tokyo's future. To be sure, there are nice buildings, fine shops, good places to eat, and fun things to do, but from physical form to the array of possible activities, it is not Japan—it's anywhere in the world, everywhere and nowhere. Modernization, internationalization, new technologies, and attention to leading fashions and global trends are all fine, but the home culture, especially one so bountiful and proud, needs to be preserved too. Despite what they say in their promotional materials, the rich and powerful concrete pourers of the new Tokyo landscape do not appear to give honest attention to that objective.

A Geographer's Approach

My own interest in Roppongi begins with a long-held fascination for knowing as well as I can both the city and the specific neighborhood where I live. This began more years ago than I care to admit during childhood when, perhaps somewhat bizarrely, I drew maps of my immediate neighborhood, and this same interest was later expressed in my doctoral dissertation about a small neighborhood in inner Philadelphia. Later I applied my interests to other neighborhoods and other cities, and then to places abroad. I moved to Tokyo for the first time in 1984 and began to study and write about that city. My 1998 book, so unrealistically overpriced by the publisher that its life was short despite positive reviews, was a product of which I continue to be proud. I returned to Tokyo in 2001, just before the 9/11 shock, and lived and worked within a short walk of Roppongi for nearly six years. I'm too old to be a full participant in the neighborhood's nightlife, but I was drawn by the action nonetheless and got to know enough key people and places well enough to get the project started.

The methodology is one that has served me well before. I spent as much time in Roppongi as a participant-observer as the constraints of my job and my pocketbook allowed, and I made a point of knowing a fair cross-section of its rhythms and activities. There are a number of bars, restaurants, and clubs that I know well and where I am known, plus many others that I made a point to learn about to round out my picture of the neighborhood. I thank a number of my younger friends for their introductions and guide services. There are also many places such as strip bars and sex clubs that I chose not to visit, as well as types of people that I deliberately kept at arm's length. Nevertheless, I made a point of meeting as many different kinds of people as practical, both workers and consumers, and took the trouble to learn Russian in order to navigate the neighborhood better. I had already learned "restaurant and taxi Japanese" and used it as needed, and I have some Japanese ability above this basic level. English is used commonly in most of Roppongi's commercial establishments that feel comfortable with foreigners among their clientele, so most of my longer and more detailed conversations in Roppongi were in English.

The research also involved reading about Roppongi (again mostly in English but also some in Japanese), scheduled interviews with key informants, and archival work for old photographs, news items, and business directories. I also employed original data from my own field surveys about Roppongi's people and businesses. This includes research in both the old, nightlife sections of Roppongi and in the area's new, privately held development projects. These surveys centered on detailed mapping of cultural phenomena (e.g., bars and restaurants by type) in the study areas and can be thought of collectively as traditional-style geographical fieldwork in a type of terrain that is not traditional for geographical work.

I think of my work as spanning some of the themes and methodologies of traditional cultural geography, the academic field in which I was trained, as well as current approaches and issues in social geography.[10] Accordingly, I have given considerable attention to the look of Roppongi—that is, on landscape or cityscape. This emphasis stems from my broader interests in the relationships between built environment and society and reflects a belief that thoughtful analysis of the former can lead to substantial insights about the latter. Urban landscapes are especially interesting in this regard because they reveal much about the people, including both present and past generations, who shaped them. The many layers of development and redevelopment that one typically finds in a city tell of that city's historical progress and the various influences from economics, politics, religion, culture, and other realms that have combined to give that place its particular character. Thus, cityscape is a readable record of urban society that should be studied. For us, the Roppongi landscape is a convenient organizing theme. This is an approach that academic geographers in particular employ in analyzing a city or urban neighborhood and relating an interpretation (Duncan 2004; Ford 1994; Lewis 2003; Relph 1987).

Research in Roppongi

I encountered quite a few specific difficulties in doing fieldwork in Roppongi that I had not fully expected. They were new problems for me, unlike the more usual challenges of urban fieldwork I had done in the past or that I had read about in the methodology chapters of works by other urban ethnographers (e.g., Gans 1962; Suttles 1968; Liebow 1967; Anderson 1990, 2003). Neighborhood ethnographies set in Tokyo were closer to home and were also outstanding, but they too helped only to a point (Bestor 1989, 2004; Gill 2001; Dore 1958; Robertson 1991). Roppongi was a special place, I learned, and getting to know it and preparing to write about it were going to be extra taxing. Anne Allison, a Duke University anthropologist who also did research in Roppongi, and in a hostess club at that, said more or less the same thing in the introduction to her book (1994).

Not the least of my problems were some personal issues, including that research in a neighborhood like Roppongi can be bad for the waistline, hard on the liver, and extremely expensive. Each of these concerns, of course, can be effectively controlled by controlling one's self, but the truth is that Roppongi can be treacherous even to a person with the supposed wisdom of advancing age and can easily win round after round if you are not careful. I lost some rounds on points but never got knocked down, and in the end I was strong enough to feel like a winner.

Other research problems should be of wider interest. One is that Roppongi changes faster than anyone can write about it. So often in the process of preparing this book I found that I needed to update something that I had just written. The months between a nearly finished manuscript and the book appearing in print have been especially frustrating, as Roppongi's motions keep driving my text out of date, forcing me again and again to rewrite this, update that, or insert information about some new incident or land development plan wherever that information seems to fit. Whatever rhythm or flow that I had in writing is constantly disrupted, and the insertions seem, to me at least, to be intrusive and obtrusive, even as they are necessary. For example, in discussing gentrification in Roppongi (chapter 6), I make mention of the opening in the neighborhood of two specific automobile dealerships selling expensive luxury cars. It's a fine example that highlights social change in the area, but it falls apart on me later as the continuing poor economy in Japan causes one of the dealerships to close not long afterward. Even more important in terms of necessitating rewriting and insertions into the text with updated information was the 2009 closing of the Almond coffee shop, Roppongi Crossing's main architectural icon and reference point for giving directions, to make way for redevelopment. I had to search for every mention of this critical landmark in what I had written and make adjustments. On many occasions, I found myself longing for a stable neighborhood and wishing that Roppongi would freeze in time.

Also very important (and another frustration) is that almost by definition, Roppongi is a place where truth is elusive and sometimes impossible to find. There are many shady people in the neighborhood with, I imagine, all sorts of delectable secrets, as well as an entire landscape of false leads, false names, and false fronts. Just asking who owns a particular bar or nightclub can be a violation of social codes, as the establishment could be a front for money laundering, a scheme for evading taxes, or owned illegally by a foreigner who is himself illegally in the country. The *yakuza*, Japan's gangsters, are a major presence in Roppongi. I can assure you from the start that I was not interested in preparing an exposé that would get me killed. Furthermore, I am not so naive to think that I would be able to get inside a criminal organization and have them tell me details that you have not heard. I also assure you that I never wanted to be questioned by police about what details I may or may not know about Roppongi's darker side. Therefore, I declare that I have nothing to offer about the inner workings of the gangster world, be it Japanese or one of Roppongi's many foreign flavors of gangsterism (we have Russian, Israeli, Nigerian, Iranian, Chinese, and Colombian but have run out of Brooklyn and New Jersey), know nothing about sources of drugs, prostitutes, and other illegal activities, and have very little knowledge about who is boss to whom or how the money flows. I saw and learned a lot, yes, but was always mindful that learning too much or asking the wrong kinds of questions could be dangerous, and that declaring publically in advance that "I know nothing" can be intelligent strategy.

It was not just the gangsters that I avoided. I also did not want to attract the attention of police. They, too, are a major presence in the neighborhood, with a large and very busy police station just a few steps from Roppongi Crossing, and are seen quite plainly patrolling the streets in force and trolling for miscreant foreigners. I knew to not break the law, of course, but was also wary that some police officers might be on the wrong side of the law or prejudiced against foreigners. There is evidence of past cozy relations between police and yakuza in Japan, and even more evidence of special problems faced by foreigners in Japan's criminal justice system, beginning with anti-foreigner attitudes by Japan's police forces. Chilling documentation of this difficult and controversial problem, including details about events in Roppongi, is found in the work of Debito Arudou, a naturalized Japanese citizen who is a leading crusader against anti-foreigner discrimination in the country (e.g., Arudou 2004; Arudou and Higuchi 2008; and his blog at www.debito.org).

The police station in Roppongi has a particular reputation for being tough on foreigners, probably because there are so many tough foreigners in Roppongi. I've had friends and acquaintances who were not so lucky and spent time locked up at the Azabu Police Station (as the Roppongi office is called) for a variety of charges including visa violations, narcotics offenses, and fighting, as well as one case of theft, which was probably a setup, and one case of murder related to international drug dealing, in which the police were almost certainly on target. Some of those friends and acquaintances became informants for this study. I also wanted to avoid being interviewed by police about my contacts and their activities and for a time feared that I could be called in to disclose what I knew about Roppongi characters who might have my phone number or business card in their possession.

Likewise, I found Roppongi to be a difficult place because it often went against my conceptions of what is right or proper. There is a lot that goes on in the neighborhood that many people find objectionable or even reprehensible, not to mention activities that are also illegal. Not only are there are the illegal drugs of various sorts, prostitution on the streets and via clubs and escort services, and various types of con artists, pickpockets, and other criminals, but there is also considerable drunkenness and late-night vomiting, occasional barroom or street brawls, meat-market sex, and other unsavory activities that most people would stay away from. How close do I want to be to activities or individuals that I would normally avoid in order to get the story? Do I need to see everything with my own eyes in order to report on it, or can I take as fact that stripping goes on in strip clubs, that the massages I am offered on the street late at night by smiling Chinese girls aren't just to relax tired muscles, and that there is something shady about the prosperous-looking young guy wearing sunglasses after midnight in his shiny Hummer? Thus, not only did I stay away from yakuza because I didn't want to be killed, and away from police to avoid arrest or interrogation, but I also kept a respectable distance from strip clubs and hostess clubs, bars full of drunks, and other places where either the services offered or the clientele disagreed with me. However, sometimes it was necessary to visit such establishments and even spend a bit of money because I needed to understand something better or see something with my own eyes. I kept such evenings to a minimum and avoided becoming a regular in places in which I would not want to be with my adult children.

There were also places that I was not part of either because I knew I would not be welcome or because I knew that I did not belong. For example, among the many types of bars in Roppongi are the "members' bars" or "members clubs." Many of them are tiny establishments on the higher floors of tall, narrow "entertainment buildings," while a smaller number are larger in size, with a stage and with entertainment such as strippers and sex shows. They have a regular, returning clientele, and only members and invited guests are able to get in. In turn, to become a member you need a proper introduction and a large entry fee. You also probably need to be Japanese. This is the private world of Japanese businessmen and high-placed government bureaucrats and their interactions, as well as their interactions with the young women who are paid to entertain them. To my eyes, it is also the world of shady-looking characters who control access. Architectural cues such as out-of-the-way locations on high floors and small, Japanese-only signage also make it clear that outsiders, most especially foreigners, should go elsewhere. I did get some roundabout insights into this world: through employees that I met by happenstance offsite who would tell a bit about what's inside. Thus, "leaked information" occasionally came my way from people in the kitchens, from waiting limousine drivers, and from some of the women who are paid to be private entertainment.

Other types of places where I did not feel particularly welcome or comfortable were young people's clubs such as those that specialize in hip-hop. Foreigners might be plentiful in such places, but certainly not those my age. Besides, hip-hop doesn't particularly appeal to me. So, except for the shortest of peeks into some of the most popular and central of young people's spots, I chose to stay away. I had learned my lesson about the age gap some time earlier, still in the United States, when I entered a club of twenty-somethings (or were they even younger and underage?), and someone wisecracked loudly, "Someone's dad is here looking for them." For insights to hip-hop clubs and other genres with which I was not familiar, I relied on my students for advice and on my colleague Kyle Cleveland, an accomplished sociologist of hip-hop, with whom I had dozens of conversations about Roppongi and the clubs in other parts of Tokyo where he has done his research.

Many ethnographers get to like the people about whom they write. In Tokyo, for example, anthropologist Ted Bestor had warm and friendly relationships with the people of Miyamoto-chō, the name he gave to the blue-collar residential neighborhood that was the subject of his first book, and warm relationships again in Tsukiji, Tokyo's fish market district, which he wrote about in a subsequent book (Bestor 1989, 2004). On the other hand, I never got to like Roppongi's yakuza, even after considering that if I met individual members outside their work environment, for example, as residential neighbors, they might actually be pleasant human beings. I also never got warm feelings about highly placed Japanese bureaucrats and salarymen who came regularly after work to Roppongi, spending huge sums of taxpayers' or company money on girls and drink, or about the most obvious and obnoxious cocksure males from prosperous Western countries for whom Roppongi was nothing more than an easy sexual hunting ground. The types of foreign guys who brought inebriated Japanese girls to men's rooms in bars for quick sex, or who insisted on fondling their inebriated dates in public, were not to become my friends. (I didn't particularly care for their girlfriends either.) Yet, all these people, plus other types of undesirables (to my taste), were key parts of the Roppongi scene. To learn the neighborhood, I had to interact with them at least a little. It was a bit of a juggling act to hang around where I felt uncomfortable and a challenge sometimes to bite my tongue.

Nevertheless, I did manage, quite naturally and easily it turned out, to make many friends in Roppongi, including a number of very close friends who I am sure will be with me for the duration. I told them early on that I was working on a book and asked for help. Some friends were Roppongi consumers—regular customers of particular clubs or restaurants who shared insights with me and introduced me to other insiders, who in turn gave me access to still others. Many other friends were workers—owners and managers of clubs and restaurants and employees such as bartenders, wait staff, kitchen helpers, and bouncers. I also got to know and befriended several hostesses and escorts (also females), as well as former hostesses and escorts, who took me around Roppongi to show me their particular ropes. Quite a number of my new friends spent time with me outside the neighborhood (and even far beyond Tokyo) discussing Roppongi and related topics. Because we had become friends, my particular interests in Roppongi became interests for them, and some were kind enough to go quite far out of their way to provide insider peeks at what goes on. I was especially happy to be able to go often as an escort to the so-called models' bars, where models and hostesses and other beautiful women (and male models) drink for free to bring in the crowds. I wish that I could insert at this point a photo of me in some hot club in the company of one or more hot women in order to brag about my status as a Roppongi insider, but that would definitely not be cool, and my children would not be proud.

Just for the record, I add that I was never once a client of these friends (or of anyone else in Roppongi). My close friends and I were comfortable with one another other as individuals, not because of our professions or any provider-client relationships, and we continue to be personal friends even now after I've left Japan. My access to this particular world was through a long chain of rewarding personal introductions that began with the first of these individuals, still a close friend, whom I was lucky to meet on my own. Fans of the classic American television series *Seinfeld* will understand what I mean in saying that, like George Costanza, I was admitted to the "forbidden city" and had my hand stamped forevermore thanks to my own circle of Jillians, not photos but real spirit and flesh.[11] Had I shown interest in having sex or a romantic relationships with any of a number of my contacts in Roppongi, those friendships and conversations would have been over and my hand unstamped. For people who get hit on as a lifestyle, and maybe even a livelihood, a warm friend who prefers the inner person to the person presented in public wins trust and gets the edge.

I was also fortunate to link into various ethnic networks. In addition to the many Japanese contacts and friends, there were Americans and other Western expatriates who worked at career-step jobs in the office buildings nearby for multinational corporations, or who lived nearby in the many better apartment complexes and who came to Roppongi after hours to relax. Also, there were officials and employees from foreign embassies nearby, including the very large U.S. Embassy. I also got to know quite a few U.S. soldiers, although their stays in Tokyo were almost always short, and our conversations would be for one time only. The U.S. military played a huge role in the initial shaping of Roppongi into a nightlife spot, as the neighborhood has long been a popular R&R (rest and recuperation) spot for American military personnel in Asia. Given the dangers to which American soldiers are being put these days in Afghanistan and elsewhere, I was often motivated to buy drinks for individuals or pairs of soldiers who looked lost and out of place in Roppongi, and who were clearly far from home.

Other networks were with many Third Worlders, most of them workers. In a later chapter I introduce them as "Roppongi's proletariat." There were people from Mexico, Brazil, and Colombia, as well as from Iran, Sri Lanka, West Africa, and various countries in Southeast Asia, all working in clubs and restaurants or as hostesses and escorts. But far and away, my most numerous and strongest contacts were with East Europeans—both men and women, but especially women from Poland, Romania, Ukraine, and Belarus, and with Russians from East Europe and Asian Russia. Being of Ukrainian background myself and speaking Ukrainian from childhood, I felt a cultural affinity to these people. Because Russian was the language that bound many of my friends together, I made efforts to improve my college Russian, paying for lessons from a close Russian friend from Ukraine who was especially adept at scolding me for Ukrainian vocabulary and accent when I was supposed to be speaking Russian. A fair assessment is to say that I am conversant. Like the American soldiers who were happy to meet a supportive friend far from home, I made most of my close and lasting friendships in Roppongi with Russian and Ukrainian speakers who also were far from home and in need of a friendly face and personal support. If there was any exchange that was made in these friendships other than what I paid for my language lessons, it was this: I offered my sympathetic, dare I say "fatherly," ear about their many difficulties in Japan in exchange for information about their work life in Roppongi and places like it and introductions to still more new friends.

Somewhat ironically, as I was working on this section of this chapter on my laptop in a favorite Roppongi Starbucks, a stripper-prostitute from a Latin American country asked to join me at my table. There were other seats available, but she wanted to find out who I was. All of us Roppongi regulars look familiar to one another, particularly if there is something distinguishing about one's appearance, and she explained that she had seen me around in some of the places I do visit (not the place where she works) and noted that I keep attractive company. Who am I and what am I up to is what she wanted to know. She may have just been curious about me, exactly as she said, or she may have been prospecting for gold, most probably a well-rehearsed pastime for her. Regardless, the exchange opened a door to yet another avenue of information and insight, and to a new network. Had I shown any romantic or sexual interest, the conversation would have stopped, except perhaps possibly to take a provider-client turn. I didn't do that, and the result was a good conversation and the start of a small but short-lived friendship that lasted until, it seems, she left Roppongi and perhaps Japan altogether. Had I been good at her native language, the friendship may have become closer, or I may have become friends with one of the several compatriots to whom she introduced me. But without the natural connection that comes with sharing a language in an alien country, as there was for me with the Slavs, this particular exchange yielded only so much toward this book.

Research in the New Roppongi

Not all of the research was about nightlife. The other major aspect of Roppongi, New Roppongi, represented by the large new redevelopment projects with giant office towers, international hotels, upscale shopping malls, and new art museums and concert halls, is also a significant part of this two-story book. This newer and more formal Roppongi—the Roppongi of the suits and ties—is also international and also a case in point of "Roppongi Crossing." It is as interesting from an ethnographic standpoint as the rhythms of the Roppongi night. I look at this side of Roppongi too in this book, beginning with chapters near the end where the new Roppongi is introduced in part as a convenient and deliberate strategy to wipe away a nighttime Roppongi gone bad and to usher in what powerful political and business interests in Japan consider to be a higher level and more appropriate form of internationalism. The inhabitants of this Roppongi are a different crowd than that among the nightclubs. They are not always in suits and ties (or the equivalent dress for women), but they are always well dressed nonetheless, very self-consciously so, even when in casual attire, and are always sober, well behaved and well mannered. Probably most are also well-heeled. Age levels are generally older than those for the Roppongi night crowd, with many individuals being even older than I am. There are also well-heeled and well-dressed younger people, say those in their twenties, enjoying the high culture and elite shopping of the New Roppongi. Both they and their middle-aged and older co-culturalists represent a new kind of urban lifestyle in Tokyo, of which they are very much aware and which they promote with confidence and enthusiasm. Therefore, they too get studied and written about.

This part of the research also involves ethnographic work and participant observation. However, the focus now is not on bars and nightclubs (except perhaps some meat-market singles bars that are built into the new office tower complexes to attract yuppies after work), but instead on social routines in glitzy new shopping centers, fancy hotel lobbies and restaurants, other new upscale restaurants (some of them elegant, French, and very expensive), and in the three new art museums in Roppongi, the new concert halls, and other new performance venues. Indeed, sometimes it seems that there have been two study areas for this research, both worlds apart and very different from one another, yet separated by blocks and half-blocks rather than miles, and by the clock: the old Roppongi is that of the night while the New Roppongi populates the neighborhood during the day.

In contrast to the nightclub world, for which one has to dig and dig again for information, there is a considerable public record about the shaping of Roppongi's big redevelopment projects, about builders' plans and intentions, and about new people, events, and other topics. One can dig, too, for deeper details about the developers, financing arrangements, political deals, and other insider information, but my analysis of "New Roppongi" did not go that far. For my purposes, it was enough to demonstrate how and why Roppongi was changing and to introduce in a general way its new denizens and their rhythms without taking on the separate project of uncovering details about the redevelopment process and its actors. In fact, I wonder if I would have gotten very far at all if I had attempted a more energetic analysis of, say, the inner workings of the Mori Building Company. I suspect that I would have continuously been fed the same diet of public relations information that was available with less output of energy, and that true insider information would have been as difficult to obtain as insider information about the shōgun's private activities when he was shaping Edo.

I am satisfied that even without privileged access I am able to provide a fair and accurate picture of Roppongi's newer aspects. I was a participant-observer and note-taker since the opening of every successive project, and I have studied the extensive public record that Roppongi redevelopment has generated. Among other sources, I benefited from advertising and publicity documents provided by the developers, some new books that have come out about the new projects (mostly of a promotional nature), newspaper and magazine articles about the projects and about the news-making events that have taken place there (e.g., a young boy had his head crushed by a malfunctioning revolving door at the entry of Mori Tower; see chapter 6), Internet Web sites and blogger commentary, and the formal tours that one can purchase to learn about architecture, design, and other local details. Also, it helped that in contrast to the nightclubs, which for me were an entirely new experience, much of New Roppongi was familiar to me from the outset. Its designs and styles have been in place for some time in other cities around the world and were known to me personally in such cities as New York, Philadelphia, Vancouver, and Singapore. Furthermore, I have experience in both Philadelphia and Vancouver in studying urban planning and project promotion documents as cultural texts (e.g., Cybriwsky 1988; Cybriwsky, Ley, and Western 1986), and I felt comfortable in applying the methodological approaches that served me with success for insights to similar changes in Tokyo. Finally, I was familiar with a large academic literature from North America, West Europe, and elsewhere that helped me put the neoliberal transformation of Tokyo into broader context.[12]

Truth and Accuracy in Roppongi

In the early stages of my inquiries, when I was just beginning to meet insiders in Roppongi and getting my first glimpses behind the scenes, I was at a small party in a private apartment and asked one of the other guests, a young Russian male, what he did for a living. "What do I do?" he shot back at me. "You ask me what I do? Let me tell you something: never, ever ask a Russian what he does! The answer for all of us is the same: we do whatever it takes to make a living." He was angry that I would ask a personal question, the answer to which was privileged information, and was perhaps surprised at my naïveté in asking it. But an hour or so later he softened, maybe because he felt bad about having spoken so sharply to an elder, or perhaps because my friend who had brought me to the gathering had vouched for me, and he responded by telling me about his import and sales business. He had found a niche commodity that could be bought cheaply abroad, imported legally to Japan, and sold at a huge markup to a particular slice of the Japanese consumer market. I was greatly impressed at how clever he was to have developed this particular angle, as I never would have been able to identify such an opportunity, and I understood as he told me that he had not wanted to provide the information earlier because of the need to protect business secrets from potential competitors. But as he spoke, my internal BS detector was quietly telling me that I was getting the polite answer, but not the whole answer. In the following months, as I got to know this person better and developed something of a friendship, I learned that the business about which he had told me was one that he had already essentially abandoned because competitors—Russians and other foreigners—had entered the market and undercut his income. I saw, instead, that this entrepreneur seemed to make his living from many sources—a little business deal here, another one there, a modest income pipeline somewhere else, and a one-shot opportunity in still another venture. Indeed, he may have identified still another niche commodity to import but was telling no one anything at all about it. It was just as he had said: he was doing whatever it takes.

A second story about truth concerns one of my closest Roppongi friends, now certainly a friend for life, an important contributor to my understanding of the neighborhood, and a source of multiple personal introductions that proved to be extremely valuable. She also lied to me at the start of our relationship, but her reasons were different than those of the Russian businessman above. Her biggest lie was about her name. It was only after about a month had passed and we had already gotten together about a half dozen times that she confessed, with great embarrassment, that she was not really "Masha" and that the cell phone number that she had given me was for her "other phone," one reserved for the out-world, people she did not know well and could not trust or people she might want to exploit. She genuinely liked me now, she said, and was switching me to her in-world, if I would forgive her. I did, although I still tease her by introducing her as "Masha" to people she'll never see again, and I entered her real-people number into my phone. Lots of people work in Roppongi behind false names because lots of people do shady things. She had thought on the first day that our relationship might be one of hostess-client, only without the base of a hostess bar. Since that experience, I have seen many Roppongi hostesses juggling not one, not two, but three cell phones, maintaining different identities to protect privacy, and maximizing opportunities for mining gold.

The reason for telling these stories is to illustrate that even in a circle of friends, as opposed to the murky world of gangsters and other strangers, truth can be hard to come by. In a competitive environment, as well as in an environment where one doesn't know for sure who is who, it is often wise to guard the truth, as the Russian fellow had done. It might also be strategic to be downright untruthful at times, as "Masha" was with me for a short while. Researchers everywhere face this kind of challenge, but as I have said, I found Roppongi to be especially difficult in this regard. That's one of the reasons why it was necessary to make close friendships in the study area. In establishing genuine personal relationships with people engaged with Roppongi, I was provided insights that I would not have had otherwise and that, I think, are critical ingredients for an interesting social-geographical profile of the neighborhood.

The "truth and accuracy" situation is a bit different with respect to the New Roppongi. Yes, the nightclub world is murky and full of lies, false leads, and misdirection, while the New Roppongi offers Web sites, informational brochures, friendly interviews, and cheerful responses to requests for information. Yet, a BS detector is needed in the New Roppongi too, even much more so than in the world of the night. At least when it is night, you expect darkness and act accordingly. The New Roppongi, however, is not necessarily more transparent and can be even more deceptive. It is a publicity machine operated by publicity professionals, and it comes at you with the same publicity message in different ways from different directions. Thus, it is easy to mistake message for fact. In the world of the nightclubs, one can build personal relationships, gain trust, and eventually get somewhere close to the truth. In the corporate world of the New Roppongi, by contrast, there can be nothing that is heart to heart, because on their side, at least, there is no heart; instead, there are only filters, spinmeisters, and official versions standing between the researcher and the real story.

Identifying People and Places

"Masha" is my pseudonym for the false name that my friend mentioned above had given me when we first met. I'm not even offering a pseudonym for her real name, as I have decided not to write about particular individuals directly and not to name names. I did this to promise confidentiality to specific informants precisely because I needed to gain their trust. People do have secrets of all kinds: about how they earn their incomes and how much there is, about their visa status, about their personal relationships, and, as I have just said, even about their real names, and they want those secrets to be kept. Most of these details, even those that are innocent and not against any laws, are no one else's business. Besides, what is said about Las Vegas (in current advertising to draw more visitors to the desert city) is also said of Roppongi: what happens there stays there. For many of the people I came to know, Roppongi provides a diversion from daily routines and freedoms from social controls such as those by employers, spouses, and society at large. If I were too telling, I could get some people in trouble. Moreover, I realized that I could conceivably be in a position someday to be asked for details about people I know by authorities with official interests in them. As long as my study area was to be known publicly, meaning that I could not disguise Roppongi with a false name and location as authors have done for their less famous fieldwork sites, it made sense that I be as discreet as possible about the identities of my contacts.

There were special concerns with regards to photography in Roppongi. I am an avid picture taker and have thousands of digital images from the neighborhood, both from the day and the night. The jpegs record data and help jog my memory as I write. Quite a few of the photographs show privileged details and could greatly enrich this book were it not for matters of confidentiality and respect for their subjects. It has been a struggle to select the exact photographs to insert in the book, because of conflicts between a desire to back up what I write with photographic evidence and a need to protect people's rights to privacy. The latter need is a higher priority, so with respect to scenes such those of policing in Roppongi, illegal activity, public inebriation, the action in nightclubs, and the Roppongi proletariat at work, all my hard-earned best shots have to remain in my personal files. Unfortunately, this applies as well to photographs that I would have wanted to use to present a sympathetic portrait of specific subjects—for example, to show the hard, honest work that occupies most members of the Roppongi proletariat. Furthermore, I am not the police and did not want to publish photographs of a type that police take with their now-ubiquitous security cameras in the neighborhood and their own surreptitious photographers.[13] The photos with recognizable faces that I do include in the book are printed with permission or with an understanding that the scene is innocuous and no one is shown in any compromising situation. In other photographs, darkness and distance help to maintain privacy.

On the other hand, there were those individuals who saw the preparation of this book as a chance for personal publicity. This was particularly true for owners and managers of business establishments who expressed interest in having me write a positive "review." Not only was I not willing to do that, even for the best of friends in the best of establishments, because it would call into question my objectivity and motivations, but I also did not want to provide any free advertising for places that I found disagreeable. And most certainly, of course, I do not want the book to be considered as a guide for where to find what in Roppongi. The Internet, published guide books, paid advertising, and aggressive street touts take care of that need. And to the several informants who expressed disappointment that they themselves would not be identified in the book ("But I've always wanted to be in a book!"), I explained why and assured them, as I repeat now, that even though their names and other identifying information are not here, they are indeed very much a part of this book. With very few exceptions, the only true names that are given are for individuals and business establishments that are no longer on the scene; the exceptions are for good reason.

I anticipate receiving criticisms from readers for my not knowing every aspect of Roppongi and for having made deliberate choices about where to go in the neighborhood and where not to go. Indeed, the social scientist in me says that I need to cover every part of the study area equally and objectively, and that it biases research to follow personal preferences about any categories of activities, types of people, or types of places. However, the better social scientist in me understands that one cannot be a genuine insider in every part of a complex, competitive, and tension-filled social world, no matter how small it is geographically. One needs to do what I tried to do: gain as broad a knowledge as possible of as many aspects of the study area and its diverse social worlds within the larger social world, but then learn well at least one of those smaller social worlds, one that is important in the study area and generally not well understood. Thank you, "Masha" and, before her, "Irina," for getting me started in Russian Roppongi, and for the leads that Russian Roppongi gave me to its overlapping social worlds that are discussed in ensuing pages—those of African streetmen, professional hostesses and professional models, and the worlds of what I call the "Roppongi proletariat," the great many people, many of them economic migrants from developing countries, who work extraordinarily hard as wait staff in restaurants and bars or as bartenders, cooks, dishwashers, and other occupations that make the Roppongi playground possible.

I also expect to receive criticisms from readers who can't find themselves or their own particular Roppongi worlds in these pages. "How can he claim to know Roppongi," their argument would go, "when he hasn't been to [critic's favorite bar] or has not apparently interviewed [the king of all Roppongi insiders as defined by the critic]?" Even more, "Who is he?" the questions might continue, "I've never met him and I am in Roppongi all the time." I've thought about these issues a lot and have discussed them as openly as I could, including one time in a very well-attended public presentation that I (very cleverly) entitled "Trying Fieldwork in Roppongi" at a conference in Tokyo of the organization Anthropologists of Japan in Japan.[14] My answer is that no two writers' or scholars' books about Roppongi would be alike, that Roppongi is so complex and has so many aspects that all researchers would be forced both to make choices about subtopics and to be guided by whatever "breaks" for them as they get to know the neighborhood. I might also wonder if such critics might not be delusional in thinking that Roppongi centers on them and their particular worlds. There are no "Kings of Roppongi" except for the self-enthroned, and no crowns to fit such heads. The district centers on no one and on no specific type of activity. The better measure of the worth for a work like this is not the completeness of its inventory or the specific place where it finds its center, but rather the quality of the selected stories that it does tell and the soundness of lessons or interpretations that are drawn from those stories. It is in these areas that I hope not to disappoint.

I learned through my work that research in Roppongi requires a good internal BS detector, a long time commitment, and many sources of information. It requires as well accepting the fact that the full truth, a completely rounded picture, or the whole story can never be known. The best one can do is to present certain slices of the Roppongi apple. Someone else may have cut the apple differently. No one can be in all segments of Roppongi equally; every researcher would have her or his own stance in the neighborhood. Let's say that there is someone else working on Roppongi at the same time on similar questions, independent of my presence. Let's say that this researcher is a she, is younger, speaks Japanese really well, or is Japanese, and also speaks English and, say, Farsi, opening doors wider to the many Iranians in the neighborhood. Or maybe this person speaks Mandarin as an additional language, facilitating access to the many newcomers to the area who know only that language. Other things being equal, would our books be the same? Of course not. Would our books be contradictory of each other? Let's hope not. Let's hope that we both write truths and provide interesting insights, even if they are different truths and different insights. And let us hope, too, that we both write fairly about the New Roppongi, giving credit where it is due, but also being careful to evaluate what we see, hear and read. Both researchers, we need to understand, are equally vulnerable to and depend on the same powerful publicity machine for information.

Organization of Chapters

I have organized my presentation into seven chapters. This chapter introduces the study area and its basic social contours and makes a first-level distinction between Roppongi, New Roppongi, and the reshaping of Tokyo in general into New Tokyo. The orientation to the study area continues in the next chapter,

"Roppongi Context." It begins with an overview of what Tokyo living is like for many of its residents, with a focus on aspects that need reform. Next, I locate Roppongi within Tokyo, not just on the map, but also in the context of the spatial and social ecology of the city specifically and the context of Japanese society more generally. I discuss how Roppongi has long been a better address in Tokyo, and how it continues to be physically near and culturally well connected to the main centers of political and economic power in Japan. I also connect Roppongi to the storied tradition of adult entertainment districts in urban Japan, to Japan's traditions of geishas and hostesses, and to the history of foreigner population and foreigner entertainment districts in Japan. In chapter 3, "Roppongi Rises," I trace the history of Roppongi, focusing mostly on how and why the neighborhood became an entertainment district. I beginning with early history when the land housed the estates of important samurai and other elites in the government of the shōguns, trace Roppongi's rise as a base for Japan's military, and then examine the time after World War II when U.S. occupation troops were based nearby and came to Roppongi Crossing for relaxation and social diversion. The chapter ends with a look at the Japanese economic bubble in the 1980s to early 1990s, when disco was king and Roppongi embodied the excesses of a newly rich Japanese society gone wild.

Analysis of contemporary Roppongi begins with chapter 4, "Roppongi Rhythms, Recently." I tour the neighborhood's nightclub district to discuss the various kinds of entertainment and diversions that it offers today (or at least before the New Roppongi deluge) and to get a sense of the ebb and flow of activities over the course of a typical day and night. I introduce some of the people in Roppongi, most particularly the foreign workers who provide much of the neighborhood's entertainment, wait on tables, serve drinks, and labor in kitchens. The word *Recently* was added to the chapter title as an afterthought because Roppongi changes faster than I can type, and because I want to cover myself for those eventualities when specific details are no longer accurate after the manuscript has left my hands.

Chapter 5, "Roppongi Troubles," is divided into three sections about the neighborhood's decline: (1) Roppongi's transition from widely popular playground to various problems such as rising crime, prostitution, and drug abuse; (2) a middle section about police action and other strategies to reclaim the neighborhood from "bad elements;" and (3) "Receding Rhythms," a section about resultant declines in the local nightlife economy. Considerable attention is given to the much-discussed (in Japan) but not proven correlation between the growth of trouble and the presence of "bad foreigners" in the neighborhood. In midchapter I reflect on the role of the yakuza in Roppongi's troubles, and on why so little of the discourse about fixing Roppongi points in their direction.

In chapter 6, "Roppongi Remade," I examine the completion of various upscale, mixed-use megastructure urban redevelopment projects. The new landscape now surrounds the entertainment district, which is receding as a result of being squeezed from all directions. In addition to the new physical form, there is a new population in Roppongi—consumers, yes, but also residents in the neighborhood and highly paid employees in new slices of the Roppongi economy. The last chapter, "Roppongi Reflections," offers some concluding thoughts about Roppongi and links the neighborhood's transitions to processes of urban change more generally. It is there that I impose a final kibitz about the "possible end of Japan" subtheme.

CHAPTER TWO

Roppongi Context

"The Tokyo Problem"

Perhaps the most enduring images of life in contemporary Tokyo are those of its notorious commutes to work. For millions of people each day, this is a journey by bus, train, or subway, sometimes all three combined plus walking at either end, that takes an hour, two hours, or even more just one way. During rush hour times on the most crowded lines, the conditions can be nothing less than awful as riders stand packed in moving train cars like sardines in an upright can. They are barely able to move, much less read a newspaper or converse, and are jabbed again and again by briefcases, umbrellas, and elbows. "Pushers" in white gloves work some of the most crowded train platforms at peak times, using polite muscle power to jam still more passengers and their belongings into seemingly nonexistent spaces before the sliding doors close. People find solace in the music they pipe through personal earphones or the games they play on their hand phones, but all in all, day after day, year after year, the ride to and from work and school in the Tokyo metropolitan area is misery for the masses of the metropolis.

A root cause is that Tokyo is so big. With a population of more than thirty million in the metropolitan area and a commuter shed that extends more than a hundred kilometers from the center, the Tokyo metropolis is the biggest in the world, and its center is the world's single largest commuter magnet. People live far away because living closer in is overly crowded and expensive. Rents and house prices fall with increasing distance from the center, so budget-minded families and individuals trade time and comfort for space, affordability, and perhaps some extra greenery. Things have gotten somewhat better with more trains and faster rides, and for women with the introduction of women-only passenger cars on certain train lines during peak times (an antigroping measure), but only marginally so. Tokyo keeps growing in size, commutes continue to be long and arduous, and commuters continue to suffer.

In an effort to make things better, Tokyo planners have long advocated plans for the decentralization of the geography of work and schooling in Tokyo. The goal would be bring retail and office districts, industrial establishments, college and university campuses, and other commuter destinations closer to where Tokyoites live. One moniker for this type of strategy has been "multinodal metropolis," the promotion of an alternative spatial form for Tokyo that depends less on an enormously oversized and overpriced central business district (CBD), and more on array of satellite centers at commuter interchanges and other designated locations at various distances from the CBD. Since the 1960s, when this tack was first formally articulated in metropolitan planning documents, these satellite alternatives have included various specific older business centers outside the CBD that were specially targeted for significant expansion, as well as several brand new "subcenters" that were grown in planned and orderly ways from the ground up in expanding suburban zones or on entirely new Tokyo land. Several of the favored subcenters, most especially Shinjuku and Shibuya on Tokyo's near-west side, have grown to enormous size, rivaling and even surpassing in various aspects the CBD itself. Other prominent achievements of the multinodal plan are Makuhari, a new cluster of high-rise office towers and other business in suburban Chiba Prefecture; Odaiba, a glitzy new commercial and recreation zone on a close-in island reclaimed from Tokyo Bay; and Minato Mirai 21, an enormous redevelopment project along the waterfront of Yokohama, Tokyo's neighbor city in next-door Kanagawa Prefecture. As a result of such construction, a smaller percentage of all Tokyo-area commuters now go to the Tokyo CBD, with more people traveling back and forth instead between other destinations. The benefit is corresponding reduction in crowding levels on many train lines and a reduction in average distances between commuters' homes and commuter destinations.[1]

Still, however, Tokyo life is commuting life (see Allinson 1979, 1984). What suffers most critically is married life, family life, even personal life in the case of those who live alone. Time spent not commuting would be time available for other activities, and the energy that is saved is energy that can be applied to work, study, building one's business, enjoyment, personal health and fitness, and various personal and family relationships. I know this personally as I have lived in Tokyo both with and without commuting. For some years my family and I lived quite far out in Tokyo's western suburbs, and I commuted to work near the city's center (as did my wife) and hated it. Several years after that, during a later long-term stint in Tokyo, I lived near the center of the city (near Roppongi) and walked or bicycled to work, saving time, strength, and hassle. As expressed by the Mori Building Company, a central character in this book and an enormous and powerful land development company that is engaged in a messianic remaking of Roppongi and other parts of inner Tokyo, the argument is this: "On average, people working in the greater Tokyo Metropolitan Area spend about 140 minutes per day commuting. Assuming they work 20 days a month, that totals approximately 560 hours, or about 23 days a year. . . . If only those 23 days could be used to meet interesting people, learn and experience new things. . . . Just imagine the possibilities" (Mori Building Company 2007). The company's CEO, Minoru Mori, another major character in this book and, in fact, either a hero or villain depending on how you see things, has elaborated with some telling statistics:

> More than 70% of Tokyo workers commute more than one hour each day.
>
> More than 70% of Tokyo workers sleep 6 hours or less per night.
>
> Of married workers, 41% spend 15 minutes or less talking with their spouses, including 10% who did not speak with their spouses at all. (Mori, Yamagata, and Mau 2001)

Other aspects of "the Tokyo Problem" include the small size and poor quality of typical housing units, be they in the city itself or in the commuter shed (the size of personal living space is 60 percent less than that in New York), a comparative lack of greenery and open space in comparison to other cities of global stature (30 percent of London is devoted to parks; the comparable percentage for Tokyo is 5 percent), and a general lack of attention over the long haul in Tokyo to community and neighborhood planning, landscape design, and urban aesthetics (Mori, Yamagata, and Mau 2001). Tokyo is a very clean, safe, and orderly city, but it is by no means pretty or charming. Some people say that it is downright ugly, even as there is little or no litter: a city of mostly soulless buildings, incompatible buildings jammed one against the other, exposed power and utility wiring overhead, pollarded trees, and sad rivers encased in concrete, among other observations (Kerr 2001). Improvements such as neighborhood parks and playgrounds or community social services centers are many, but they are hit and miss as determined by officials' decisions and financial means in each of Tokyo's twenty-three "special wards" (*ku*) and its twenty-six cities (*shi*), five towns (*machi*), and eight villages (*mura*), and such improvements have typically not been accomplished in the context of any comprehensive city planning or grand strategies.

Yet, despite the shortcomings, Tokyo costs more. The city ranks consistently among the most expensive places in the world, particularly for its high rents and prices for purchased housing, but also for food; transportation; home heating, cooling, and lighting; and consumer items ranging from clothing to cosmetics to kitchen cleaners and beyond. I can think of very few bargains in Tokyo in comparison to shopping elsewhere, and I know to fill my suitcase with things I will need as I return to the city from travel abroad. The most recent (2009) Mercer Cost of Living Survey, which compares the world's cities to New York City, to which it assigns a score of 100.0, puts Tokyo at the very top with a score of 143.7 (that is, 43.7 percent higher than New York), far ahead of number two, co-Honshuite Osaka (119.2); number three, Moscow (115.4); number four, Geneva (109.2), and number five, Hong Kong (108.7). High costs, in turn, make Tokyo less competitive as it strives to maintain high rank as a global business center and have caused the city to lose ground to urban rivals, even those within Japan. If London was the global city of the nineteenth century and New York that of the twentieth, Tokyo is learning that its head start as the capital of the twenty-first century, the "Asian Century," has slipped, and that Shanghai, Hong Kong, Singapore, and now Mumbai have all been disturbingly ascendant.

There are other challenges to Tokyo too, including those that are demographic. Like Japan as a whole, Tokyo has an aging population (its percentage of residents aged sixty-five and older has zoomed from an already-high 10.5 percent in 1990 to 13.0 percent in 1995, 15.8 percent in 2000, and 18.3 percent in 2005, and no doubt is above 20 percent now), and all the extraordinary special needs and financial obligations that are entailed, including those for housing, transportation, medical care, and pastime activities. At the same time, there are low birthrates and reduced percentages of the population that can be taxed to support such needs. Even in a bad economy, a mark of both Tokyo and Japan as a whole since the bursting of the bubble economy in the 1990s, there are shortages of labor and even greater worries down the road as to who will do the work that is necessary to keep the country going, much less pay support for an aged population with rising longevity. Indeed, in Tokyo and elsewhere we see many older people, presumably once retired, back at work, if only part-time, as parking-meter attendants, school crossing guards, supermarket checkers, and orderlies in bicycle parking zones, among other jobs, in order to supplement their incomes and, perhaps, to fight personal isolation.

To a certain, contained extent, Japan (and Tokyo specifically) has turned to young immigrants for help, most famously those from Brazil, Peru, and other countries who happen to have paper proof of Japanese ancestry. One sees them (and other immigrants too, such as those from China) in the automobile factories and other industries, at constructions sites, in restaurants as servers, cooks, and dishwashers, and as counter clerks in convenience stores, among other places of employment. Roppongi cannot function without what I call in a later chapter an "immigrant proletariat." It is clear, however, that Japan is not yet ready for large-scale immigration and worries greatly about the impact that such a change would have on traditional Japanese culture, on routine ways of living in the country, and on public safety. Even supposedly sophisticated Tokyo pins many of its social ills on the supposed negative effects of having more foreigners than other Japanese cities. In many neighborhoods where foreigners are present, not just in Roppongi, there is bilingual and multilingual signage that reveals what many Japanese think about foreigners: warnings against shoplifting and other crime, litter, and excessive noise, as well as information about proper disposal of trash and good manners on subways and subway stations platforms.

And then, of course, there are great concerns in Tokyo (and other Japanese cities) about social problems of Japan's own making, including a rise in bad manners, crime, and other ills within its own, Japanese population. There is, for instance, the "lost generation" of Japanese youth, now sadly pushing two generations, of disaffected men and women who have never had full opportunity to enter the economy with gainful employment, or who do not want to do so because they abhor the strict routines and high expectations of the formal economy. Many subsist as short-term contract workers or jugglers of multiple part-time jobs. Many other young Japanese become social dropouts and live in isolation or in their parents' homes, losing touch with social skills and reality, and are dependent on various "escapes" such as computer games, anime, or pornography. A new word, *hikikomori*, has entered the vocabulary to describe the syndrome. It blends *hiku* (pull) with *komoru* (to retire) into "pulling in and retiring" and applies to a population of socially withdrawn shut-ins, about 80 percent of whom are males, who can no longer be ignored as side effects of Japanese society and who are a growing minority in Tokyo's population (Zielenziger 2006). In addition, there is a new generation of in-your-face young Japanese who seem to ignore whatever they may have been taught about common courtesies and ways of behaving in society, and who act in public as if they and perhaps their circle of close associates were the only people on the planet who mattered. Wherever we are in this world, we all have our complaints about declines in civilities: in Japan, though, and most particularly in Tokyo, I think, the problem is jarring because standards have always been high, and the declines are so sharp and recent.

Thus, "the Tokyo Problem" comprises many issues, and there can be no easy fix. For many observers, however, this geographer included, as well as the Mori

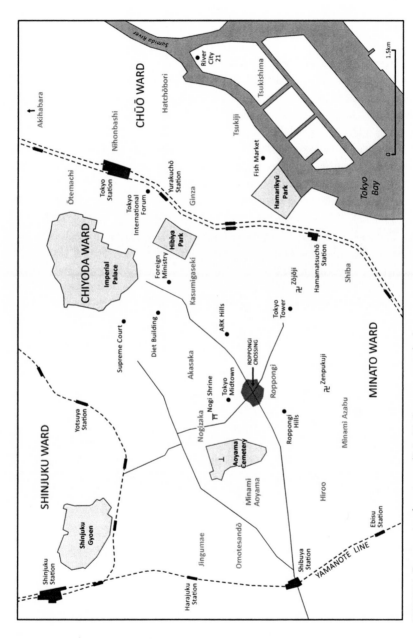

FIGURE 2.1 Roppongi and environs. (Erin McCann cartographer)

Building Company and its CEO Minoru Mori, both spatial thinkers, many of the city's repairable problems are related to urban form and diurnal division of space. The CBD and other business centers are jammed during the day on work days but empty at night and on holidays, while outer-ring districts are bedroom zones only, filled at night, but devoid during the day of family members who are part of the commuting scene. Not only is this inefficient in terms of land use and commuting energy, but it has unnecessarily separated family and other household members from one another, leading to a myriad of personal and social problems—everything from couples' needs for sexual intimacy to the challenges of bringing up children and teaching them to integrate fully into society to providing activities and companionship for the many retired people in an aging demographic structure, and more. How much better life would be if only people could live where they worked, and if those places had as well the kinds of cultural, recreational, and entertainment facilities that people prefer! That is how Tokyo needs to be reshaped and where a "New Roppongi" comes in as a demonstration project to presage as "New Tokyo." There are many benefits to urban life as presented in New Roppongi, not the least of which is eradication by bulldozer of the haunts of trouble, but new trouble, both unexpected and not, has arisen for citizens to deal with in the new urban landscape.

Roppongi's Location

Roppongi is located near the center of Minato Ward, one of the inner-most wards of Tokyo's twenty-three inner wards. To the east, it is close to the city's traditional downtown business district with its famous Ginza, Marunouchi, and Nihombashi districts, as well as near Tokyo's national government district in Kasumigaseki and Nagatachō and the grounds of the Imperial Palace, the enormous "empty center" around which this great and unusual city turns (Barthes 1982, 30–32). In the other direction, Roppongi is close to both Shinjuku and Shibuya, the giant rail-subway interchange commercial districts on Tokyo's west side that have surpassed the downtown in importance in retailing and other commerce. Their tall buildings and explosions of neon are icons of Japan's consumer society and Tokyo's bustle after dark. Other neighbors are the famous fashion centers of Harajuku, Aoyama, and Omotesandō. Where there are still residential blocks, the aura is one of tradition and prestige. The land is extremely valuable, so anyone who owns a single home, no matter how modest, is a millionaire, while many of the newer condominium towers in the area are pricy even by Tokyo standards and signal a high-income population.

TABLE 2.1 Three definitions of *Roppongi*

DEFINITION	GEOGRAPHY
Roppongi machi	Formal definition; made up of 7 chōme
Roppongi Crossing	Informal definition: the irregularly shaped zone in the vicinity of the main street intersection that is known for nightlife activity
Roppongi Station	Informal definition: similar to Roppongi Crossing in size and shape, but defined as the area around the Roppongi subway station, nightlife, and other activities

Three Definitions

There are at least three ways of defining *Roppongi* (table 2.1). First, the word *Roppongi* refers to a formally defined subsection of Minato Ward, a local administrative district referred to as Roppongi machi, or Roppongi Town. This district is then divided into seven smaller districts called *chōme*, each of which is named by sequential number: Roppongi 1-chōme, Roppongi 2-chōme, and so on up to 7. Both machi and chōme are extremely important elements of Tokyo's citywide address system, which is based on a hierarchy of spatial units, and the city's spatial units for compiling records such as census data. Roppongi machi is a comparatively large, formally defined neighborhood, and each of its seven chōme is a smaller neighborhood unit within. People who know Tokyo well can identify just where Roppongi machi is and can also describe its major characteristics, including perhaps specific details about one or more of the numbered chōme. Roppongi 1-chōme, for example, is known for prestigious office addresses such as the Izumi Garden development; 2-chōme is mostly the residential complex of the U.S. Embassy, and 6-chōme has long been the location of the studios of TV Asahi and now contains the glitzy Roppongi Hills redevelopment complex. Roppongi machi measures almost exactly one square kilometer in area and has a residential population of 7,394. The daytime population, which counts office workers, shopkeepers, and others employed in the neighborhood, is more than five times higher: 40,833 (table 2.2).

However, most people in Tokyo associate the word *Roppongi* with a second definition—one that is informal and loosely bounded. Under this definition, Roppongi is a nighttime playground and commercial district that is centered on Roppongi Crossing or Roppongi *kōsaten* (Roppongi intersection). From this nucleus, the district stretches for a few blocks somewhat east

TABLE 2.2 Roppongi population by chōme, 2008

CHŌME	AREA (KM²)	RESIDENTIAL POPULATION	DAYTIME POPULATION
Roppongi 1-chōme	0.15	1,138	4,766
Roppongi 2-chōme	0.07	232	1,516
Roppongi 3-chōme	0.18	1,373	7,753
Roppongi 4-chōme	0.12	933	4,146
Roppongi 5-chōme	0.19	1,686	6,402
Roppongi 6-chōme	0.20	473	7,962
Roppongi 7-chōme	0.24	1,559	8,288
TOTAL ROPPONGI MACHI:	1.15	7,394	40,833

Source: Minato Ward Office.

and west along Roppongi-dōri, the busy street beneath an elevated express-way, and a few blocks again somewhat north and south along Gaien Higashi-dōri, the nearby small streets that run irregularly within each of the quadrants formed by the central intersection and that also figure in Roppongi's nightlife.

This informally defined Roppongi has no fixed geographical limits; it simply grades into neighboring districts with distance from the well-defined center. To the west, the grade slopes steadily downward from Roppongi Crossing to the next big intersection along Roppongi-dōri, that at Nishi Azabu Crossing about 750 meters away. To the east, the boundary is with Akasaka, itself a neon-lit nighttime playground that is even closer to Japan's centers of political and economic power than Roppongi. To the north, Roppongi runs past the former site of the National Self-Defense Forces headquarters (Japan's "Pentagon"), now the location of Tokyo Midtown, to Nogizaka, a neighborhood also some 750 meters away. It is a quieter area of upscale apartments and condominiums and foreign embassies, although it is a neighborhood of high-rises just like all the surroundings. Nogi's Slope is named after General Nogi Maresuke (1849–1912), Japan's hero of the Russo-Japanese War (1904–5), who lived in an old wooden house along Gaien Nishi-dōri with his wife Shizuko until they both committed ritual suicide on the day of the funeral of the Meiji Emperor. To the south, Roppongi runs, first, into Azabudai, home of both the Russian Embassy compound and the American Club that was built next door, and then into Shiba-kōen, the park that is the site of Tokyo Tower. The Eiffel-like landmark is slightly more than a

FIGURE 2.2 Tokyo Tower as seen from a point near Roppongi Crossing down Gaien Higashi-dōri. The tower is an important Tokyo landmark and a reference point for orientation in Roppongi, as well as a symbol of Japan's construction state.

kilometer from Roppongi Crossing and is a clearly visible architectural feature, day or night, as one looks south from Roppongi Crossing (figure 2.2).

The third definition of *Roppongi* is with reference to the subway system rather than to streets. This is especially appropriate since it is by subway that most users of Roppongi, both workers and consumers, come and go. Roppongi is the name of a subway stop for the neighborhood, and the district Roppongi then is the area within a short walk of the multiple stairways and exits of Roppongi Station. Because the station is essentially directly beneath Roppongi Crossing, the geographical extent of "Roppongi Station Roppongi" is for all intents and purposes identical to "Roppongi Crossing Roppongi." The more heavily used of Roppongi's two subway lines is the Hibiya Line, which arrived in Roppongi for the Tokyo Olympics in 1964, and which winds under central Tokyo in a contorted pattern to connect Ginza, Akihabara, Ueno, and other popular destinations. The other line is the Ōedo Line, one of Tokyo's newest subway lines, the twelfth. It opened on the twelfth day of the twelfth month of the twelfth year of the reign of the Heisei emperor (2000) and connects Roppongi with Shinjuku Station, Tokyo's busiest commuter station, only nine minutes away.[2]

As reported in the *Tokyo Statistical Yearbook* for 2004, some 21,895,000 passengers got off the Hibiya Line in Roppongi in that year, an average of about 60,000 persons per day. That is a higher number than for any of the twenty other stations on the Hibiya Line except for the terminals at either end. The Ōedo Line contributes an additional 11,843,000 departing passengers per year to Roppongi Station, about 32,500 passengers per day. Thus, the total number of people getting off the subways in Roppongi on an average day approaches 100,000. Along the Ōedo Line, too, Roppongi ranks as one of the top stations, particularly among passengers who purchase single-trip tickets as opposed to those with commuters' passes, an indicator that for many riders the neighborhood is a "special destination neighborhood." That Roppongi is changing can be seen when one is still below ground and beginning to negotiate the maze of stairways to the surface. Almost all of the directional signs point riders to the area's new attractions: Roppongi Hills in one direction, Tokyo Midtown and another new development, the National Art Center, in another, and only the most detailed signs say anything at all about the heart of the nightclub district, Roppongi Crossing.

Spatial Ecology

Before getting into additional details about Roppongi, it is helpful to understand just how the district fits into Tokyo's spatial ecology and social organization, as

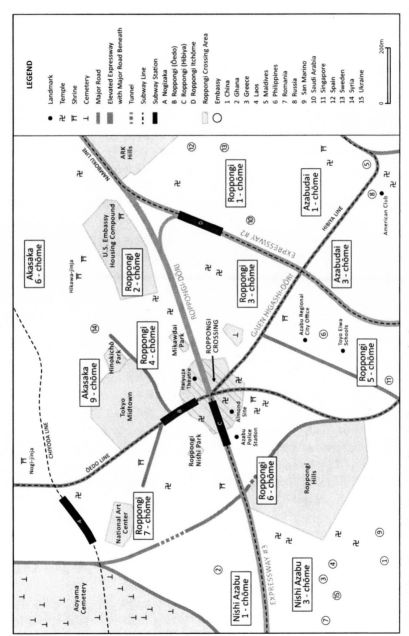

FIGURE 2.3 Roppongi orientation map. (Erin McCann cartographer)

well as into the context of Japanese society more broadly. Even though it is a one-of-a-kind place, being the city's preeminent foreigner-Japanese nightclub district, it shares social characteristics and historical experience with a broader side of Tokyo, as well as characteristics with other, more distant parts of the city (and other Japanese cities), both present and past. This chapter focuses on places that provide geographic and historical context for understanding Roppongi today and ties some key social aspects of Roppongi to longstanding Japanese cultural traits and experiences. There are five broad subject areas in this chapter: (1) Roppongi as a prestigious "high city" neighborhood; (2) Roppongi's nearness to Japan's centers of political and corporate power; (3) Roppongi in the context of Japan's "construction state" character; (4) Roppongi in the context of urban Japan's tradition of specialized nighttime entertainment districts, including the geisha tradition and its modern-day cousin, the hostess industry; and (5) Roppongi in the context of foreigners in Japan and districts where foreigners have been most numerous in the past and are most numerous now.

High City

Roppongi's central location in one of the world's largest, wealthiest, and most influential cities has been a critical factor in how the neighborhood has evolved. The key reference point within Tokyo's center, point zero for understanding how the city is laid out, is what is today the grounds of the Imperial Palace, the huge green space beyond moats and walls and without many buildings around which the city turns. This was the site of Edo Castle (Edo-jō), the citadel that brought the city into being. The first castle was built in 1457 by a minor warlord named Ōta Dōkan, the city's founder, but it was run-of-the-mill by the standards of Japan's castles, and the city, named Edo at the time, was not very distinguished. Things changed beginning in 1600 when Tokugawa Ieyasu, soon to be the first in a long line of hereditary shōguns, gained control of all of Japan and presciently selected the site to be his citadel. The Edo Castle that he built on the same site was perhaps the biggest that the world ever knew, and its very construction quickly turned Edo into an enormous city. Other than the castle itself and its complex, spiral pattern of fortifications and internal social spaces, the city had two clearly understood divisions, shitamachi and yamanote, both identified simultaneously by topography and social status.

Shitamachi, meaning "low city," was at the foot of the castle near Edo (Tokyo) Bay, on the low-lying flats amid the city's river mouths and multiple canals. This was the excessively crowded home of craftsmen and laborers who came from all over Japan to build Edo Castle, as well as the quarters for merchants and others from among Japan's common people who came to be called *edokko*, the children of Edo. As the city grew, shitamachi expanded to new land reclaimed from Tokyo Bay, much of it formed in the early years by the shōgun's decree to level nearby "Kanda Mountain" and haul its soil to the edge of the bay. *Yamanote*, by contrast, translates loosely as "in the direction of the mountains" and is commonly referred to in English as the "high city," apparently after the lead of Edward Seidensticker's brilliant history of Tokyo (1983). It comprises five distinct ridges of higher ground north and west of the castle that protrude toward the castle and its nearby low city neighborhoods like five fingers on a hand. This hilly terrain came to be the domain of Edo's elites. Throughout the city, today as in the past, the juncture between shitamachi and yamanote is marked by steep stairs from one level of neighborhood to the other and by steep slopes, many of which have proper names that today recall people, events, and activities from the city's history (Enbutsu 1993; Jinnai 1988, 1995; Waley 1984).

What is today Roppongi is on a yamanote highland called the Azabu Hills, located about five kilometers to the southwest of where Edo Castle stood. Its first recorded residents were samurai and other elites who were assigned this better land for their estates by the first shōgun. Indeed, the very word *Roppongi*, which is translated as "six trees," comes not from any particular trees than may have stood in this forested area, but probably from the names of six influential *daimyo* (feudal lord) families who had their estates among the district's slopes. It was coincidence that their family names all happened to be the names of types of trees. Roppongi's part of yamanote was also one of the designated districts where the shogunate directed the construction of temples that came to be centers of influence, and where other temples were relocated by decree from the overcrowded and fire-prone precincts of shitamachi.

The presence of these temples, as well as the elite residents, gave yamanote a superior prestige that has never waned. Most of today's residents and business owners take pride in being there and pay premium rents for the land (or volume of air space) that they occupy. Real estate developers, most notably the giant Mori Building Company, itself a homegrown product of yamanote's Minato Ward, have capitalized on the area's luster and have constructed upscale commercial and residential developments that can be afforded only by the top end of Tokyo's market. Many of Mori's biggest local construction projects, such as Roppongi Hills, Omotesando Hills, and Atago Green Hills, were given names to evoke the conflux of lofty social status and topography. Perhaps not wanting to be outdone and in what can only be described as a delectable example of "Japlish," another developer, one I had never heard of, named his residential project in a neighboring ward "Respectable Hills."

Many of the Buddhist temples that were constructed in and near Roppongi in Edo times still remain. Often, the temples are close neighbors to multistory apartment-condominium complexes and modern-day shopping streets, and receive worshipers, seekers of urban quiet, and visitors exploring local history. Some temples, like the enormous Zōjōji complex, are large and well known and are featured in every guidebook to Tokyo in any language. It was a favorite of the Tokugawa shōguns, six of whom are buried on the grounds, and was once the centerpiece of a tight cluster of hundreds of temple buildings, monasteries, and other religious buildings that stood behind walls in what is today Shiba Park. Today, only several buildings remain, as the prestige of Zōjōji waned with the 1868 end of the shogunate, but the smaller-scale 1974 reconstruction of the original main temple after it was destroyed in the 1945 air raids is impressive nonetheless. The new Zōjōji finds itself next to an interloping neighbor, Tokyo Tower. The juxtaposition affords visitors a fine opportunity for a "cliché photo" of traditional Japan and an icon of modern Japan in the same frame.

A little nearer to Roppongi Crossing is Zempukuji, once an extremely powerful temple with considerable influence in medieval Japan and still an active center of Buddhist worship. Near the end of the Tokugawa suzerainty, the temple was taken over by the American legation to Japan as its base. A memorial stone in the courtyard commemorates Townsend Harris, the first American consul. In the neighboring cemetery is a 750-plus-year-old ginkgo tree, the largest in Tokyo and quite storied, and the tomb of Fukuzawa Yukichi (1835–1901), the great intellectual-modernizer of Meiji Japan who had urged Japan to learn as much as possible from the West in order to meet the challenges that superior Western technology and military power presented. Mori Building Company's odd-shaped, prestigious residential tower, Moto-Azabu Hills, is the interloper next door, affording still another set of opportunities for "old Japan–new Japan" photography. As represented by Moto-Azabu Hills, the new Japan looks like a gigantic empty ice cream cone instead of the Eiffel Tower.

It is something of a rule of thumb in central Tokyo that wherever you spot the tops of a cluster of larger trees poking from behind today's buildings, there will be an old temple or shrine there, and perhaps a burial ground as well. There are four or five temples or burial grounds located within a one- or two-minute walk from Roppongi Crossing, and at least ten or so more within five minutes. They are all "behind things" and essentially invisible to the neighborhood's party crowds. However, Tokyo history buffs and geographers know they are there, as well as, I suppose, what few religious faithful they seem to have. Often in good weather on mornings and afternoons, one sees groups of older Japanese, presumably retired from their jobs, undertaking history walks in and near Roppongi, cameras and long lenses in tow, and following routes outlined in various guidebooks or brochures. I personally recommend visiting Hikawa-jinja, a shrine in a wooded area of Roppongi that was once called Hinokichō ("place of cypress trees"), not far from the district's border with Akasaka. As an institution, the shrine dates to 951 and was moved a short distance to the present location in 1730 by the eighth Tokugawa shōgun, Yoshimune. The main building is simple and austere as he directed. There are three giant gingko trees on the property, each about three hundred years old. They are especially beautiful to view in autumn when the leaves turn bright yellow (Moriyama 1993, 256).

Other aspects of Roppongi's setting are more in tune with larger numbers of today's Tokyoites, particularly its many affluent young consumers. While the neighborhood itself is not known as a center for high-fashion shopping, most of Tokyo's most fashionable and most expensive shopping districts, such as Aoyama, Omotesandō, and Harajuku, are nearby in other parts of Minato Ward or in adjoining Shibuya Ward.[3] Omotesandō-dōri, sometimes referred to as Tokyo's Champs-Élysées, is the main street of a glitzy shopping district at the juncture of both wards and is lined with giant, new glass-covered emporia selling the full lines of designer fashions by Prada, Chanel, Louis Vuitton, Burberry, Gucci, and other pricey brands popular with label-conscious Japanese. Each of these "transparent temples of design" was itself designed by a prestigious architect.[4] Also, each shop positions one or more formally attired doormen at the entrance to greet customers and open doors.

Also on Omotesandō-dōri are the retail stores specializing in top-end Japanese designer brands such as Hanae Mori, and Omotesando Hills, the city's most upscale shopping mall. Opened in 2005 and designed by world-renowned Japanese architect Tadao Ando, the mall is still another profit-seeking development project by the Mori Building Company. There are more that 130 shops and restaurants, including the likes of Yves Saint Laurent and Dolce & Gabbana, as well as plenty of resentment and controversy over the project's elite-shopper orientation and its displacement of a tight-knit residential community and unique, historic housing (Devlin 2005). The side streets have still more fashion outlets, including a great many small start-up boutiques with unique product lines and, sometimes, bargain prices. The neighboring shopping district of Harajuku is especially popular with price-conscious and fashion-minded young people.

Centers of Power

In one of a great many fascinating details about Tokyo's history, Edo Castle (Edo-jō) did not last long despite its enormous scale. It burned in 1657 soon after it was completed, in a great fire that started in a temple in another part of town and all but destroyed the entire city. The castle wasn't rebuilt, mostly because it was no longer needed, and came to be mined as a source of stone. It had already fulfilled its task of cementing the shōguns' power via the all-consuming construction process that so taxed the nation and tested loyalties, and there was no one, domestic or foreign, who was going to attack. Many of the stones from the fortifications that were removed were used in foundations and construction elsewhere in Edo (and later, too, in Tokyo), giving genuine historical foundation for the city's character today as a place of construction atop construction.

> Wherever you go in today's Tokyo
> You're always among stones from old Edo-jō.

After the fall of the *bakufu* (the shōguns' government) in 1868, the newly established Meiji government chose to build its institutions of government to the west of the castle grounds, now the emperor's palace, on land that had been samurai estates. This was the beginning of today's national government district of Nagatachō and Kasumigaseki, about half as close to Roppongi as was Edo Castle. This geography, too, would forevermore impact Roppongi by bringing it even closer to the center of power in Japan and by creating demands for office space, close-in residences, and after-hours places for bureaucrats and government official to wine, dine, and strike deals.

So, too, the first semblance of a commercial downtown (central business district or CBD) developed during the Meiji Period (1868–1912), initially just to the south of the main gate of the Imperial Palace, in an area that came to be called Marunouchi. Developed by the founders of the Mitsubishi family of companies, it was designed by a hired-gun architect, Englishman Josiah Conder, and patterned after London's Kensington district. For a while, it was referred to as Mitsubishigahara (Mitsubishi Fields) and then Mitsubishi Londontown. From that nucleus, the CBD spread south into shitamachi to cover old merchant and craftsmen's districts such as Nihombashi and Ginza, and then starting early in the twentieth century, it began expanding as well toward the government district and to the close-in yamanote neighborhoods on Tokyo's west and southwest sides, including, of course, our Roppongi.

Thus, for most of the twentieth century, Roppongi's history, checkered in so many ways, was to be at the advance of the west-southwestward migrating central business district. This was, of course, to become one of the biggest business districts in the world, so its impact on Roppongi would be enormous. Two periods of sustained economic growth during the course of the twentieth century fed the business district and its ripple effects on surrounding neighborhoods. The first occurred before the Great Kantō Earthquake of 1923 and then continued with the reconstruction afterward, while the second commenced with the rebuilding of Japan and its economy after the destruction of World War II and continued for decades thereafter. Tokyo's CBD became enormous as well because the city chose to develop itself into a gigantic commuter hub focused on the intersections of multiple train and subway lines and their networks of interconnecting stations, famously crammed during peak times with silently suffering commuters. A landmark event occurred in 1968 with the opening of the thirty-six-story Kasumigaseki Building, Tokyo's first modern skyscraper, on the west side of the CBD, heralding a commitment to CBD growth (as opposed to a fresh-start business district in another part of the city) and west side expansion.

Westward (i.e., Roppongi-ward) expansion of the CBD continued as postwar reconstruction gave way in the 1970s to the enormous export wealth of exports-based Japan Inc., and then gained heads of steam as economic growth became an unprecedented economic joyride. The bubble period covered the 1980s and into the early 1990s and transformed central Tokyo into a city of high-rises on the most expensive land in the world. Some of the most spectacular construction took place outside the immediate center, in response to a much-publicized plan to transform Tokyo into a "multinodal metropolis," most notably in Shinjuku, located at a critical commuter rail juncture a little further to the west of the most central neighborhoods. There, starting in the 1960s, where the local geology was more suitable than elsewhere in Tokyo, Japan's answer to the high-rises of Manhattan was developed. In 1991, the district was capped with a new tallest building in Tokyo, the spectacular headquarters of Tokyo Metropolitan Government designed by Kenzo Tange. It was referred to sometimes as the "New Edo Castle" because of its high costs and extravagances in construction materials and "artscaping," as well as the "Tower of Taxes," again a reference to the capability of government authority to require that their subjects pay for their headquarters. Whether shown in day with Mt. Fuji in the horizon or at night with its bright lights, by the 1980s the Shinjuku skyline became a prime symbol of the economic might of Japan, the primacy within Japan of Tokyo, and the great powers of Japan's politician and business leader–led, construction-fed growth machine (Coaldrake 1996, 266–77; Kerr 2001, 13–50).

Construction was so rampant in Tokyo during the bubble years that several of the nodes of the multinodal metropolis, including Shinjuku, started to look more like extensions at the edge of the central business district than alternatives to the CBD. The residential spaces between the CBD and those nodes were displaced by more and more commerce in tall buildings, particularly office towers and international hotels in showpiece redevelopment projects. All of this was facilitated by government policy initiatives that favored private-sector urban construction and redevelopment as a stimulus for the overall economy. Specifically, we can point to a policy called *minkatsu* for short, which translates from the full term as "the active use of the dynamism of private enterprise" and which makes use of relaxed zoning rules and easy disposal of public land as specific mechanisms for getting things done (Waley 2000, 138–39; Hayakawa and Hirayama 1991). Because of location, Roppongi and its next-door neighbors were prime targets for such development. Major Japanese companies that have impressive office headquarters in Minato Ward, the ward in which Roppongi is situated, include Dentsu, Mitsubishi Heavy Industries, Mitsubishi Motors, Morinaga, NEC, and Toshiba, while many other famous Japanese corporations such as Sony are in neighboring wards not far away.

Unquestionably, the most significant bubble-period icon in this regard was the construction of a mixed-use, multibuilding, "megastructure" redevelopment project called ARK Hills, on a yamanote slope just east (i.e., on the CBD side) of Roppongi, where Akasaka, Roppongi, and Kasumigaseki come together. Opened in 1986, this unified cluster of office buildings, hotels, residences, and cultural facilities, all set apart by design from the immediate surroundings, was the creation of Taikichiro Mori, founder of the Mori Building Company, a fascinating person and a fascinating company. In opening ARK Hills, Mori advertised it widely in posters and print ads with unrestrained confidence with the slogan "Where Tokyo is Headed." The claim may have been an understatement because Mori and his son Minoru Mori, who succeeded him in 1993 at the helm of Mori Building Company, as well as some of their competitors, would all continue to greatly transform central Tokyo to this day, having especially an enormous impact on Roppongi.

Centers of Play

Where there are prominent political and business pooh-bahs and their corridors of power, there are also great centers of play. That is probably true almost everywhere in the world, and it is especially true for Japan. All larger Japanese cities have excellent examples of bustling pleasure districts, as the society has a deeply engrained tradition of frequent and lavish nights out by men in positions of power and influence, and each city has a rich history that can be written in ample part by focusing on one or more of its large, lively, and immensely popular entertainment or amusement districts. Some of the most storied such places are in Kyoto, the ancient Japanese capital, and include the famous geisha quarters of Gion and Pontochō (Dalby 1983; Dougill 2006). In Tokyo, specialized entertainment districts became part of urban life from the very start of that city as Edo and flourished in tandem with urban growth. In 1617, still during the time of construction of the city's giant new castle, the first "licensed quarter" was established. It was named Yoshiwara (plain of reeds) and was created specifically as a place for men's enjoyment in which officials could regulate prostitution and other vices, and where agents of the shōgun could spy on any nighttime plotting against him. Similar motivations led to the establishment of Shinmachi in Osaka in 1624 and Shimbara in Kyoto in 1640, the first officially licensed pleasure quarters in Tokugawa Japan's two other biggest cities.

From such beginnings, Edo and then Tokyo (as well as other Japanese cities) saw the successive rise and fall of numerous nighttime pleasure districts of various sorts, of which Tokyo's Roppongi emerged in the twentieth century as a unique subtype. The pages that follow give quick looks at a selection of famous Tokyo playgrounds from different times in history. Welcome to Yoshiwara, Asakusa, Ginza, and, as a pair, Shinjuku and Shibuya. This detour is important, I think, because in order to understand Roppongi it is necessary to know something about its ancestors and living cousins.

Yoshiwara

Yoshiwara was originally in the muddy flats adjacent to Edo Bay, just downriver from "Japan Bridge," but it burned along with most of the rest of shitamachi in the Great Meireki Fire of 1657. A replacement, Shin Yoshiwara (New Yoshiwara) was soon built in the paddy fields directly north of the temple town of Asakusa, a short distance up the Sumida River from the city center. Almost immediately, it came to be called simply Yoshiwara and served both Edo and Tokyo as a licensed prostitution district until well into the twentieth century (De Becker 2000; Hane 1982, 207–17; Longstreet and Longstreet 1988; Seigle-Segawa 1993). It was marked by a large main gate (Ōmon) through which customers entered and left, and also by a rectangular moat that surrounded the district to prevent customers from leaving before paying. The moat also helped to confine captive sex workers, many of whom had been sold as young girls by impoverished families. Other fires periodically devastated the district, contributing to a long-term downward slide. Prostitution was outlawed in Japan in 1958 in the reforms that emanated from the American occupation (1945–52), although the legislation defined it very narrowly as coitus only, and the district was formally shut down. Long before that time, however, Yoshiwara's early charms, such as they were, had vanished, and the district's reputation had sunk to a place of cheap prostitutes by the thousands, quite a few of whom suffered from syphilis. Many of the last lawful customers of Yoshiwara were American soldiers during and after the occupation of Japan.

The name *Yoshiwara* is no longer on the map of Tokyo except for historical markers associated with the old district and one street intersection named Yoshiwara Daimon, "the great gate of Yoshiwara." The original distinctive street plan, however, askew from the pattern of surrounding streets, is still there, as is the slightest hint of the moat and old gate and several streets of tacky "soaplands" and other thin fronts for yakuza-run prostitution. The new, nonsuggestive name for the district is Senzoku 4-chōme, a part of Taitō Ward. The neighborhood is worth a peek from at least the outside for the sake of social-scientific inquiry and a study of architectural kitsch. At least one of the establishments is distinguished by a large plaster frieze of Julius Caesar, while others have all manner of shapely mermaids, horses with wings, Grecian columns, and bunches of grapes, among other adornments, as well as an amusing assortment of loopy signs in loopy English written primarily for people who do not read English but respond to the looks of the script.

On the whole, Senzoku 4-chōme is a low-class vice den that operates twenty-four hours a day. The sex workers are mostly Japanese and Southeast Asian women, generally older than sex workers in other parts of the city; the clients are overwhelmingly Japanese males (as opposed to foreigners), many of them blue-collar workers; and the brothels are generally ornate on the outside and have names like Silky Doll, Pretty Girl, June Bride, and Soapland Aladdin. The usual routine is for the male customer to receive a thorough soapy washing in a shower room from an unclothed female attendant, with special attention being given to genitals, followed by an erotic, lotion-lubricated body-to-body rub and oral sex. None of this is considered prostitution. Coital sex is doubtlessly common in these establishments too, although those arrangements are private between customers and their attendants. Gangsterish-looking doormen are posted outside around the clock to call in customers and, in my experience, also to give the evil eye to passing foreigners. However, if you act naive and ask politely in Japanese "What is soapland?" even the meanest looking doorman can mellow and try to nicely explain the terrain.[5]

Asakusa

Asakusa also became a popular entertainment quarter, with merrymakers from Edo's center often combining a visit to the Kannon Temple and its precincts with a stay in a Yoshiwara pleasure house in one daytrip. The district then prospered as a favorite destination in its own right during Japan's time of modernization and innovation after the 1868 demise of the bakufu and enjoyed a heyday of a decade or two on either side of the ensuing turn of the century. In contrast to the elegant refinement of early Yoshiwara, the emergent playground was plebian, brash, and spontaneous, and its diversions were of a new sort and many. Edward Seidensticker (1983) and Donald Richie (1999) both have written entertainingly about the district's attractions, citing an 1891 guidebook for foreigners as follows: "the grounds of Asakusa are the quaintest and liveliest place in Tokyo . . . performing monkeys, cheap photographers, street artists, jugglers, wrestlers, life-sized figures in clay, vendors of toys and lollipops of every sort, and, circulating amidst all these cheap attraction, a seething crowd of busy holiday-makers" (Richie 1999, 116).

There was also kabuki theater and opera, movies and more movies, Japanese and foreign, bare (Japanese) flesh on stage in chorus lines and strip tease shows, acrobats and bareback riders, elephants and bears, shooting galleries, a carousel, the Hanayashiki amusement park, restaurants with exotic foreign foods, places for gambling, and an assortment of bargain-priced brothels. Asakusa also boasted of the Panoramakan, a long wooden building with life-sized models of soldiers and generals from the U.S. Civil War (yes, the U.S. Civil War) and then, starting in 1903, the Denkikan, "electricity hall," the first of the many movie theaters that would become an Asakusa staple (Waley 1984, 183).[6]

The main landmark, looming even higher than the great temple itself and the pagoda next door and representing the playground aspects of the neighborhood, was a curious new-style building called Ryōunkaku, the cloud-scraping pavilion. It was also descriptively called the Asakusa Twelve Storeys, or Jūnikai. I later draw some parallels between it and today's equally curious skyscraper, Roppongi's Mori Tower. Seidensticker introduced his discussion of this Asakusa structure with a quotation from the Japanese author Kubota Mantarō: "In the days of old, a queer object known as the Twelve Storeys reared itself in Asakusa" (Seidensticker 1983, 71). It was an odd structure indeed. Erected in 1890, it was Tokyo's first tall building after the ephemeral central keep of Edo Castle, which had disappeared some two and one-half centuries earlier, and the first in Japan to have an elevator. The tower was octagonal, made of brick, and tapered from a broader base to a twelfth-floor outdoor observation deck with a distinctive peaked cap above it. From there, visitors who braved the shaky ride up could view the panorama of the city and spy details through telescopes. The various floors of the Twelve Storeys were a compendium of shops with goods from abroad, bars, restaurants, and other amusements. Near the top was an art gallery. A lively woodblock print by the artist Kunimasa IV (1848–1920) illustrates the structure's unusual outward features from both the outside and, by cutaway, floor by floor on the inside. There are crowds of people coming and going on the street below, while in the skies he painted a busy landscape of parachutists, balloonists, and flying kites.

Suddenly, on September 1, 1923, with no warning at all, at almost exactly noon, the end came for most neighborhoods in Tokyo and more than a hundred thousand souls who died as a result of the Great Kanto Earthquake. Centered south of Tokyo in Sagami Bay, the quake violently shook buildings all across the Kantō Plain and started multiple fires that spread wildly on this windy day, destroying everything in their path. The greatest damage was in Yokohama and the shitamachi neighborhoods of Tokyo, with Asakusa being one of the worst affected. Despite having been reinforced after a lesser earthquake in 1899, the Twelve Storeys broke spectacularly at the eighth floor, showering bricks to the pavement below. Other popular entertainment districts of the time were also destroyed by the disaster, including those at either side of the long bridge across the Sumida River between Yanagibashi and Ryōgoku, the amusement quarter at the approach to the bridge at Edobashi, and the one that had sprung up at Ueno Hirokoji, "Ueno Broadway," the widened firebreak street that had been cut through the city precisely to prevent such a disaster. Tokyo's residents started to blame the Koreans among them for the fires, and in Asakusa and other neighborhoods mobs of Japanese began to attack them at random on the streets. Several thousands were killed (Lee and De Vos 1983; Ryang 2003). The Ryōgoku district eventually managed to recover its distinction as the city's sumō center, although some of its other attractions such as riverside fireworks displays and starting point for hundreds of *yakatabune*, "roof-shaped" pleasure boats crowded with partying passengers that plied the river in the summer months, gravitated after the disaster to other river ports. Other *sakariba* (nightlife districts) never recovered.

Asakusa, however, was rebuilt, albeit with quite a few new open spaces that were not there before and that are now parks and parking lots. It continues to function as both a temple town and an entertainment zone, although the dominance that it had before the earthquake as an entertainment venue was lost forever as other venues, based on newer fashions and activities, eclipsed the old neighborhood. The temple still attracts worshippers almost every day, as it has genuine religious significance for believers, and is jam-packed along with its approaches on Sundays and holidays. In summer months, foreign tourists, most visibly from China and Korea, add to the crowds, stopping at shop after shop along Nakamise-dōri ("street of the inside shops") to purchases Japanese souvenirs and such Asakusa tchotchkes as hand fans, key chains, replica swords, and images of Kaminarimon, the iconic gate of the thunder god that guards the temple's approach. The streets with movie and stage theaters have been rebuilt and modernized, although the fare seems heavily tilted nowadays toward pornographic films and burlesque, and the largest crowds, mostly aging men, are seen at the large new palace for off-track betting on horse races that stands on the site of the Twelve Storeys. The Hanayashiki amusement park had been rebuilt too, but clearly some time ago as its rides are old-fashioned and no longer draw big crowds.

Among the newest attractions in Asakusa are tours of the neighborhood by rickshaw, a recently established "retro" service designed to create a more authentic historic atmosphere. The pullers are strong, young Japanese men and (some) women, while most of the riders, it seems, are foreign tourists. There are new events too, also designed to bring family crowds back to Asakusa. For example, every August, near the end of that sweltering month, the neighborhood hosts a huge Rio de Janeiro–style carnival parade. There are thousands of dancers from Brazil in full feather costumes and skimpy glitter-encrusted bikinis parading down the main streets to a salsa beat, as well as tens of thousands of Japanese samba enthusiasts, men and women, also in full feather, following the Brazilians' lead. Japanese Brazilians, a major and fast-growing immigrant group, are also part of the action. The number of onlookers is more than a million, including quite a few aging men with long-lens cameras, making this carnival one of the key money events in Asakusa's economic revival calendar.

Ginza

As Asakusa struggled with recovery after the earthquake, it was Ginza that emerged as the city's next entertainment hotspot. Located near the main downtown office districts and originally Edo's silversmiths' quarter, the district had been remade after a huge fire in 1872 into Ginza renga-gai (Ginza Bricktown), Tokyo's showpiece of Western fashion and style. It was given cobbled streets, sidewalks lined with trees, and buildings of brick with doors on hinges. Those who came there to see and be seen wore Western fashions, sipped coffee instead of Japanese tea, and, after the first one opened in 1899, drank beer in any of several cavernous beer halls. The loan words *mo-bo* and *mo-ga*, meaning "modern boys" and "modern girls," eventually came into use to refer to Ginza's habitués. There was also traditional-style entertainment in Ginza and a clientele who would otherwise have belonged in Asakusa. For example, from 1889, with the opening of the spectacular theater, the Kabukiza, the east side of Ginza became Tokyo's premier venue for kabuki theater, which at that time was itself undergoing of considerable innovation and reform.

The transformation of Ginza was illustrated with delightful detail as early as 1874 (just two years after the fire) in the triptych woodcut by Utagawa Hiroshige III with the expressive title "A Scenic View of Tokyo Enlightenment." In addition to new fashions and borrowed architecture, the print showed the passing of Tokyo as a city of canals, with the focus of activity clearly now being on the bridge over a barely seen canal and on the new wide street. As with Asakusa and so many other neighborhoods, the 1923 earthquake wrecked it all, but recovery in Ginza was relatively speedy and resulted in an expanded reputation for the district as an up-and-coming shopping and relaxation center. It was not long before the modern boys and modern girls returned to Ginza, resuming their favorite pastime of *ginbura*, "aimless strolling in Ginza," as business entrepreneurs opened more and more restaurants, bars, beer halls, dance halls, movie theaters, and other places for their enjoyment. Kabukiza was rebuilt by 1925 and still stands as a rare, older architectural gem in the center of Tokyo and a popular destination for both Japanese and foreign tourists. A recent book by Miriam Silverberg (2006) provides a richly detailed account, complete with reproductions of delightful old posters and photographs, of Japanese modernity between the time of the earthquake and the buildup to war in China and the Pacific in the celebrated leisure and entertainment worlds of both Asakusa and Ginza.

As Japan recovered from the devastation of World War II and its economy soared through the 1970s and 1980s to global status, Tokyo's downtown came to be the most valuable real estate in the world and home turf for countless of the world's new richest companies and richest men. A lot of the excess wealth was spent in Ginza, particularly in the hundreds of hostess clubs that came to be a staple of the neighborhood. There were hostesses in other neighborhoods, including in nearby Shimbashi and Akasaka, in Ueno, emerging Shinjuku, and Ikebukuro, and in other districts, but Ginza was the acknowledged lodestone. Think of Ginza in the years of Japan's bubble (1970s into the 1990s) as where Japanese corporate executives and well-placed politicians came the short distances from their offices to continue their work days in a lounge atmosphere. They came after work and even during normal working hours, met in pairs or groups as business meetings called for, and enjoyed comfortable seating along with music, alcoholic drinks, and the company of pretty young women who were paid to say nice things to them, light their cigarettes, and keep beer and cocktail glasses filled. Sometimes such "meetings" lasted long into the night, and sometimes there were multiple meetings per night in club after club. Many customers found specific hostess clubs that suited them best and became treasured regulars in these establishments, even "members," spending big again and again each time they returned. They also developed personal attachments to favorite hostesses and showered them with money and gifts.

The side streets of Ginza came to have hundreds of hostess clubs and thousands upon thousands of young, pretty hostesses. The money that supported this economy was almost never one's own but was from excessively copious corporate and government entertainment accounts that the bubble both allowed and expected. In fact, it was (and still is) common for no cash to be exchanged at the end of an evening, but for the tab to be added to a monthly bill that the club issues directly to the companies for which the club-goers work.

Some clubs enjoyed high prestige status and were the exclusive domains of *ichiban* clients, that is, first-rank individuals such as company presidents, section chiefs, and high government officials, along with their special guests, while other clubs that were cheaper were subscribed to by companies for the business entertainment of lower-level executives. Companies that wanted to impress clients or build stronger business relationships had choices in how lavish they wanted to be in entertaining their clients, ranging from full-blown parties in private clubs with high-cost hostesses to just dinner and drinks in a nice restaurant. In his fun book about the "pink side" of Japan in the bubble, Nicholas Bornoff cites what he describes as a long-standing joke about the pricing formula in Ginza bars: "Just for starters it's 10,000 yen to cross the threshold, 10,000 to sit down, ten for a glass and 10,000 each for the ice cubes" (1991, 258). An exaggeration, yes, particularly about the ice cubes, but with table charges, hostess fees, and other costs, total nightly tabs of 100,000 yen per person (in round number US$1,000) were (and still are to some extent) quite normal.

Today, Ginza is also known for its department stores, exclusive art galleries and clothing boutiques, and gleaming new emporia, one after the other, with brightly lit displays of some of the world's most overpriced fashions. On Sundays the main street is closed to vehicles and becomes a pedestrian paradise for today's modern boys and modern girls, for dog owners and their beloved dressed-up dogs, for families, and for tourists. As seen at night, the side streets are still all restaurants and clubs, including private restaurants and clubs, piled one atop the other, six floors, eight, ten, or twelve floors, building after building, block after block, still hundreds of them. They start filling at dusk, first with the arrival of hostesses, still thousands of them (but maybe fewer thousands) arriving by taxi or walking a block or two from a subway exit, and then by their businessmen clients, also still numbering in the thousands, also arriving by taxi and subway, but very prominently as well in shiny black company cars, being dropped off by their drivers, who then wait patiently nearby. More than a decade of economic troubles in Japan, plus reforms affecting the uses of expense accounts, have meant that there is less money than there once was to support the extravagances of the past, but the hostess clubs of Ginza are still there nevertheless. There has also been a shift in Tokyo to higher proportions of foreign hostesses, in part perhaps to save labor costs, but also because of new tastes among some business executives for the company of tall blondes. That fact is especially relevant to Roppongi today.

Shinjuku and Shibuya

Both Shinjuku and Shibuya are huge commercial centers about three kilometers apart on Tokyo's west side and are built around cavernous interconnected train and subway stations where commuters change between train lines to bedroom communities more or less to the west, southwest, and northwest and subway lines that run beneath central Tokyo. They are also principle stations on the Yamanote Line, the famous ultracrowded rail line that loops around central Tokyo. That line, color-coded yamanote green, appears on a map a bit like an irregular twenty-nine-pearl necklace that has been laid somewhat asymmetrically on a flat surface, each pearl representing in sequence one of the twenty-nine stations along the circuit. The differences in size and luster of the pearls correspond to the size and prestige of each of the stations. Along with Tokyo Station, the largest stations are Shibuya and Shinjuku. The necklace is pushed outward a bit toward the west, where the Yamanote Line runs along the margins of inner Tokyo directly through our two large-pearl stations, and is pushed inward on the east side where it runs through Tokyo Station and other stops in the heart of the CBD. You can think of Roppongi as being in the space within that pearly confinement, somewhat to the west and south of dead center, two stations by subway from its closest pearl, Ebisu Station.

Shinjuku is by far the bigger of these "subcenters." Along with Shibuya and Ikebukuro, another west-side commercial center on the Yamanote Line, it had been designated by Tokyo planners in the 1960s and 1970s as a preferred site for new commercial development to take some of the load off the overcrowded CBD (hence the term *subcenter*) and to bring jobs and retailing a bit closer to the huge commuter population in west-side neighborhoods and suburbs. It grew to become the biggest subcenter because of its favorable location at a well-established crossroads and site advantages such as unique available space for new construction. Its complex rail station handles more than 3.2 million passengers per working day, making Shinjuku the city's busiest commuter station. The impressive skyline of tall new office buildings in the vicinity of Shinjuku Station has been called "Tokyo's Manhattan" (Popham 1985). The retailing sector in Shinjuku, ranging from department stores and electronics emporia to restaurants, pachinko parlors, movie theaters, and extraordinarily large numbers of sex businesses, exceeds both in sum and in many individual categories that of any other commercial center in the metropolis. Shibuya ranks second, being especially popular with a huge niche market of affluent young consumers, while Ikebukuro has its own characteristic mix of offices, department stores, and nightlife destinations huddled around its commuter station.

As commercial centers built around train-subway stations, these two centers, as well as Ikebukuro and Ueno on the other side of the Yamanote loop, have many features in common, including similar mixes of land uses and corresponding internal spatial patterns (Cybriwsky 1988). They also have major centers of play that have emerged over recent decades as Tokyo's biggest, surpassing all of the entertainment districts just discussed, including hostess-rich Ginza, and much bigger by far (in numbers of establishments, numbers of customers, etc.) than our Roppongi. Much of their popularity can be attributed to the advantages of their crossroads location where millions of commuters pass daily as they move between home and work or school, and a favorable location on the Tokyo rail and subway network that allows for groups of individuals who live, work, or go to school in different parts of the metropolis to come together at a place that is convenient for all.

Like in the other entertainment districts, the crowds begin to build in the evenings after work or school hours, as customers arriving from different directions pour from trains and subways at their respective commuter station nodes and then filter en masse, in rush hour mode, from station gates toward their respective playgrounds. These places are also busy on nonwork, nonschool days, most especially Saturday and Sunday afternoons and evenings. This bit of time-space geography is most clear at Shibuya, where its mostly young clientele exit the station into a large staging area plaza in front, where they tend to wait for others in their party, and then cross the famous main intersection in Shibuya (Shibuya Crossing) by the thousands with every light change, heading to where they plan to have fun. Many of them enter the Shibuya playground through an arched open gate at the far end of the intersection marking the start of Shibuya senta-gai (Shibuya Central Street), a brightly lit and raucous main pedestrian street through the heart of this young people's entertainment district. There are other gates in Shibuya too, to other entertainment zones near the station, and gates as well in Shinjuku, Ikebukuro, and virtually all other sakariba in Tokyo. Roppongi, however, has none.

The best known of the entertainment districts in these three west-side sub-centers is Kabukichō in Shinjuku. The name means "place of kabuki theater," but the planned theater was never built. Instead, this is Tokyo's main "sin city," a gigantic urban fantasyland for adults, a total escape, if only for a few minutes or a few hours, for the tens of thousands who enter on a given day, from all the ills and oppressions that surround them (Cybriwsky 1998, 159; Pons 1984). It is most famous for its several hundred sex businesses: sex-selling hostess clubs, strip shows, peep shows, "no-panties coffee shops," pornography emporiums, *telekura* stations, and, of course, the ever-popular soaplands.[7] A lot of what goes on is kinky (Van Hook 1989). That would be the case for the *nozoki-beya* in which customers pay to peek "in secret" at actresses representing "mama/big sister/auntie taking off her dress," and at establishments where salarymen can have their diapers changed and derrieres baby-powdered by a young female "nurse" in uniform (Richie 1999, 96–98). There are also a great many "host clubs," a rather new kind of establishment in which women pay for the company of attractive young men, inside the club or outside. Interestingly, many of the clients are hostesses who feel a need to be on the other side of a club's table, being on the receiving end of flattery instead of always giving it. At least one such club in Kabukichō has Korean hosts instead of Japanese to capitalize on Japan's "Korea boom" and Japanese women's crush on heartthrob actor Bae Yong Joon (Schreiber et al. 1997, 108–9).

There are also "legitimate" diversions in Shinjuku such as movie theaters, bowling alleys, games arcades, pachinko parlors, baseball batting cages and cages for slamming golf balls, karaoke clubs, and lots of fine restaurants, but the emphasis and reputation of Kabukichō is on sex. The customers are mostly middle-aged salarymen, Japan's legions of dark-suited male office workers, as well as younger Japanese males, while the sex workers are mostly young Japanese and Southeast Asian women. Sadly, their numbers have also included schoolchildren in their teens, attracted to such work by the premium prices that older men are willing to pay for their services and by perceived needs for purchases of expensive consumer items such as clothing and accessories, foreign travel, and concert tickets. Kabukichō is a gangsterish place as well, with tough-looking touts and doormen at the front of many establishments, distinguished by dark suits and ties, punch perm hair, and stern looks. That foreigners are generally not welcome is evident in the glares that we receive from said doormen and in the signs that are posted outside establishments that read "Japanese Only" or "No Foreigners Allowed" (Arudou 2004). Ironically, and completely bizarrely as well, one such den of discriminating discrimination, with a "Japanese only" sign written in English at its front door, has the name American Crystal. That, too, is written on the front door, but only in Japanese. Still another establishment with a Japanese-only policy sports a sign on the door that it is an "American and British Club."

A prominent entertainment district of a different sort in Shinjuku is the area known as Shinjuku Ni-chōme (Shinjuku 2-chōme), or simply Ni-chōme or Nicho. It is Tokyo's premier gay-lesbian district. It has a reported two to three hundred gay and lesbian bars of various kinds within a relatively small area, possibly making this district the densest concentration of gay and lesbian bars per block in the world. Most of the establishments are Japanese, as one would expect, but several have a decidedly foreigner orientation in which English is the first language. Nicho also has several restaurants and cafés that have mostly gay or lesbian clientele, massage parlors and saunas, gay- and lesbian-oriented retail shops, some streets and street corners where cruising is common, and office bases for gay-lesbian social-political activism and publications. There are other concentrations of gay and lesbian bars in Tokyo as well, including several in Roppongi that are not very widely known, some in Shibuya, others in Ikebukuro, and still others elsewhere in the metropolis (Ueno, Asakusa, Nakano), but those other concentrations are all much smaller than Nicho and do not qualify as "gay districts." There is a book still to be written about Shinjuku Ni-chōme in particular and about gay and lesbian social geographies in Tokyo more generally. An excellent introduction to the topic is the essay by Mark McLelland, "Japan's Original 'Gay Boom'" (2006) and his two books on the subject (McLelland 2005; McLelland, Suganuma, and Welker 2007).

There is also reason for someone to write a book about Shibuya. Second only to Shinjuku as a retailing and entertainment center in the metropolis, its clientele are mostly high school and college-aged avid consumers. Instead of the sins of salaryman Kabukichō, the attractions of Shibuya are shopping and more shopping for anything and everything in fashion, seeing and being seen by like-fashioned peers, and perhaps the chase to find a like-minded partner. That some of the money that is spent in Shibuya is money earned in the "water trade," or *mizu shobai* (a popular euphemism for the nighttime pleasures industry), of Kabukichō or other "pink" centers would have center stage in one of the chapters of that book. An iconic landmark that symbolizes Shibuya's young consumer world is a multistore, multistory shopping center named 109 (a pun in Japanese) that looms over a prime street junction within sight of Shibuya Crossing and is a focal point for shoppers, especially young women, of the latest fashions in clothing and accessories. Among the more interesting bits and pieces to read about Shibuya culture are the brilliant insights by the dean of prolificacy on Japan, Donald Richie, particularly in his book *The Image Factory* (2003), sociologist John Clammer's many references to the neighborhood in his study of Japanese urban consumption (1997), and the recent flurry of pair-written fun books about fashion in Shibuya and its fashion-conscious neighbor Harajuku by Godoy and Vartanian (2007), Keet and Manabe (2007), and Macias and Evans (2007).[8]

As a nighttime entertainment center, Shibuya caters to primarily a younger crowd in comparison to Shinjuku, although there are people of all ages, and one specific small area is a mini-Kabukichō with sex shops, soaplands, and pachinko. For the most part, Shibuya Center Street and other youth-oriented pleasure zones are a medley of games arcades, karaoke parlors, movie theaters, fast-food restaurants (Shibuya probably has more McDonalds restaurants per unit area than any other place on earth), and dance clubs and bars with the music of the times for young people. Nowadays it is hip-hop and electronic music that seem especially popular, although the variety of genres available in Shibuya is wide and also includes R&B, reggae, metal, various more acceptable forms of rock, and Japanese pops, among others. There are many start-up bands and new singers of all kinds among Tokyo's restless and creative youth, and there are plenty of venues in Shibuya that are willing to give them a stage in hopes that they might draw a crowd of paying customers.

For couples in a romantic mood, as well as those engaged in commercial sexual exchanges, both Shibuya and Shinjuku have large subdistricts of quiet streets lined with discreet hotels that rent fantasy rooms by the hour. In Shibuya the main such district is called Dōgenzaka, adjacent to a bar and nightclub district that could serve to put couples in the mood, while in Shinjuku it is Shin-Ōkubo, immediately adjacent to Kabukichō. The hotels used to be called *love hotels*, but in Japan's ever changing, self-correcting lexicon, the terms in favor now are *leisure hotel* and *fashion hotel* (Richie 1999, 100). In Tokyo as a whole there are some three thousand such rental establishments, testament to both the great size of the sex industry and the inconvenient location and inadequate arrangements for privacy in people's homes and apartments. A recent book by Sarah Chaplin (2007) has explored the sociology of the love hotel phenomenon in urban Japan, complete with illustrations about architecture, interior decor, and in-room facilities and equipment. As for me, I am getting back to Roppongi.

Geishas and Hostesses

In the return to Roppongi from this tour of Tokyo's famous entertainment districts through time, additional background information about the large hostess clubs economy in urban Japan is helpful to distinguish it from its cousin predecessor, the geisha tradition, and to explain some details about how the contemporary Japanese institution operates. Hostessing is a major part of the Roppongi scene and, in fact, is vividly appropriate to the book's title, *Roppongi Crossing*. This is where young women's needs to earn a better income intersect in interesting ways with both the workings of Japan's corporate world and the personal needs of many Japanese men; it is also where many of the informal "international crossings" that take place in Roppongi are most sharply seen. In that regard, we observe that nowadays many Japanese clients prefer the company of foreign hostesses, if only for a short-term, new experience, and that there is demand along these lines for hostesses from many nations, along with the continuation of traditional preferences for Japanese hostesses in Japanese (i.e., not international) settings. There are also non-Japanese clients in hostess establishments, some as the guests of Japanese businessmen-hosts, but also some who are "shopping" or "playing" independently. However, in Japan foreign men comprise only a small minority of hostesses' clients. This section provides general background information only, leaving discussion of the rhythms of hostess-client interactions in Roppongi specifically for chapter 4.

First, although there are similarities between the two, hostesses are not geishas and vice versa. The geisha tradition goes back about three centuries to the middle of the rule by the Tokugawa line of shōguns (1603–1868) and began with male entertainers as opposed to *onna* (female) geisha, who emerged later and came to define the profession. They were well-trained and highly accomplished singers, musicians, dancers, storytellers, and game players who spent the early years of their youth in preparation for entraining male companions in special tea houses (*ochaya*) and restaurants (*ryōtei*) and then ascended through various stages of accomplishment to higher ranks. The occupation was organized into discrete groups called *hanamachi* (flower towns), where every geisha maintained registry and through which she received assignments. Sex services were not part of the job, although individual geisha were free to be intimate with favorite or favored clients. Such relationships were always discreet, as their personal reputations and the reputations of the hanamachi to which they belonged were at stake. It was also common for an individual geisha to accept a special client as her patron (*danna*). Normally, he was a very wealthy man who could afford to support her and her cultural studies as well as to support his own family;

geisha-danna relationships often became exclusive and personal and were also discreet and private. The geisha occupation has been declining in Japan. In the 1920s, there were some eighty thousand geisha in the country; now the total is below ten thousand with the largest numbers being in the traditional geisha districts of Kyoto (*Japan*, 1:446). In Tokyo, the remaining geisha are mostly in the Ginza-Shimbashi area, in Akasaka, and in Kagurazaka, but not in Roppongi.

There are popular misconceptions outside Japan that associate geisha with prostitution, perhaps high-class prostitution. The erroneous impressions are likely to be partly attributed to confusion of genuine geishas with "geisha-girls" who provided sexual services to U.S. military and occupation personnel after World War II. They were also called *pan-pan* girls, a term whose origins are obscure (Dower 1999, 132; Seidensticker 1990, 186), and "geesha", as the word was mispronounced by foreign language–challenged Americans. There were quite a few prostitutes in postwar Japan, driven by the desperation of poverty, all charging low prices, and occupation forces far from home were exceptionally willing clients. Those relationships may have altered from then on what many Western men, especially Americans, thought of Japanese women. The confusion was compounded by the fact than many "geesha" dressed in kimonos specifically to have potential clients think of them as geisha, adding to their marketability. But even well before the sad time of the occupation, there was confusion about geisha and prostitutes. In the Yoshiwara of old, for example, there were geisha who entertained men with music and stories and other well-prepared arts, and those who made motions in those directions but were more truly sex workers. As Yoshiwara declined, it was largely because the geisha traditions were being lost to geisha pretender prostitutes, to a point where now there are no longer geisha pretenders but only soap specialists.[9]

Hostessing emerged in the twentieth century in conjunction with the rise of corporate Japan, but its history has yet to be written. What hostesses have in common with geishas is that they entertain men with conversation, which can often be skilled conversation, and sex is not part of the job. There is little if any training for hostessing, although intelligent hostesses do learn to improve their abilities to please men with words and smiles, and informal coaching among hostesses and by the *mama-sans* (typically former hostesses) who manage them is a daily routine. In the case of many foreign hostesses, even conversation does not take place, as quite a few have very little facility with the Japanese language, so communication is through smiles and body language only, and perhaps also by cleavage and thigh. In Elena Shpak's recent film *Hallucination*, there is a poignant scene where a new hostess, just arrived from Russia and speaking no Japanese, is asked by clients in English, "Where are you from?" She responds with one word, "Rossiya", which causes the clients to exclaim in return, "Vodka!" That then produces a bottle of vodka for the table from which a sweet-smiling "Mira" (played by Antonina Revenko) continually pours shots for the salarymen at her station, who keep raising their glasses and shouting, "Vodka! Horosho!" (Vodka! Good!), because that is all they know how to say to her.[10] Foreign hostesses who have the right looks and are good at Japanese are in great demand and earn very high, essentially nontaxable, incomes.

Like the geisha who preceded them, hostesses are not prostitutes, unless one defines prostitution to include the "sale" of sexually witty or suggestive conversation. That's what skilled hostesses do: they "sell" fantasies about sexual relationships that will never happen, and smile and pour drinks. Some show cleavage as they work. Some hostesses do exchange sex for cash or gifts, although the exchange is not as direct as in more common prostitution exchanges and is almost always discreet and private to protect the hostess, the club that employs her, and the customer. In most establishments, there are extremely strict rules about appropriate versus inappropriate behavior, as business reputations are at stake, and employees and customers who are in violation of standards are not welcome back. Even hugs and touches can be off limits, much less kisses or other physical expressions of affection. Words and body language only, please. The job of hostesses is to entertain clients with conversation, the more interesting and the more flattering the better. While some men enjoy discussing politics, current events, movies, or literature, many others want just banter and what Allison referred to as "breast talk" (Allison 1994, 46–49). Maybe the largest numbers of men simply want to be flattered and want assurance that, yes, their bosses are jerks and that, yes indeed, their wives don't understand them. As hostesses encourage clients to prolong such conversations, they keep pouring more and more drinks, have clients purchase (weak) drinks for themselves, and keep running the night's tab and their own commissions higher and higher.

There are several excellent sources of written information about the hostess industry in Japan, including about how the system works, how it fits into Japanese society and business routines, and the various dos and don'ts of hostessing, particularly those written by women who once worked as hostesses. The best study is the previously cited scholarly social anthropological explication by Duke University professor Anne Allison and happens to be set in Roppongi in a club that she called Bijo (Allison 1994). The book originated as a doctoral dissertation and focuses separately on various aspects of the hostess club: the women who work in the clubs, the actual establishments, and the men who are the clients; she explains how they all fit together in the unique context of Japanese society. I also recommend a short and informative newspaper article by Samantha Culp, which includes a brief tour of Roppongi's hostess clubs (Culp 2006); the chapter called "Jackie: The Hostess" in Karl Taro Greenfield's portrait of different subcultures among contemporary youth in Japan (1994, 227–43); and the wide-ranging discussion of Japan's "water trade" in the book *Pink Samurai* by Nicholas Bornoff (1991). A short, handy guide to what being a hostess is all about, called "So You Want to be a Hostess?," is an anonymously posted online article that seems accurate and provides some realistic details.[11] Still another source is the recent exposé by Japan visitor Clare Campbell (2009). Finally, I also recommend some outstanding films that are centered on the Tokyo or Roppongi hostess world.[12] My comments in this section of the book and in "Hostess Heaven" in chapter 4 come from these and other sources and, of course, from my own research interviews, observations, and casual conversations in Roppongi.

The subject of the hostess economy in Japan is complex, sensitive, and controversial. While this is not the place for a full-blown treatment of the subject, I make some overall comments that outline differences of opinion about hostessing and provide needed context and explanation. Arguments on the negative side stress that the hostess economy is inappropriately lookist, valuing young women for their physical appearance and their presentation of sexiness instead of other attributes, and that it unfairly exploits those attributes for the benefit of men who themselves are no longer competitive because of age and perhaps paunch, but who command disproportionate power because they are wealthy or on expense accounts. Furthermore, there are arguments specifically against the expense account aspects of this economy, saying that in the end it is all consumers in Japan who pay for men's enjoyment in hostess bars, as the expenses that hostesses' clients ring up are passed on to consumers in the form of higher prices. Even worse, until recently when controls were tightened, it was possible for government bureaucrats to "conduct business" in hostess establishments on expense accounts in the public sector, meaning that taxpayers had been paying for those bureaucrats' nights out. Still other arguments point to dysfunctional aspects of family life in Japan that are exacerbated by the hostess phenomenon, saying that the habit of late nights out in hostess bars for men, typically justified as "working late," is detrimental to the obligations of marriage and fatherhood, and that having aging men cavorting socially with much younger women is abnormal, unhealthy, and distortive of reality.

On the other hand, hostessing has enjoyed several generations of popularity in Japan as a modern-day descendant of traditional geisha services, and it is possible to counter some of the criticism and even make arguments in favor. For one, the most successful hostesses are distinguished not necessarily by physical appearance as much as by intelligence, personality, wit, humor, and an ability to make another human being feel comfortable, and that hostesses grow in these skills with coaching and experience. Second, what exploitation goes on is less exploitation of pretty young women by moneyed, aging men than it is exploitation of vain or vulnerable men with deep pockets by smart, sweet-talking women who know how to extract cash and expensive gifts from them. Third, even though hostessing work is hard, encompassing late hours and frequent long conversations with people who might be considered dull, stupid, egocentric, or unnervingly creepy, that is actually not much different than work in many other occupations, including those of many of the hostesses' clients, and the pay is quite good, particularly for someone at a fairly young age and with no other professional skills as yet. In fact, hostessing pays quite a few college tuitions, making the difference for many young women as to whether they obtain a higher education or not. Even more, I have been told a number of times about instances in which the material learned in a university class was applied successfully to "hostess bar talk," with appropriate rewards for the brainy hostess.

Shifting the focus from hostesses to their clients, it can be said that in the high-pressure and excessively hierarchical world of Japanese business, there is a legitimate need for male employees to spend time in fantasy worlds, however banal, to relax and stay sane. Second, although the vast majority of clients in hostess bars are Japanese, in Roppongi at least there are also significant numbers of foreigner clients, mostly, I am told, young, unattached men who make enormous incomes in high-pressure finance jobs and need no-pressure personal relationships to relax. Furthermore, some might argue that comfortable and relaxed settings such as hostess bars are advantageous for entertaining business clients and for speaking freely about complex business issues, and that good hostesses actually perform valuable functions in helping the Japanese economy operate more smoothly. Allison observed that most businessmen clients of hostess establishments consider one primary function of the hostess assigned to their table is "to smooth the conversational path between men" (1994, 47). Finally, visiting hostess bars is a smaller vice than what many men are capable of doing, so hostess bars might be doing society a service by keeping certain individuals safely indoors at night and engaged in conversation with skilled professionals who are proficient in certain aspects of masculine psychology.

Foreigner Flavor

The character of Roppongi and its surroundings also derives from Tokyo's history of international contact and settlement. That history can be traced first to the occupation of Zempukuji, the powerful Buddhist temple on a hilltop just south of Roppongi, by uninvited American diplomats as the shogunate was in its final gasps, and then later to another uninvited occupation, that by U.S. forces of Japan as a whole between 1945 and 1952, during which time Roppongi was home to thousands of American soldiers. Now, the Roppongi area is one of the country's prime concentrations of foreigner residence and employment, particularly at the top end of pay scales and prestige. Foreigners from Western nations such as the United States and those in Western Europe are especially numerous. Many are employed in high-paying, white-collar occupations in corporate offices, financial institutions, and foreign embassies, although there have been significant declines in all of these categories in recent years because of a slumping global economy. There are also many foreigners who work in Roppongi's nighttime economy who live in the area, but this is a fairly new development and might be changing. By contrast, foreigners from developing nations who work in factories or construction tend to live in other parts of the metropolis. Minato Ward, of which Roppongi is near the center, is a leader in Japan in numbers of offices of foreign companies and institutions and employs more foreign "bosses" than any other jurisdiction in Japan. Within or very near Roppongi are (or were) the Japan offices of such investment companies as Lehman Brothers, Goldman Sachs, and Credit Suisse, major manufacturing companies of well-known consumer products such as IBM, Motorola, Samsung, and Mercedes-Benz, and world headquarters of joint Japanese-foreign companies such as copy industry giant Fuji Xerox. Japan's biggest foreign university, the Tokyo branch of Philadelphia's Temple University, is also near Roppongi.

Perhaps the clearest demonstration of the Roppongi area's upscale international character is the distribution of foreign embassies in Japan. They are all in Tokyo, of course, the national capital, but within Tokyo, 79 of the 146 embassies (54.1 percent) are in Minato Ward, with those of the Russian Federation, Spain, Singapore, Saudi Arabia, and the Philippines being in or immediately adjacent to Roppongi. The large U.S. Embassy is near Roppongi too, in Minato Ward's Akasaka district, and its residential compound, the largest embassy residential compound in Japan, has a Roppongi address and is only a short walk from Roppongi Crossing (table 2.3).

Over the years, I have met about a dozen ambassadors to Japan from various foreign countries, either in Roppongi or nearby. This number includes three or

TABLE 2.3 Foreign embassies in Tokyo by ward

Minato	79
Shibuya	19
Chiyoda	18
Meguro	12
Shinagawa	7
Setagaya	6
Shinjuku	3
Chūō	1
Taitō	1
14 remaining wards	0
TOTAL	146

Source: Compiled from directory of Tokyo's foreign embassies and consulates.

four ambassadors from the world's largest or most powerful countries; I met them in connection with ceremonial functions related to my university employment. For me, that was a new kind of interaction. However, in Roppongi, I made friends informally with three or four ambassadors from small countries, grey-haired men like myself, "regular guys" who pass time in a Starbucks or other non-night establishments and are happy to strike up a conversation with a person at the next table.

Minato Ward publishes a running count of its total population and its total foreigner population every month on its Web site, the data coming from the registrations at local government offices that that are required of all residents, most famously of foreigners. The most recent numbers as of this writing, for September 1, 2008, showed a total population of 218,845 for the ward and 22,098 foreigners, 10.1 percent of the total. That is the highest foreigner percentage in any of twenty-three the wards in central Tokyo, an area of about 8.8 million people and 3.4 percent foreigner population. Three other wards, Shinjuku, Adachi, and Edogawa in decreasing order, each have more foreigners than Minato Ward, but their total populations are much larger. Within Minato Ward, the largest population of foreigners are Americans, with 4,608 of the total, nearly one in four of all foreigners in the ward. They are followed in descending numerical order by Koreans (2,978), Chinese (2,397), United Kingdom passport holders (1,562), Filipinos (1,028), and Australians (916). Minato Ward ranks first among the twenty-three wards in numbers of Americans, UK passport holders, Australians, and Indians, and second in numbers of French residents. This ethnic mix reflects Minato Ward's character as a place where residents are typically higher paid, white-collar workers in comparison to the more blue-collar nature of other parts of Tokyo where the foreigner population includes more immigrants and guests from developing countries, with employment in the lower-paying service sector, manufacturing, and construction.[13]

Uneasiness with Foreigners

Urban Japan has a long history of designated districts for foreigner settlement, and the Roppongi area can be considered a modern-day manifestation of this tradition. Formal segregation decrees aimed at foreigners no longer apply, but the complex workings of urban economics and Japan's continual unease with foreign residents and foreign visitors have combined to create a social geography landscape that concentrates foreigners into a relatively small number of neighborhoods, leaving the majority of urban terrain essentially Japanese-only. In this section, I cast light on Roppongi's status as a place where foreigners congregate by reviewing the history of foreigner concentrations in Japan (for other aspects of the history of foreign settlement in Japan see Yamawaki 2000). There will be intriguing parallels between that interesting history and the specific history of Roppongi.

During the Tokugawa shogunate (1603–1867), the small numbers of foreigners who lived and worked in Japan were heavily concentrated on Dejima (or Deshima), a small, fan-shaped artificial island constructed in 1634–36 in the waters off Nagasaki (Kyushu, Japan's large southern island) specifically for this purpose. In the early years, the residents were Portuguese, but then after 1641, when the Portuguese were sent off to join their Catholic brethren in Macao, the island housed mostly Dutch traders, the only Westerners who were permitted by the shōguns to do business in the country. Dejima was the only place in Japan where Westerners could reside until 1856, when a new era began to take shape. During the time of isolation, travel within Japan outside Dejima by Westerners was rare and strictly controlled. Moreover, except for prostitutes who came to service the foreign traders, it was rare as well for Japanese to enter Dejima.

With the opening of Japan to other nations after the arrival in 1853 and 1854 of Commodore Matthew Perry's "black ships" in Edo Bay (now Tokyo Bay), the center of foreigner population switched to Yokohama. That settlement had theretofore been a quiet fishing village, but it was designated as the foreigners' trading city in 1859 and began to grow quickly as an international settlement, gaining evermore international notice. It was close to Edo, soon to be renamed Tokyo, the national capital, but was thought to be far enough outside the capital to keep it safe from the intruders.

Early Yokohama was divided into discrete parts for foreigners and locals, with Kannai, meaning "within the barrier," being the officially designated foreigners' district. Most of its residents were Americans and Europeans. It was separated from Kangai ("outside the barrier") by Nihon-dōri (Japan Street), a broad tree-lined boulevard along which foreigner and Japanese trading companies faced each other from opposite sides. For play, the foreigners were invited to visit Miyozakichō, a licensed quarter for prostitution that had been laid out across a canal in a vacant area beyond the city's edge. The confines of Kannai did not hold for long, and soon other foreigner districts emerged in Yokohama, most notably the Bund, a waterfront commercial and trading street, and Yamate, an attractive residential neighborhood that grew along with the foreigners' wealth on a prominent hilltop. Several blocks back from the waterfront, a "Chinatown" developed in Yokohama, reflecting yet another lineament of emerging segregation patterns. Not far away were dubious little districts nicknamed "The Swamp" and "Blood Town" that were crowded with sailors' bars and unlicensed brothels.

But even as the Bund and Yamate were in their first stages of development in the 1860s, it became clear that Yokohama would not be able to hold the capital district's foreigners, and that the "blue-eyed barbarians" would soon be encroaching on Tokyo. Accordingly, Japan's defenders ordered that Tsukiji, a district of reclaimed land along Tokyo's waterfront, be prepared as a foreigners' settlement. Like Kannai, it was gated. The district was opened in 1867 and housed several of the foreigners' legations, including that of the Americans. There was also a Frenchman who was described in an 1872 list of residents as an "equestrian acrobat" (Seidensticker 1983, 36). As was the case earlier in Yokohama and Dejima, there was concern in Japan about foreign men having their ways too freely with Japanese women, so a special district of brothels and teahouses was created. A major objective was to please foreign diplomats who might then become inclined to negotiate more favorable treaties with Japan. This special district was New Shimabara, opened in 1869. It took its name from the famous licensed quarter in Kyoto. Ironically, Shimabara was also the name of the district in Kyushu, Japan's large southern island, which was home to the country's main concentration of foreign missionary activity and convert population in the sixteenth century, before the shōguns closed Japan to such influences. The foreigners were said to have come in to New Shimabara in large enough numbers to look, but they did not pay (Seidensticker 1983, 38–39). Consequently, New Shimabara, like Christian Shimabara, was short lived.

A second landmark connected with the Tsukiji foreigner settlement was the Hoterukan, a large hotel opened in 1868. Located across a canal from the main part of the foreigner settlement, it was a curious-looking structure that combined a pseudo-Western façade with traditional Japanese architectural foundations. Even the name was a blend, with the first syllables coming from the Japanese pronunciation of *hotel* and *kan* being the Japanese word for "inn." These choices reflected the building's purpose: it should be a meeting place for foreigners and Japanese. This experiment failed too. The building was sold at a loss in 1870 and was then consumed in the devastating fire that swept the city in 1872. A lasting legacy, however, one that was to have great impact on modern Tokyo, was that the Hoterukan was a construction project of Shimizu Kisuke, the founder of Shimizu-gumi, one of the largest and most influential construction companies in Japan.[14] As previously discussed, Roppongi has had a special link to the inner workings of Japan's construction state.

Following the early experiments at Tsukiji, foreigners began to settle more freely over wider areas in Tokyo, particularly in the better districts where foreign legations were established and near the places of their employment. In contrast to the missionaries, traders, and shipwrecked sailors who constituted the first waves of foreign arrivals, the immigration that arrived after April 1868, following promulgation of the Charter Oath calling for Japan to gain knowledge from around the world, consisted heavily of foreign teachers and technical advisors. Referred to as *oyatoi gaikokujin* (hired foreigners), these migrants numbered in the several thousands and hailed from more than two dozen nations. Most of them, however, were Americans, British, French, and Germans. Many, such as the architect Josiah Conder, mentioned earlier in connection with the design of Tokyo's first office district, Marunouchi, came by specific invitation from Japan's modernizers and contributed greatly to the country's technological progress and internationalization. They settled primarily in Tokyo, which had been designated as the nation's classroom for the learning of foreign ways, often near the offices of Meiji government and schools that employed them. For example, many foreign government workers were assigned housing in the "Kaga estate" at what is today the Hongō campus of Tokyo University (Seidensticker 1983, 36).

The Tsukiji foreigner settlement was closed in 1899, ending forever Japan's official zoning of foreigner geography. Interestingly, however, segregation policies continued to be applied to foreigners' earthly remains, if not their addresses in life, with many of the most prominent oyatoi gaikokujin being buried in a special section of Aoyama Cemetery, just to the north of Roppongi, that was reserved for foreigners. The site of the Tsukiji foreigner settlement, on the other hand, would eventually be set aside for dead fish and fish about to die, as it became the famous "fish market at the center of the world" (Bestor 2004).

There is one other short-lived chapter of Tokyo foreigner geography to mention, that of a celebrated place called the Rokumeikan. Established in the early 1880s at the insistence of Foreign Minister Kaoru Inoue, who saw it as potentially a valuable asset for his diplomatic efforts against the hated unequal treaties, the Rokumeikan was a large, two-story guest house and gathering hall for social mixing between the upper crust of Tokyo's foreigner population and Japan's cosmopolitan set (Seidensticker 1983, 68–70, 97–101). It was designed in an Italianate style by Josiah Conder and featured a dance hall, an opulent dining room, a reading room, and other venues for "equal" social exchanges. The Japanese government promoted it as a place where Japanese could both learn and then display foreign ways such as Western dress and cuisine, classical music from Europe, and the finer points of waltzes and ballroom dancing. The "Rokumeikan Era" did not last long, ending before the 1880s ended, in part because of anti-foreigner feelings after the 1886 Normanton Incident.[15] Nevertheless the Rokumeikan is remembered fondly for its opulence, sense of romance, and fashionable styles and has been celebrated many times in Japan in film, TV drama, print, and lithographs. The Rokumeikan is a kind of "proto-Roppongi," a place where foreigners went out for good times and met Japanese peers with the same goals.

Awkward Steps

It is likely, however, that the dancing at the Rokumeikan was mostly awkward and stiff, as the majority of Japanese who attended weren't comfortable with the new steps, and more than a few of the foreign guests only pretended to know what they were doing. The specialist instructors from abroad may have been experts, but their charges, both Japanese and foreign, probably tripped up often and were not the best of students. What's more, some of the instructors may have been pretenders, as the curious pattern of foreigners who were not successful in their home countries but then became "big in Japan" after moving abroad has deep roots. Those who live in Japan know quite well the phenomenon of rock or hip-hop bands that could not make it back home but are successful in Japan, second-rate baseball players from the United States who become stars in the less demanding Japanese big leagues, and somewhat eccentric individuals who would seem to have difficulty finding or maintaining employment in their home countries but who manage successful careers in Japan as teachers of foreign languages or other subjects, in technology, or other fields. Even today there are people teaching English in Japan with not only little or no training for that difficult profession, but also with very little facility for correct, native English of any stripe. They are hired because they say they can teach English and, to naive Japanese employers, they look like they speak English.[16]

Like the Rokumeikan was, Roppongi is a place of social interaction between foreigners and Japanese, and not unlike the Rokumeikan during its short life, today's Roppongi and the Roppongi of the recent past have been more or less ascribed the task of being an international contact place. In both settings, too, are parallel social topographies: some Japanese clustering together here, in this corner of the dance floor or in this nightclub or that bar, foreigners clustering in another corner of the room or in different bars and clubs, and a variety of places for cross-cultural mixing. Sometime the interactions are spontaneous, natural, and equal, while others are tentative on account of barriers of language, unfamiliar etiquettes, and sometimes deep-seated cross-national suspicions and mistrust.

From the start of Japan's opening up to the world in the mid-nineteenth century to the present, Japan has been amazingly accommodating to foreigners, welcoming, polite, and uncommonly tolerant of whatever eccentricities or peccadilloes they display. At the same time, Japan has learned to be at least a little wary of foreigners and their intentions and to know that at least some foreigners misrepresent themselves and can bring harm. A step beyond that is prejudice or racism against foreigners, which exists also in Japan, often quite blatantly, both despite of and alongside Japan's welcoming nature. In some cases those prejudices are equal opportunity and apply to all foreigners more or less equally, while in other cases (or among other Japanese), there is more prejudice felt against certain groups of foreigners (e.g., those from poor countries) and less prejudice against others (e.g., those from more prosperous parts of the world). As ensuing chapters discuss, it is understood that in Roppongi the contact is to be on Japan's terms. When foreigners gain ascendancy, either in terms of sheer numbers or in terms of behaviors that are out of synch with Japan or are thought to threaten its cherished orders, Japan has ways to respond as it did in the Normanton years.

Therefore, a central theme in this Roppongi narrative concerns growing perceptions among powerful people in Japan's government and business leadership that foreigners in this particular neighborhood are responsible for more and more problems, that the situation is no longer to be tolerated, and that the Japanese state should respond, leading to a growing police presence in

Roppongi, selective application of immigration laws to cull the foreigner population, and especially big-business redevelopment as the most effective way to introduce a new kind of international flavor into this international district. At the same time, there are the many problems in Tokyo and Japanese society that have been made worse by a life of commuting and spatial separation. The cleanup of Roppongi is a chance to bring improvements in these areas too. Thus, "New Roppongi" is the most natural and most effective response by a construction state to the ills of Roppongi, to Tokyo's persistent commuter malaise, and to other aspects of "the Tokyo Problem" as well.

Other Districts, Other Cities

Roppongi is, of course, not the only district in this huge city that has been targeted for remaking, and Tokyo is, of course, not the only city in which an energetic and strategic remaking of a problematic neighborhood has been undertaken. "New Tokyo" has been taking shape at various fronts simultaneously in this construction-happy city, and there are examples from around the world, some of them quite momentous, where zones of nightlife have been unreservedly erased in favor of a new order. This is not the place for a full account of Tokyo's redevelopment projects because that would require a book of its own, as would an account of analogous cases of strategic redevelopment in other cities and other countries. However, a brief overview of redevelopment trends in Tokyo in general and a few redevelopment stories from selected cities around the world that in one way or another have parallels with events at Roppongi Crossing.

With respect to Tokyo, it is safe to say that no other district in the city parallels what is happening in Roppongi. The city's other famous nightlife zones such as Kabukichō and Shibuya have problems of their own—some of which are quite distinctively criminal—and attract considerable police attention, but they are not as yet targets for sweeping redevelopment and do not carry the "bad foreigner" label to the extent of Roppongi. Where redevelopment does take place in the city, which is in a great many places, it is for reasons other than neighborhood misbehavior. For example, some areas fall to developers because they are in the way of downtown expansion (e.g., inner-ward residential neighborhoods give way for construction of office buildings); other districts are erased because they represent a shift of Tokyo's economy away from industrial production to still more tertiary economic activity; and still other parts of Tokyo are remade as a result of emerging priorities for higher standard residential environments and new goals for increasing urban greenscapes and recreation spaces. At

Odaiba and Toyosu, for example, sizable islands that were reclaimed recently from Tokyo Bay, there are new waterfront and skyline-view residential neighborhoods, upscale and roomy shopping malls, and wide streets with plenty of parking for vehicles of residents and visitors alike. There are also new parks and sandy beaches, new tennis courts—even new hiking trails. Collectively, they all add up to good living near the center of Tokyo and, for those who can afford it, an answer to "the Tokyo Problem."

As could be expected, the emergence of the New Tokyo has attracted a growing academic literature that seeks to explain its source and to fathom its specific contours. If Roppongi gets specific mention in this literature, it is because the district is home to two of the most famous New Tokyo projects, Roppongi Hills and Tokyo Midtown. My own topics of nightlife that might be out of control and foreigners who are not welcome are but footnotes in this literature if they are mentioned at all. Instead, the redevelopment in Roppongi is seen to be taking place because of location alone: the neighborhood is hot real estate in Minato Ward; it is the midpoint between the city's bulging central business district and prosperous commuter centers to the west along the busy Yamanote Line; there were sizable blocks of strategically sited land that could be had fairly conveniently. In fact, thus far the literature is notably ageographic, not focusing on any case study or specific case studies within the Tokyo metropolis, but on macroscale processes instead: economic transitions, political alignments, flows of capital, and the construction state. All of these work together to keep Tokyo current and competitive with other global cities (or even its work-hard rival in Japan, Osaka), with the balances between economic forces and political forces, and between domestic stimuli versus those that are external to Japan being presented differently by different authors. The key studies to consider are those by Andre Sorensen (especially 2002, 2003, 2010), Paul Waley (2002, 2007), Kuniko Fujita (2003), and, a bit presciently, Takashi Machimura (1992, 1994, 1997).

But if Roppongi is unique in Tokyo (and Japan, too) for justification of redevelopment because of alleged misbehavior in the target neighborhood, there are some prominent cases where precisely this has taken place in countries abroad. Perhaps the most obvious example is the famous remaking of Times Square in Manhattan in the last two decades of the twentieth century. There were banners that heralded the "New Times Square" as the makeover moved forward, just like exultant new signage announces the New Roppongi. In Times Square, the victory was one against the drug dealers and prostitutes who had taken over 42nd Street, the pickpockets and armed robbers who preyed on commuters and theatergoers, and the district's large collection of X-rated magazine and video stores, stage performances, and movie theaters. Redevelopment efforts began under the administrations of Mayors Ed Koch (1978–89) and David Dinkins (1990–93), and then gathered steam under tough-guy mayor Rudolph Giuliani (1994–2002), who increased the security presence of the neighborhood and conducted a very public war against the purveyors of pornography and drugs. He also took on those poor New Yorkers who made their living off passersby, most symbolically the city's notorious "squeegee men" (tough-looking men who washed windows of cars stopped in traffic in expectation of tips). Now the "Crossroads of the World" is a fun and safe place and once again a popular tourist destination. "Mom, pop, and the kids" go there from the American heartland, as do visitors from around the world, all of them enjoying new shops and theaters in the shells of the old and reveling in one of the world's greatest shows of animated light—a display that New Yorkers call "spectaculars" and "jumbotrons." For the happy visitors, the criticism that Times Square has been "Disneyfied" is irrelevant.

Other cities have also tackled problem districts in similar or related ways or are now in the process of a makeover: in my own memory and experience in North America we have the old "Baltimore Block" in that revitalized Maryland city, the aptly named "Combat Zone" of Boston, the Broadway entertainment strip in San Francisco, the less and less seedy Hollywood and Vine area in Los Angeles, and both Yonge and Granville Streets in Toronto and Vancouver, respectively. More momentous, however—even revolutionary in the most literal sense of the word—is what transpired decades ago first in Shanghai and then in Havana, Cuba. In the former case, a city that had come to be known as an unparalleled (and notoriously inequitable) international playground (Dong 2000; Field 2010) was shut down and reeducated, first in the wake of the 1949 establishment of the People's Republic and then even more so with the start of the Cultural Revolution in 1966. (The fact that Shanghai is now "back" once again as a nightlife center is still another story.) In the case of Havana, it was the sins of mob-owned casinos and other entertainment emporia, as well as of corrupt politicians from Fulgencio Batista on down, that helped energize the small band of angry patriots who had gathered in the country's remote Sierra Maestra and led them to plot the revolution that eventually succeeded on January 1, 1959 (English 2007). The retaking of Roppongi from the forces of international partying will not be as permanently etched among the landmarks of history as the cases of Shanghai and Havana, if only because the revanchists do not hail from the grassroots, but it is a remarkable revolution nonetheless, albeit one that is local and does usher in new authority and new sets of rules.

CHAPTER THREE

Roppongi Rises

Six Trees

In Tokyo, it is common for subdistricts of the city, major streets, key bridges, hillocks, slopes, and other bits of geography to have names that are instructive about local history. In Roppongi, which means "six trees," it is often assumed that the reference is to specific trees that stood there in the past. As previously mentioned, these "trees" are actually the family names of six feudal lords who had their mansions in the district in the early years of the Tokugawa Shogunate: Uesugi (upper Cryptomeria), Kutsuki (rotting tree), Takagi (tall tree), Aoki (green tree), Katagiri (wayside Paulownia), and Ichiryū (one willow) (Waley 1984, 384–85). They were among the many elites who lived on this somewhat elevated and leafy side of Edo (old Tokyo) that we defined earlier as *yamanote*, "the land in the direction of the mountains." Although not much is known about the specific properties of the six "tree lords," their houses (and those of their neighbors) were almost certainly large and lavish, and their grounds were carefully landscaped in accordance with expectations for persons of their status.

Many of Roppongi's place-names are reminders that this heavily built-up urban district was once green and leafy. For example, there is the district name *Hinokichō*, an old name still in use that predates *Roppongi* and means "place of cypress trees." The ancient shrine Hikawa-jinja, famous for its enormous gingko trees, is in Hinokichō. It is approached via Hinoki-zaka, "Cypress Tree Slope." The word *Hikawa-jinja* means "frozen river shrine" but does not apply to local conditions; instead, the name had been transported to the neighborhood along with the shrine from elsewhere in early Edo times. Other nature names in and near Roppongi include "Raccoon Slope," "Darkness Slope," "Lone Pine Tree Slope," and "Potato-Washing Slope." The name of Roppongi's neighbor, Azabu, means "place where asa (hemp) is grown"; it has had this name from before the time of the shōguns (Waley 1984, 384). The many trees that are girdled with small signs reading *Minato-ku hogoju*, "Minato Ward Protected Tree," are further reminders that the area was once forested. This designation is given to trees with a trunk circumference of one meter or more (Moriyama 1993, 249–50). A grouping of such giants indicates that the site was once the estate of someone important.

Early Roppongi was also the domain of many temples and shrines. In addition to the "Frozen River Shrine" mentioned above, there were also Zōjōji, the huge roadside religious complex on the far side of Tokyo Tower from Roppongi that was mentioned in chapter 2, and Zempukuji, a powerful old temple just south of the neighborhood in today's Moto-Azabu 1-chōme. Zempukuji was described in chapter 2 as the base of operations beginning in 1868 for the first American delegation to Japan and its leader, Townsend Harris. Other temples and shrines are less famous but have also been longstanding ingredients of the Roppongi mix. Many of them were established in Roppongi in response to a decree after the huge fire in Edo in 1657 that religious institutions should vacate the crowded city and find space instead amid the verdure of yamanote. Their approaches were typically lined with shops, refreshment stands, and other businesses, and behind those lanes emerged narrow lanes and alleys with the crowded wooden homes of shopkeepers and the religious proletariat. A great many of the temples and shrines have or had burial grounds. A theme explored later in the book is that some people in Tokyo today believe that Roppongi's current problems are linked, at least in part, to a history of developers' disrespect for the necropolis: to make room for their buildings, they removed cemeteries altogether or perhaps even built atop them.

Old maps of the area show interesting topographic associations. The most important of the daimyo and other military ranks had the highest elevations, with homes directly on hilltops or arranged one after the other along ridge lines. Many enjoyed southern exposures. Their gardens stretched along the slopes below. Lesser officials also lived on the slopes, typically in group housing arrangements referred to as *kumiyashiki*. Roads followed the valleys, and along them were shops and the houses of working people. The brilliant anthropologist of Edo and Tokyo cityscapes Hidenobu Jinnai referred to commoner districts in the valleys as "the low city within the high city" (Jinnai 1995, 61). Builders of temples and shrines also sought the hills and were sometimes accorded land from the larger estates. There was also a pattern of fairly straight "branch roads" that split off from the main roads and connected the commoners' settlements in the valleys with loftier social strata above. A specific case in point is the street that climbs the upper reaches of Torii-zaka, named after a shrine's gate, from the once-low but now prestigious neighborhood of Azabu Jūban to Roppongi's heights. Originally the road was lined with daimyo residences and gardens on either side, but today in their place are large-footprint institutions of

FIGURE 3.1 One of the many cemeteries along Roppongi's back streets. The cemeteries, as well as temples and shrines, recall the neighborhood as it was during the Edo Period.

various kinds: the International House of Japan and its gardens, Tōyō Eiwa Girls' School, a prestigious private club, the Embassy of Singapore, the Embassy of the Philippines, and a Minato Ward community center.

Modern City

Tokyo changed dramatically after 1868, and so did Roppongi. That was the year the shogunate fell, imperial rule was restored, the name *Tokyo* replaced Edo, and Japan's modernization began after some two and a half centuries of imposed isolation. The daimyo had become redundant decades before, as power and prestige had been shifting for some time to a rising class of merchants centered in old shitamachi neighborhoods that were becoming the nucleus of an increasingly modern, big-city downtown. The emperor himself, referred to as the Meiji Emperor (r. 1867–1912), moved to the city from Kyoto and settled where the shōguns' castle had been. Much of the land to the immediate west and south of the new Imperial Palace became headquarters and ministries of the new government and military grounds. Roppongi specifically became mili-

FIGURE 3.2 Japanese soldiers on parade along Gaien Higashi-dōri, 1938 or 1939. This particular block is now one of the main centers of Roppongi nightlife. (Photo by K. Kato, courtesy of Minato Ward Creative Arts Council Executive Committee, from their book *Minato Ward: A Story of My Town and I [Minato-ku: Watashi to machi no monogatari]*, 1:152)

tary land, an association that it would retain until well into the second half of the twentieth century. Very early in the transition of government, land that had housed daimyo estates was taken over by the imperial army; much of that was put to use as drill grounds to replace previous drill grounds on the site that is now Hibiya Park. Later, in 1882, the War College of the Japanese Army was established in Roppongi, modeled after a parallel institution in Prussia and staffed with German officers on contract as instructors of modern military techniques.

The Japanese military was the essence of the Roppongi district until its defeat in 1945. We see this in figure 3.2, a rare shot of Imperial Japanese soldiers marching in 1938 or 1939 along a block that today houses one of Roppongi's main strips of nighttime activity. Tokyo residents of the time associated the district with the military and referred to is at as *heitai machi*, a "soldiers' town." In the always-eloquent words of Paul Waley: "Look at any map of Tokyo in the years between 1868 and 1945 and you will be struck by how much of the city was occupied by military facilities, but nowhere is this more so than in the Aoyama-Roppongi area. A city of military complexion is here stained a deep martial hue" (Waley 1984, 382). It is interesting to ponder, then, that so many of the bloody and tragic events that took place in Korea, China, and elsewhere in East and Southeast

Asia before and during World War II have roots in Roppongi, and that the same
district would soon be occupied by the military forces that vanquished Imperial
Japan. Before long, the American soldiers who were stationed in Tokyo's old
Japanese Army barracks would look to the main street outside, Gaien Higashi-
dōri, for rest and relaxation, thereby beginning the remaking of Roppongi into
a nighttime pleasure zone.

It is worth pointing out that before all that took place, the Roppongi barracks complex was the starting point of still another critical juncture in modern
Japanese history, that of the February 26 Incident, known in Japan as *ni-niroku
jiken*. On that date in 1936, some 1,400 junior military officers came out of their
Roppongi bases and engaged in a bloody revolt against the civilian Japanese
government, in an attempt to gain more power for the emperor and more government attention to problems in the domestic economy. They took over several key buildings in the city, carried out the assassinations of three cabinet
members, including the finance minister, and made near-miss attempts on the
lives of several other top officials, most notably Prime Minister Keisuke Okada.
Indeed, there was the possibility of civil war. In the end, the rebellion was put
down quickly on orders from Emperor Hirohito, martial law was imposed, and
the rebellion's leaders were executed. One of the immediate results of the entire episode was the strengthening of the most militaristic factions in Japan's
government and a more aggressive foreign affairs posture that helped lead the
nation to war (Shillony 1973). Yukio Mishima's celebrated novella *Patriotism*,
written in 1952, explores the complexities of the incident from the perspective
of a fictional army officer based in the Roppongi military complex.

The larger concentration of military land uses was to the north of Roppongi
Crossing, in the direction of Nogizaka (Nogi Slope), the next neighborhood to
the north from Roppongi. That slope is named after General Maresuke Nogi
(1849–1912), who lived there in connection with his military position. He is
the general who led Japan's forces in the Sino-Japanese War (1894–95) and the
Russo-Japanese War (1904–5) and who committed ritual suicide along with his
wife on the day of the funeral of the Meiji Emperor. His house still stands amid
a thicket of trees just off Gaien Higashi-dōri on land that was in late Edo times
the estate of Takayoshi Kido. He, in turn, had been one of the key individuals
behind the scenes in the fall of the shogunate and the restoration of imperial
rule. In 1923, a new shrine, Nogi-jinja, was built on the Kida-Nogi tract to honor
the celebrated general.

By contrast, the southern part of Roppongi, that is, south of today's Roppongi
Crossing, became increasingly urbanized over the Meiji years and afterward
with dense concentrations of shops and residences. Roppongi-dōri was fash-

ioned from preexisting roads to connect the center of Tokyo with Shibuya and other growing areas on the elite west side of the city and emerged as a major commercial thoroughfare, as did parts of Gaien Higashi-dōri, Sakurada-dōri beyond Roppongi's southern edge, and other bigger streets nearby. When trolley lines were built beginning in 1883 and then electric tramways in the early twentieth century (there was some service in 1903; more service was added by 1911), the commercial character of these streets became forever sealed. Moreover, any available real estate that was nearby was converted by developers into housing for the growing Tokyo population. Although there initially had been a substantial drop in the city's population when the shogunate ended, as many of Edo's residents were finally free to return to home provinces, the loss was quickly recouped, and Tokyo began to grow spectacularly. The emerging industrial economy of the modernizing city and Tokyo's growing dominance in virtually all aspects of Japanese life together assured that the city would become a magnet for migrants from every corner of Japan. Forevermore, there would never be enough room in Tokyo for everyone who wanted to be there.

Some of the old estates survived in modern Tokyo as private homes for privileged bureaucrats, industrialists, or successful businessmen. For example, we read a historical marker beside a stone wall on Torii-zaka stating that here was the site of an old Edo-era estate that had been remade in the early twentieth century into the modern home and extraordinary traditional gardens of Koyata Iwasaki, a former president of the Mitsubishi industrial empire. Many other samurai estates were converted into foreign embassies or other institutions or yielded their land for such development. Other land from old-order estates was acquired by speculators and developers and was subdivided into the dense urban fabric that is Tokyo's vernacular. As the precincts at the foot of what had been Edo Castle developed into a modern downtown, close-in districts like Roppongi and Azabu came to be trolley line–based bedroom neighborhoods for shopkeepers and shop workers and for the growing rank-and-file of office workers (Jinnai 1995, 38). Some of the available land was developed in interesting ways with a distinctive personality. An example is the "curious section called Spanish Village" where Roppongi borders Azabudai to the south (38). Most of the development, however, followed a standard Tokyo model of land division and finer land division, profit-seeking construction, and ever-higher population densities.

The enormous earthquake of September 1, 1923, and the fires that followed destroyed many of the remaining Edo period buildings, but the Roppongi area as a whole was not as severely damaged as the rest of the city. Instead, the bigger impact of that disaster on Roppongi and neighboring districts was the arrival of refugees from those parts of Tokyo that were completely destroyed. This necessitated ever denser and taller new construction and urbanized more of what had previously been green. The main streets came to be much more fully lined with shops and, apparently, in some places amid the shops, with amusements and diversions for the soldiers living nearby. Thus, by the time Roppongi and most of the rest of Tokyo were destroyed again just a generation later in the 1945 bombing raids, the neighborhood had evolved into a typical Tokyo mix of residences and commerce, older houses and new, nice homes and hovels, all somehow distributed into their appropriate spaces according to topography and solar aspect. The more closely you look at old maps and compare them with the streets today, the more such patterns become apparent and the more we recognize a hidden order amid Tokyo's chaos.[1] If Roppongi was different from other nicer neighborhoods on the yamanote side of town, it was because of the presence of the soldiers, their barracks, and, quite certainly, places on the main streets nearby where they gathered to drink and make merry.

And Tokyo did indeed make merry, certainly before the war, as was its ingrained culture, and according to the fascinating first-person recollections of Robert Guillain, a French journalist who had entered Japan in 1938 and was trapped there, mostly in Tokyo, until after hostilities ended, it continued to make merry even well into the time of the bloodiest battles and heavy casualties outside of Japan. One chapter of his memoir entitled "Tokyo at Play" (chapter 4) is devoted to the euphoria in Tokyo in 1942, when the war was going Japan's way and the empire was expanding. He didn't mention Roppongi by name, as it was not yet one of the top entertainment districts in the city, but he did refer to another "soldiers' town" not far away, Kagurazaka, site of Japan's War College, as one of the city's many "half-hidden little pleasure districts where the latest Japanese victories were celebrated nightly" (Guillain 1981, 49–50). I can imagine that the bars along Gaien Higashi-dōri in the Roppongi soldiers' town were no different, and that Guillain may have been thinking about Roppongi at least a little when he wrote these words:

> Evenings in Tokyo [in 1942] were an Oriental carnival. The nights belonged exclusively to men; the women stayed home. Eating well and drinking too much was the minimum program for the thousands of men who gallivanted off at nightfall. In the narrow streets, fittingly darkened by the blackout, almost all the passersby entering or leaving the restaurants were either tight or tipsy. They staggered, bawled patriotic songs in staccato rhythms, dragged their wooden sandals and scuffed shoes dreadfully as they zigzagged from bar to bar. (49)

The text continues with the observation that unlike other national capitals that might have had three or four districts specializing in nightlife, Tokyo had a minimum of thirty. Some were known for restaurants and drinking bars, others for theaters or movie houses, and in still others "the lights of countless bars and cafés blinked in tiny buildings." Elsewhere, there were geishas, tea houses, and rickshaws, while still other districts were "merely red-light districts" (49). Roppongi at the time was probably near the bottom of that mental list of thirty, if not even lower, but it had a fair share of small bars and cafés nonetheless. Like in all the other nighttime pleasure districts of the city, there were also places in Roppongi where a soldier could go from time to time to satisfy bodily appetites of a more personal sort. Before long, however, the war would begin turn against Japan, the city's euphoria would die, and almost all the soldiers would be gone, having been called as reinforcements to the war's fronts. Soon after that, the situation would become even worse, and Tokyo would experience its darkest days.

The 1945 air raids were most cruel in the low-lying river wards in Tokyo where topography, high building density, and wooden construction assured that the fires would consume virtually everything and everyone. However, Roppongi and other yamanote neighborhoods were also destroyed. Roppongi was designated as a target of the B-29 bombers because of the presence of the military facilities, which the bombs left in shambles, and also because of other targets nearby, including an industrial corridor along Tokyo Bay and its port facilities to the south. As the bombs fell in the Shiba neighborhood, also just south of Roppongi, they destroyed Zōjōji and its huge adjacent complex of monasteries and other religious structures. Almost all of what stands there today is a reconstruction. According to an aged eyewitness, the falling bombs sounded like rain as they fell on the streets around Roppongi Crossing, where they spread flames and turned the entire area into burned ruins. Only the Azabu Police Station and a few other concrete buildings were left standing (Koike 2005a).

By the time the war ended in August 1945 and the first planeload of victorious Americans arrived on the twenty-eighth of that month, most of Tokyo resembled a barren moonscape. The basic pattern of streets and their intersections still remained, providing a template for the reconstruction that would follow, but many of the thoroughfares were still covered by rubble from the bombings, only a few buildings were standing or could be salvaged, and most of Tokyo's residents were living in crude shelters amid the detritus. Where debris had been moved aside, vegetable plots were being tended to help feed the starving survivors. The Japanese citizens that those first 150 Americans met on August 28 were reportedly dazed, exhausted, impoverished, and demoralized, as were those encountered two days later by General McArthur, his entourage, and the American troops who landed that same day. The previously technical term *kyodatsu* soon entered the popular lexicon to describe their clinical condition: as a whole, Japan's survivors were diagnosed as "distracted," "dejected," and suffering from "physical or emotional prostration" (Dower 1999, 89).

I spoke at length with a person who was among the Japanese who had gathered in Atsugi, Kanagawa Prefecture, just outside Tokyo, to witness the arrival of that first U.S. plane. He was a Roppongi resident, still lives nearby, and is still in Roppongi almost every day. He had survived the war by sheer luck and because he was doing work for the imperial government in a location out of harm's way. Yes, Roppongi and all of central Tokyo were in complete ruin, he told me, survivors were selling their valuables just to eat, and without exception every family was grieving for those who were dead and was searching for the missing. They also wondered whether their loved ones who had been deployed at the war's front lines would return home alive. But there was shock and trepidation too, my informant described, among the first Americans as they deplaned. There was initial hesitation to step off and away from the plane for fear of being shot at from within the crowd, but soon enough there was the first direct, face-to-face encounter between the victors and vanquished. The Americans had never seen such despair, my elderly witness said, and did not know how to respond except to reveal a sense of shock at what they were seeing. The first conversation was in English between one of the American soldiers and my English-speaking informant, but it quickly switched to the Russian language, as the American turned out to be a Russian American and my informant, who had been singled out from the crowd for questioning because he was a tall Caucasian, was Russian. He had been brought up in a Japanese-occupied part of China and had moved to Japan before the outbreak of the war for university study. His story is still not written and requires an expert to record, substantiate, and integrate it with existing first-person accounts of Japan at war and the postwar occupation. I have some notes of my own from interviews, but this is not my subject.[2]

The American Era

Within days after that first encounter, planeload after planeload of Americans would arrive in Tokyo, and the occupation would commence in earnest. Its official dates are recorded as from September 8, 1945, until April 28, 1952, the date of the formal restoration of Japan's independence. Within months, by the end of 1945, some 350,000 U.S. troops were based in Japan, along with about 40,000 troops of the British Commonwealth Occupation Force from the United

Kingdom, Australia, New Zealand, and India. A short time later, by mid-1946, the number of foreign personnel in Japan attached to the occupation reached a peak of about 600,000. By 1950, the number of Americans had been reduced to 136,000, as U.S. General Headquarters (GHQ) was finding a comfort level in the number of troops needed for the work of monitoring Japan and enforcing change, but the onset of the Korean War in that year soon required another escalation in military population. As a result, by 1953 the number of Americans who were based in Japan had grown to about 209,000. There were even more in Korea, the great majority of whom had arrived there via layover in Japan. In Korea, the numbers of American troops zoomed from only 510 in 1950 to 327,000 in 1951 and remained at about that high level for the duration of the war. It was reduced to 226,000 in 1954, the year after the cease-fire, and then dropped still more year after year afterward. In 2005, the round-number totals were about 35,000 U.S. troops stationed in Japan and 30,000 in Korea.[3]

During the Korean War and in the years just afterward, American soldiers typically unwound in the safety of Japan when on break. In addition, those who finished their tours of service often unwound during homebound layovers in Japan, many in Tokyo specifically by choice. Ginza and nearby Yurakuchō were probably the most popular American playgrounds, but Roppongi was also attractive. Early in the occupation, the Sanno Hotel was opened nearby by the U.S. Navy. It housed military travelers when on visit to Tokyo. Its successor, the New Sanno Hotel, is still in the neighboring district of Hiroo, a short walk or quick taxi ride from Roppongi Crossing. As is well documented in books about Japan in the 1950s, the Korean War was a boon to reconstruction in the country, creating a demand for goods and supplies needed at the war's front, kick-starting Japanese industry, and providing jobs in construction, manufacturing, and services, among other economic sectors (Kohama 2007; Nakamura 1995).

To the surprise of no one, a great many of the service jobs turned out to be in Japan's "water trade," now also attentive to the bodily desires of foreign soldiers on Japanese soil. Indeed, Japanese officials began preparing for this eventuality even before the Americans set foot on Atsugi's tarmac, wanting to head off an explosion of lust and protect the women and female children of the nation. This led to the creation of an extraordinary Japanese institution that was called the Recreation and Amusement Association (RAA) and the founding of a national network of "comfort stations" in which as many as 70,000 young Japanese women provided sexual services to American GIs (Takemae 2002, 68). There were at least thirty-three state-run brothels in the Tokyo area, the first of which opened on the very day that the first Yankees landed in Atsugi. It was in a district called Ōmori on the way to the city center from Atsugi and was named

Komachien, commonly translated as "Babe's Garden." The biggest brothel, on the other hand, was developed in Chiba, in the suburbs on the opposite side of Tokyo. Named the International Palace or simply "IP," it became famous for an assembly-line character in which American clients stood in orderly lines on one side of the building as they awaited their turns to enter, and then they picked up the freshly shined shoes or boots that awaited them on the other side as they departed in turn after finishing their business. Another name for the place among Americans was "Willow Run," after the productive and highly efficient giant bomber factory of that name that the Ford Motor Company had established during the war (Cohen 1987, 126). Other large brothels were Bordeaux and Oasis in Ginza, Paramount in Shinagawa, Officers' Club in Sangenjaya, and Paradise in suburban Tachikawa (Takemae 2002).

The majority of the tens of thousands of young women who worked in the state-run brothels had been recruited for the task by Japanese officials. They came from the lower classes and from postwar poverty and were called upon to provide the patriotic, self-sacrificing service of safeguarding the daughters of the well-born and middle classes by engaging the lustful foreigners and keeping them within geographical confinements (Takemae 2002, 68). It is estimated that each RAA conscript provided services to between fifteen and sixty U.S. servicemen a day (Dower 1999, 129). Yet, even with these extraordinary precautions in place, the worst happened: in nearby Kanagawa Prefecture, for instance, there may have been as many as 1,336 rapes committed by U.S. troops in just the first ten days of the occupation. Other terrifying statistics tell of 931 "serious offenses" committed by Americans in just the Yokohama portion of Kanagawa Prefecture in the first week of the occupation, including thefts, armed robberies, and rapes (Takemae 2002, 67).

The RAA facilities were closed by GHQ in January 1946 on orders from General MacArthur. However, many of them continued to function for a time under new guises such as "Café Associations" and "Tea Shop Sanitation Associations" (whatever that might be), and prostitution was rampant. In addition, there were also tens of thousands of so-called pan-pan girls, who worked the streets independently. As mentioned in the previous chapter, Americans also called them "geesha," confusing them and what they do with geisha and mispronouncing en masse that short and not very difficult Japanese word. Prostitutes charged very low prices, and could be found in every commercial district of the city, in the amusement quarters, and, of course, near the gates of occupation bases. Ginza and Yurakuchō were especially notorious for prostitution, the latter so much so that even today one still hears it being referred to by the derived sobriquet Rakuchō, meaning "Pleasureville," but the Americans also found companionship in Shimbashi, Ueno, Shinjuku, Shibuya, and all (or almost all) the city's other thirty-plus pleasure districts (Seidensticker 1990, 187). A good number of the Americans lived a playboy lifestyle, flitting from girlfriend to girlfriend like butterflies, to use a term that was applied to them at the time. However, there were also quite a few steady relationships between U.S. soldiers and the Japanese women they met—and many marriages. Cohen estimated that in 1946, as many as 40 percent of the men in GHQ had "regular" Japanese girlfriends (1987, 124).

Such was the situation with respect to Roppongi. Soon after they arrived in the city, the Americans began requisitioning the land and buildings that were required for the occupation. Among them were the Imperial Army's Roppongi barracks, or what was left of them. They were immediately repaired or replaced as needed, were renamed Hardy Barracks, and were put to use as housing for U.S. soldiers of the 1st Cavalry, almost all of them men.[4] The Americans continued to live there until the barracks were returned to Japan in 1959. A portion of the same tract became the headquarters of *Pacific Stars and Stripes*, the military newspaper for servicemen and –women in the Far East, an operation that continues to this day. When not on duty and not spending time in the bigger playgrounds such as Ginza, many of the Hardy Barracks soldiers relaxed together in what few bars and cafés existed nearby. They may even have frequented some of the very same establishments along Gaien Higashi-dōri that had previously been popular with soldiers of the Imperial Japanese Army, although I have been unable to verify this. It is from this beginning that Roppongi had its quiet start as an international playground.

Another dimension of that beginning was in the form of "ex-Occupationaires," to borrow Whiting's term (1999, 43), who had served their tours of duty with the U.S. military and then stayed on in Japan or returned to the country after a short trip home. Some may have grown to like Japan and others fell in love with Japanese women, but for many the deciding factor about staying in Japan to make a living was the realization that there was big money to be made from the chaos. In the first decades after the war, there was a shortage of virtually everything in the country, and anyone who could lay their hands on a supply of no matter what stood to make a bundle in resale, particularly if the goods could be pilfered from the plump food larders, PX inventories, and supplies shipments of the U.S. military. Japanese gangsters had gained control of the many black markets that had sprung up around Tokyo, while a class of small-time American gangsters and shady entrepreneurs emerged during the occupation and shortly afterward to help feed this Japanese pipeline with American products, the more cheaply obtained the better.

Perhaps the most brazen of the ex-Occupationaires was a fast-talking former

Marine sergeant from New York named Nick Zappetti (1921–92). The subject of an engaging and popular biography by Robert Whiting from which this specific section of the book is drawn and in which he is accorded status as "the mafia boss of Tokyo" (Whiting 1999), Zappetti was an opportunist-entrepreneur who began his Tokyo career with small-time smuggling and sales of lighter flints and gum balls and then branched to bigger scores, often in partnership with Japanese mobsters, as well as to various legitimate (or almost so) business adventures. Huge swings in financial success had him spending lavishly like a millionaire playboy one day and then hiding from creditors and begging to borrow money the next. At various times, he supplied a Korean-Japanese gangster in Ginza with prizes for his pachinko parlors and with stolen ball bearings from the U.S. military for the actual machines, participated in an ill-fated diamond heist in the Imperial Hotel, got caught up in the shady business of Japan's professional wrestling boom (*puro-resu bumu*), and opened a mink farm, a hog farm, and a sausage factory.

Most importantly for us, however, Zappetti was responsible for a fresh slice of modern Roppongi history when, in 1956, he opened Japan's first pizza restaurant. There was not much in the way of restaurants with Western-style fare in Tokyo when Zappetti began to consider opening an Italian restaurant to accord with his own upbringing and favorite foods, and only one in Roppongi, a greasy spoon diner called Hamburger Inn. He settled on pizza because one of the investors said he craved for it, and located a spot in a building occupied by a tailor shop near a major street corner, Ikura-Katamachi Crossing, just south of the little strip that was becoming Roppongi. He named it Nicola's. It happened to be close to the Embassy of the USSR (now the Russian Embassy) and nearly midway between Roppongi Crossing and the site where Tokyo Tower was beginning to take shape. A favorable review by a columnist in *Stars and Stripes* is said to have propelled Nicola's to local fame. It became a hangout for the staff of *Stars and Stripes* and for foreign diplomats, and then for Japanese who wanted exotic cuisine and an international atmosphere. Before long, Nicola's became the place to be and be seen. Calling it "the Toots Shor's of the Far East," Whiting lists an impressive array of Hollywood personalities who dined there during their Tokyo visits: Elizabeth Taylor, Mike Todd, David Niven, Harry Belafonte, Connie Francis, Frank Sinatra, William Holden, and Xavier Cugat, among others (1999, 78).

Important Japanese personalities also patronized the restaurant, some becoming regulars. It helped that in 1959 a large television studio, that of TV Asahi, opened nearby on a rise in Roppongi 6-chōme, bringing new media stars to the neighborhood and a full assortment of star groupies, star watchers, and star wannabies. Zappetti typically covered the tabs for the biggest celebrities himself, for which he was probably repaid many times over by increased business from the lines of diners who waited outside for a slice of his pizza and, hopefully, a peak at someone famous. The most well-known such celebrity was the wildly popular professional wrestler Rikidozan, an on-screen fixture during the early years of Japanese television broadcasting and the darling of the nation because he always defeated his American opponents. It did not matter that he was controlled by mobsters and that matches were fixed, nor did it matter that he was in reality not even Japanese; he was Korean. Rikidozan was the era's top media star, Nicola's was his favorite restaurant, and he always arrived with a sizable entourage of other stars and beautiful women.

Also famously, Crown Prince Akihito, the present emperor of Japan, frequented the restaurant with his future wife during their courtship. However, they must have come for the pizza and checkered tablecloths only, rather than for camaraderie, because it is reported by Whiting and a source of my own who remembers that the restaurant was always emptied before they arrived and the tables reassigned to the emperor's security detail. Finally, there were the mobsters who frequented Nicola's. The most prominent were Hisayuki Machii (1923–2002), the burly Korean Japanese commander of a small army of mostly Korean gangster thugs that comprised the Tosei-kai syndicate of the yakuza, and Yoshio Kodama (1911–84), a drug-smuggling, ultra-right wing, nationalistic, staunchly anti-Communist organized crime figure who was probably the most powerful *kuromaku* (behind-the-scenes power broker) in Japan for about three decades after the war until his career crashed in the 1970s when he became caught up in the center of the notably sleazy U.S.-Japan Lockheed scandal.[5]

However, things began to change for Nicola's with the mid-1964 opening of the Hibiya Line of the subway. Ironically it ran more or less beneath the restaurant (or at least beneath its door stoop) as it snaked through Roppongi, but the local station was put in quite a bit north, at Roppongi Crossing. That is where the center of gravity of nightlife began to shift, marginalizing Nicola's and its neighbors in the old center closer to Tokyo Tower, even as Olympics-period crowds began to fill the neighborhood. Furthermore, as the Japanese economy strengthened from the Olympics boom into the time of the bubble, more and more restaurants opened in Roppongi, including others that served pizza, both with and without the gangsters. Some of the new competition was stronger because it was backed by the added power of chain restaurant companies. Finally, as the economy in Japan nosedived with the bursting of the bubble in the early 1990s, and as Zappetti's own profligate spending habits and lousy money management brought him to the brink of bankruptcy, Nicola's closed in 1992 with its sale to a popular chain of Indian eateries.[6] Later that year, Zappetti died. The story of this restaurant gets us started with the development of modern-day Roppongi; Nicola's eventual decline shifts our attention to other aspects of Roppongi and developments closer to Roppongi Crossing.

None of this is meant to imply that Nicola's was the central attraction of Roppongi. It was the center of Nick Zappetti's world, to be sure, and for many of his hangers-on and lovers of Tokyo's first pizzas, it may well have been a favorite spot. But there were other popular places too, including those quite different in flavor, style, and ethnic identity. As established earlier, Roppongi has many faces and many sides, and no one aspect, much less any one place of business, can represent it. Seryna Restaurant, for example, still a landmark in the neighborhood, opened in 1961 and is one of Tokyo's largest and most famous choices for shabu-shabu and other Japanese meat dishes. It too has a history of foreigner and Japanese celebrity clients and its own "Kings of Roppongi." Another example was Chianti, a close neighbor of Nicola's and also an Italian restaurant. It served more pasta than pizza, though, and gained a reputation as a gathering place for Japanese intellectuals. The writer Yukio Mishima (1925–1970), for example, is said to have come there often to debate lofty topics late into the night with other lofty minds (Koike 2005b). As far as I can tell, Chianti also suffered the marginalization fate; it adjusted by moving to Shibuya.

Likewise, there was the "supper club" Crazy Horse. Opened in 1970 by Rieko Ikeguchi, a proprietress who had previously worked in the clubs of Ginza, it was said to be a key spark for the popularization of Roppongi for an upscale Japanese clientele. According to the memoir book by Ryoji Sugi (2005), a long-time-bartender-turned-club-owner in Roppongi who was described in an afterword to his book as "the emperor of the Roppongi night," the neighborhood's watering places were mostly of the small, old wooden building variety until the late 1960s and early 1970s and had no pulling power for a nonlocal clientele. The change came when Rieko Ikeguchi and other Japanese entrepreneurs, including Sugi, began to open stylish clubs for stylish people. The first wave of these establishments were called "after clubs" because clients tended to arrive after midnight, following an evening out in one or more of the nightspots in nearby Akasaka or Ginza. They came to the supper clubs for a late meal and to meet. Indeed, according to Sugi, for a time Roppongi was referred to as *afta-no-machi*, "the city of after" (Sugi 2005).

Seidensticker's history of twentieth-century Tokyo refers to Roppongi as "the earliest of the [city's] brassy, amplified entertainment districts" (1990, 242). The neighborhood started to gain fame by the early 1960s because of the TV facilities nearby and increasing numbers of popular nightspots and soon developed its own returning crowds of dedicated, like-fashioned merrymakers. They referred to themselves as the *Roppongi zoku*, the "Roppongi tribe," and were described as such in media accounts and other public discourse of the time. In Seidensticker's words, early 1960s Roppongi was where "young people went to ogle, and to imitate, and to dance and eat pizza" because there "the pizza and dancing were exotic, and the people of television were the bright cutting edge of progress" (1990, 243).

Roppongi's Heyday

The opening of the Hibiya Line and its station at Roppongi Crossing was instrumental in propelling the neighborhood from small beginnings as a nighttime hangout to one of the city's premier entertainment districts. Even though the neighborhood was close to the center of Tokyo, it had always been regarded as somewhat of a "desert island on the ground" because of inconvenient bus and streetcar access (Koike 2005b), but beginning in March 1964, when the Roppongi part of Tokyo's third subway line opened, the crowds began to arrive. With fast subway connections to the Ginza Line and the Marunouchi Line, as well as to the heavily used surface rail lines, Roppongi suddenly became accessible, and business could grow. The first four exits (stairways to the surface) were at the four main corners of Roppongi Crossing, which instantly became prime property. Some of the area's first taller buildings, at that time about six stories maximum, were built in conjunction with the impact of the subway. The iconic corner Almond coffee shop, said to be the first establishment in Japan to offer *oshibori* (moist hand towels) to customers as they got settled,[7] opened at about the same time in 1964 in one of those newer structures and was reportedly overfilled from the first day. It too had a celebrity clientele, drawn in part from the TV Asahi studio nearby. It might be argued that the choice of Roppongi Crossing as the location for the neighborhood's subway stop was itself a result of the presence of the television facilities.

The new subway line was timed for the 1964 Summer Olympics held in Tokyo. The games were the city's (and indeed the nation's) coming-out party to the world after the defeat of war. They marked Japan's reentry into the community of nations and showed off to foreigner and Japanese visitors alike new technologies and a modernizing, fast-rebuilding city. Most of the largest venues were near the center of Tokyo, not far from Roppongi, and in October, when the competitions actually took place, the city was packed with visitors. Roppongi was one of the attractions: it offered places to unwind in an international atmosphere, a checklist ride on the new subway, and an alternative gateway to Tokyo

Tower, about a twenty-minute walk down Gaien Higashi-dōri from Roppongi
Crossing. The tower had debuted several years earlier, December 23, 1958, as
perhaps the first major tangible symbol of Japan's rehabilitation, and immediately became one of the city's premier tourist attractions. Locals and international visitors came in big numbers to see the structure up close and ride
its elevators to the top. During the Olympics month, the lines for tickets were
exceedingly long. Those who had invested in Roppongi bars and restaurants
where especially pleased; their places of business were crowded too. As a result,
there was a scramble to open still more bars, restaurants, and other fun places
near Roppongi Crossing, and there was plenty of business for developers and
the builders of pencil-thin, multistory bar buildings and other forms of multitenant, cram-them-in types of commercial configurations.

The international character of Roppongi was bolstered with the opening of
many foreign embassies nearby. As mentioned earlier, this was the better and
more prestigious side of Tokyo and was near the center of Japanese government. Some of the embassies established themselves in Roppongi, only a few
minutes walking distance from Roppongi Crossing, while almost all the rest
located in neighborhoods that abutted Roppongi (see chapter 2). Roppongi's
American character continued to be disproportionately large: the U.S. Embassy
is Tokyo's largest, and its imposing new building was built close to Roppongi in
the next-door Akasaka neighborhood, while the majority of its many American
employees and their dependents came to live even closer to Roppongi Crossing
in a spacious housing compound in Roppongi 2-chōme.

To move a little ahead on the timeline, on American Independence Day (July
4) 1983, the American ambience was solidified, if you will, with the opening
of yet another iconic landmark, Tokyo's first Hard Rock Café. The company
behind the Hard Rock phenomenon is actually British, and the first Hard Rock
Café opened in 1971 in London, but the character and food fare are definitely
American, and until that 1983 opening of the Tokyo branch, almost all other
locations of the chain were in the United States. The distinctive logo with glittering neon guitar on the façade of the building is a Roppongi icon, as is the go-
rilla climbing the side of the building and peering into a second-story window.
Some other American chains opened nearby, giving rise to the nickname "Little
Beverly Hills" for this small subdistrict of Roppongi. Originally there were palm
trees lining the alley that leads to this bit of Los Angeles, but now only several
survive, in not such good health at that, and the nickname, I think, is known
only to old hands.

Another distinctive ingredient in the Roppongi stew, with an aroma all its
own and separate from the international flavors, was that of gangsterdom. There

is no way to quantify how many yakuza may have done what in Roppongi over the years, but suffice it to say that their impact has almost certainly been significant and direct in the construction of many of the commercial buildings in the entertainment district, the ownership and management of many of its places of business, and the shaping of those parts of the Roppongi economy that involve commercial sex, narcotics, and violence or threats thereof as a technique for land acquisition. The punch-permed set has also had an active hand in Roppongi's many hostess clubs, perhaps especially the racier ones, and then later in the 1980s and 1990s in the explosion of strip clubs and other sex-on-stage establishments that the neighborhood experienced.

I would expect that normally gangsters would keep a low profile and want to conduct their business under the radar. In the case of Nick Zappetti's friend Hisayuki Machii, however, the exact opposite was true, at least with respect to his relationship to Roppongi. He made the neighborhood the headquarters for his multifold legal and shades-of-gray operations and built for those purposes an imposing six-story structure that, according to Whiting, was "by common agreement the most elegant building in all of Tokyo and . . . the ultimate symbol of Japan's postwar recovery" (Whiting 1999, 183). Opened in mid-1973 and located within a block or so of Roppongi Crossing, it was named TSK-CCC, the letters standing for Toa Sogo Kigyo (Eastern Mutual Enterprises)—Celebrities Choice Club. The first three letters corresponded to the new corporate-sounding name that Machii gave his business empire, as well as by design to the initials of Tosei-kai, the old gang name. Yoshio Kodama was the new TSK chairman of the board. CCC, meanwhile, was the name of the expensive, private membership club that occupied a part of the building. Upon joining, a member also gained access to sixteen exclusive private clubs in exclusive Ginza. In keeping with his characteristic bravado, Machii had an enormous logo for the organization with those six letters affixed at the top of the structure. He once described his paradise as "an oasis in the desert of dry, contemporary human relationships" (Kaplan and Dubro 2003, 230).

At various times I have been inside different parts of the building but, sadly, only after the glory had faded. Whiting's description is best:

> Contained in the building's 19,000 square meters was an array of Dionysian delights—a cabaret, a disco, restaurants specializing in Chinese, Korean, Japanese and Continental cuisine, banquet halls with authentic rococo, Spanish, German, and Roman motifs, wedding salons, private lounges with deep leather armchairs, tatamied mah-jongg parlors, and a sauna imported from Finland. The lobby and various sitting areas were outfitted with expensive furnishings imported from

Europe and the Middle East, while priceless ancient Korean vases, porcelains, stoneware, and calligraphy were showcased in alcoves along the building's many lushly carpeted corridors and caverns. On display in the main vestibule, lit by an enormous chandelier, was a giant Picasso. (Whiting 1999, 183–84)

This remarkable place is revisited in the next chapter in a tour of Roppongi's rhythms and then again in chapter 6 when considering the progress of redevelopment in Roppongi.

There were many other noteworthy builders and proprietors. Some had recently made fortunes in the "water trade" of Ginza or Akasaka and were now eager to expand to the emerging new entertainment district of Roppongi, where returns on investments promised to be quick and huge. Such was the thinking of Gensiro Kawamoto, a fast-moving entrepreneur who had abandoned his family's kimono business in Kyushu, Japan's large southern island, to invest in Tokyo's construction boom, and who soon came to be referred to as the "King of Ginza Real Estate." In approximately 1975, he developed at least two of his signature "Marugen" buildings, numbers 12 and 22, just down Imoaraizaka (potato-washing slope) from Roppongi Crossing, thereby helping to move Roppongi in the direction of being a new center of hostess clubs and other similar nightspots. The buildings were marked by Kawamoto's distinctive logo: a red and green neon circle with a number inside that identifies each building by sequence of construction.[8] As with his other Marugen buildings in Ginza, Akasaka, Shinjuku, and elsewhere, numbers 12 and 22 were busy beehives of hostess bars, private clubs, and other types of bars, all jammed one atop the other and even several per floor, in newly constructed buildings. By 1987, around the time of the peak of the economic bubble, he had come to own some 3,500 properties in Tokyo and elsewhere in Japan (only some of which were part of his Marugen chain), as well as 800 more in Hawaii and California, and had become one of the half-dozen richest people in Japan.[9]

With an ever-stronger Japanese economy and changing consumer tastes, Roppongi was able to progress beyond the "city of after" reputation and began to emerge by the mid- to late-1970s as a prime first destination for Japanese consumers (Sugi 2005). It had something for everyone, it seems. Some of Tokyo's biggest spenders, normally habitués in the top hostess cabarets of Ginza and Asakusa, began to visit Roppongi as well and spent lavishly. The entertaining personal memoir by underworld denizen Manabu Miyazaki referred to them as "bubble gents" who routinely dropped the equivalent of tens of thousands of dollars in a single night on entertainment and tips in the neighborhood's most exclusive clubs (Miyazaki 2005, 375). For others, Roppongi came to be identified as the most international of all the city's nighttime playgrounds and as the main concentration of popular dance clubs. This was particularly so with respect to disco, which caught on in Japan first and foremost in Roppongi and sustained a sizable fraction of the neighborhood's business all through the bubble and even beyond. Some of the most popular clubs of the time were Neo Japanesque, Déjà vu, Vietti, Cleo Palazzi, Rajah Court (an "Arabian theme" disco), and Lexington Queen. The last of these opened in 1980, is still in business, and is still tended to by a local-celebrity American with a deep knowledge of Roppongi and its bubble-period history. At one time, Japanese and foreign media stars, popular singers, and other celebrities could be seen almost nightly at "the Lex," arguably making the club the most glamorous in-spot in the neighborhood.

There was an ambience of high fashion and exclusivity that appealed to consumers. The Lexington Queen and other clubs would compete to attract professional models, especially female, to their dance floors, not charging them admission or for drinks. Many clubs also employed scouts or agents on the streets to identify the best-looking or best-dressed passersby and entice them with free passes, discount passes, and other inducements. People stood in lines to enter the most popular clubs and paid as much as ¥5,000 ($50 in round numbers) as door charges. As was the case with the disco phenomenon more generally, looking good and being recognized for it were especially important. I personally remember young Tokyoites from the 1980s who took pride in their collections of club invitations and coupons from the weekend before and showed them off to others, as well as those who trash-talked about gatekeeper doormen at specific clubs that were supposedly "full" when they tried to get in or that had denied them any special deals.[10] If the line at a particular club was too long, the door charge too high, or if the doorman had somehow failed to see your obvious curb appeal, there were always other clubs to try. Often club-goers flitted from one establishment to another, taking advantage of special promotions to check out the newest clubs or simply moving from one place to the next in search of that elusive special atmosphere or special someone. One could often flit even within a single building: the Roppongi Square Building, the Roppongi Forum, and Roi Building, for example, were among several larger buildings in the neighborhood that housed multiple clubs for multiple tastes.

Roppongi also had quite a few live music venues with performers of various genres: blues and soul, jazz, oldies, rock and roll, and others. Many of the musicians were Japanese, of course, but as Sugi wrote in his book and as others have told me as well, there was special interest and a special premium on imported musicians. They were seen as authentic; they also internationalized Roppongi's ambience. African American musicians had special magic in these regards and played an oversized role in shaping Roppongi's character in sound-stage clubs such as Ink Stick and Roppongi Valentine, among others. However, unlike with dance clubs, where the neighborhood gained first ranking among Tokyo's' many nighttime playgrounds, Roppongi was but one of several districts in the city with a reputation for the best and latest in live music. Shibuya and Shinjuku each probably had (and still have) more music venues.

As mentioned earlier, sexual interactions in Roppongi are most overtly of a heterosexual nature, as certain other parts of Tokyo are known as the places to go for GLBT (gay, lesbian, bisexual, and transgendered) atmosphere. Indeed, Tokyo has a long history of places of entertainment for sexual minorities, even quite openly. I can't say how far back such places existed in the Roppongi area, but I do know that the neighborhood's traditions of openness and "anything goes" enabled establishments that cater to sexual minorities to thrive from early in the postwar buildup of Roppongi as an entertainment district. By the time of the neighborhood's heyday during the bubble, there were quite a few GLBT clubs and bars in operation in Roppongi, albeit a small minority of the total number of establishments. An essay in the collection by McLelland, Suganuma, and Welker mentions Roppongi quite prominently, particularly with respect to its cluster of so-called *densō* (dandy) bars that appealed to various categories of transgendered and mixed-gender clientele. Establishments that were named Meme (Budding Woman), Don Juan, Gin no Kishi (Silver Knight), and Hoshi no Ōjisama (The Little Prince) were among other spots that they singled out, mentioning the popularity of these bars among *onabe*, women who want to love women not as lesbians but men (McLelland, Suganuma, and Welker 2007, 160–63). In the mid-1970s, Roppongi gained some exciting publicity along these lines when it was revealed that Rumiko Matsubara, a "Roppongi Girl" beauty contest winner, was a *nyūhāfu* (new half), a person of mixed gender (321).

The story of Roppongi's heyday would not be complete without mention of its Playboy Club. Although it was just one of the many nightspots that have come and gone over the years in the neighborhood, it did have extra visibility during its time and, among some people, special cachet. Located on a high floor with large windows and great city views in the newly constructed Roi Building, the club opened December 9, 1976, and was Tokyo's first and only branch of that famous, multi-bunnied icon of sexual pseudorevolution from America. It was operated as a franchise. Japan took to the Playboy Club concept, and other clubs in the chain were opened in Osaka, Nagoya, and Sapporo in 1978, 1979, and 1980, respectively.

Even though it was an import from afar with unique characteristics, the Playboy Club seems to have fit many aspects of Roppongi quite well. Its business plan of selling memberships and giving "keys" to dues payers meshed with the members-only practices that had emerged in many Japanese clubs and pubs, as did its marketing of exclusivity and a sense that one was uniquely welcome into a world behind closed doors. The Playboy Club, however, was all glitz inside and out, with ample publicity and hoopla, while typical Japanese member clubs tended to be unobtrusive, with their glamour being kept from public view. Indeed, the very presence of the Playboy Club in Roppongi helped to set or maintain a tone that marked the neighborhood's nightlife: "We were all playboys then," recalled a Japanese friend from my generation who was in his twenties in the 1970s and had both played and courted in Roppongi. He was never a member of the Playboy Club, nor had he ever been there, but he recalled exactly where the place was and remembered fondly what Roppongi was like at the time, even as his much-younger foreigner wife sat beside him: "We were all playboys. There was a different girl every night. It was easy. It was innocent. It was fun. Every weekend we would head to Roppongi to the most popular dance clubs for the best bands and the best looking girls. We had jobs and we spent our money in Roppongi." The "we" in his sentences refers to the "tribe" of former Roppongi-goers of which he was part and that characteristically looks back with nostalgia on a time of happy nights.

And then there were the people who were quite famous in Roppongi as local personalities. In Roppongi's parallel worlds of Japanese and foreigners, some of the stars were Japanese and others were from the United States or elsewhere. One such foreigner was an American named Rick Roa (1932–2006). It might be fitting to close this section about the neighborhood's history with some thoughts about him and the neighborhood he knew, borrowing insight from his autobiography, a thin little book that he narrated in one of his last years to his friend Tony Teora (Roa 2004). I had met him once, and our paths crossed occasionally, but I never got to know him. His book and his reputation are the basis of my remarks here. His recollections are also those of a former playboy, actually an inveterate playboy, with fond memories. The value of his book is in verifiable details from an insider about places and personalities in the neighborhood at its peak and its portrait of heyday Roppongi as a rollicking place with playboy ambience. Indeed, the Roppongi Playboy Club gets star billing. Mostly, however, the narrative is about Rick Roa himself, as befits autobiography, and about the person that he wants us to see. The book is actually much like Roppongi itself: there is a lot of show, but the substance is thin. Likewise, the book reflects its neighborhood in that it is hard to tell what is real, what is braggadocio, and what is misdirection.

Roa was born in Brooklyn and was introduced to Asia via the Korean War. Later, he took employment for an American company near Clark Air Base, the huge American outpost that once reigned supreme over notorious Angeles City in the Philippines, where he remembers sex "in all shapes and sizes" (Roa 2004, 25). In 1968, Roa agreed to a reposting to Tokyo, his first visit to Japan, where he would eventually live out the rest of his life. He arrived in the city only after he had been assured that its nightlife would not disappoint him (26), and upon arrival he was drawn immediately to Roppongi. There, he worked variously as bar-to-bar salesman, hostess club bartender, and bar manager, and continued to enjoy a not-so-private private life. Eventually, he says, he became "King of Roppongi" and was often referred to as such.[11] "I was famous in the Playboy Club," he wrote. Within its doors, he was "ambassador to the Ambassadors," bestowing his choice of foreign diplomats with company-given Playboy Club memberships so that they would have a welcoming place to entertain high-level guests. The serendipitous similarity between his family name *Roa* and the name of the large, prosperous-looking building in which the Playboy Club was a major tenant, the Roi Building, served Roa's public image well, as many people thought that he owned the complex (57).

The Tokyo Club Playboy Club closed in 1990, victim of declining business during a weakening economy. It died as well because of financial and public image problems suffered worldwide by the Chicago-based parent company. Put simply, human bunnies were no longer popular, the once-glamorous magazine had become passé, and the company's own bubble burst. The last of twenty-two Playboy Clubs worldwide closed in Manila in 1991. As for Roa, he aged and mellowed, as reflected in the published narrative, and then, in 2006, he passed away. During his nearly four decades in Roppongi, he came to know many people and places in the neighborhood, including lots of visiting celebrities with whom he posed for photographs, and was known by even more people. I have no doubt that he is missed and remembered fondly by his old friends, and that he will be regarded by some for a long time as an icon of a fun and carefree time that is past.

Beyond the Bubble

This chapter is now close to the present time. The goal here was to trace the neighborhood's origins as an entertainment district and its rise to popularity. I have done that. I have described how the neighborhood's boom period coincided roughly with the time of Japan's greatest economic prosperity; next I trace the decline of Roppongi that followed the bursting of the nation's bubble sometime in the early 1990s. I begin in the next chapter with Roppongi's routines as I witnessed them personally, which, as I now understand, reflect stages of Roppongi's eclipse. My choice to end "Roppongi's Heyday" with the memories of Rick Roa, of all people, emphasizes the excesses of that time and the high levels of confidence that swirled about the neighborhood before the change. That special time is remembered fondly by participants. It was when Japan was king, when Roppongi was king (Ginza and Akasaka and other playgrounds were kings too), and when Roa was king of Roppongi, as he confidently tells us. Nick Zappetti was Roppongi's king also. So was Rikidozan. Ryoji Sugi, introduced in his memoir as the "Emperor of the Roppongi Night," was king too. There were other "royals" too, some still alive and still commanding what they command. That may have been one of the charms of Roppongi: a fine place of entertainment allows everyone who wants to be king (or prince or queen or princess; even the Duke of Earl) to be just that, if only through the lenses that only they wear, or if only for that one, most memorable Roppongi night.

Something about how Roppongi has changed and has become somehow spiritually empty may have been captured in a conversation overheard in a local restaurant by Australian professor Robin Gerster. His short essay, "Conversation in Roppongi," encapsulates much of what I think about the neighborhood.[12] Like the popular American television series *Seinfeld*, which was pitched as "a show about nothing," the conversation at the next table was also about nothing. It was between a middle-aged American businessman and the much younger Japanese female that he was hoping to seduce during his overseas trip, and like so much else that Gerster was observing in postbubble Japan, it was vapid (Gerster 1999, 146–49). As he eavesdrops and watches the two "thumb wrestle," there is something just not right about the match: he's a liar trying to score; she's lost and confused and hopes that "Dan" will marry her; everything that is said seems low-level and pointless (his ex-wife did not understand him; he would like his date to give him a massage; their waiter can't pronounce English correctly). At least *Seinfeld* was funny. The conversation represents Roppongi extremely well—perhaps most pointedly the transmogrified Roppongi that took shape after Japan was no longer king: the bounce and optimism were gone; the future was uncertain; there was no more trust; exploitation ruled. Gerster's disapproval is evident; perhaps it is the same uncomfortable feeling that I admitted to having about the Roa book.

It is, indeed, hard to put a finger on exactly what changed in Roppongi after the bubble burst and how that led to some sort of decline, but there is no dispute that Roppongi old-timers say again and again with lament that the place is no longer what it used to be. One piece of the story has to do with the passing of the popularity of disco, removing what had been a popular underpinning of Roppongi's nightlife. But that is just a wee part of the story; I would never go so far as to suggest that Roppongi's woes are because disco died. More important is that elusive "there is no longer a 'there' there" quality—a missing sense of special place—that I am trying to describe. With the headiness diminished, Roppongi went flat, the liveliest nightlife went elsewhere, and problems increased. Drugs entered the neighborhood, not for the first time by any means, but in greater quantity and with greater danger. As well, there may have been more of an X-rating to the new Roppongi nightlife: increased strip shows and VIP room raunchiness, fetish clubs, and the familiar exploitation of the schoolgirl image that is almost an icon of off-color Japan. Scary characters increased as well, some spilling over perhaps from Kabukichō, where police had been doing battle with some of the most troublesome gangsters and pimps. For some Japanese, the tipping point may have been the increasing numbers of foreigners in the neighborhood. There are certainly those who will argue that Roppongi's problems today are because of too many foreigners of the wrong kinds. But these developments, too, would be only part of the story.

Whatever the reasons, it seems clear that many discerning Tokyoites, Japanese and foreigners alike, began to avoid the district sometime in the 1990s, turning instead to Shibuya and other hangouts further west on the yamanote side of Tokyo, and that at about the same time the number of faces that were visibly non-Japanese increased. It is this Roppongi that I got to know face to face and that I describe from personal experience in the next chapter. I saw lots of excitement in the neighborhood as I got to know it, as Roppongi is not yet dead, but I did not know at the start of my encounters that the Roppongi of the time was but a "next stage" after a heyday. It makes me wish that I had been there from the start. But even if I had missed the best, the next stage of Roppongi's biography promises to be interesting as well.

World Cup 2002

There is, however, what might be one last hurrah to report from Roppongi before the good old days were gone forever. That took place between May 31 and June 30, 2002, when Japan and the Republic of Korea jointly hosted the FIFA (International Federation of Association Football) World Cup tournament. The game venues were scattered among various cities in both countries, and the final match, won 2–0 by Brazil over Germany, was in Yokohama, but all through the events, as well as for several days before and after the tournament, Roppongi was one of the most popular gathering places in Japan for international visitors and for fans of the thirty-two national soccer teams involved. I was in Roppongi at World Cup time, and although not much of a soccer fan myself, I became one during that exciting period, being caught up in the merriment and camaraderie. Celebration parties spilled from sports bars with big television screens onto the streets, making Roppongi great fun during that month. (Shibuya was also an especially popular place to be.) The nights following Japan's victories over Belgium and Russia were especially boisterous. All month long, even those who supported teams that had just lost joined the happy crowds, wearing national colors and waving flags.

It is worth mentioning these things because Japan had expected the worst from the world's soccer fans. As *sokka feeva* (soccer fever) built up in anticipation of the games, there was also something approaching national hysteria, in at least some quarters in Japan, about possible mayhem by foreign soccer *furigan* (hooligans). There was pre-visa screening to identify potential troublemakers and keep them out of the country, as well as talk about closing schools near game venues and likely celebration spots such as Roppongi to shield children from the riots and crimes that would almost certainly take place.[13] In addition, there were reports of various extraordinary precautions by Japanese authorities such as gluing down stones along railway tracks in Kobe and Osaka to prevent them from being hurled as projectiles by out-of-control hooligans, and a Japanese Coast Guard drill near Niigata with helicopters and commandoes to subdue "mock hooligans" who had taken over a ferry ship. I had also heard of plans by the Justice Ministry to charter a large ferry to transport arrested hooligans from Hokkaido to jails in Tokyo and deportation's doors.[14] In Kawaguchi, a suburban Tokyo town that hosted a game between Sweden and the notorious England, the head of municipal disaster prevention efforts said that bicycles and signboards would be removed from the streets before the game to prevent them from being used as weapons (Wijers-Hasegawa 2002). There was even a much-publicized (and, from other quarters, much ridiculed) warning by a Japanese politician that there would be mass rapes committed by foreigners against Japanese women, followed by a spike in births nine months later.

None of the terrible things happened, of course, and the number of incidents of excessive partying and the uptick in the numbers of crimes were all within reasonable levels. The naysayers were proved wrong, and Roppongi, generally considered to be the most likely spot for the worst occurrences, turned out to be an admirable mix of fun-making Japanese and foreigners from around the world. Japan (and Korea too) shone during the games, and those who witnessed the parties at Roppongi Crossing (still being shown in YouTube clips) have happy memories (Darling-Wolf 2003). It is interesting to consider that Roppongi's birth as a proper international nightlife locale was aided by one set of games, the Olympics of 1964, and that its possible last triumph in this regard was with a second international athletics competition.

When the world came to play
That's when Roppongi had its best day.

Roppongi Rhythms, Recently

Crow Time

Early in the morning, Roppongi belongs to the crows. At least that's the case on this June day during the crows' mating season. They are enormous crows, black as can be, with mastodonic beaks, strong, mean, and smart. I've never seen crows anywhere in my travels like these Japanese crows (*Corvus macrorhynchos*). They have been known to stop trains by piling stones on rails, attack people and kill small pets, and crack nuts by dropping them onto the path of traffic. They are Tokyo's scourge, feeding on the leftovers of a well-fed city, scattering the contents of street-side trash bags, and cawing so loudly during their first-light gatherings that entire neighborhoods cannot sleep. Aggressive crow-control efforts have made things better in some districts, but still the back streets of Roppongi, where bags of fresh trash are piled from just a few hours before, are the domain of King Crow, the regency of Roppongi's raptors.

If the early morning is a Saturday or Sunday, or a national holiday, the crows have considerable company. There are all-night Roppongi-goers every night of the week, but Friday and Saturday nights as well as holiday times fill the streets, clubs, bars, amusement arcades, karaoke parlors, and almost every other kind of fun establishment that the neighborhood has to offer, with a much larger percentage of clientele staying out until crow time. Most of the partygoers seem perfectly functional, some having regained their faculties after some earlier loss of control, but many more were always in command of themselves and are now anxious to go home. The first subway train out of Roppongi is at 5:08 a.m., and hundreds of people are waiting to board. It's like the famous Tokyo sardine-can rush hour, but not quite. There are plenty of passengers in now-rumpled business suits carrying briefcases, but there are also people in party finery, as well as those in T-shirts and jeans. And very importantly, there are also many, many people who have worked all night, providing for the happiness of their fellow passengers: bartenders and wait staff, cooks, nightclub hostesses, touts and bouncers, strippers, and many others. Everyone is tired, few are talking, and quite a few, especially those lucky enough to have seats, are sound asleep. It's some time before the train is far enough from Roppongi for passengers to begin getting off. In the meantime, as it pulls into station after station, almost no one boards or gets off: these are not action neighborhoods where people have stayed up all night, and they are not where Roppongi's early morning train-riders live. This is the "Roppongi Special," running the full route of the Hibiya Line but filled only with those who saw Roppongi's crows.

That first train would make quite an interesting sociological study. So would other subsets of Roppongi's population, most particularly those unfortunates who did not board the Roppongi Special but probably should have. They are the ones who linger endlessly in the Roppongi morning, past first light and then sometimes into the 9:00–10:00 a.m. morning and beyond. At first they share space with the crows, many of them literally among the bags of scattered trash and empty beer cans, and then they outstay the crows and the trash cleanup. They simply can't get themselves together enough to make it home. Some are sprawled motionless along the sidewalks or in doorways, others are staggering, taking a half-hour or more to advance a single block, while still others are so "in love" with their companions of the night that they can't seem to part, but just kiss, kiss, and kiss again. These are people still in their business suits from yesterday, or the overdressed or barely dressed nightclubbers in sequins and miniskirts, or young hip-hop fans sporting baseball caps with graffiti. I'd start my study of them with a review of the scene and the question, "Who are these people and what the heck happened here?" and work my way backward to cover the rhythms of the previous hours.

However, instead of focusing on the morning I'll take the more conventional approach and start with people arriving in Roppongi in the evening. This makes it easier to give a fuller account of the many different kinds of people who come to enjoy themselves in Roppongi and their activities, and to more properly explain Roppongi's roles in the rhythms of Tokyo life more generally. I return to the colorful crow people later, as this section of the chapter winds down. Then in separate sections, I (1) explain that the Roppongi night is but one aspect of the neighborhood and that there have been other, very different people in Roppongi and with different ways of using the neighborhood over and above any reference to a New Roppongi; and (2) focus not on the people who come to Roppongi for enjoyment but on the large number of people who come to the neighborhood to work, in fact to produce enjoyment for its consumers. That is a key "crossing" for this book.

Evening Ballet

I begin the evening in Roppongi at Roppongi Crossing, the center of the neighborhood, the title of this book, and the symbol of all the cross-cultural, international, First World–Third World, economic, sexual, urban-makeover, and other interactions for which Roppongi is the stage. Also, the intersection of Roppongi Crossing is the traditional meeting spot for people going out in Roppongi (see figure 1.3). There are subway exits directly at the intersection, and people often arrange to meet their dates, companions, or business associates at an appointed time at a specified spot nearby. As mentioned in chapter 1, until recently the easiest landmark for meeting was the pink and white striped awnings of Almond coffee shop at one of the corners, so "See you at Almond" was a familiar refrain (Schreiber 2002). (Almond no longer stands, having been knocked down in Roppongi's redevelopment, but as of this writing its new building is under construction.) For many years, a low clock tower at a bit of widened sidewalk kept time as people waited, but now with ubiquitous cell phone use, people know exactly when their appointments will arrive or how late they will be, so no one seems to pay much attention any more to the clock. The space in front of where Almond stood is usually overcrowded at peak times, so some people plan ahead by meeting at one of the other corners or down the block. There is a selection of coffee shops within a one-block radius, including a temporary Almond and at least two Starbucks, so Roppongi-goers also arrange to meet there, particularly during inclement weather or if the wait is to be indeterminate.

Roppongi starts to fill in the early evening hours, between about 6:00 to 8:00 p.m. or so, after people get off work and make their way individually, in pairs, or in groups, by subway, by cab, or on foot from any one of the many workplaces nearby, to meet up with others and have a good time. There are Japanese and "visible foreigners,"[1] twenty-somethings and older people, men and women in business suits, and men and women dressed casually. There are also touts working for local bars, clubs, and restaurants, drumming up business and passing out leaflets. Most of them are Japanese, both males and females, but as the section about Roppongi's working class indicates, many of the most visible and most aggressive touts are males from Africa. So, too, there are lots of young women, black-haired and blonde, who turn heads because they've dressed to work as hostesses and escorts, strippers or dancers, or prostitutes and pickups. It's a fascinating scene to watch as Roppongi builds energy throughout the evening, until a crescendo is reached at about 10:30 or 11:00 p.m. when crowding and noise levels peak and sidewalks become barely passable. Friday and Saturday

FIGURE 4.1 Evening crowd gathering in front of Almond at Roppongi Crossing. Note the striped awning and the clock.

nights are the busiest and Sundays perhaps the quietest, but it's a nightly scene of partying, drunkenness, sex, and drugs, seven days a week, every day of the year.

The crescendo is the first of two each night and lasts until about midnight, when many of the merrymakers leave to take the last trains home. Those are happy trains, full of drunks and also worthy of sociological (and photographic) study. But Roppongi does not empty with the departure of the "Orient Excess." All evening long, other revelers have been arriving with plans for staying later. There is even a small "reverse rush" at about midnight, as new cohorts head for Roppongi on the last trains to spend the rest of the night there. Taxis line up by the hundreds, some having just arrived in the area with revelers from Ginza, Akasaka, or some other sakariba. By midnight, almost every vehicle on the streets is a taxi, and every taxi driver is hoping for a big score—a Japanese customer who lives far away, knows his way home, has missed the last train, and is willing to pay a premium for the ride. (Foreigners tend to not live as far, and in the opinion of many taxi drivers they might be problem customers because of language barriers.)

Sometime after midnight, a second crescendo is reached, the crowds having built up again with reinforcement arrivals, this time with more of the truly dedicated and thoroughly experienced partygoers. No more couples standing on the corner with a restaurant guide in hand, deciding which way to go, as hap-

FIGURE 4.2 One of the side streets from Roppongi Crossing; leafleting for a restaurant.

pens during the first arrival rush. Now, late at night, everyone knows where they belong, and everyone knows which dance club or bar is the current hot place within their own particular social subset. To be sure, people also flit from one nightspot to another, but in doing so they usually adhere to a circuit of familiar places and do not experiment. Many people leave Roppongi as the night goes on whenever they are ready, jumping into the nearest taxi that is not trapped by double-parkers, but a great many of Roppongi's most dedicated bacchants stay until first light to board the train that I describe as the Roppongi Special.

The earlier part of the evening is dinner and drinks, taken in either order, but sometimes the focus is on just one and not the other. As at any sakariba in a large Japanese city, the choices are manifold and include places for couples on dates or for quiet business conversations, and places that cater more to groups, including quite large ones from the office, from college reunions, or for old friends gathered to celebrate a birthday. There are also postwork singles' bars— or "meat markets," if you prefer that terminology—typically Western-style places where men and women seek compatibility over drinks. Increasingly, such places sprout up at street levels of the new office building–oriented redevelopment complexes that are being built in and near Roppongi and have that "New York yuppie" feel. In fact, one of the newest establishments in this genre takes its name from a Manhattan landmark and advertises the slogan "A New York Style Restaurant & Lounge." Much of the action is a "ballet within the larger ballet" between Western men and Japanese women, mostly in their twenties and thirties on both sides, who are chasing each other. This, of course, is a long-established routine in foreign relations within Japan, dating back at least to the time of Japan's opening to the world in Early Meiji and reaching full flower with the arrival of U.S. occupation forces after World War II. Single Western women in Japan often complain about the single-mindedness of their male counterparts and are resigned to receiving inferior attention in such places or stay away altogether.

There is a range of prices, cuisines, and atmosphere to choose from in Roppongi, as well as places that are established and famous, and new places that are just getting started and hope to find a niche. Because there are so many bars and restaurants and so many potential customers, there is something of an industry that has developed to bring the two together via "where to go" magazines, Web sites, and guidebooks. Restaurant reviewers abound, some honest and professional, others scamming for free meals and payoffs. Patrons also explore on their own as they set out from Roppongi Crossing, pondering the menus that are posted outside of restaurants as they pass, looking at the Japan-iconic, brightly lit plastic replicas of food dishes and desserts in restaurant windows or in special display cases that invade the sidewalks, and reading the leaflets they are handed on the sidewalks by restaurant workers drumming up business. Whatever place they select, chances are that they will be satisfied, as the restaurant and bar business in Roppongi is extremely competitive, and those establishments offering poor quality or poor service, or whose inflated prices do not correspond to their level of cachet, do not last long.

The choice of after-dinner establishments is even greater. For most people that means drinking. Groups often linger at the group-friendly restaurant where they ate, continuing to order beer, *shōchū* (a popular Japanese drink distilled from barley, rice, or sweet potatoes) or *sake* (brewed rice wine), content in already having seats for everyone, enjoying the increasingly boisterous conversation, and knowing that the restaurant welcomes them to do just that. Although Roppongi is not as well known as other entertainment centers for having *izakaya*, a traditional type of group-friendly eating and drinking establishment whose name means "remain" or "linger" and "sake shop," there are some popular ones in the neighborhood nonetheless. Typically, they combine a nonstop array of Japanese finger foods such as *edamame* (boiled and salted soybean pods), skewered meats and vegetables, and *karaage* (bite-sized pieces of fried chicken), with nonstop alcoholic beverage service, usually at fairly low prices. What is more, even some of the U.S. chain restaurants in the neighborhood that serve Western foods, such as Hard Rock Café and TGI Friday's, can act as izakaya in that they too seat sizable groups, keep the food and drink coming, and sanction amiable rowdiness.

It's not possible to list all of the types of places, with alcohol or without, that thrive in Roppongi, nor would it be interesting reading if I tried. The list is too long. I do, however, want to stress the great variety of going-out places that are available and to say something about some distinctive categories of places for which Roppongi is best known. I've undertaken various inventories of what is to be found in the neighborhood, almost always getting lost in the literally hundreds of establishments that I logged in via building-to-building, block-after-block field surveys, and I was able to conclude that there are, in fact, many parallel Roppongis existing side by side for different types of people, different interests, and different spending abilities. A person from any one subset of the Roppongi population would have a mental map of the neighborhood's attractions that is quite different from, and even in conflict with, the mental maps of people from another subset. Not only do the twain never meet, but they are barely aware of each other's existence, even as they cohabit the exact same short stretch of block. Consider, for example, the setting below. It's the start of a small tour.

Roppongi Tour

About a five-minute walk from Roppongi Crossing and still fully within what is the Roppongi night zone is a particularly crowded little area around the intersection of two small streets that come to abrupt dead ends only a few meters away. One sphere of activity focuses on dozens of young people, mostly in their twenties but also seemingly younger despite the law that says you need to be at least twenty years old to purchase alcoholic beverages. They drift in and out of a large, noisy nightclub, brightly lit in neon on the outside but dark inside, drinks in hand, getting more and more inebriated as the night continues. The music is hip-hop, the DJs have star status, and there is considerable skilled dancing, although it is beer that rules supreme. A large hip-hop style graffito behind the bar reads "What Do You Want?" while other signs posted prominently throughout the establishment warn that you must keep drinking in order to stay. Despite low drink prices, as indicated by a huge neon sign advertising "Happy Hour" specials, many of the people outdoors are drinking even cheaper, picnicking if you will, by consuming beer and other imbibements from a nearby convenience store. No one in this young crowd looks like they have a lot of money; if any-thing, they look "studentish."

There are many Americans here. They come to Roppongi to meet up with others from back home, but also to meet Japanese. Some of them are military personnel from U.S. bases near Tokyo, but more of them are college students in Study Abroad programs in Japan or young, poorly paid English teachers also in Japan for the experience. There are many young Japanese patrons too, those who are very clearly enamored of certain facets of American popular culture and fashion. They've dressed more American than the Americans they imitate, wearing either "hoodies" or Allen Iverson or Kobe Bryant jerseys, heavy chains of bling, and oversized baseball caps askew. Many of the men have those stupid-looking "droopy drawers," and some carry skateboards as accessories. This is Cultural Exchange 101: the foreigners get to practice their Japanese lessons, and male foreigners also get to chase young Japanese women, while for Japanese it's an escape from their normal routines and lessons about what's current or cool from those who have just come from the United States. As one of those young Japanese women who is a frequent chasee explained: "This is great. I get to speak English here. It's like having free lessons and having a party at the same time. It's the first place where I met black people. I feel like I'm in America."

On the same block are other worlds. Exactly where Cultural Exchange 101 meets outdoors is another Roppongi subset. Twenty or so luxury cars and lim-ousines are parked illegally on that same block. I take note of their low, single-digit license plate numbers and know immediately that somewhere nearby are people of some wealth and influence. I can't tell by looking from the street in which establishment or which building they are located; I have to ask. The drivers waiting beside their vehicles for their bosses won't tell, so I have to ask around Roppongi, finding people who work in the service sector in kitchens, behind bars, or as bar hostesses to find out that, yes, these are yakuza, Japan's storied gangsters, and that, yes, they come here to gamble in an underground casino in that building, to play with young women in a club in a building across the street, or to meet face to face over drinks at a private "member bar" on a high floor in the casino building. I could wait for a gangster to arrive and then follow him inside wherever he goes, but that's not recommended. It's better to ask someone who is on my side.

Wow! A little yakuza playground sharing space with the hip-hopsters! Well, I'm told that they are yakuza, although I can't know for certain. If the hip-hop crowd looks "studentish," then the nattily attired, evenly tanned, alpha-looking fifty- and sixty-somethings getting out of their Nissan Presidents and Toyota Centuries can be said to appear "positively gangsterish," which is close enough to yakuza for me. There are molls too, half the age of their male companions, beautiful, appointed in designer labels, with beauty shop hair and, it seems, puppy-dog devotion. They are Japanese, but the Japanese gangsterish clan also likes foreign girls, perhaps increasingly so. Beautiful blondes who can speak Japanese are especially popular. I suppose that is who I would encounter if I were able to get into an intimidating-looking private club in one of the gangsterish buildings that is called CCCP Girls. (Presumably, "CCCP" is in Cyrillic.) The logo shows a nude female silhouette riding a Soviet sickle within the framework of a Soviet star. There are cameras that watch you enter the building and ride the elevator to the appropriate floor, and more cameras to inspect you again as you ring the bell beside the club's faux-gold front door. Unfortunately, the doors would not open for me, even when I tried entry with a beautiful blonde companion.

There is more. Also within this interesting little venue, where yakuza drivers buff cars amid America's and Japan's futures barfing beer, is a still another world, a favorite restaurant of mine, moderately upscale, with a great wine list and a tasty, healthy cuisine from a happy, sunny part of the world.[2] It's on a higher floor above and overlooks the street below through floor to ceiling windows that allow patrons a view of the goings-on from their dinner tables. I've done that several times because I am a geographical spy. However, other diners seem to completely ignore the social geography craziness at their feet and exist only in their own world of moderately upscale yuppie dining. At least that is their public presentation, as Japanese can be quite good at making it seem that they don't see what they see. The oldest person I know personally in Japan, a foreigner, a Roppongi institution who has seen it all from before the devastation of World War II and was himself a part of history in several decades, including as a foreigner seven decades ago in a colonial territory of Imperial Japan, dines there regularly (see chapter 3). He has his usual window-side table but also ignores the view. When I ask him about the goings-on outside, he dismisses the topic, making it clear that those worlds are not his, and that his own (remarkably interesting) understanding of Roppongi encompasses entirely different sets of people and activities.

I leave this little corner and take a five-minute walk to another side of Roppongi Crossing to contemplate still another complex little world in the chaos below, across the street, beyond the double- and triple-parked limousines, in the thickest part of the hip-hopping nighttime picnic crowd. It's OK to come closer; no one sees me because I am not of them. There is a sign that is worth seeing. It is in English although there is an identical one in Japanese immediately adjacent. It's an official type of sign, on a thick sheet of galvanized steel and supported by a metal pole planted in the volcanic Japanese earth, painted "caution yellow" with big-font black lettering. It reads: "Be quiet! You are disturbing the neighborhood." That's a scream. We also see graffiti everywhere. It's not in Japanese and it's not in English; it's not in any script I can decipher. It must be in hip-hop-ese. Yes, that Japanese party girl was right: I feel like I'm back at home in America.

The Tour Continues

I round the corner and enter Gaien Higashi-dōri, the wide street that takes me back to Roppongi Crossing and then to another side of the district beyond. The sidewalks are packed with pedestrians and loiterers, the street is jammed with waiting taxis, and neon is everywhere. This is quintessential nighttime Tokyo, those famous and inviting scenes of traffic and bustle and colorful lights that look so good in films such as *Lost in Translation* (2003) and *The Fast and the Furious: Tokyo Drift* (2006). Hollywood's Tokyo is usually shot in Shinjuku, Shibuya, or Ginza, but nighttime Roppongi fits the scene requirements too, with its glitter, excitement, and tall, tall columns of neon. There are so many buildings, mostly multiple-story buildings but with narrow street frontages, and with so many commercial tenants inside that the way to convey information about contents is with signs that run the vertical length of the buildings, separately identifying, floor by floor, the names of the establishments that are just behind and giving perhaps just a hint about what's inside. Many buildings also have multicolored, illuminated directories of their contents at street level, hoping to attract passerby inside.

It's an interesting form of commercial architecture that all of these after-dark playgrounds have in common. Peter Popham, author of a favorite book about Tokyo that is now unfortunately hard to find, calls them "bar buildings" and focuses his description on Shinjuku's notorious Kabukichō district, introduced earlier, and a representative building called Ichibankan. The description is more than twenty years old, but is so on-target about the essence of Tokyo playgrounds at night that it is still current and could be a description of where we are standing today instead of Kabukichō during the bubble: "The section of Kabuki-cho that [Ichibankan] stands in is full of these bar buildings, structures of five or six or more stories crammed with small pubs, clubs and "snacks" from top to bottom, separated by inches and single-mindedly devoted to shouting each other down. Ichibankan has forty-nine bars, yes forty-nine, distributed through eight floors, and joins in the scrimmage in deadly earnest" (Popham 1985, 110).

TABLE 4.1 Business establishments, 2006

CHŌME	NUMBER	EMPLOYEES
Roppongi 1-chōme	146	5,158
Roppongi 2-chōme	59	1,423
Roppongi 3-chōme	631	9,591
Roppongi 4-chōme	514	4,712
Roppongi 5-chōme	295	3,374
Roppongi 6-chōme	548	16,955
Roppongi 7-chōme	879	7,822
TOTALS	3,072	49,035

Source: Minato Ward Office.

How many bars are there in Roppongi? My best answer is "hundreds." According to data published by Minato Ward, Roppongi has more than three thousand business establishments (table 4.1), but that count covers all seven of Roppongi's chōme as a unit, an area somewhat larger that the nightlife district that is the focus of this book (see chapter 2). It does not help to consider any of the seven chōme or a combination thereof as a surrogate for the study area, because chōme boundaries are drawn in way that does not work for this. The study area includes parts of six of the seven chōme, and in each of those six, substantial territory is outside the main area of focus. Furthermore, the survey covers wide categories of enterprises, including bakeries, pet stores, hair salons, and other businesses that are not relevant to the question, although the single largest category is doubtlessly "eating and drinking establishments," and the drinking places doubtlessly outnumber by a substantial margin those that are primarily for eating. Hence, my best reply to the question is "hundreds." My own field surveys, in which I walked every street and photo-recorded building directories and the signage outside buildings, also point to an answer of "hundreds." How many hundreds, though, I can't say because I can't tell from just the names what kinds of establishments are there, and because I doubtlessly missed many enterprises as well. There is no doubt, however, from this painstaking methodology that drinking establishments are indeed the most numerous of Roppongi's businesses.

"Hundreds" of bars in a small area is quite an impressive concentration, made possible architecturally only by the cramming of a great many of them one next to the other, "separated by inches," and then atop one another in multistory "bar buildings." Many of the places are also very small, quite a few of them with seating for only ten customers or even fewer. The variety is almost infinite. It seems that the business plan for a great many of the establishments is to fit a niche market and to charge high prices to offset low volume. Many customers are happy to pay a premium for a cozy setting with attentive personal service, all the more so perhaps in response to the hugeness and anonymity of Tokyo. Quite a few establishments, not just in Roppongi but also in Ginza, Akasaka, Shinjuku, and other sakariba, are small, intimate "member clubs" that give clients a sense of belonging in exchange for dues that have to be paid in addition to the night's tab. Being a member club, in turn, means a greater degree of privacy for both clients and proprietors, which then in turn means opportunities to address niche markets that, let's say, actually require privacy. That fact, in turn, drives prices still higher, which in subsequent turn attracts still more entrepreneurs to open businesses and to think creatively about niche opportunities.

The result is a bewildering array of places. Some serve an exclusive world of aficionados of highly specialized consumer products and services such the best wines or cigars, special tastes in music, or the narrow interests of avid hobbyists. One establishment, located on Gaien Higashi-dōri, serves two menus as you arrive, one for drinks and the other for your selection of realistic replica guns to shoot in the behind-glass firing range behind the bar. Many establishments exist outside a genuinely public domain, and I can only begin to describe what is behind the curtains. Lots of it has to do with sex and perhaps with loneliness too. Typically, such bars are oriented to male customers, with hostesses catering to clients' needs by sweet-talking them as they pour drinks and, in some of the more private establishments, perhaps by providing other, more intimate services as well.

There is already much written about the great range of kinkiness in Japan's huge sex industry and about the many kinds of specialized sex establishments in the service and retailing sector of the country's economy, so I do not need to repeat details here. Nor did I feel a need or a desire to include this aspect of Roppongi in my research. Instead, I refer readers again to books by Bornoff (1991), Richie (1999), and Schreiber (Schreiber et al. 2007), among others, some sections of which can be quite titillating. None of these books are about Roppongi specifically, as other districts, most notably Shinjuku's Kabukichō, are better known for this side of Japanese life, but Roppongi has its share, and some of what goes on there, day and night, is of that vein. Specific examples include places with sadomasochist role-playing and decor, so-called no-pan establishments in which young female employees in miniskirts and no panties

TABLE 4.2 Number of bars in Roppongi by music genre

Karaoke	10
Piano Bars	8
Jazz	6
Latin	4
Oldies	3
Rock	3
Beatles	2
Reggae	2
Soul	2
Blues	1
Disco	1
Hip-Hop	1

Source: Field survey.

work on glass floors, places with participatory sex on a stage or on the bar, and places where the hostesses and sex workers are dressed as schoolgirls (and in fact might actually be schoolgirls and be underage). For those with a different bent, there are even places that specialize in mother-image hostesses.

In those street-by-street field surveys in which I found that the number of bar-type establishments was in the hundreds, I was able to make some classifications by type. Again, it is variety that stands out as a hallmark. Take, for example, the mix of bars classified by genres of music. At a bare minimum, there are at least twelve choices (see table 4.2). The numbers are a serious undercount, as they show only those places that identify their kinds of music on exterior signage. Many places have no information at all posted about music or any other activities inside.

The ethnic or international variety is even greater, as is the number of establishments that can be identified as having a particular ethnic or national orientation. Roppongi prides itself as being an international crossroads, so it follows that many of its business establishments would aggressively reflect that theme. I counted 88 restaurants that could fairly be identified from outside as ethnic because of the name, a national flag, or posted words about the cuisine, and 33 ethnic bars.[3] The 88 restaurants included 24 different ethnicities, while the 33 ethnic drinking establishments included 19 different ethnicities. Table 4.3 gives details.[4]

TABLE 4.3 Restaurants and drinking establishments in Roppongi by ethnic/national identity

ETHNIC/NATIONAL RESTAURANTS		ETHNIC/NATIONAL DRINKING ESTABLISHMENTS	
Chinese	19	"Latin"	5
Italian	11	American	4
Indian	8	English	4
French	7	Brazilian	2
American	6	Caribbean	2
Korean	6	French	2
Thai	5	Iranian	2
Japanese	3	Jamaican	2
Mexican	3	Australian	1
Vietnamese	3	Belgian	1
Cuban	2	Chinese	1
Spanish	2	Irish	1
"African"	1	Italian	1
Belarusian	1	Korean	1
Brazilian	1	Philippines	1
German	1	Romanian	1
Greek	1	Russian	1
Hungarian	1	Spanish	1
Iranian	1	Thai	1
Jamaican	1		
Russian	1		
Swedish	1		
Tahiti	1		
Turkish	1		

Source: Field survey.

My five-minute walk takes much longer because of the jammed sidewalks. People are moving slowly, are busy in conversation, and are constantly being stopped by touts for bars and clubs. It's a scrimmage all right as Popham's imagery from Kabukichō describes, with the touts and the establishments they represent being the players—on both sides. People on the street are the ball, getting pounced on from all sides, bounced and tossed around, and carried across the line. Many of the touts are Africans, mostly from Nigeria. Quite a few of them represent strip clubs owned by fellow Africans who had come to Tokyo a bit earlier. The touts are a head taller than many of the other people on the street, all the better to spot approaching males and position themselves in advance for the sales pitch. They are good at breaking into conversations, blocking the way, and tagging after you if you try to ignore them. The way is also slowed by greetings that I exchange with people I know. Roppongi has a great many regulars, including I suppose yours truly, and just two main drags, one of which we are on, so one continually sees familiar faces when walking from place to place during peak hours.

There are other distractions on the way: some are tempting just enough for a peek inside; what's it like, who is there tonight? I cross the street by the McDonald's, marveling that with so many choices about where to eat there are so many people in line at this particular establishment. A sizable fraction of those in line look Americanish. The Hard Rock Café is nearby. There, the music redeems the food, and the honest-sized drinks can redeem the music. In summer when the tourist season is at its peak, there are Americans one after the other photographing the HRC, buying souvenirs, and posing for "I've been to Japan!" snapshots in front. There's an Irish pub on the next block in the basement of the Roi Building, one of the biggest footprint buildings in Roppongi and once a Tokyo showpiece. Honest drinks too, and a place to scan the foreigner clientele for friends. The Playboy Club of Japan (see chapter 3) used to be at the top of this building (the thirteenth floor), but it's gone now, replaced first by a stylish Thai restaurant with great views from the enormous windows and then by a nightclub. The building is also a great place for pool and darts. Lots of people come to Roppongi not to drink, dance, and mate, but for sport. Some are serious players. There is also a posh Internet café on one of the higher floors with low lights and rather private booths, some with "love seat" furnishings that do nicely as an inexpensive place to sleep until trains begin running again in the morning or as a venue for other activities often associated with hotel rooms. The place has showers too.

The opening of a new restaurant-cum-nightclub attracts my attention. I have been handed an "invitation" by an African streetman and am dazzled by the scores of huge "good luck" bouquets of hundreds of fresh flowers each that are piled along the approach and at the doorway. There are African doormen in tuxedos at the door and African floormen in tuxedos keeping an eye on the floor. It's too early in the evening for a crowd to be at the dance floor, but the music seems nice, the dance floor is large, and a few couples are already dancing. The restaurant looks expensive. There's a section of tables with a good view

FIGURE 4.3 Performers on stage at nightclub opening.

of the dance floor. I decide to have a drink. I sit down at a vacant table, and a waiter comes over and tells me to leave the area. It's all reserved. I take a better look and whoa, the men at the other tables look positively gangsterish. The nearest one has a double-breasted white suit with thin, dark vertical stripes and an arm extended just enough to show the Rolex. There are three women with him, also Japanese, about half his age and, like with the molls described near the secret casinos, "they are beautiful and are appointed in designer labels, beauty shop hair, and puppy-dog devotion." In fact, they are probably the same gangsters and the same girlfriends. Other occupied tables look more or less the same, with a three-to-one ratio of gangsterettes to punch perms. As I leave, I sneak a flashless photo, but it does not out work well. I then depart this aptly named place altogether; on the way out I ask a tuxedoed African doorman "Yaks?" (yakuza), and he replies "Yes." A good detective would have taken down the names from the cards of all those who sent the good luck bouquets of flowers that I pass again as I leave. Each bouquet is larger than you and me together.

Nearby is another building with multiple distractions and multiple African streetmen, doormen, and floormen. It has an inner courtyard arrangement, so that as one enters the courtyard and stands inside to survey the opportunities over two and a half floors, there is plenty of advice being offered about where to go. The biggest sell is for a strip bar with a fresh stock of dancers from Romania.

FIGURE 4.4 Popular Roppongi strip club.

Those places scare me. The prices they charge are bad enough, but who knows what additional adventures my credit card number would take after I've paid at such a place? What is more, the entry looks like a dungeon, perhaps appropriately so if the new arrivals from Romania are not doing exactly what they thought they would be doing when they signed on to work in Japan. I have some personal knowledge about human trafficking from the nongovernmental organization (NGO) side in Tokyo and know not to patronize places like this. I've been in other establishments in Roppongi with strip shows, but only a few. Those were places where I knew one or more dancers personally beforehand or where the African owner was a friend I knew to be an honest man. I always spent as little money as possible, and I always came only for geographical reconnaissance.

I duck into one of the bars that the Africans do not represent. It's a foreigner-friendly drinking bar with a small alcove that is a stage for bands. The music varies nightly, but usually it's some form of rock music: classic rock, progressive rock, sometimes rising artists performing their own compositions. The quality of show varies, sometimes within a single evening, as on weekends two or three acts are booked per night. You never know what to expect. Will the place rock or will it be dead? Tonight turns out to be a quick one-drink-and-out night. The band is one of those "Big in Japan" phenomena—something that could not possibly succeed back home but seems to have a following here. It's a so-so classic rock band with an outgoing, fine-voiced, Japanese woman lead singer, three young Japanese males on drums and guitars, and, somewhat incongruously, at the very front, a twice-their-age Caucasian male playing, of all things, the bongos. He works up quite a sweat as his hairy arms and fingers dance in a blur across the drums to the band's rendition of "She Bop," Cyndi Lauper's paean to you know what. Again and again he surveys the crowd as he taps, grinning from ear-to-ear, obviously content as can be that he is a rock star.

Another place in the same complex is a very popular dance club, but it's way too early for it to be crowded. I stop in nonetheless to "register." It's always smart to chat with the staff while they still have time, to become known, and then to receive personal attention (a better table, perhaps) during peak hours later. Having personal relationships with staff and management in popular places, however fleeting, is a key to apparent social status in Roppongi, and something "Roppongi climbers" cultivate. The owner of this establishment happens to be African, the staff mostly Japanese, and the clientele comes from everywhere in the world. I know that some nights are "Russian nights," in which a large corner of seating is reserved in advance for members of the large Russian–East European workforce of nighttime Tokyo. Word spreads via text messages that the gathering will be in this particular establishment on a specified night, guaranteeing a sizable turnout for the establishment and some cachet as an in-spot for beautiful foreign women. The Russian clientele, in turn, gets dedicated service in a preferred seating area among friends.

I will eventually make my way to my destination, another corner of nighttime Roppongi where I want to highlight another set of experiences, but distractions keep getting in the way. One of the newest distractions, now seemingly incessant particularly late at night, is the solicitation from Chinese streetwomen for "massages." As I try to dodge them, I pass games arcades and a pachinko parlor, and I am tempted by the former to see the newest fantasies of shoot-'em-up, automobile larceny and digital race horses, and by the latter to seek an explanation for the sign stenciled neatly across the sliding front door: "Americans take showers all the time. I know that from experience and physique magazines. Kinshichō [this one word in red; the name of a district in Tokyo] for an artist this interest in showers is obvious: the whole body is always in view and in movement . . . gracefully usually, as the bather is caressing his own body." I know in advance that the words are nonsense, just decoration, and that no one inside this essentially Japanese-only world would actually be able to read them, much less know their origin or meaning. Besides, like in every other of the estimated 14,600 pachinko establishments across the Japanese islands, everyone inside is in a pachinko stupor, lost deeply in the noise around them, the color and flashing lights of the machines that own them, and the endless cascades within of thousands upon thousands of identical little steel balls that drop this way or that.[5] They don't look up, never notice me, could not hear my question if I asked, and would not understand if they did.

By this time, after 10:00 p.m., there are drunks on the street, often an amusement in their own right and another Roppongi diversion. It used to be that the first casualties of the evening in Roppongi were young American soldiers, at eighteen and nineteen too young to drink alcoholic beverages legally both back home and in Japan, but on leave from nearby bases or visiting ships and anxious for a great time in an exotic land. To get more bang for their limited money, many of them drank on the streets, having purchased beer or sake from convenience stores or vending machines. Now, however, very few U.S. military personnel are to be seen in Roppongi, as more and more of them are engaged differently in other exotic lands and as base commanders in Japan have issued orders against visiting Roppongi and other nightspots because of the trouble. That leaves Japanese as the new first casualties of a Roppongi evening, and it is they who are most numerous as the toll of drunkenness escalates as the evening wears on. There is plenty of silly and loud behavior, vomiting, and people passing out on streets, stairways, public toilets, subway platforms, and wherever else inebriated bodies may have dropped. Sometimes the casualties are looked after by companions; others are alone and abandoned. The toll includes young men and women who look like they are students, salarymen in business suits with a hand on their briefcases, "Office Ladies" who have been out with their equally drunk coworkers, and others. At times, this aspect of the evening ballet in Roppongi is funny, maybe even positive in the sense that it's nice to see someone who needs it having a good time. Far too often, however, it is a sad and depressing picture when good people are so not in control of themselves, perhaps because they so needed an escape from their Tokyo days. It is sad, too, because as discussed in the next chapter about Roppongi as a problem neighborhood, sobriety-deficient Roppongi-goers can be especially vulnerable as victims of crime.

Across Roppongi Crossing

I return to the tour and at long last cross the big intersection beneath the "Roppongi High-Touch Town" (now "Roppongi Roppongi") sign to reach another cluster of targeted destinations. I make my way up a darkened side street to another short block of glitter. The side street is dark because on one side still stands a Buddhist temple and a small grove of trees from Edo time, one of the many such places still hidden away amid Roppongi's bright lights and bustle, and the other side is a demolition-construction site wherein some more of yesterday's Roppongi has passed and where some more of the new Roppongi will rise. I talk more about that in chapter 6, "Roppongi Redevelopment," but it's worth pointing out now on this little tour that what stands behind those bright-white cordons was once a very famous nexus of Roppongi activity.

That ghost of a building that looms above the protective wall is none other than the remains of TSK-CCC, Toa Sogo Kigyo (Eastern Mutual Enterprise)— Celebrities Choice Club, variously described as "the gangsters' castle," "the gangsters' palace," and "the castle of decadence." As mentioned in chapter 3 in the discussion of Roppongi during the bubble, this was headquarters for a powerful yakuza group called Tosei-kai, the "Voice of East Asia," that was founded by "the Ginza Tiger," Hisayuki Machii. Arguably, it was once the most opulent building in Tokyo—a multistory maze of power and pleasure set in Italian marble. Now it is about to be demolished. It's amazing how fast empires, even those in the underworld, can rise and fall, and interesting to see this particular complex, once the epitome of Tokyo cool, now smothered in darkness. By the time I return to this small street in chapter 6, the building is gone completely, and there are new plans for the site.

Some of the last tenants of TSK-CCC have survived. I knew them before, occupying a part of the building that had thus far avoided the auction block because of a technicality in real estate records about the property, and I know them still as they have moved under changed names, also because of a legal technicality, to new quarters in separate buildings a short distance away. My lasting memories of the inside of their part of TSK-CCC are images of yesterday's cool: red velour and red carpeting in a hostess club, chandeliers in a common corridor, and a golden lion guarding the doorway to a sports club. Most impressively, though, was the huge company crest, TSK-CCC, looming high above from a darkened part of the building whose fate had already been sealed. As with the hip-hop and yakuza corner, my interest in visiting the displacees from TSK-CCC in their new furnishings is with Roppongi's diversity and its complex patterns of social space. It also allows for a transition to the next section of this chapter, the world of work in Roppongi.

I hope that the TSK-CCC crest was spared the demolition and is safe somewhere. They moved the lion. He now has an awkward perch beside an indoor stairway, but he still marks the sports bar. Its name is different, but much of the staff is the same, and so are the routines. Even the customers made the move down the block. I recognize people immediately, and they recognize me. There are several sports bars in Roppongi, all of them, I think, popular, and variously oriented to clientele from different parts of the world. The TV screens in some places seem more focused on American football and baseball, while in others they show more soccer and rugby. There is overlap too, as well as sports variation depending on season of the year. And because this is Japan, there's golf showing on sports bar screens everywhere all year round.

People go to sports bars after work for drinking (they also serve food from limited menus), socializing, and maybe some darts or pool playing. They can be good places to linger until late and can serve as overnight havens for the postmidnight crowd. Because of time differences, sporting events in Europe or North America are televised live during the midnight-to-dawn period in Tokyo. Whenever there is a particularly important match, no matter which sport, avid fans gather to cheer their teams. Usually in this international setting that means fans of both teams at once in the same place, cheering for opposing results. And because this is Japan, the rivalries are almost always polite and civil, no matter how boisterous the crowds and how crowded the bars. I recently spent a full night in the sports bar to which I am heading, watching with friends (and writing into a notebook) as Russia beat the Netherlands 3–1 in extended overtime in a critical match leading to the European soccer championship (subsequently won by Spain). The place was packed, mostly with Dutch fans decked out in orange. However, more and more Russians arrived as the night continued (they work later), so that by the end of the match the room was balanced numerically, and the Russians' chant of "ro-si-ya, ro-si-ya" was loud, clear and, in the end, triumphant.

I have met people from thirty or more countries in this one bar alone. In addition to the Japanese, Americans, and Russians that are most numerous in my own subsets of Roppongi, there are others from East Europe, such as Ukrainians and Belarusians, a full array of European Union nationalities, Canadians, Colombians and Brazilians, Nigerian streetmen on break, Turks and Israelis, Iranians, and, from South and Southeast Asia, Sri Lankans, Indians, Bangladeshis, Singaporeans, Thais, and Filipinos, among others. But nationality does not matter much here, except perhaps during the excitement of a football match. This is international Roppongi, the language is English and Japanese mixed, and we are all the same except for the visible ethnicity or race badges we carry. Moreover, this is "lookist Roppongi." It's just a sports bar, but it's in a setting where the social structure is based disproportionately on physical appearance. Like the hip-hopsters and yakuza sharing space without seeing one another, here inside this small, crowded bar with multiple TV screens and one always-in-demand pool table, space and interaction are based mostly on who has the looks and who does not. This is a theme that is elaborated on in some detail in various ethnographic studies of the intersection of youth culture and nighttime entertainment (Chatterton and Hollands 2003; Grazian 2008; Malbon 1999; Wilson 2005).

The lead is set by the many professional models, males and females, most of them Caucasians from North America, Europe, or Down Under, who come here to be with one another and relax in a nonthreatening environment. Some of the models are quite famous, seen on TV, on posters on subways and trains, or on the ubiquitous billboards advertising expensive fashions that loom over this prosperous side of Tokyo. The bar welcomes them with free drinks, a brilliant business strategy in that it keeps other customers coming in but costs very little as the models rarely drink much. They are amazingly self-aware, cliquish, and do not seem to see beyond their sphere of beautiful friends. Yet, if you happen to look in their direction a little too hard, either the back turns to you or you get the "What are you looking at?" look. As the evening goes on, the models crowd flits back and forth between a dance club down the street and the sports bar, never staying in one place long enough in a stretch to finish a free drink. There are also strippers (Caucasian females) from another establishment down the street and bare-breasted mermaid-swimmers from giant aquarium tanks in the restaurant-lounge next door who pop in for timed smoke breaks from work. Professional hostesses filter in as well after finishing their shifts at saying flattering things to men twice their age, and also flit back and forth between the sports bar and favored hangouts nearby. They seem to have no interest at all in more conversation with men not already in their circles. For those at the top level of cool, or for the really big spenders, there is a VIP room with VIP staff. Those of us who are not part of this beautiful world interact freely and enjoyably among ourselves, sharing the same floor, the same TV monitors, and the same toilets with people who are much better looking, and understand that the line has been drawn against communication.

If a sports bar can be a tough environment, then imagine what it's like in an all-night dance club frequented by the "modelish" classes. I am truly out of my element in such an environment but responded nonetheless to the call of fieldwork. Particularly late at night, when Roppongi belongs to the experienced clubbers, people know where they belong and where they do not, and dance floor lines are perhaps the clearest drawn of all. I don't even try. It's a steep price to be admitted to this particular club unless you are a model playing for free, and drink prices are steep too. The doorman can be a hurdle too, but I know some tricks and, of course, have some connections too. The goal is a perch on the balcony that overlooks the dance floor. From there I can observe a very "special" subset of Roppongi in action.

Again, the clientele is highly international, and even more than in the sports bar nearby, it looks like this club has a lock on looks. The Web sites and blogs that discuss this place all confirm this. The professional modeling community in Tokyo is one of the largest in the world and is made up mostly of people who are far from home and who do not speak the language of the country where they are working. Many of them know one another from countless times together on assignments and from showing up again and again at the same auditions. The females especially suffer a lack of privacy in public because of the double whammy of being "visible foreigners" and being extra striking to boot. Even Japan stares as they pass. That helps to explain the cliquishness and apparent disinterest in people from outside their circle. It's not surprising, then, that perhaps even more than those of us from the "nonspecial" public, they would be drawn into places of escape and togetherness. Malbon's study of the world of clubbing in London, and some of his observations about the motivations of women clubbers in particular, cast some light on this complex topic (Malbon 1999, esp. 38–46).

I see just that from the balcony. This being a weekend, the place is crowded, and the bar area, dance floor, and seating zones all seem to be more group oriented than I would think is typical for a nightclub. Yet, I am reminded that the very word *clubbing* itself connotes notions of group identity and belonging (Malbon 1999, 37), so I shouldn't be surprised to see the little world below as one of social spheres and subsets and status symbols. There are a number of clusters of several persons each, mostly women but also some groups that are mixed. It's obvious that these are people who know one another and feel comfortable together. They stay more or less intact as they move from, say, the bar area to the dance floor, and then back to the bar a few cuts later. Groups of women dance as groups. There are individuals and pairs too, but it's the group scene that strikes me most. I recognize one group as Russian women models and another group of young Russian men and women, as well as a young French male whom I know to be a student and part-time model. He might not even be old enough to be in a place that serves alcohol. He's in a group too, three men and two women, all of whom look Schengenish. The club has hunters too—men who come alone or in pairs looking to meet women. What club doesn't? They seem to be from Tokyo's large headhunters and hedge fund crowd, well-dressed young men with good incomes and high aspirations. For some, chasing Japanese women is no longer a challenge: the best trophy is the blonde on the billboards. A pleasurable part of my entertainment from the balcony is watching the ballet of approaches, rebuffs, and new approaches.

Throughout the club there are people who are lost in the music. There are individuals dancing alone, others in the tables area who are also visibly engaged with the beat, and two beauties near us at the balcony railing, putting on a show for those below. The music alone seems worth the price of admission. It's a commercial house genre, and the DJs must be excellent because it seems like the in whole place is in motion. It is likely that some, or maybe even quite a few, of those who are dancing are fueled by energies other than sound, light, and alcohol alone, as that is part and parcel of the club scene anywhere, even in antidrug Japan, but I won't open that door any wider for now. This particular club, though, has a clean reputation, and the security personnel at the door are probably charged as much with maintaining that reputation as with separating those who are cool from those who are not. Some clubs of this type display very explicit signs (in English) about a no tolerance policy for illegal drugs.

The highly competitive marketplace of Roppongi seems to function correctly: good sounds, a good floor plan, and a masterful blend of movement, color, and illumination in lighting, plus a constructed atmosphere that makes you feel special—they all add up to a quality establishment that has earned its crowds. Even I, in my inexperience at clubbing, can distinguish between what is good from the bad. There are dives in Roppongi too, lots of them, but this place is many cuts above. There are other top places too. Readers who know Roppongi already know the famous establishment that I've been describing; they also know some of the other upscale places that I know, some of the dives that I could be describing, and some of the places that are nothing but trouble. More about the trouble topic soon, but first there is one other, critically important aspect of Roppongi's rhythms that I want to introduce on this particular corner, Roppongi's very prominent hostess industry.

Hostess Heaven

There are scores of hostess bars in Roppongi, maybe a hundred or more, and every evening hundreds of professional hostesses are hard at work serving hundreds more, maybe a thousand or more, male clients. Again, details about numbers are impossible to know because of problems of definition, the variety of places, and the curtain that surrounds many of the establishments in this category. It is, however, a very large category, a big part of the Roppongi rhythm and the Roppongi reputation, and a major element in the Roppongi economy. It is also an excellent topic for two transitions that I am making, first to a section in this chapter about the world of work in Roppongi, of which hostessing is one aspect, and then, in the next chapter, to the ways in which Roppongi is changing. At least some aspects of the hostess economy might be in danger in a "New Roppongi" and are already facing decline. Nevertheless, for now Roppongi is still a "hostess heaven," meaning that it is a fruitful place for young women interested in engaging in this line of work to become employed, and a ripe place for clients in search of young hostesses who meet their tastes and with whom to spend time.

A hostess's workday can start well before the evening crowds begin to arrive at Roppongi Crossing. If there are no other obligations such as college classes or a child at home, much of an afternoon is often given to necessary, time-consuming and expensive appointments at hair and nail salons, possibly a tanning salon, and working out on a treadmill or with weight equipment at a fitness club. The fitness club I know best in Roppongi is packed every day with hostesses and strippers until the 5:00 p.m. price jump for the postwork rush and the arrival of a mostly male clientele.[6] The afternoon is also a time for shopping. Roppongi has several specialty stores for makeup and other beauty products, accessories, lingerie, and the kinds of dresses that hostesses are required by their clubs to wear. It seems that many Japanese clubs employing only or mostly Japanese hostesses require evening gowns (although they can be fairly cheaply made as most men won't know the difference), while many of the establishments that specialize in foreign models expect miniskirts and cleavage. A hostess cannot wear the same dresses again and again, as regular customers expect to see wardrobe variety, so there is a need to keep buying, if only at "recycle shops" where used clothing is bought and sold, and to share clothing and accessories with coworkers.

As afternoon turns toward evening, ambitious hostesses with no special "appointments" that night or those working for demanding clubs turn to their cell phones and call clients they had met earlier to drum up business. I've seen this routine many, many times up close, both by being with friends who are hostesses as they get ready for work, and by witnessing and overhearing the routine as repeated by stranger-hostesses. In fact, the idea for this particular paragraph comes from what I see unfolding at the next table in one of the Starbucks cafés where I have been doing much of my writing. My neighbor is a very attractive Japanese woman in her twenties, obviously a hostess, revealed by her beautiful, long, and stylishly coiffured auburn hair (I think it's described as pompadour with ponytail), her way of dressing and accessories, and the small carry-on suitcase on wheels that is beside her. I know from experience that the bag contains changes of clothes and every conceivable need in makeup. Her table is so close to mine in this Japanese setting that I can actually read the *meishi* (business cards) that she has arranged neatly on her tabletop beside her two cell phones. She has her appointment book out too, one like mine in which any two facing pages represent the seven days of one week, and I can see that her book is much more full on a day-after-day basis than mine. Thankfully, my laptop is at an angle away from her, and she cannot see that I am typing about her. She arranges her stock of business cards one way and then in a different pattern, consults her appointment book again and again, looking at past weeks, this week, and next week, and then starts calling:

> Hello Murata-san, this is Aoi. You remember me from last week at Club Montmartre? I have not seen you in a few days and wonder if you will be coming in again soon. Can you come tonight? I think that it will be quiet and I can spend a lot of time with you. I want to hear more about your trip to Hong Kong, and also I want to ask some advice about a problem I am having with my apartment. You said that you know about real estate law. . . . I told that joke that you told me about the [whatever] to my friend Ayumi in my English class. She loved it and said that you must be a very funny man.

That's a "composite" conversation rather than an exact quotation, and all names are fictitious. She calls client after client, employing the same kind of approach and seeking the same objectives in each case, with only the details differing from one person called to the next. I see that she has handwritten notes on the backs of calling cards, apparently reminding her of who is whom and various key facts about each of her contacts. Before she clears her table and leaves, she wheels her little suitcase into the restroom, where she spends at least fifteen minutes, and moves then to the washbasin-cum-mirror, which is in a corridor that is visible from the establishment's seating area, where she spends another quarter hour or so working on makeup and perfecting the bounce in her hair. Then, a few minutes before 7:00 p.m., she leaves, with just enough time to walk the two blocks to her club.

On many evenings, clubs require their hostesses to go out on a *dohan*, an arranged date with a client who has expressed interest in spending time outside with a particular employee. The client pays a substantial fee to the club for the privilege, a part of which is returned to the date via a complicated pay scale formula that most clubs use. The date itself is usually nothing more elaborate than dinner together in a restaurant nearby before the client escorts his companion back to club (or is it the other way around, with the hostess escorting the client to the club?). The hostess, in turn, encourages the client to stay at the club, where he would continue to spend money. Quite a few of the nicer restaurants in Roppongi do a brisk early evening business of hostess-client dinners. This is especially so in the case of some of the restaurants with ethnic fare, as it is not unusual to see a Japanese male client with a young foreign hostess in restaurants that correspond to their date's nationality. Oh, how many times have I overheard conversations in a favorite European restaurant of mine about the ethnic cuisine, the national brands of beer, "the capital of my country," who the prime minister or president is, and exactly where on the map of Europe the country is located! This restaurant even keeps a supply of maps and tourist brochures on stock to help with such conversations.

The hostess who is working a dohan has incentive to keep the customer happy because her income will rise as he keeps coming back to the club to ask for her. A skillful hostess will know how to squeeze her client for ever more expensive gifts, typically by making him think that his lucky day, that is, what he is secretly fantasizing about or asking for directly, is just around the corner.[7] A common ploy by hostesses is to request the same exact designer bag as a gift from the client as one has already gotten from another client or multiple clients in the past, because the duplicate bags can be sold for personal gain, and one original is kept to make every client think that it is his bag that she is carrying. Roppongi has some stores that specialize in the sale and resale of designer handbags and other popular gifts for hostesses, and some part of a hostess's afternoon can be spent in taking care of such banking.

Club work is also hard and calculating work. While many times I hear back from hostesses about a fun evening at the club with interesting clients, lively karaoke, or other games and entertainment, for the most part it is pasted-on smiles and friendliness atop banal conversation. How much fun could it be to see again and again, as I once did for about two hours when I was an invited guest of a small, private club, a relooping video on the flat-screen TV called *British Girls Gone Wild*—a film about U.K. girls on holiday break in the Mediterranean exposing their breasts while drunk in a bar? In a newspaper article that she submitted to the *Japan Times* as her "confessions" from the job, former Roppongi hostess Ivy Emerson (2007) had this to say about her work routines:

> Some nights I'd meet up to 10 different men. Each introduction meant having the same boring conversation once again. Where do you come from? When did you come to Japan? Do you like Japanese food? Do you like Japanese men? Do you have a boyfriend? Oh, you're Canadian; can I ask you to sing Celine Dion?
>
> The same questions, answers and karaoke songs, for three to eight hours a night, six nights a week.

FIGURE 4.5 A foreign hostess (actress Antonina Revenko) at work in a Tokyo hostess club. (Photo courtesy of Fedotova Productions, from the film *Hallucination*)

One-on-one time at a table or comfortable seating area with a special client is part of the required routine, even if the client is a boor, but even more required is the spirit of the club, where hostesses work together to entertain clients and keep them happy. In Japanese-staffed clubs, one often sees groups of several hostesses (or even the entire staff!) step outside to escort big-spending clients into taxis or to the street leading to the subway stop, bowing their thanks and appreciation in unison as is the Japanese way, and waving cute good-byes, also a Japanese way.

In many clubs the work starts at 7:00 p.m., 8:00 p.m., or 9:00 p.m. (a precise time is established) and runs until after customers have left to take the last trains home. Some clubs allow their employees to leave early for their own last trains, but in many places the work lasts longer because of late-staying clients. Some clubs compensate hostesses for late-night cab fare home. Also, however, one often encounters hostesses on their own time in predawn hours in Roppongi, relaxing with other hostesses in places like the sports bar or nightclub described above and waiting for the first trains of the morning. Some have pocketed the cab fare they had been given. One of the Russian restaurants that I know strips the tablecloths and rearranges the furniture at about last-train time; then it

FIGURE 4.6 Japanese hostesses escorting a favorite client to a taxi as the evening closes.

changes over to something that resembles a coffee or tea shop, backed up with Russian MTV, for its late-night in-group clientele of hostesses, strippers, and other Roppongi workers waiting to go home. Unlike some of the many drunks who stagger out of their own cubbyholes in the morning to start their winding ways home, the hostesses and other night workers who are seen on the street at crow time are sober and make a beeline straight for the subway. I know for a fact that some hurry home to wake up their children for school and prepare their breakfasts.

Immigrant Proletariat

Most of the people who work in Roppongi and places like it in Japan are Japanese, of course, and someone should take the time to write their stories, particularly in this time of economic slowdown, reduced opportunities for advancement, and harder work with fewer benefits and less job security.[8] However, my interest here is primarily with foreign workers in Roppongi, as their stories are even less well understood, not just with the hostesses discussed above, and the strippers and the African streetmen, who are so visible in the Roppongi night, but also the behind-the-scenes people—the cooks, dishwashers, wait staff, bartenders, kebab-truck operators, and others, who along with their Japanese peer workers make Roppongi's rhythms possible. Slowly, Japan is becoming a country that depends on a migration of foreign labor to function (Noguchi 2006). That story and the story of the immigrant experience in Japan are still new and untold, but already there are things to learn and immigrant contributions to appreciate. Unfortunately, I can only begin to tell this story here, because like with so many other of my subtopics in this book (namely, the hostess economy), the full story is a book and more in itself.

There is some shaky ground here from the standpoint of both research methodology and the presentation of research results. There are no existing data about how many of what kinds of people do what jobs in Roppongi, whether from census sources, tax rolls, immigration records, or other potential archives, so all my information for this section has to come from my own field work. Furthermore, for logistical reasons a data snapshot at any one time is not possible, making my personal observations over a prolonged period, backed up by field notes and photographs, into my only alternative for information about national or ethnic niches in the local economy. But "observing" people's national or ethnic status is tricky and inconsistent, and generalizing about ethnic or national groups is always troublesome. Sometimes it is immediately clear and obvious that a person of interest is Russian or Japanese or Korean or something else, and sometimes it is not. You can't usually tell someone's ethnicity simply by looking, except perhaps to a certain point, and it is not always possible to engage in conversations or other explorations that fill information gaps. Likewise, what can be said about any ethnic or national group is not always true, as there are inevitable significant exceptions and examples of the opposite. With time, however, it is possible to see patterns that seem to hold up again and again, and that can be cross-checked by others who are familiar with the scene.

What I have done, then, is to construct impression-based profiles of who works in Roppongi in general and of employment in Roppongi in particular occupations, both formal and underground, by ethnic or national status. The information is from months of mental notes, typed field notes, and photographs about these very subjects, and from the "editorial advice" of others in Roppongi with whom I discussed these subjects. On the latter point, I was particularly careful to check my observations with individuals in the very categories that are identified in my profiles. Even so, I am not completely comfortable with what I am about to write. Generalizations about ethnic groups are always dangerous and sensitive: there is always something that was overlooked or misinterpreted, and patterns observed at one time can change to something new later. Furthermore, I fear that of all the many things I have to say in this book, this will be the one topic that readers remember most or will relate to others as being representative of my work, when, in fact, I am stating that this is where I am most clearly on a limb. I put myself there voluntarily, knowing the risks, because I think that having even an imperfect work-ethnicity profile of Roppongi is extremely important for having a sense of the neighborhood. Having said that, here goes.[9]

First, who works in Roppongi? There are certainly more Japanese than non-Japanese, although in some establishments the majority or even all of the employees can be non-Japanese. That seems to be the case particularly in ethnic restaurants where ethnic menu fare, decor, and staff define the business, but it is also seen in some bars and clubs that are patronized mostly by a foreigner clientele. Whether the workers are Japanese or of foreign extraction, they include both men and women, with the twenties to thirties age group being far away the most numerous. Those who are older tend to be managers or owners of establishments rather than frontline workers or workers in kitchens. Among young Japanese, there are quite a few individuals who fit the category called *freeter* (also *furita*), a word related to "free" or "freelance" that describes young, part-time workers who roam more or less freely from job to job as desired, giving no or little long-term commitment to employers and expecting in return few job benefits and little job security. They constitute a fairly new phenomenon in Japan, being the result of a prolonged period of weak and uncertain economic conditions and of a growing sense of detachment or independence from Japanese norms on the part of many younger Japanese.[10] There are also many other kinds of part-time workers such as college or university students, Japanese and not, who work nights in Roppongi to sustain themselves and pay for the costs of their studies. The most numerous occupations are service jobs: waiter staff, bartenders, kitchen staff, retail clerks, and clerks or counter staff at establishments such as pool halls, karaoke parlors, and movie theaters. There are also jobs that require specific skills such as those of DJs, musicians, and singers, and jobs that are gender specific (women or men only) and require a certain look to carry out. Women's jobs in this category include hostesses, strippers, and dancers,[11] while the only men-only jobs I can think of are those of tough-looking bar and restaurant bouncers and doormen.

In the formal economy of Roppongi, foreigners do more or less the same jobs as Japanese workers and include in some cases bar-restaurant managers and owners. A few even work in the police department, although not at the highest ranks but as translators and perhaps as undercover operatives. Most foreigners, though, are in frontline positions in bars, clubs, and restaurants and behind the scenes in kitchens. Most work legally, but there are many who do not, some of whom have deceived their employers about their visa status. They are self-sorted according to ethnic or national affiliations, as well as by gender, into specific occupations or specific categories of work, reflecting a combination of the power of ethnic networks in finding work and, in some occupations, Japanese consumer tastes in terms of what country's foreigners they prefer for what specific services.

A good example of ethnic sorting and how it changes concerns the occupation of hostesses, a topic introduced discussed in this chapter. Roppongi's foreign hostesses come from many countries but have recently included larger numbers of young women from Russia, Ukraine, Poland, Romania, and other parts of the former USSR and East Europe. This is so because of connections to such jobs that were forged earlier by pioneer arrivals and because of agent-recruiters who work for Japanese interests in that part of the world, knowing that attractive young women from these countries are now in fashion among Japanese businessmen-consumers. There are also hostesses from Southeast Asian countries such as Thailand and the Philippines, as there have been for decades in Japan, and from Latin America (Brazil, Colombia, Mexico, and other countries). When the Japanese economy was stronger, and before the famous tragic case of Briton Lucie Blackman in 2000 (see chapter 5), there were more hostesses from First World countries: the United States, Canada, the United Kingdom, Germany, Australia, and so on, almost all of them Caucasians. However, the number of First Worlders declined with the decline of the yen in the 1990s, new competition from the post-Communist world, and post-Lucie fears about dangers on the job. Now, too, there seems to be the beginnings of a decline in the number of hostesses from Russia, as the Russian economy has started to take off and Russia is becoming a place of new opportunities and a magnet for migrants. In addition, entry requirements to Japan have tightened for young women from East Europe. In their place, it seems, are more Latin Americans (Brazil, Mexico) and perhaps a first wave of young women from Africa.

Other jobs by foreign women in Roppongi include work as strippers and dancers and, as part of an underground economy, work as prostitutes. Some of these occupations overlap, of course. The ethnic contours are a bit different than those for hostesses, with the most numerous and most visible prostitution being by young women from China and secondarily by Latin Americans, particularly women from Brazil and Colombia. The latter case almost certainly involves instances of human trafficking and exploitation, if not cases from the other countries too. Other underground work by women includes furtive importing and sale of jewelry and accessories, clothing items, and other goods—sometimes as sidewalk vendors, sometimes through consignment selling, and sometimes as off-the-record sellers to established retail outlets. Russians and Israeli women (with an overlap there) seem to disproportionately occupy this niche.

Among foreign men, the most visible are the Africans who work the neighborhoods sidewalks as touts for Japanese and foreign-owned bars and nightclubs and as doormen–security personnel. I write about them in a separate section below. Most of the Africans are from Nigeria, but some are from other African countries as well, in addition to some Africans from European Union countries, most notably Great Britain. Some of the Africans are said to be involved in illicit narcotics sales and as go-betweens in prostitution, although here there is almost certainly more hearsay than direct evidence. The Africans have stepped in to a niche that was once the domain of Iranian males until a massive immigration sweep that started in 1992 resulted in large numbers of deportations (Komai 2001, 45–49, 54–57; Morita 2003). That was when Iranians had a particularly bad reputation in Japan as sellers of drugs and counterfeit telephone cards and were Japan's largest group of illegal immigrants. Some Iranians who survived the deportations did so by marrying Japanese women. They then opened businesses, including some night spots in Roppongi that now employ African men and foreign women, as well as some popular restaurants, busy retail shops, and other enterprises. Some Iranians are still working in the underground economy of Roppongi, engaged as sellers of illegal goods ranging from drugs to pirated DVDs to possibly guns. There are also Russian and Israeli men in such trade. The kitchens and dishwashing stations in Roppongi also employ foreign men, sometimes legally and sometimes despite the lack of proper work documents. The foreign ethnic-national groups that are most represented in these behind-the-scenes occupations are Chinese, Burmese, Nepalis, and Sri Lankans.

Table 4.4 is a summary of foreigner employment patterns in Roppongi. It is illustrative rather than exhaustive, and needs to be considered with caution because it is based on impressions from observations and not hard data and because there are exceptions to just about everything it shows. However, it was field tested among representatives of various occupations and ethnic groups that are listed, and shows accurately that Roppongi's proletariat is a genuine mix of ethnic and national groups. Most of the foreigners are from the Third World and from the post-Communist economies of Russia and East Europe and occupy specific niches for employment and illegal economy.

TABLE 4.4 Foreigner employment patterns in Roppongi by gender, ca. 2005–2006

MALES

FORMAL ECONOMY

Bartenders, wait staff, kitchens, etc.	From anywhere in the world
Owners and managers of clubs	Iranians, Nigerians

UNDERGROUND ECONOMY

Narcotics sales	Iranians, Nigerians
Touts for Clubs	Nigerians, other Africans
Pimps/Recruiters	Iranians, Nigerians
Pirated DVDs, etc.	Israelis, Russians
Kitchen staff (illegal workers)	Sri Lankans, Burmese, Chinese

FEMALES

FORMAL ECONOMY

Bartenders, wait staff, kitchens, etc.	From anywhere in the world

UNDERGROUND ECONOMY

Prostitution	Colombians, Brazilians, Chinese
Hostesses	Russians, Ukrainians, Romanians, now in decreasing numbers
	Decreased numbers from Australia, UK; North America
	Others from Thailand, Philippines, South America
Strippers	Russians, Ukrainians, Romanians, Israelis, Brazilians and other Latin Americans; recently Africans
Unlicensed sales of jewelry, etc.	Russians, Israelis
Kitchen staff (illegal workers)	Chinese, SE Asians, East Europeans

Source: Field surveys and interviews.

"You tell me, is it prostitution and is it so bad?"
Asks Margareta, an in-demand blonde, in Terminal One,
Boarding a flight to go home, moving a small fortune in cash.
"You tell me what I've done that's so wrong,
To take two thousand dollars for a tolerable hour or two,
From tolerable men, in Japan's better clubs,
When my family at home, hard as they work, all of them combined,
Can't pay the bills that are due in that oligarch economy of ours?
Does the sin sit with me?" she asks rhetorically,
"Or is it the very shape of the world that's a sin?
You tell me," affirms the traveled Margareta, decisively.

African Streetmen

I begin a series of short profiles of Roppongi's immigrant proletariat with the neighborhood's African streetmen. In some ways, their stories need to be told most, because there are the most misconceptions and false stories about them. On a busy night there are fifty or more men, visibly from African descent, mostly in their twenties and thirties, working along the sidewalks in the nightlife zones of Roppongi as promoters for the specific bars, dance clubs, and strip clubs that they represent. There are Caucasians, Japanese, and others working alongside them, sometimes in competition, sometimes for the same employers, but it is the Africans who stand out the most. They also work as doormen to clubs, as floormen, and, in general, as club security. I suppose that has to do with the fact that many of the African men are big in size and perhaps have an aura of toughness. Those who have worked hard and been frugal, I am told, have managed to purchase bars and clubs of their own, or to rent facilities and open their own, original establishments, at which point they become employers of African men who have followed them to Japan. Some Africans own multiple establishments and display their personal wealth accordingly. The chrome-heavy Hummer parked outside is an example. Outright ownership of nightclubs is actually difficult for foreigners in Japan, so I understand that many of the African-owned businesses have Japanese owners as fronts or own businesses through Japanese wives.

The majority of Roppongi's African men are from Nigeria, having arrived in Japan often via connections of an extended family sort with Nigerians who preceded them, but there are also Africans from Ghana and other countries, as well as others of African ancestry. My own conversations with "Africans" have included African Americans, a Jamaican, and a Frenchman. Not all of them, I am sure, are in Japan legally or have permits for employment, as they would tell me if I inquired, but I know that quite a few, probably the majority, do, in fact, have proper documentation. Many had worked in other countries—Israel, the Arab Middle East, Western Europe—before circumstances brought them to Japan. Perhaps a majority support family back home and cannot wait to earn enough money so they can return there for good. Others are in Japan for the long haul and have Japanese wives and children. Apparently, a common route into Japan for Nigerians is to go first to the European Union, where they acquire documentation as international refugees or even some European nationality, and then to enter Japan on ninety-day tourist visas, which they overstay. Quite a few of them marry Japanese women, sometimes within those ninety days, which allows permanent residence status and permission to be employed. I have seen published accusations that Nigerians and other Africans deliberately impregnate Japanese women they meet as "one-night stands" in order to be married and stay in Japan (Kamiyama 2005), but I have seen no data to support such claims and suspect that they might be rooted in Japanese racism and sexual stereotyping more than anything else. A sympathetic short article about Africans in Tokyo, containing information from a series of articles by Jinichi Matsumoto that had appeared in the Japanese-language newspaper *Asahi Shimbun*, was published not long ago in the *Japan Times* (Brasor 2007).

Roppongi's Africans come from poor backgrounds but with enough advantages, it seems, to have gotten educations and an orientation to opportunities for them elsewhere in the world. Some of what they earn in Japan is remitted home to support relatives. Some streetmen have wives and children back home in Africa whom they miss greatly and with whom they long to be reunited once they have saved a nest egg of Japanese earnings and can open their dream business back home. Still others work to bring their families to Japan and enroll their children in Japanese schools so that they can have a future in a more stable society. As mentioned, other Africans are married to Japanese women and have children by them. For some, the student visa route has been a preferred entrée. In my own position at a university, I have been able to see perfectly legal immigration documents from Africans employed as streetmen in Roppongi and to follow the successful academic progress of these new residents of Japan as they work toward degrees in higher education.

I say these very basic things about Roppongi's African men specifically because there is so much misinformation about them that corrections and basic definitions are necessary. "They are all drug dealers" is the kind of comment

FIGURE 4.7 Streetmen at work.

one hears frequently about them from both Japanese and non-Japanese in Roppongi, always without proof or justification. Likewise, there are accusations that an "African mafia" has emerged in Roppongi, selling protection and shaking down legitimate businesses. While there probably are some Africans, maybe even more than just a few, who deal drugs or engage in other illegal activities, just as there are such people in any sizable population group, the key fact is that there are no reliable data to support accusatory generalizations of any kind against this particular population. Yet, no less a person than the current governor of Tokyo, Shintarō Ishihara, is guilty of gratuitous blanket condemnations of these individuals. As quoted in Bloomberg.com, February 20, 2007, "Roppongi is now virtually a foreign neighborhood. Africans—I don't mean African-Americans—who don't speak English are there doing who knows what. This is leading to new forms of crime such as car theft. We should be letting in people who are intelligent."

I continue with observations to the contrary for the record. As described in chapter 1, I recognize that this is Roppongi, a place where lies abound and where one always needs to weigh carefully what one is told, but there are some things that I know for sure. About Africans' knowledge of English, I testify that I have spoken with dozens of Africans in Roppongi over the years, always in English, as the great majority of them are from countries where English is widely used, and only rarely have I encountered an African who does not have excellent English-language facility. Furthermore, to the discredit of Ishihara's understandings, quite a few of the Africans are, in fact, highly educated, often in technical fields and engineering, mostly at colleges and universities in Africa, but also in some cases at those in Japan. I know that personally and directly. I also think that the Africans I have met seem to be intelligent and that I have never met one in Roppongi about whom I thought differently. In addition, many of the Africans in Roppongi speak passable Japanese. The fact that many of them work the streets of Roppongi as touts for girlie bars and "who knows what" is in large measure (but not exclusively) because they have been hired by Japanese bosses to do so, and because discriminatory hiring practices in Japan have not allowed doors to open for other employment, including the professional positions for which many of the Africans had trained.

Having said all that, I add that only some of the African men in Tokyo work the streets of Roppongi and other neighborhoods of the night. Many others who are seen in Roppongi are actually customers, not touts, and despite the roadblocks against them, they have earned their beer money in trade and other professions. And to be completely accurate, quite a few are very religious (both Christians and Moslems) and don't actually drink alcohol. The term "bachelor sojourners" has been applied in immigration literature more generally to describe such young, ambitious, and hard-working men who build a life far from home.[12]

AFRICAN STREETMAN

"Come to my club, I give you discount.
Just have a look, look inside for free.
Beautiful Russian girls, yes, we have Japanese.
No cover charge, your first drink is free.
For you a discount, just have a look and see."
That's what the streetman from Ghana,
And one from Nigeria too
And a tall one from Congo, in a beautiful striped suit,
That's what the streetmen, working Roppongi's club street,
Pitch night after night, African streetmen, pitching entreaties to me.

Russian Roppongi

As used in Roppongi, the word *Russians* is a catch-all for Russians from Russia, Russians from Siberia, Kazakhstan, and other parts of the former USSR, Ukrainians, Belarusians, and others from that East European/North Asian, mostly Slavic part of the world. Although Ukrainian and other languages are spoken by these people, Russian is a language that binds, as it was once the common language known by all these people. Like the Africans, they are economic refugees. However, unlike the Africans, most of whom are men, the majority of Russian migrants are women. Most arrive in their twenties and find the kind of work that young, beautiful women can find easily in Japan: as models, hostesses, strippers, and sex workers. Sometimes it seems that there are so many Russian women in Japan there can't be any left in Russia, until one remembers the huge size and large population of that country. But then I've met so many women migrants from just one city, Khabarovsk, a medium-sized city in Eastern Siberia near Russia's border with China, that I have to wonder if there are any attractive women in their twenties left there. A similar joke that has circulated within Japan's Russian population makes the same point. There are also many migrants from Nakhodka and Vladivostok, which are actually quite near Japan, but also from Minsk, Kyiv, St. Petersburg, Magnitogorsk, Ufa, Chita, and a great many other cities and small towns across that vast terrain.

"Oh, you are writing a book about Russians in Roppongi," a young Russian woman exclaims. "Please tell them that we are not all prostitutes and such, be-

cause that's what they think of us here." So again, there's a need for basic definitions and the clearing up of misconceptions. Yes, there are Russians in Tokyo
who earn their living at prostitution, but they are but a small fraction of the
Russians in Tokyo and a small fraction as well of all sex workers, the large majority of whom, without doubt, are Japanese. And yes, the majority of Russians
in Tokyo are women. Japan has welcomed them and their distinctive look with
employment in the looks-based occupations that I have mentioned. Therefore,
it's probably fair to say that the majority of Russian women in Tokyo (or Japan
more generally) found their opportunity to migrate because they have the kind
of physical appearance that is now in demand. It's quite common to hear comments in Tokyo by Japanese and others that the Russian and Ukrainian women
and other women from those parts of the world are especially attractive. I can
add that they certainly know how to dress and present themselves.

There is so much more to the Russian–East European community than attractive women: there are men, of course, as well as families with children,
women whose main self-definition is mother and wife, Russian women married
to Japanese husbands, Russian men with Japanese wives, and a whole lot of people, women and men, who earn their living not primarily by how they look but
by how they think and what they can do in terms of creativity, entrepreneurship,
technological acumen, and other skills. There are writers and journalists, teachers, professors, engineers, computer specialists, singers, designers, artists, poets,
and priests. There are also plenty of Russians engaged in business, particularly
trade. Imports to Japan include Baltic amber, Moldovan and Georgian wines,
Russian vodka and caviar, Ukrainian honey, freshwater fish from Siberian rivers
and ocean fish from Russia's Pacific waters, Siberian cats and Siberian timber,
and many other products and resources. Exports to Russia focus on automobiles and electronics. Russian businessmen and –women are especially keen at
exporting used cars, motorbikes, and bicycles from Japan to Russia, and certain aspects of Japanese design and home decor for the booming housing and
condominium market among wealthy "new Russians" in places like Moscow.
There are also under-the-table businesses, including the trafficking by Russian
and Japanese mobsters of young women to work in the sex industry. There is
fierce competition in Japan-Russia trade of all kinds as well as a lot of money
to be made, so the number of Russian investors and businesses keeps growing,
even as information about who is doing what for a living is not always freely
shared.

Most of the Russians and other East Europeans in Tokyo have short-term visas and have plans to return home after reaching financial goals such as money
to purchase an apartment or open a business. Others have made long-term

FIGURE 4.8 Dinner party in a restaurant popular with foreigners and Japanese.

commitments to Japan and are raising families as immigrants in a new coun-try. This is particularly true for the large number of Russian women who have married Japanese men and gained permanent resident status. Most of them learn Japanese quite well and raise children either with Japanese as the primary language or bilingually. The marriages come in all flavors including many that begin with introductions through Internet services and those that result from personal relationships that began as hostess-client relationships. There is a fas-cinating story to be told about the sociology of Japanese-Russian marriages, or even marriages between Japanese and any foreigners in Japan—another book subject waiting for an author. I have my own observations on the subject, many of them coming from Russian women who are unhappy and lonely as wives of Japanese and come sometimes to Roppongi for a break. One quotation from someone I came to know well haunts me: "The number of us [Russian women] who married Japanese is thousands. The number who are happy is five." There is hyperbole here, of course, as those who know this community can personally count many more marriages than five that seem perfectly happy, but sadly the assessment is rooted in the reality of significant cross-cultural difficulties within many mixed marriages and is a plea for understanding.

Roppongi is an important part of Russian life in Tokyo not just because many young women happen to work in the neighborhood's nightlife industry or enjoy it as consumers, but also because the Russian Embassy happens to be in Roppongi. In addition to diplomatic functions and consular services, the grounds house a school, elementary through high school, to which Russian children commute from all over Tokyo, if only for once-a-week Russian classes, and there are quite a few embassy personnel and their families who live within compound walls and go into Roppongi daily for shopping and other routine errands. There are also some restaurants in Roppongi that specialize in Russian and Belarusian cuisine that thrive at least partly because of the coethnic population and serve as friendly venues for birthday parties and other community gatherings. Russian Orthodox church services are held in at least two other parts of Tokyo, but Orthodox services in the Ukrainian language now take place on a regular schedule in a borrowed church just outside Roppongi next to Tokyo Tower.

I want to emphasize that most of Tokyo's Russians, Ukrainians, and other post-Soviets do not work in Roppongi, as their offices, studios, and classrooms can be anywhere in the metropolis, and some venture to the neighborhood only rarely. In fact, I promised to mention that some of these immigrants, maybe most, hate Roppongi for its style of nightlife and reputation, and they bristle that associations are made between the neighborhood and their national groups. So there, the promise is fulfilled.

Restaurant Proletariat

I could continue with "Russian Roppongi" by writing about the people who work in the Russian restaurants that I know well and where I am known well, but the number of such restaurants in the neighborhood is few, they are easy to identify and find, and the privacy of people who have come to be my friends would then be compromised. Therefore, I have made it a point to eat elsewhere as well and to make friendships in other immigrant-based restaurants (and bars) so that I can describe some of what goes on behind the scenes for a wider group of people and without worries about breaking trusts. As I describe earlier, Roppongi is ethnic bar-restaurant paradise. Among establishments where I have comfortable personal relationships with immigrant workers who have contributed to my observations in this section of the book are places that specialize in Indian, Mediterranean (purposely vague here), Chinese, Filipino, and

Middle Eastern–Iranian cuisine, in addition to those excellent Russian places. There are also drinking establishments with ethnic themes such as Australian, Belgian, English, German, and Irish beers and at least some workers from those countries, as well as many other places with bartenders, wait staff, and kitchen workers who are from abroad. In fact, it would not be out of place to wonder if Roppongi could function successfully as a nighttime entertainment magnet without the labor contributions, with and without proper documentation, of foreigners in Japan.

Restaurant work is hard work. In Japan, there is what would seem to be an additional disincentive for such work in that there are no tips to be gained by providing fast, friendly, and accurate service, no matter how busy the night or how ill a worker might feel. Yet, that is what Japan expects and almost always receives. Standards are high for food and drink servers, bartenders, cooks, and everyone else connected with feeding hungry consumers and quenching their thirst, and the competition between the great many establishments that consumers have as choices assures that pressures and standards for the highest-quality service will never relent. Pay is low too, about ¥1,000 per hour, or about US$10, in round numbers, and hours can be long into the night. Conditions seem ripe for an immigrant labor force, especially behind the scenes in the kitchens and at dishwashing stations, which is exactly what I see developing in Roppongi. There, the conditions of work are perhaps the most taxing of all Roppongi workplaces: confined quarters; heat from the stoves, the ovens, and the dishwasher; few or no breaks, but a constant pressure of order after order, each needing to be perfect. The people who shoulder all this come from everywhere that is poor: Sri Lanka, China, the Philippines, Nigeria, Peru, you name it. They also come from Russia and its "partner" countries. Once, on a rare night when I needed help getting home from a favorite restaurant, I was escorted in a taxi by the dishwasher, a young man who was supporting his family in Mexico. Another favorite restaurant, one that specializes in pasta and pizza, amplifies the ethnic diversity of Roppongi's restaurant proletariat: in the years that I have been eating there, it seems to have had only Africans and South Asians in the kitchen and a wait staff that has included young men and women, many of them university students, from at least the following countries: Germany, Austria, Brazil, Mexico, Peru, the United States, Nepal, Poland, Morocco, Greece, and, of course, Japan.

As with the Nigerians who work their way up to ownership of bars and clubs, other ethnics have succeeded in rising to management or ownership of restaurants. Roppongi has multiple Indian restaurants owned by Indians, plus at least one each of the following: a Brazilian restaurant owned by Brazilians, a Turkish restaurant owned by Turks, a Thai restaurant owned by Thais, an Iranian restaurant owned by Iranians, a Greek restaurant owned by a Greek, and other similar permutations. Iranians seem to be especially adept at bar and restaurant ownership. As mentioned earlier, there was quite a large migration of Iranian male laborers to Japan in the 1980s and early 1990s. Most of those individuals have long since left, many having been deported for overstaying visas and for shady business activities, but many others have remained and turned entrepreneurial acumen into ownership of restaurants, bars, shops, and other businesses. Some of the restaurants they own have neither Iranian nor Japanese identity, but "third country" identity such as Russian and Italian restaurants. As with the Africans, it has been helpful along the way to be married to a Japanese citizen. That status furnishes one with legal residence in the country and an entrée for business ownership. Ownership of a restaurant or bar, however, can be just the beginning of a life of worries, as competition is fierce, profit margins can be small, and many businesses fail.

The Rest of Roppongi

I imagine that there are readers who, if they have had the patience to get this far, would say that despite the many pages I've written, I have still not described the Roppongi that they know. Exactly! Roppongi is many places, even within the world of nightlife, and it is not possible to give a completely exhaustive account. I just hope that if the comment pertains to nightlife, it is not followed by a criticism that the Roppongi I have described is in conflict with the nighttime Roppongi that these readers know. That would be a problem.[13]

It is also appropriate at this point for a reminder that Roppongi is not only about nightlife. For one thing, there is the New Roppongi in the making that will occupy much of the rest of this book. It emphasizes the daylight, nine-to-five world as opposed to the world after nine at night and is defined by the corporate culture of multinational companies in their New Roppongi office towers, new art museums, theaters, and concert venues in the neighborhood that cater to an upscale brand of international culture, new residential zones within Roppongi for the rich, and large new shopping centers dominated by global chain stores and expensive designer fashions. All of these aspects are discussed later in the book. But there are also long-established and long-thriving aspects of non-nightlife Roppongi that also need to be introduced to round out the profile of this complex neighborhood. A more complete roll call of what is in Roppongi reveals some of these other aspects.

My own introduction to the neighborhood was more than a quarter century ago, when Japan was still enjoying the bubble, and Roppongi was one of Tokyo's premier places for the lavish, playboy life. I was oblivious to that. Instead, as I wrote in the preface, for me and for my family Roppongi was where every Sunday morning we went to church. That was always followed by brunch at the children's choice of either a McDonald's or a particular Indian restaurant that I still occasionally patronize. We lived far away and commuted by three trains, but the church was our community and our Sunday enjoyment—a routine that we maintained for several years until returning to the United States. The children are grown now and on their own, and my wife, sadly, has passed away, but the Franciscan Chapel Center is still there, and I still attend when I am in Tokyo. It has served Tokyo's Roman Catholics since 1967 when it opened, and it has an international membership. Americans are the most numerous, but there are also many Europeans, Latin Americans, Filipinos, and others, as well as Japanese Catholics.

Filipino Roppongi

The Filipino community is quite large and can be presented separately as another aspect of Roppongi. Most Filipinos are Roman Catholic, as is most of the Philippines as a whole, and the Franciscan Chapel Center (FCC) is a principle Filipino community center, although it is not the only Roman Catholic church in the city with Filipino parishioners. There are masses in Tagalog at the FCC, as well as other activities. One reason for the presence in Roppongi of many Filipinos is that the Embassy of the Philippines is nearby, closer to Roppongi Crossing than the Russian Embassy, already mentioned. It is a place where Filipinos live and work, as well as where many Filipinos need to go from time to time for citizen services. There are also many Filipinos who work in Roppongi in the bars and restaurants, including some specialty restaurants with Filipino food, and whose labors were among those that I had in mind in writing "Restaurant Roppongi" above. There are also young women from the Philippines who work in the nighttime industries of Roppongi and other Tokyo neighborhoods as hostesses and strippers and at other jobs. They had been coming to Japan since long before the Russian boom. Some were trafficked in the worst ways, tricked by unscrupulous agents into thinking that they would be working as waitresses or in child care and then forced into prostitution. That exploitation, unfortunately, still continues, although now there are greater protections and better publicity against it and increased penalties against those found guilty of such crimes. Quite a few Filipino women who came to work in Japan in years past are now married to Japanese husbands and are mothers of children being raised as Japanese.

Many more women from the Philippines work in Tokyo as domestic servants and child care specialists, particularly among the city's highly paid foreigner households on expat employee packages that include such benefits, and in health care, including elder care. One often sees Filipino women in Roppongi walking the foreign children in their care to and from school, entertaining them at one of the many local playgrounds, or engaged in grocery shopping for the nearby foreign households that employ them. On Sundays after Mass and on holidays, many Filipino women are in Roppongi enjoying a day off together. They meet at a place like one of the Starbucks, where they converse for hours, or they visit Roppongi's new museums, tour the gardens that have been built in connection with the upscale new redevelopment projects, or shop for gifts to send to family members back home.[14]

Some Prominent Roppongi Institutions

Various prominent institutions present still other sides of Roppongi. Toyo Eiwa Jokaguin, for example, is a prestigious girls' school in the neighborhood, located next to the Embassy of the Philippines, that dates back to 1884 and boasts a long and distinguished list of alumnae.[15] Founded by Martha Cartmell, a missionary sent by the Methodist Church of Canada, the school still provides a Christian-based education to mostly Japanese girl students. The Roppongi campus now runs from kindergarten through the completion of high school. Sadly, every morning and then again late in the afternoon, one can see its distinctively uniformed students file past unpleasant and inappropriate aspects of Roppongi's less delicate side. The morning arrival is especially troubling because the students almost always have to negotiate their way past some of the worst leftovers from Roppongi's "night before" as they make their way to classes. Thankfully, the girls seem to be well trained and pretend not to notice, continuing their cheerful conversations as they scamper past.

Still other slices of Roppongi are represented by two "odd-couple" neighbors, the Embassy of the Russian Federation, formerly the Embassy of the USSR, and the Tokyo American Club, which is safely and suspiciously tucked behind it. TAC is now, like so much else in Roppongi, undergoing a wholesale renovation and reconstruction. The Russian Embassy, in the meantime, is an important community resource for the fast-growing Russian population in Tokyo, many of whom live or work near Roppongi. The Russian school on the embassy's grounds is particularly important, not just for the high standard of education that it provides to Russian-speaking children through high school, but also as a meeting place and network builder among the children's parents. There are quite a few Russian families who live within the embassy compound. For them Roppongi is where they do the routine chores of daily life, including grocery shopping and taking laundry to the dry cleaners. The housing compound for employees of Tokyo's U.S. Embassy is on the opposite side of the neighborhood from the American Club and is even larger than the Russian facility.

Roppongi also has quite a few old Buddhist temples and burial grounds, as well as Shinto shrines, scattered throughout. As mentioned in chapter 2, there are four or five temples or burial grounds within a one- or two-minute walking distance from Roppongi Crossing, and at least ten or so more within five minutes. The originals of some of these buildings date back to the Edo period. Typically, they are hidden behind Roppongi's other buildings and can be found now by following the flight of crows who return from Roppongi's garbage to nests amid the clusters of tall trees on temple grounds. Other temples like Zōjōji and Zempukuji, located near Roppongi rather than within the district, are famous and in all the guidebooks. The shrine Hikawa-jinja near the U.S. Embassy housing compound is also well known. Just south of Roppongi along the way to Tokyo Tower, on a side street in neighboring Azabudai, is Reiyukai Shakaden, a fairly new (completed in 1975), oversized, and highly unusual temple of red Brazilian granite and stainless steel that is also a famous institution. *Reiyukai* is a popular "new religions" Buddhist sect with origins in the 1920s and a reputation for carrying out various charity programs, while the building, *Shakaden* (the dwelling of the Shakyamuni Buddha), is an architectural wonder or a monster of architecture, depending on one's viewpoint. Many people see it first from the Tokyo Tower observation windows, are startled or puzzled, and then feel compelled to have a closer look after returning to earth. How to describe this place? Peter Popham's book did a good job: "There, wedged into the little street is this monstrous thing . . . What is it? A dinosaur in a tight spot? A helmeted samurai warrior with his tongue hanging out? The mating of Buddhist temple and a flying saucer? Or is it, as the Reiyukai people themselves suggest, 'Two hands placed together in an attitude of prayer'?" (Popham 1985, 68–70).

Still another side of Roppongi is seen in a visit to U. Goto Florist. I had said that I would not be promoting any businesses herein, and I don't intend for these passages to be read as a promotion for this particular florist's shop (which does not need my help to attract customers), but U. Goto is such an institution

FIGURE 4.9 A scene from the dance review at Roppongi's Kingyo Club. Here, an innocent Japanese girl in white is about to be descended on by lecherous American GIs.

and so well known that any discussion of Roppongi almost has to mention it, so one might as well identify it by name. It is one of the most celebrated of all florist shops in Japan, a country that knows flowers well, and a Roppongi institution at its present location almost exactly at Roppongi Crossing since 1892. In fast-changing Tokyo, that is a significant longevity. Founded by Umanosuke Goto (hence, *U. Goto*, its name since 1947), it was originally named Hanauma in Roppongi and then in 1919 was renamed Goto Youbana Ten, a phrase that identified it as Japan's first shop for Western flowers. The store still has amazing floral creations by specialists from several countries (including Japanese specialists) who work there and gorgeous window displays. They sell flowers on a retail, walk-in basis, as well as arrangements for weddings, banquets, and other major events, including those attended by world leaders. There are also classes in the U. Goto Professional Florist Academy. One of my points here is that that the clientele of U. Goto Florist probably has next to nothing to do with the Roppongi of the night I have been describing.

There are also other businesses that qualify as strongly Japanese Roppongi institutions, even as their work is conducted mostly after dark. Notable examples include the aforementioned restaurant Seryna (chapter 3); the Edo-theme restaurant Gonpachi housed in an old storehouse just down the street from Roppongi Crossing in neighboring Nishi Azabu;[16] and the old Haiwa Theater, a stage theater with a long and checkered history in the neighborhood. Most interesting is an unusual and fascinating little theater called the Kingyo Club (or Kingyo-gurasu; "the goldfish glass"). Located in an aging building on a side street amid the world of nightclubs, this mainstay from the past presents a highly entertaining professional dance show two times each evening and three times on Fridays and Saturdays, with the last show starting at 1:30 a.m. I used to see it every so often because one of the dancers was a friend. The English page of the Kingyo Club's Web site says that the show is "Japanese entertainment we send to the world from Roppongi."[17] I visited the club again recently and was thrilled to see an eclectic show that ranged from Michael Jackson's "Thriller" to Irish step-dancing and Queen's "We Will Rock You", and that at the same time revealed Japanese music and dance traditions and considerable Japanese patriotism. I was allowed to photograph the performance for publication and selected figure 4.9 as the scene to print here because this particular dance number relates to my earlier text. The scene is from post–World War II Tokyo and contains a moving stage in which the previous (happy) scene is receding below and two U.S. servicemen appear on the stage from above to prey on the innocent Japanese girl in the white dress. Then, in the scene that follows, Japanese women are shown as pan-pan girls. Soon, however, to the delight of the snacks-and-drinks audience that roared its appreciation, Japan's honor is restored by virtue of the country's remilitarization, and the young girl in white is able to resume a normal life with a Japanese boyfriend.

CHAPTER FIVE

Roppongi Troubles

Roppongi's Reputation

The word *gaijin* is the colloquial Japanese word for "foreigner," and nowadays, most of the news that comes from Roppongi is bad news, mostly about crime, and very often about foreigner or *gaijin* crime. Many people think of the neighborhood as Tokyo's most dangerous district and avoid it. That is probably why there is so much of the other kind of media reporting from Roppongi too, that about campaigns by officialdom and grassroots organizations to clean up the neighborhood, about immigration actions against "bad foreigners," and about upscale and "proper" events that signal the birth of a "New Roppongi," such as museum openings and sales in designer-made shopping malls. But even the new development projects, unlucky Roppongi Hills in particular, generate bad news too, so the overall weight of the media presentation about the neighborhood is negative.

Consider as a start the following short news item from the Web site Crisscross News Japan dated September 8, 2005:

FOREIGNER INJURED BY SWORD IN ROPPONGI FIGHT

TOKYO—A male foreigner was slashed by what appears to be a Chinese broadsword after a fight broke out among 5 to 6 foreigners in Roppongi around 9 a.m. Wednesday morning. Police received a call that there was a fight outside a restaurant. When they arrived at the scene, a man in his 30s was lying on the ground, bleeding from a wound to his stomach. Police are looking for two foreigners who fled the scene of the crime. ("Foreigner Injured" 2005)

It is a just a small incident and unusual because a sword seems to be involved, but it represents the flavor of Roppongi's troubles: once again something has gone wrong in Roppongi; once again it is something bizarre; and once again it is foreigners who are in the midst of whatever is wrong. Not only that, the incident took place not during the dangerous night hours but early in the morning when things are supposed to be normal. Roppongi, unlike routine-fixed Tokyo, is unpredictable: you never know what will happen or when. Bloggers (in this case non-Japanese) responded with comments that could be expected: for example, "Roppongi is a low-class trash heap" in which foreigners who kill one another are "doing Darwin's dirty work," and "Roppongi is a 'gaijin zoo.'"

Indeed, most of the blame for what has gone wrong in Roppongi is placed on a "bad element" of foreigners, probably deservedly so to a point. As a result, much of the campaign to take back Roppongi and make it safe again is a campaign that touches on Japanese immigration policy, the visa status of troublemaking foreigners, and distinctions that are made, often with racist overtones, about "good foreigners" versus "bad foreigners." In this chapter I discuss Roppongi's fall from grace by looking at some of the crime and other incidents that now mark the neighborhood, as well as at some of the discourse in Japan about how to reclaim the district. I then look at a variety of specific efforts to turn things around on the streets: (1) a crackdown by police and private security forces against crime, rowdy behavior, and actions such as vandalism and litter; (2) the implementation of neighborhood beautification and landscaping; and (3) an extraordinary use of signage to both inform the public about Roppongi's dangers and warn potential miscreants about the earthly consequences of their sins. That discussion sets the stage for some final words about "Receding Rhythms" in Roppongi and then for the examination of remaking Roppongi via urban redevelopment projects in chapter 6.

I pause in midchapter to reflect on what is not being said about the troubles: that Roppongi has long been a haunt of Japanese mobsters, the yakuza, and that they continue to hold huge and seemingly unobstructed sway in the district. The animated discourse about reclaiming Roppongi from trouble is not about them, it seems, even though it is widely known that they occupy the root of illegal narcotics distribution, as well as guns, gambling, prostitution, and other ills that bear directly on the neighborhood's troubles. No, the war against trouble in Roppongi focuses on foreigners, a much easier target, and the yakuza, as shown in the nighttime tour of the neighborhood in chapter 4, go about their business unmolested, as if they were in a parallel universe that others occasionally see but can do nothing about.

Dangerous Terrain

Thankfully, there are not many swordfights on Roppongi's streets, whether with Chinese swords as was first reported, or with Iranian swords as a blogger later corrected. Instead, there are lots of other bad incidents, more routine, less comical, and oftentimes more dangerous. There are assaults, occasional murders, thefts and robberies, narcotics offenses, the doctoring of drinks in bars to steal a victim's money or to take sexual advantage, and many other crimes. There are also mountains of litter that accumulate on Roppongi streets during the course of any night, as well as the graffiti and other vandalism that are now simply part of the backdrop. Foreigners do indeed deserve a disproportionate measure of the blame for the problems, as the neighborhood can be thought of as a "gaijin zoo" with much more crime and other misbehavior than is normal in Japan. Many young foreigners, some fellow Americans included, seem to act as if Japan's laws and any normal standards of civility do not apply to them. Foreigner-on-foreigner crime occurs often enough to be a serious threat, although there are Japanese criminals to be wary of too, as well as Japanese victims of both. There has even been a turf war between two rival factions of the Japanese yakuza, the Yamaguchi-gumi and the Sumiyoshi-kai, that, quite famously, resulted in a gang killing just down the street from Roppongi Crossing in the 10 a.m. daylight of February 6, 2007.

Even Japan's traditional and once sacred sport *sumō* is not safe. The sport has been suffering a downward spiral in recent years on account of scandals related to match fixing and abuse of steroids, competition from other sports, and perhaps some wounds to national pride because more and more of its stars are foreigners. Now the sumō world has been further rocked by the revelation that one of its up-and-coming foreign wrestlers, Wakanoho, a twenty-year-old Russian whose birth name is Soslan Aleksandrovich Gogloyev, was arrested August 18, 2008 (just a few days before this writing) for possession of marijuana, a quite serious offense in Japan. He has admitted buying the substance from a foreigner in a Roppongi nightclub and has been expelled from the ranks of the professional sumō association, the first active wrester to ever be so punished. This is national news and the source of considerable public clucking about yet another foreigner miscreant and yet another nasty incident in this particular neighborhood. And then on September 3, 2008 comes news that two other foreign wrestlers, the brothers Rohō and Hakurozan, born in North Ossetia in the Russian Republic as Soslan and Batraz Feliksovich Boradzov, have both tested positive for marijuana in a random urine test ("Roho, Hakurozan" 2008). Subsequently, I add still more recent news, this time about the Japanese sumō wrestler Wakakirin (Shinichi Suzukawa) who was arrested for marijuana possession, a substance he said he bought from a foreigner in Roppongi ("Wakakirin Admits" 2009).

There is no shortage of other examples of trouble among foreigners in Roppongi. A quick search of electronic archives via the LexisNexis service turns up the following mix of incidents:

May 11, 2005: A twenty-year-old student from the Kingdom of Tonga and an eighteen-year-old Japanese student, both of them rugby players, are arrested for attacking a woman professional wrestler on a street in Roppongi, punching her in the face.

May 17, 2005: A rugby player from New Zealand was arrested for punching three nightclub employees in Roppongi after they challenged him for insulting and touching a woman patron.

September 20, 2005: A sixteen-year-old girl from Brazil, a frequent visitor to Roppongi from her parents' home in the Tokyo suburbs, is found dead on a back street of the neighborhood, apparently the victim of a drug overdose.

March 8, 2006: A twenty-four-year-old Russian boxer is arrested for punching a Japanese man and a Colombian man at 5:15 a.m. on a Roppongi street after an argument in a restaurant.

Not just foreigners cause troubles. For example, other sources indicate that Roppongi figured prominently in a series of gang rapes committed by members of Super Free, a twisted social club of Japanese male students from Waseda University, the University of Tokyo, and Keiō University, the three most prestigious Japanese institutions of higher learning. The club leader, once a student at Waseda, considered gang rape as a means to "create solidarity among members" (Wijers-Hasegawa 2004). At least two of the dozen or more young women who are known to have been among the club's victims were attacked in separate incidents weeks apart in April and May of 2003 on the same landing of a nightclub building in Roppongi. As of the time of the article in the *Japan Times* (November 3, 2004) that is my source, a total of fourteen young men had already been sentenced to prison terms for taking part in the attacks.

Among other embassies in Tokyo, the U.S. Embassy, which is located nearby, warns its citizens that Roppongi is a deceptively dangerous place in otherwise ultrasafe Japan (U.S. Department of State n.d.).

CONCERNS REGARDING ROPPONGI, TOKYO:

The majority of crimes reported by Americans have occurred in Roppongi, an entertainment district that caters to foreign clientele. Incidents involving U.S. citizens since spring 2004 include murder, assault, overdoses on heroin allegedly purchased in Roppongi, theft of purses and wallets at bars in clubs, exorbitant bar tabs and drugs allegedly slipped into drinks. A number of Americans have also been arrested over the past year in Roppongi for various offenses. You can read about these reported incidents in our monthly newsletter by subscribing to it or by reading it on http://japan.usembassy.gov/acs.

Please be aware that Roppongi has also been the scene of recent violence between criminal syndicates. Americans are urged to keep these incidents in mind and exercise caution should they choose to visit Roppongi.

Indeed, the monthly newsletters referred to in the notice above are replete with warnings and descriptions of specific dangerous incidents, particularly those where Americans were victims. The list below, gleaned from the online newsletter of the U.S. Embassy in Tokyo, gives examples of crimes of special interest to Americans that have taken place in Roppongi.[1] The picture is clearly contrary to what one would normally expect to see in Japan.

July 2007: Americans are warned about come-ons that get them to enter clubs in Roppongi and Shinjuku, where they might then be drugged and robbed.

May 2006: A male American citizen is stabbed to death in a public men's room in Yoyogi Park in another neighborhood in Tokyo. (The victim and perpetrator were linked as acquaintances via Roppongi.)

August 2005: An American male is drugged and robbed of his wallet. Charges of $7,000 are rung up on his credit card for drinks.

June 2005: An American female is drugged in a popular bar near Roppongi Crossing and wakes up in a nearby hotel room with an unclothed Asian male. Other foreign women reported similar assaults.

June 2005: A foreign woman employed by an embassy near Roppongi is beaten and robbed of her purse by two Asian males in a small park in Roppongi.

May 2005: Two Americans are assaulted and robbed in an elevator in Roppongi by assailants they believe to be non-Japanese.

May 2005: Several Americans report that their wallets and purses have been stolen from them in Roppongi bars and clubs.

April 2005: An Iranian male is shot dead in a Roppongi bar.

February 2005: A foreign male, possibly from Uruguay, is stabbed to death in the popular Roppongi Bar Wall Street II.

January 2005: An American citizen was murdered in an office building in Roppongi.

August 2004: Several Americans reported that purses, wallets, and passports had been stolen from them while they were in Roppongi bars.

June 2004: Several foreigners, including Americans, overdose on heroin purchased in Roppongi, resulting in three deaths.

A more recent warning by the U.S. Embassy, posted in 2009, is even blunter about dangers that lurk in the neighborhood:

MESSAGE FROM THE U.S. EMBASSY

This is to inform the American community that the U.S. Embassy has recommended that the embassy community avoid frequenting Roppongi bars and clubs in Tokyo due to a significant increase in reported drink-spiking incidents. American citizens may choose to avoid frequenting drinking establishments in this area as well.

The number of reports of U.S. citizens being drugged in bars has increased significantly in recent weeks. Typically, the victim unknowingly drinks a beverage that has been secretly mixed with a drug that renders the victim unconscious for several hours, during which time large sums of money are charged to the victim's credit card or the card is stolen outright. Victims sometimes regain consciousness in the bar or club, while at other times the victim awakens on the street.

Because this type of crime is already widespread in Roppongi bars and is on the rise, the U.S. Embassy has recommended that members of the embassy community avoid frequenting drinking establishments in this area. American citizens may consider this recommendation as it applies to their own behavior. If you, nevertheless, choose to participate in Roppongi night life, we urge you to remain extra vigilant of your surroundings and maintain a high level of situational awareness. Establishments in the area of Roppongi Intersection . . . have had the highest level of reported incidents.

I can discuss at least two Roppongi crimes in detail from personal contacts with the victims, the first being the robbery mentioned above on August 2005. A young American law student, in Japan for the first time on a special study abroad program in international law, met two beautiful French models in a busy nightclub. It's his lucky night, he thought. The women suggested moving to a quieter bar that they knew, where conversation would be easier. The student barely remembered that second bar. The next thing he knew, he woke up on a Roppongi backstreet in the light of morning, sans wallet. He soon learned that his credit card had been active all night. The police made some minimal efforts to solve the crime and managed to produce the French models, who turned out to be Russians and who were probably victims themselves of a sort. They claimed that their only role was to bring customers into the bar, for which they would get a cut of the spending, and that they had nothing to do with the apparent drugging and robbery that took place afterward. They and the American victim said that the police showed no interest in investigating the Japanese bartender or other Japanese at that Japanese-owned bar and the case simply fizzles away.

In a second incident, a man in his thirties from a beer-loving central European country got drunk in a Japanese bar with other European friends. As they got ready to leave, they are handed their coats by an employee of the bar who had stowed them on the coat rack. A Japanese customer suddenly complained loudly that the European had his coat. The inebriated European checked, and indeed, he had accidentally put on a coat that was not his, albeit the coat that he was handed by the employee. There are apologies and an exchange is made, but then the Japanese complains even louder, this time about money that is missing from a pocket—more than the equivalent of $10,000 in Japanese yen cash. The police are called. Companions of the Japanese say that, yes, there was such money in the coat, because they had all pooled money earlier that evening and given it to the victim. Despite a search, no money is found, and the Japanese tell the police that there had been a foreigner who left quickly at the time of the commotion, probably a confederate of the drunken European, and that he had been handed the money surreptitiously. The European was arrested and was questioned for more than three weeks before being released. He told me that he got out of detention only by paying the money to the Japanese man in exchange for a dropping of the charges. For him, the result was not only that he lost the money, but that he also lost his Japanese job as a computer specialist because of his unexcused absence from work and the suspicions about him that were raised by the whole episode. He wound up leaving the country to start afresh elsewhere.

Everyone who knows Roppongi well can relate similar stories about people they know who have been victimized in the neighborhood, about their own bad experiences, or about what they saw as witnesses. Those same people also understand that what I reported above for both incidents may not be true in every detail, because, as indicated in the first chapter, Roppongi is a place where truth is elusive and I could have been lied to. In both cases, though, I am comfortable with what I was told, and I have some independent corroboration. In that same vein, a friend who has been updating me by email about activities on the street where he works recently described an incident in which he challenged an inebriated Japanese male who was vandalizing some private property late one night. After police arrived, my friend found that Japanese witnesses attempted to pin the damage on him simply because he was a foreigner on the scene.

I have been lucky and have avoided personal trouble, even as I sometimes seem to ask for it. Instead I am alive and could elaborate about even more victims of Roppongi crimes and more types of scams. I could even talk with authority about some Roppongi felons. I know several individuals personally who have been arrested and served jail time for narcotics possession in the neighborhood, and I know quite well the convicted murderer of the American victim who was mentioned above under May 2006. I think it's ironic that the only murderer that I, an American from a large U.S. city, know personally is one who committed his crime in low-crime Tokyo. It was an argument about narcotics, and the killer was from a compactly shaped South American country beginning with the letter *C* that is well known as a source of illegal narcotics trafficking and gratuitous violence. He is now in a Japanese prison for the rest of his life.[2]

It has been said that, until recently, police in Tokyo looked the other way when it came to Roppongi. It was a foreigner's zoo, and if foreigners went about scamming and robbing one another and piercing each other with a foreigner's swords, then who cares? This seems to be confirmed by an almost-too-juicy-to-be-true quotation given by an unnamed officer at the local police station to a reporter writing for *Metropolis* magazine:

> It used to be that crimes against foreigners by other foreigners or by Japanese did not concern us. It's not worth the trouble and the paperwork to arrest them. Crimes against Japanese by foreigners—that becomes an issue, of course. Other than that, this is an area where we always look the other way. For most Japanese, Roppongi isn't part of Japan and Japanese standards don't apply. It's like that area in Saudi Arabia where all the foreigners live and ignore Saudi rules. (Noblestone 2004)

Regardless of just exactly what a Japanese-speaking police officer said to the reporter (I again express my caution that truth about Roppongi can be hard to come by and that BS detectors always need to be switched on), Tokyo police attention was always more on Kabukichō, where both perpetrators and victims were much more likely to be Japanese. Indeed, one of the theories on the street about Roppongi is that it has picked up some of the worst elements from Kabukichō who have been chased out of that district by relentless cleanup campaigns. The result may be more drugs in Roppongi, more furtive gambling dens, more guns, and more gang shakedowns. I am in no position to elaborate or even to be completely certain that I am correct in what I have just written. There is certainly an increase in open prostitution, which can be estimated by the number of times one is approached on the street for "massages" and more direct come-ons. In my experience in Roppongi, it is mostly women from China and Colombia who inquire about doing business with me, with the number of aggressive Chinese prostitutes apparently growing quite rapidly.

I know from the nongovernmental organization (NGO) side of things that there are quite a few young women in Tokyo from Colombia specifically who had been tricked into coming to Japan as "entertainers" or restaurant workers, and who were then forced to pay off huge debts to traffickers by working under duress as prostitutes. They are threatened with beatings, disfigurement, death, and even harm to their families back in the home country. I heard this directly as well in 2005 from "Patricia," a young Columbian woman who spoke alongside supportive social workers from her embassy at an antitrafficking conference in Tokyo. She had fled her Japanese captors and was getting ready to return home. The Colombian Embassy estimated that there were as many as 3,500 women from Colombia working as prostitutes in Japan at that time (not all of them trafficked, and only some of them in Roppongi), and that as many as 60 flee to the embassy for safety each year (Onishi 2005). Since its founding in 1989, a women's shelter named Women's Home HELP—cofounded by Mizuho Fukushima, a prominent women's rights activist, Japanese Diet member, and, as of 2010, chair of the Social Democratic Party of Japan—has helped thousands of foreign women who have been forced into prostitution or who have been assaulted or beaten, or abused in Japan in other ways. Most of them are from Southeast Asian countries, but increasingly the desperate clients have been women from South America, Russia, and Eastern Europe. A common complaint is that police are often no help because the victims are in Japan illegally (Wright 2001).

Indeed, just as many Japanese associate rising crime rates in Roppongi and elsewhere in the county with foreigners, many experienced foreigners know that Japan, particularly shady places like Roppongi, can be dangerous for them specifically because of Japanese criminals who target them as victims. There are Japanese scam thieves and scam artists who know how to take advantage of noncitizens' weaker position with respect to the justice system and victimize them with relative impunity in everything from routine business dealings to transactions regarding rents, security deposits, travel agency purchases, and various kinds of paperwork and legal documents. In today's bad economy in

Japan, and in the anonymous terrain of a neighborhood like Roppongi, any and every person, Japanese and not Japanese, can be a crook, no matter how sweet the smile and how true the eyes. Just ask my fully-legal-in-Japan Russian friend who lost a substantial inventory of dresses and fashion accessories that she had made over many months of hard work to a cheating consignment agent. He had sold her goods with great success via a top-shelf department store, but he never paid her and then disappeared. Not only was her substantial investment in labor and materials lost, but her Japanese creditors (landlord, health insurance, utility companies, etc.) still had to be paid. Could she get help from the police or the department store? Forget about it.

Yakuza Roppongi

There is another, extremely important aspect of Roppongi as "dangerous ter- rain" that so far I have only alluded to: the role played in the neighborhood by Japan's organized crime networks, the *yakuza*. It is an enormous topic, and one where, admittedly, this book comes up short. I said at the start that I had made a deliberate decision to keep this aspect of the neighborhood at a distance, not just because of any concerns I might have about my personal safety, but also because I was not so naive as to think that any digging I could do into this closed world would unearth new information. As promised, there are no exposés of gangster activity in Roppongi to be found here. Yet, we know that gangsters are everywhere in the neighborhood and see them regularly, read and hear about them in the media, and learn tantalizing details from researchers whose work has brought them closer to the topic. We know as well that it is gangsters even more than bad foreigners and their tag-along Japanese miscreant friends who underlie Roppongi's troubles, and who are involved more than any other group in some truly despicable activities. For instance, the human trafficking activity in Japan introduced above is yakuza territory, with or without the assistance of criminal elements from point-of-origin countries.

An interesting peculiarity about Japanese organized crime groups is that there is nothing particularly secret about their presence in Japan, and that at least the outlines of their activities are there for all to see. Mobsters in other countries operate undercover and might deny being gang members, but Japan's yakuza are organized into named groups with crests or logos and have head office buildings and branches with registered addresses and signs outside just like any other company office. Members often dress for the role and even have distinctive hair styles, not to mention body tattoos from collar to ankle. Already described is the "ghost" of the gangsters' castle TSK-CCC, a once-opulent building that stood just a healthy stone's throw from Roppongi Crossing and even closer to the busy main door of the local police headquarters. If you danced at Vanilla, played pool or watched big-screen sports in the sports bar with the lion out front, or visited with strippers or hostesses in some of the other businesses in the complex, you were doing business with the mob.

That particular empire of the Tosei-kai eventually met its demise from too many high-priced Picassos and other financial miscalculations, a cameo role in the famous Lockheed bribery scandal of 1976, and a measure of police pressure, among other factors. Instead, for some time now Roppongi has been the territory of the Sumiyoshi-kai, presently one of the two largest yakuza groups in Japan and the main organized crime presence in Tokyo specifically. They had negotiated a truce about turf with their former rivals, the Kakusei-kai, whose headquarters happened to be just a few minutes from Roppongi Crossing in fashionable Azabu Jūban, where I was their neighbor, and gained from them the run of Roppongi vice. There were strip clubs, sex shops, intimate massage parlors, illegal gambling dens, pachinko arcades, and many of the hostess clubs. There was also probably narcotics distribution, other prostitution, and still more shady business such as loan sharking and coercive real estate dealings. Their presence in Roppongi is obvious; just off Roppongi Crossing there is even a tall office building that boldly bears the gang's name. What is not known is the full inventory of the gang's holdings: exactly which business or which piece of land is or is not theirs, and what stake they may hold in any particular business. There is also the matter of non-yakuza businesses that routinely pay the Sumiyoshi-kai for the privilege of staying open in Roppongi. Of course, how many businesses pay for protection and where they are located are proprietary information.

If there was anyone in Roppongi who did not know that the neighborhood was mob turf, they certainly learned differently on February 5, 2007, when media everywhere blared the news that a "Yakuza War" had started in central Tokyo. Just after ten o'clock that morning, in full view of more than sixty passersby on busy Roppongi-dōri, two men wearing motorcycle helmets walked up to the black Toyota Century limousine owned by Sumiyoshi-kai kanbu (director) Ryoichi Sugiura and shot him dead with three bullets fired through the rear window. The witnesses scattered, police and the media descended on the district, the scene was festooned in yellow "crime scene" ribbons, and everyone soon learned the details: Japan's largest yakuza group, the Yamaguchi-gumi, were in town. Based historically in the Kansai region of Japan (Kobe and Osaka), this 39,000-member criminal organization (Sumiyoshi-kai membership is about 10,000) had for several years been making entrepreneurial forays into the Tokyo region, seeking to expand their business and influence as counter to postbubble declines in revenue. As early as 1990, the two gangs had been shooting at one another in the distant western suburbs of Tokyo, and for a while the "front" stood at the Tama River, a waterway in the suburbs that divided the Sumiyoshi-kai stronghold of central Tokyo from ground that had been gained by the invaders from Kansai. "We will never let them cross the Tama River," a Sumiyoshi-kai boss is reported to have said (Kaplan and Dubro 2003, 185). For a time, the gang gunfire in cross-Tama Hachioji, a prosperous and leafy suburb known for its many university campuses and research institutions, was so intense that school children were issued detour maps for walking to and from classes, and Tokyo was likened to the Chicago of Al Capone.

The murder of the Sumiyoshi-kai kanbu proved that the Tama had been crossed for good and that central Tokyo was now contested turf. What had happened was that some two years earlier in August 2005 the Yamaguchi-gumi had taken over the Kakusei-kai, negating any pact that had existed before, and announced with their three shots that they were ready to reclaim from the Sumiyoshi clan the lucrative territory of Tokyo's prosperous "high city." They had already taken over the slices of Roppongi nightlife that Kokusai-kai had retained for themselves and made inroads as well into the heart of gangster territory in Ginza. Now the Yamaguchi-gumi wanted more. Roppongi-dōri connected Roppongi and the huge commercial center of Shibuya not quite two miles to the west, and the murder was well placed almost halfway between, near the main intersection of Nishi Azabu, the next big crossing in that direction from the Sumiyoshi-kai's headquarters at Roppongi Crossing. That there were some ten foreign embassies (mostly Latin American nations) in the building just beside the murder scene added to public understanding that a war was on, that more shootings were to come, and that anyone could be in the crossfire. Roppongi had become "dangerous terrain" indeed.

The much anticipated "blood balance sheet" killings never materialized, at least not to public knowledge, and the two killers are apparently still at large as of this writing. The police are in possession of one gun that has been matched to the shooting and the killers' abandoned motorcycle, but maybe not much else. The peace came from something internal to the gangs and was actually announced to the police. Even while the soul of Ryoichi Sugiura was still in the midst of forty-nine days of straddling our earthly world and whatever lies beyond, a score was settled on February 25, 2007, when the body of seventy-year-old Kokusai-kai chairman Kazuyoshi Kudō was found in his own apartment. In atonement for the bloody mess that began when he reneged on the Sumiyoshi-kai and shared ritual sake with the leadership of the Yamaguchi-gumi, he had taken his own life. The blogosphere would have us think that he had used a sword, but the suicide was, in fact, accomplished by a single gunshot wound.

Somehow the Sumiyoshi-kai and Yamaguchi-gumi have carved up Roppongi among themselves, and all of the rest of us simply live with it. Depending on where you go and what you buy, you pay one group or the other for your purchases, or maybe no mobsters at all. They are there among us in Roppongi, part of the background, pulling strings when they need to, and making business decisions that are none of our business. As indicated in connection with the tour of Roppongi in chapter 4, they inhabit a different universe that is somehow parallel to ours. How else to explain the little side street in Roppongi shared by yakuza limousine drivers on call with loudmouthed American and Japanese hip-hopsters outside drinking beer? The gambling dens and member clubs of the yakuza playground are from one world, while the garish hip-hop club and restaurants and other business at that same point are from other, nonintersecting worlds. The same was true when visiting in chapter 4 a new Roppongi nightclub the evening it opened. We were welcome to have fun and spend money, but not at an empty table in a section just above the bar and dance floor; it belonged to a different world.

Yakuza gangs also control Japan's enormous and highly lucrative pornography business, including the production and distribution of pornographic DVDs. Years ago when I lived near Shinjuku's Central Park, I used to occasionally come across filming in progress. It was almost always very early in the morning before there were many other people outdoors, and in all but one memorable case the scenes I encountered were those that were clothed and nonintimate. I thought it strange then that pornographers would use public spaces for their work but imagined that, yes, even pornographic movies need scenes that provided context, if not occasional outdoor sex scenes. Then, not long ago, as a result of another encounter with the making of pornography, those experiences came into a different focus. I was near Roppongi, walking home from a dinner outing, when I saw a sex film being made on a high floor of an apartment building that I had long associated with mobsters; the room was a flood-lit beacon against the night sky, and the actor couple was hard at work directly against the floor-to-ceiling windows. Yes, parallel worlds, I thought; they live and work in theirs, and with apparent impunity, and unless we get in their way, the rest of us are in a world different from theirs and simply do not matter.

Roppongi is dangerous terrain indeed, and sword-fighting foreigners have helped make it so. So have quite a few other foreigners, as well as various thieves, pickpockets, drink spikers, drug addicts, and other miscreants in the neighborhood, be they from foreign counties or native Japanese. The yakuza, however, underlie it all. But like the pornographers I saw in the park and in the night sky, they work with seeming impunity as if in a parallel and impenetrable universe. There are, of course, sincere efforts by Japanese law enforcement to rein them in and make Japan safe from at least the worst of their offenses, and yakuza members do get arrested and are sent to prison. Indeed, since May 1991 there has been strengthened police authority to take on the *bōryokudan*, the official Japanese term for organized crime groups, in the form of a law that is commonly referred to as *bōtaiho*, a shortening of what is called in English the "Law Regarding the Prevention of Unjust Acts by Bōryokudan Members" (Hill 2003). In Roppongi, however, few fingers point openly at the yakuza-bōryokudan; instead, the noise about trouble is noise about foreigners. The yakuza-bōryokudan are simply there as a matter-of-fact and all-encompassing background.

In the course of many years of work in the Japanese language as a crime reporter for the leading national newspaper *Yomiuri Shinbun*, American writer Jake Adelstein got a lot closer to understanding the yakuza and the damage that they bring to society than I could. I applaud his recent memoir *Tokyo Vice* in which he took on the yakuza, including named individuals in Roppongi specifically, and the foreigner gangsters with whom they work in their role in human trafficking (Adelstein 2009). Whatever minuses his book might have, I commend him for reminding us all that there in that all-encompassing, parallel universe inhabited by the yakuza is true evil, bringing the worst of misery to trafficking's victims. Adelstein spoke from the floor at the antitrafficking conference in 2005 where I met Patricia from Colombia, and he scolded Japan for being a major world center of sex slavery and for failure not just to do something about it but also to acknowledge it. He refers to the country in his book as "The Empire of Human Trafficking." Indeed, I have personally picked up enough bits and pieces about individual foreign women who have worked in Roppongi to have that sick feeling that some of the neighborhood's "proletariat" that I describe in chapter 4 were, in fact, involuntary workers. Adelstein's anger about the situation is palpable; he has stirred my anger too, not just at the yakuza and their associates, and not just at Japan for what is an inexcusable failing in that otherwise very fine country, but mostly at myself for the choice I made not to probe deeply from one parallel universe into the other. That may have been irresponsible. The "Never ever ask a Russian what he does for a living" advice that I was given (see chapter 1) could also have been a warning to keep one's nose out of the activities of a gangster.

Lucie Blackman

That Roppongi is increasingly a netherworld is seen most clearly in the famous and tragic case of the murder of Lucie Blackman. It dates to mid-2000, so several years have passed since she was killed, but her demise is still a rallying point in calls for reform, a spark for some national soul searching in Japan, and a story to never forget. She had been a flight attendant with British Airways, but at age twenty-one she was already tired of back-and-forth flights between home in London and airports in Africa and North America and wanted to see much more of the world. She had heard from a friend of a friend that an attractive blonde such as herself could make big, easy money in Japan simply by chatting it up with expense-account Japanese salarymen in Tokyo hostess clubs, so she quit her job and arrived with another adventuresome British female, her friend Louise Phillips, at Narita Airport on May 4, 2000. She soon found a hostessing job at a club named Casablanca, right on the main drag in Roppongi, on the floor above Seventh Heaven, one of the city's biggest strip bars. On July 1, 2000, not yet two months after arriving in the country, she disappeared, never to be heard from again.[3]

Hostesses disappear often from work. They change their minds, find something better to do, zip off with a boyfriend who insists on no more hostessing—whatever, they simply don't come back. Those who are working illegally in Japan, as Lucie was, are even more unpredictable about what they might do and where they might go. But Louise Phillips knew to be concerned, particularly since Lucie had called to say that she'd be back soon. Within days, Lucie's parents and sister had flown in from England and began a search. Some thirty thousand leaflets were printed with Lucie's photo, and Roppongi and other Tokyo night zones were blanketed with family members, friends, and a growing cast of supportive members of the public (mostly foreigners). Police helped, but from a distance and only to a point, lacking enthusiasm for a lost hostess and an illegal foreigner at that. They said that they were not able to trace the origins of Lucie's last phone calls, saying that it was not possible technologically. In the end, the technology suddenly appeared after an appeal for help from then–British prime minister Tony Blair to his Japanese counterpart, a substantial Japanese police search force was assembled, and the trail led to Jōji Obara, the forty-eight-year-old man with whom Lucie had gone out that night on a dohan (date with a client) arranged by Casablanca. He was a regular customer of the club and of other hostess clubs as well, and was the target of previous accusations by foreigner hostesses that he may have drugged them while on dates and sexually assaulted

FIGURE 5.1 Lucie Blackman's younger sister Sophie in front of Almond at Roppongi Crossing during the search for Lucie with poster showing Lucie's image. (Photo courtesy of Associated Press, Koji Sasahara photographer, dated 8/31/2000)

them. However, he was rich and a treasured customer with big-spending ways, and it took some time for fingers to point directly at him.

Lucie had disappeared on July 1, 2000. Her remains were found months later, February 9, 2001, in a beachfront cave outside Tokyo that had already been searched by police but not very thoroughly. The body had been cut into pieces by chain saw, and her severed head was encased in cement. The remains were so badly decomposed that the cause of death was impossible to establish—even gender could not be identified. A match was made because strands of long blonde hair were intact within the block of cement. The cave was only a minute's walk from the front door of the beachfront apartment building where Obara maintained one of his several residences. A search of his belongings turned up the spooky writings of a profoundly sick man: "Women are only good for sex," and "I cannot do women who are conscious," among other appalling passages. There was also the intact body of his German shepherd dog in a freezer next to frozen roses and frozen dog food. Most disturbingly, police found hundreds of self-made videotapes of Obara, dressed only in a Zorro mask, sexually abusing women who were sleeping or passed out. An untold number of them were Westerner blondes. Police think that he might be Japan's most prolific serial rapist ever. There were all sorts of warnings about him, including a 1998 arrest for attempting to videotape a woman using a public toilet that he had entered dressed as a woman (an episode for which he was found guilty and fined the equivalent of about $75), but no one connected the dots that could have saved the life of Lucie Blackman. Police had missed another opportunity as far back as 1992 to recognize Obara as a dangerous psychopath when they failed to properly investigate the death of Carita Ridgeway, a former Ginza hostess from Australia, whom Obara has now been convicted of killing (Norrie 2007).

Obara was first arrested for Lucie Blackman's killing on October 12, 2000. Police had found strands of her hair in one of his apartments and photos of her taken at the beachfront apartment, but since there was as yet no body he was not charged with murder. Rape charges were brought against him instead as a result of evidence on his videotapes and testimony by victims who were starting to come forward. He was finally charged with her death on April 6, 2001, some months after the body was found. His trial ended April 24, 2007. Incredibly, he was found not guilty of killing Lucie, because forensic evidence never linked him to the body. Yet, there was evidence of chain saw and cement purchases at the critical time, and police who had been called to his apartment because neighbors had complained about extraordinary noises saw cement on his hands on July 3, 2000, two days after Lucie's disappearance. He was convicted instead on a series of rapes, including that of Ridgeway but not that of Lucie Blackman, and was sentenced to life in prison. He was given credit for 1,600 days already served in detention toward the ten years that is required by Japanese law for life prisoners to be eligible for parole. Although he never admitted any guilt, Obara offered Tim Blackman, Lucie's father, atonement money in the amount of some £450,000—a condolence for a lost daughter. Incredibly, Tim Blackman, who had heroically led the search for his daughter, accepted the cash (Knight 2007).

Lucie Blackman's tragedy and the bizarre outcome of Obara's trial are another book that needs to be written, one of several I have been suggesting over the course of this book. The wounds from the tragedy remain open and fresh. Lucie's mother, Jane Steare, was quoted as saying after learning that the man who almost certainly killed her daughter was likely to be a free man again in the coming years: "I'm heartbroken. I just can't believe this. My worst fears have come true" ("Man Cleared" 2007). Indeed, everyone is afraid. In the words of a Nigerian club manager who was interviewed for the *Japan Today* news site: "To be honest, when I found out that Lucie had disappeared, I was relieved it was not one of my girls. I became very cautious with my girls. I told them to be careful and to not get in a taxi with a customer and so forth."[4]

Foreign women feel particularly vulnerable, believing that police can and will mismanage the investigation of even the most heinous of crimes against them, and that rapists and killers are able to go free. Foreign hostesses have cut back on dohans and on the income increments that such dates represent, and stick closer together. Recently, I've seen an increase in dohans where two women accompany the male client, probably not always as a security measure, but certainly for this reason in many cases. "There is no one to protect us," I was recently told by a hostess from one of the Russian-orbit nations. Many foreign hostesses now toss accusations that Japanese males, at least those who seek to rent their friendship in hostess clubs, are all potential Obaras (you can't tell by looking) and that Japanese police will always side against them to protect Japanese men. It might be fair to say that they see the Lucie Blackman killing as one where a weirdo Japanese social pillar trumped an illegal-foreigner-woman social pariah.[5]

Now, the atmosphere is even more racially charged. There is still another unsolved murder, that of a third young Caucasian foreigner woman, and deeper fears that Japan is crawling with dangerous men who would kill what they can't have. This victim was Lindsay Ann Hawker, a beautiful twenty-two-year-old woman from the United Kingdom who disappeared on March 24, 2007, and was killed, probably the same day. She was not a hostess but an English teacher, and in a suburban area of Tokyo at that, and her killer was apparently a private student, a young Japanese male named Tatsuya Ichihashi, whom she had taken on. Her nude body was found buried in a bathtub in his apartment. The growing attitude seems to be that anybody in this population could be a killer. The uncertainty was compounded exactly one month after Hawker's death, when the shocking verdict of not guilty was announced in the Obara trial, and when revelations came to light that police in Chiba Prefecture, where Hawker was killed, had visited Ichihashi's apartment to interview him but that he slipped away just as they arrived. He remained at large for two years, during which time there were rumors that he might have committed suicide or was hiding as a cross-dresser; women were scared. Finally, Ichihashi was captured in Osaka on November 10, 2009, while attempting to board a ferry to Okinawa. He has reportedly confessed to killing Hawker.

Japanese Voices

The discussion so far about the troubles in Roppongi has been in a foreigner's voice, naturally and deliberately so. Naturally so because I am not Japanese, and my networks in Roppongi are also primarily not Japanese. Also naturally so because I habitually read the foreign press in Japan instead of Japanese newspapers, and I browse the Internet mostly in English. It is deliberately so because foreigners' voices need to be heard about Roppongi. But it is even more deliberately so because had I begun with Japanese criticisms of Roppongi, where foreigners are disproportionate in numbers in comparison to almost everywhere else in Japan, and foreigner crime is indeed a legitimate concern, it could have looked like a case of anti-foreigner prejudice by Japanese. Racial prejudices exist, of course, in Japan and cut both ways, foreigners against Japanese as mentioned just above, and also various levels of prejudice by Japanese against foreigners. To be sure, foreigner Roppongi has long been a target of negative, stereotyped preconceptions. But to make certain that it is understood first that reasonable people, no matter what their nationality, can think of Roppongi at least sometimes as being a foreigner zoo that is out of control and can call loudly for reform, I held back with Japanese people's opinions—until now.

Let me start softly. It would not be out of line at all if a Japanese person disapproved of foreigners in her or his country on the basis of how some of them behave. While there are always model visitors and model immigrants, there are people at the other extreme too, short-term visitors, multiple-year visa holders, and immigrants who abuse the country. The list includes English teachers, entertainers of various sorts, business professionals, artists and other creative folk, factory workers, construction workers, domestic helpers, and many, many others whom Japan needs and welcomes, and who have come, understandably so, "for the money." The disapproval comes because some of these people, too many of them perhaps, give nothing of value back to Japan and show disrespect and a lack of appreciation for the kindnesses and opportunities that the country has given them. There are those who evade paying taxes, skip out on rents, telephone bills, utility bills, and other obligations, as well as committing various kinds of offenses, big and small, to Japanese customs and ways of living. There are complaints about excessive noise and rudeness by foreigners, disregard of requirements such as trash recycling or licensing of bicycles, shoplifting and other petty theft, and even personal hygiene and ways of dressing, including lack of modesty by some females. There are complaints, too, that foreigners are disproportionately responsible for serious crimes in Japan such as robbery or drugs peddling, even if those complaints are not convincingly supported by the data. There is also sexual exploitation of Japanese by foreigners. To wit, many foreign males in the country, from soldiers at U.S. military bases to Japan's corps of foreign English teachers to highly placed white-collar professionals in Tokyo's corporate world, seem to be looking for sexual conquest more than anything else in Japan and appear to be on a rampage to score with as many pretty young Japanese women as possible.

Expressed a little differently, we can say that Japanese are justified to complain that many foreigners show a lack of respect or interest in Japanese culture and do not bother to learn the language, even after many years of staying there and earning a living. Worse still, there are many whining critics of things Japanese among the foreigner population, again even among those who apply year after year for visa extensions, and a very nasty and rude habit among foreigners to ridicule certain physical attributes of Japanese, their ways of dress, how they pronounce English, tolerate alcohol, borrow from foreign cultures and mimic foreign fashions, travel in groups, and other things that amuse those far from home. We have all heard foreigners making fun of Japan and calling it the weirdest place on the planet or some such thing, even directly to Japanese who are then expected by those same foreigners to laugh along with them and agree. I think that Japan has been extraordinarily tolerant of foreigners' misbehavior; I also think that there are more and more Japanese people whose patience is wearing thin and who are no longer naive like earlier generations about how to deal with miscreant foreigners. There is still reluctance by most Japanese to be critical of foreigners on a face-to-face basis, but the feelings that many people have are now ever more directly and overtly expressed in spoken complaints and in a growing Japanese complaint literature, some of which is downright racist.

Here, we can turn as a prime example to the famous case of the 128-page "mook" (magazine-book) *Gaijin Hanzai Ura Fairu* (Foreigner Underground Crime File) that was published in early 2007 by Shibuya-based Eichi Shuppan, which is, according to Debito Arudou, "a middle-tier publisher specializing in popular culture . . . and pornography" (2007). It caused quite a stir when it came out and was eventually removed from store shelves because of possible boycotts and complaints about overt anti-foreigner hatred, but it sold quickly while it was available and is now something of an e-Bay collectors' item. It was posted in full online, apparently by critics wanting to expose the ugliness of Japan's racist side ("Foreigner Crime" 2007). The tone is set on the cover, where a headline announces that "everyone will become a target of gaijin crime in

2007!" Roppongi is identified prominently as one of the "lawless zones" (*fuhou chitai*) of Tokyo, along with Shibuya and Shinjuku, and is described individually as "a city without nationality" (*mukokuseki toshi*) where only the fittest can survive. "Documentation" is via photos that possibly originate with the police security cameras that are set up around the neighborhood. A representative illustration is one showing an unconscious person sprawled on a Roppongi street and being tended to by emergency medical personnel, while the accompanying text exclaims that "the surrounding foreigners look as though they have no concern whatsoever" (*shuui no gaikokujin tachi wa mattaku kanshin ga nai you da*).[6]

Another telling example of how foreigners and Roppongi are thought of by at least some Japanese is evidenced in a brief newspaper article that was published several years ago in a small newspaper called the *Honolulu Advertiser* (Kageyama 2002). The author is Japanese (or of Japanese descent), and the article was written for the Associated Press during the buildup for the opening of Roppongi Hills, the vanguard of the New Roppongi that has taken shape in recent years. It is not a good article and was picked up perhaps only by the minor newspaper where I found it, but I cite it because I think that it reveals exactly what the author thinks about foreigners in Roppongi, if not what her interview subject, Minoru Mori, president and CEO of Mori Building, thinks himself. We see a strong sense of anti-foreigner racism, a distinction between "bad" and "good" foreigners, and an argument that it will be Roppongi Hills that will rid Roppongi of undesirables. Specifically, we read that "Tokyo's Roppongi district [is] infamous for prostitution and shady foreigners," and that the neighborhood is a place of "lowlife" where "solicitors coax pedestrians to sleazy hostess bars between massage parlors and striptease joints." Moreover, it is where "homeless men slump in the subway station." Thankfully, the article continues, there will be "a much needed facelift with Roppongi Hills," where "Tokyo's giant developer, Mori Building Co., is courting the top-crust of foreigner population," as an alternative to "the lowlife loitering around today." The article, titled "Tokyo Targeting the Rich," goes on to gloat about the very high rents that will be charged for Roppongi hills apartments, the high membership fees for new private clubs, the shops that will sell expensive luxury goods, and the project's deliberately chosen "elitist Westernized environment." In other words, with Roppongi Hills, the bad foreigners will be replaced with rich, good ones.

One of the loudest voices nowadays in Japan about what the country needs and does not need to do and does not need is that of Shintarō Ishihara, the outspoken governor of Tokyo Metropolis (Tōkyō-to) since 1999. He is one of the best-known personalities in Japan and has a huge popular following as measured by the millions of people who have voted for him, some of them again and again, for various political offices since he started his career in public service in 1968. We can assume that he speaks for millions of Japanese, although we know as well that there is also a segment of Japan's population that does not share his beliefs. Even though his political office is local, he is listened to (or at least can be heard) across Japan, as he speaks often about a range of national issues such as foreign relations, national defense, trade policy, and immigration. He has come to be quite famous in Japan and beyond as the country's one politician who expresses most directly and most publically what many of his constituents would say only in closed circles about Japan's foreign relations, about neighboring countries China and Korea, and about the United States. China knows him especially well because of his public stance against immigration from China and lack of contrition about Japan's wartime atrocities in that country, while American foreign policy and trade experts know him for his assertive book *The Japan That Can Say No* (1991) that argues for greater independence for Japan from the United States in business and foreign relations. That publication helped establish a reputation for Ishihara as a Japanese nationalist and public patriot and won him an appreciative following among like-minded citizens. Before his turn to politics, he was already known in the country as somewhat of a renaissance man with accomplishments as a novelist, playwright, actor, yachtsman, and global adventurer. My interest in him is because of what he has had to say as Tokyo's highest political leader about Roppongi, both directly and indirectly.

It seems that Ishihara has quite a bit in common with the American politician Rudy Giuliani, the former mayor of New York City. Both men are or have been in charge of large cities, are known for frequent foot-in-mouth incidents as a result of their outspokenness, have or have had large popular followings, and seem always to be enveloped in controversy and criticism. Both also claim and are accorded credit for bringing improvements to their respective cities, even as there is a world of difference between the kinds of issues and problems that Tokyo and New York face and the severity of those problems. Giuliani is known for a tough approach to crime in New York, including a zero-tolerance approach to lesser crimes like graffiti, subway fare cheating, and unlicensed vendors and buskers, believing in the tenets of the "broken windows" theory of urban crime that small violations of law set a climate of larger violations.[7] He is widely credited for making New York, particularly Manhattan, safer, cleaner, and more civil, credit that he accepts with apparent glee and an iconic grin. Most specifically, as mentioned in chapter 2, he is credited with the cleanup of Manhattan's Times Square district, once a dirty and dangerous place known for drug trafficking, prostitution, and the sleaziest of America's triple-X sex parlors, and now a popular, family-oriented, safe, clean, and civil tourist and entertainment district (Berman 2009; Eliot 2001; Reichl 1999; Sagalyn 2001; and Taylor 1991).

Ishihara has displayed his own "get tough" approach with what is wrong in Tokyo and has targeted his city's own versions of precleanup Times Square, Kabukichō and Roppongi, for the big broom. Both men, too, have or have had ambitions for national office; Giuliani has run for U.S. president, albeit unsuccessfully, while Ishihara has been said to be positioning himself for an eventual run at the post of Japanese prime minister. Both men also seem to enjoy gratuitously goading others for political advantage, Giuliani recently at the September 2008 national convention of the Republican Party, where in front of tens of millions of television viewers he ridiculed the profession of community organizing, repeatedly laughing out loud at just the words *community organizer*; and Ishihara in 2004 with his bizarre and completely uncalled-for pronouncement that French is a failed language because, as he seems to think, "[it] is a language which cannot count numbers" ("French Outraged" 2005).

Many of Ishihara's "choicest" comments are widely quoted and requoted, much like the juiciest "Bushisms" from the United States, but unlike those of the former American president, Ishihara's shockers are not the result of any verbal dyslexia or naive ignorance. Instead, like his assessment of the French language, they are calculated and pointed insults, intended to rile and hurt. More to the point with quotations that bear directly or indirectly on the perceived need to clean up Roppongi, the Tokyo governor has expressed special concerns about China as a source of criminals, given its nearness, huge population, and low incomes, and has opined publically that Chinese think of Japan as an easy mark for quick riches. He has also blamed Chinese immigrants for drug peddling, a crime that he also attributes to immigrant workers from Pakistan and Iran. In his preparations of Tokyo for a possible disastrous earthquake, he has warned without citing any supporting evidence that immigrants from China, Taiwan, and the Korean Peninsula, people whom he referred to with the derogatory term *sangokujin* (people from "third" countries), would take advantage of the chaos and start riots. And finally about Roppongi specifically, he has singled out Africans as a cause of its ills, as already quoted. They engage in "who knows what," don't speak English, and steal cars. With such pellets of Ishihara wisdom illustrating the kinds of attitudes that are held by many people in the Japanese public, I now turn to a closer look at the retaking and remaking Roppongi.

Policing Roppongi

Another summer is just around the corner as I write this section. I've returned to Tokyo after three months away and can sense immediately that things are changing in Roppongi. The police, politicians, the public, all of them, it seems, have had enough of the trouble and are engaged full swing in a campaign to retake the neighborhood from bad elements. There are also campaigns to clean up other districts noted for trouble and vice, and as I visit different places around Tokyo I see an aggressive police presence in Shibuya, Shinjuku's Kabukichō, and the nasty side of Ueno. These campaigns coincide with heightened security throughout Japan because of a G8 summit that will be taking place in another part of the country in a few weeks, and one of the bilingual leaflets that I and thousands of other pedestrians are handed one Friday evening at Roppongi Crossing shows gory color photos of destruction from car bombs and warns of possible terrorism and violent protests. "AL-QAIDA UTTERED THAT JAPAN WAS ONE OF THEIR TARGETS " it says in English on a poster that I see on a notice board nearby.

But there is a Roppongi-specific campaign that catches my eye too, and it seems especially pervasive. What strikes me most is an almost oppressive police presence. There had always been police in Roppongi and occasional spot checks of foreigners' identification papers, but now day and night there are uniformed police officers seemingly everywhere on the main entertainment streets, a patrolling quite unlike anything I had seen in Roppongi before or elsewhere in Japan. They walk their beats in twos or threes, sometimes more, never alone. They carry guns at their sides, handcuffs, and menacing nightsticks and seem to be wearing bullet-proof vests. As I walk around a small perimeter, I feel surrounded by police: there are three walking together on this side of the street, three more across the street heading in the opposite direction, and another patrol visible a block or two away down the slope of one of the many side streets. A black and white police car cruises by. I wonder how many of the "civilians" on the street are actually police officers in plain clothes. At times, I see the uniformed police jog off to converge at a particular corner, as if called to respond to a report of trouble, scurry about among themselves like Keystone cops, and then quickly disband to resume normal patrols. Perhaps it was a false alarm, I think, or the "all-clear" had been given, or maybe it was just rehearsal. It could have been that someone reported a fight on the street. Fights happen during the drinking hours and almost as often break up quickly before police arrive. The police activity could also have been a calculated show of force. I know not to ask

FIGURE 5.2 Policing Roppongi.

them what's going on; communication with the public, even if I ask in Japanese, is not a strong suit of the Tokyo Police Department, and police operations are to be respected as professional secrets.

Many of the police officers have chips on their shoulders, literally—the kinds that power their radio communication devices. They seem to be in constant touch with the headquarters of the Azabu Police District just down the block from Roppongi Crossing or with a blue police bus laden with reinforcements and break-time tea that is parked nearby. I'd seen such police buses many times before. They show up in varying numbers at protest marches and other events where trouble might occur, and from time to time in Roppongi whenever police feel a need to show their presence. Today, however, the bus seems to be a much busier and more urgent command post than I remember from before. A favorite parking spot is on a particular block of Gaien-Higashi-dōri, the busy street that intersects Roppongi-dōri, near a larger cluster of popular bars and nightclubs. Whatever else the reinforcements do while on the bus, I'm sure that they can look through the steel-meshed windows and keep an eye on the goings-on outside.

The bus is also the staging vehicle for many of the raids by police of bars and nightclubs that are deemed to cause trouble. Such raids have been frequent since about 2005 and are usually triggered by reports of drug activity or illegal workers. They have also targeted underage drinking, although Roppongi

FIGURE 5.3 Police stop and search of a non-Japanese Asian woman in Roppongi. Such searches take place regularly very early in the morning and do not require any special reasons. She was eventually allowed to leave freely.

does not have as many carousers under age twenty as Shibuya and some other young-oriented districts where police also have their hands full. In some cases, where police are determined to put pressure on establishments that trouble them, they have cited arcane regulations that prohibit dancing after midnight (recently changed to 1 a.m.) as the reason to invade and close a place down. Apparently, there is such a provision in public morals legislation that was drawn up 1948–49 on the self-righteous advice of leadership in the American occupation. That has resulted in some paradoxical situations. A licensed nightclub in this all-night neighborhood that has invested in an ample dance floor, special effects lighting, and the best sound system for dance music is driven out of business, at least temporarily, because its customers were seen to be dancing after a senseless curfew, while at the same time all up and down the street Chinese prostitutes aggressively offer special massages, and private club after private club on Roppongi's back streets and front and center in other sakariba (e.g., in Shinjuku's Kabukichō) cater for profit to every manner of sexual kinkiness imaginable, plus some beyond the imagination.[8]

The red lights on the top of the police bus are flashing as we pass, and I make light conversation with my foreigner friend by asking: "Why are there so many police here today?" "Looking for bad foreigners," she responds. It's a glib answer, of course, even flippant, but not off target. The police would arrest Japanese miscreants too, give parking tickets, and keep order in any other way that the situation demands. They also take time to answer questions from passersby, foreigners and Japanese, who are lost, often going out of their way to be helpful. But the subject of "bad foreigners" is indeed the key for understanding why this particular police presence is quite likely Japan's largest police presence at this time. Roppongi does indeed have a good number of "bad foreigners" who break drug laws, shoplift, pickpocket, snatch bags, and get into drunken brawls, among other transgressions. There are also many visa violators. The police cannot catch them all, of course, but they do have successes, which are in turn publicized to reinforce their message. As I type these particular words, I can turn to this week's issue of the English-language "what's on in Tokyo" magazine that I read regularly, and can quote yet another very typical mininews piece about a type of event that occurs again and again on the police beat of Roppongi: "Police busted four foreigners, including a British employee of Merrill Lynch, and six Japanese, for possession and use of cocaine and cannabis after early-morning raids on Roppongi nightclubs DownTown and Odeon. Some suspects told police they bought the drugs from an 'African guy' at various bars."[9] (*Metropolis* 741, June 6, 2008, p. 03).

Ethnic Profiling

Policing Roppongi means ethnic profiling. I myself have not been stopped been by police in Japan for more than twenty years.[10] But foreigners who are younger than I am and who are not Caucasian have different experiences. Perhaps because of the frequent assertion that many males from Africa, Iran, Pakistan, and other Third World origins deal drugs, such individuals are stopped routinely by police for questions and document checks. African males driving expensive automobiles have their cars searched again and again, always politely, "just in case." From time to time, the police score and find something illegal or an expired visa. One also sees police targeting Chinese in their routine stops, as well as attractive young women who the police think might be in Japan illegally from Southeast Asia, Latin America, or Eastern Europe. As I have explained, some of these women work in Roppongi, often in the "water trade," but many more others, I estimate, are employed legally in skilled professions in the formal economy, are students on student visas, tourists from nearby countries (Japan and Russia are so close that they practically touch), or wives and mothers of Japanese. For them, it must be especially annoying to be the targets again and again of ethnic profile-based queries and searches regardless of how nicely the inevitable apology that comes afterward is presented.

A woman friend from Eastern European explains that the police always say that it's a routine precaution to make sure that visas are in order, but she wonders if she is stopped as much because of police voyeurism as anything else. The police want to know where she is from, whether she speaks Japanese, how old she is, and so on, all standard questions asked by Japanese men who approach foreign women. On the other hand, another companion from the same part of the world interrupts to say the exact opposite: "We are stopped," she argues, "because Azabu police hate foreigners. All they see from the foreigners here is trouble. They know that so many of the dancers and strippers and hostesses here are over-stayers or are working illegally while on tourist visas. To them, all of us (i.e., attractive foreign women in Roppongi) are visa violators and prostitutes." Indeed, strip clubs and hostess bars that employ foreign females are being targeted more and more for visa checks, and some have been forced to close. "Turn off the music. Everyone stay where they are. Show us your passports" is becoming routine script not just in Roppongi but also in Ikebukuro, Kinshichō, and other sakariba where foreign women are known to work. Kinshichō has been especially hard hit, forcing the closing of several clubs, particularly those run by the "M" group, a shady Japanese company with a reputation for hiring the very most beautiful Russian and Ukrainian girls, even those on tourist visas, paying them extremely well, and charging exorbitant prices for hostess and strip bar services from a moneyed clientele ("Police, Immigration" 2007).

Ethnic-profile inspections by police are few in the daytime but become quite aggressive late at night. They pick up again in the very early morning when Roppongi's all-night denizens begin to emerge bleary-eyed into the daylight. At this crow time on a Saturday morning, I watched as two police officers questioned a young foreign male, possibly Iranian or Turkish, who had emerged with his Japanese girlfriend from the depths of an all-night club. He was demonstratively outraged for having been stopped and complained very loudly in Japanese, with the occasional F-word as well in English, that he had been working all night, that he is a DJ, and that they can go up to the third floor to verify. The girlfriend tried to calm him as the police very calmly and very professionally examined his identification card and patted him down. Within a couple of minutes the incident was over as the police headed off to continue their patrol in one direction and the not-so-happy couple walked toward the subway station in the opposite direction.

Police do not stop only foreigners in their checks in Roppongi. They do so, of course, if their suspicions are about visa violators specifically, but their battles against illegal drugs and other crimes involve random inspections of Japanese and foreigners alike. Again and again at night and in the first light of morning, I observe police stopping and searching individuals of all races and ethnicities, including Japanese. They open bags, reach inside pockets, examine identification cards, and even thumb through the insides of wallets, as they are allowed to do by Japanese law. They also stop cars on the street or approach drivers of cars that are parked or idling and go through trunks, glove boxes, under floor mats, and so on.

Almost always, the police who patrol in Roppongi are males and their more "personal" inspections are of males only. Women who are stopped are usually interrogated about visa status and maybe about possible prostitution, but for them I have seen police do only document checks instead of more thorough searches. However, this does seem to be changing, for now I see more female police officers and more intrusive police interrogations of women on the street. In the case of a bleary-eyed Chinese woman who was being questioned after crow time at 10:00 a.m. by a minimum of eight male police offers, everyone waited for nearly one hour for a female officer to arrive before the searching of pockets and a pat-down. Then the "suspect" was released.

As with the foreigners who are stopped, there seems to be a profiling by age and style or demeanor when police select who among Japanese they want to question. Young males (ranging from late teens to their thirties) are the most frequent targets, especially those with casual fashions such as drooping baggy pants, hip-hop styles, and T-shirts with marijuana messages, and those seen coming out of clubs that are known to be places of drug activity or other trouble. Young men carrying small shopping bags also seem to be targets. It's almost a routine: two police offers on patrol walking one way on the sidewalk and a lone "suspect" walking in the other direction. They pass. Then one police officer says to the other, "Let's search him. That bag." You can see the words being mouthed. In an instant the police turn around, catch up to the target, and point directly to the bag. The "suspect" complies politely, often with a smile; the police look at the bag's contents without pulling them into the light, have a quick look at the shopping receipt inside, and thank the suspect; he smiles and nods back; and it's over, all in less than a minute.

Yes, the police presence in Roppongi is enormous, even oppressive. But where else in this world could I walk around all night among drunks and partygoers from all nations, conspicuous camera in hand, snapping pictures of the chaos of the streets at will as I walk, even of police in action, and have nothing to fear, experience no unpleasantries, and see nothing from the police other than polite and professional patrolling? And where else would I witness the following take place: a patrol of three police officers from the Azabu police station pass the Hard Rock Café, where a group of twenty or more young American college students, obviously on a study tour as indicated by their badges, is milling about. One of the young women approaches the police to ask if she could pose with them for a photo. They agree and begin lining up for the pose, but within seconds a dozen or so others from the group join in, also wanting to be photographed with the police. Again, the police comply. Instantly, a half a dozen or more cameras clicked away, including my own, and then the students trade places with one another, now clicking instead of posing. And then one of the officers shouts "Stop!" A car has approached. He parts the crowd and waves the car through. The photo session is resumed until the students have the pictures they wanted. I was impressed, and I hope that the young Americans were too.

Citizen Patrols

In addition to the increased police presence, there has been as well the introduction of patrolling the neighborhood by various civilian groups, some paid and some volunteers. The local business owners' association, the *shōtenkai*, has been especially active and has organized a uniformed army of its own members, mostly senior citizens it seems, to walk the streets and keep an eye on the goings-on. They wear identical navy-colored baseball caps and white shirts with official-looking, striped navy epaulets, and walk in pairs around Roppongi in the early evening as the party crowds start to gather. The lettering on their caps and shirt backs identifies them as "Security Patrols: Roppongi Shopping Street Association" (in English only). They are not armed (of course) and probably do nothing more than contact police if they see something untoward. Their time seems to be the early evening when people are still gathering in the neighborhood, and I have never seen them out late.

A separate cadre of uniformed deputies is identified in black and white. Their black baseball caps have white lettering that identifies them as members of "Executive Protection," the name of the company that employs them on contract for particular businesses or buildings. They also have "Executive Protection" sewn onto the seat pockets of their black slacks. Younger and tougher-looking than the shopkeepers' group, they stand all day and into the night at construction sites as protection and in front of the buildings whose owners have hired them. One recent early morning, I observed Executive Protection personnel escorting school children through the neighborhood on their way to school. I understood why, as the children's path was mined with inebriated post-crow-time hangers-on, morning-shift sex workers, and other characters incompatible with a walk to school. Other patrol groups wear green vests with Japanese text that identifies them as agents of the "City of Minato" (Minato Ward) who are deputized to patrol against illegal smoking. The concern in this case is with secondhand smoke in crowds, as well as cigarette butt litter and with the dangers that lit cigarettes could accidentally brush against passersby and cause injury. There are posted signs in the neighborhood that explain all this with explicit graphics, showing, for example, that an adult holding a lit cigarette while walking typically carries the "fire" at the same elevation as a child's eye. To keep smoking safe and orderly, there are designated corners where smoking is permitted, as well as a filter-fanned indoor smoking room at a central, street-corner location. (The same antismoking campaigns are underway in other wards of Tokyo as well as throughout urban Japan.)

Still another patrol is by the Guardian Angels, the famous red-bereted tough-guy street patrol group founded in 1979 in a high-crime neighborhood in New York City by Curtis Sliwa and his fellow workers at a branch of the McDonald's hamburger chain. They came to Tokyo in 1996 and opened a chapter of their group, recruiting a cadre of local toughs to keep watch over districts where crime was high by Tokyo standards. They started patrolling in Roppongi at least sporadically in the late 1990s. They continued to come and go in Roppongi for several years afterward, although I have not seen them in the neighborhood lately. Most of their attention is given to Shibuya and Ikebukuro, two other Tokyo districts known for nightlife, as well as near a U.S. military base outside the city. Their Roppongi patrols normally took place on weekends after midnight. They broke up fights, cautioned against overly aggressive solicitation, and helped partygoers who were too intoxicated to be functional. They called police when needed (Karasaki 2003). I had also seen Guardian Angels involved in graffiti cleanup.[11]

Once particular afternoon, I encountered an unusually sizable group of Roppongi patrol people and decided to follow them on their rounds. There were several different categories of watchdogs as indentified by their various uniforms. Three Tokyo police officers were in the lead, with one particular older individual of higher rank clearly being the person in charge. In addition, there were three tough-looking "Executive Protection" members, six or seven uniformed Roppongi Shopping Street Association delegates, including both men and women and one quite old male who barely had the strength to walk, and three green-uniformed parking enforcers, representing still another category of geriatric patrollers—about fifteen individuals in all. It was about 4 p.m., well before any trouble usually occurs and well past morning crow time and the regular a.m. pat down and roundup by police of leftover revelers. What were they after? The answer became clear as I walked along. They made notes and photographed places where there was litter and where trash was not arranged neatly, huddled here and there about bicycles taking up space on the sidewalks, checked signage that had been put out by restaurants, shops, and other businesses, and used a tape measure to identify which of the movable signs had been placed outside code limits. They clucked as well about illegally parked cars and trucks that were loading and unloading supplies for the night, directed a walking smoker to the officially designated smoking corner down the block, and challenged an old lady who was selling giant radishes from a bit of dead space where there was a widened sidewalk. This was a multifaced campaign for order in the neighborhood and a show of presence. The fifteen of them moved slowly en masse, greeted people they knew, ignored almost everyone else, and never seemed to notice me, my camera, or my notebook. They also never looked in the direction of the spiffy chauffeurs and illegally parked luxury cars that awaited their bosses who, as already observed, were taking their afternoon recreation breaks.

Beautifying Roppongi

Tough talk from people who have lost patience with Roppongi, merciless crackdowns by police, increased patrols of the neighborhood by neighborhood watchdog volunteers and paid reinforcements, and "everyone together" assessment and planning walks through the neighborhood are but some of the measures that are aimed to reclaim Roppongi. In the next chapter, I discuss redevelopment in Roppongi, the remaking of the neighborhood from the ground up. Those large projects are spic and span from day one. However, the interstices, the public spaces between the big megastructure developments, are often dirty, unattractive, and in need of beautification. The work being done to accomplish this is also part of "Reclaiming Roppongi." I have organized this section under three headings: (1) Infrastructure Improvements, (2) Cleanup and Maintenance, and (3) something that I call Indecent Fliers.

Infrastructure Improvements

Short of taking it down altogether, which is not practical given the needs of Tokyo's traffic flows, there is not much that can be done about Roppongi's biggest blight, the elevated highway that runs across the heart of the neighborhood above Roppongi-dōri and deprives the street below and much of

Roppongi Crossing itself of sunlight and views. That "improvement" from the cement happy 1960s is in Roppongi to stay. However, the skin that envelopes the expressway—its sound walls—has been cleaned up and looks better without the grime. So, too, officials have removed the puzzling signs that once read "Roppongi High-Touch Town," and after some debate about alternatives came up with a slick and stylized "Roppongi Roppongi" with descending and ascending letters (see chapter 1). That logo is now part of Roppongi's new look.

There are many other physical changes. Minato Ward as a whole is a prosperous and attractive part of Tokyo, but the core of Roppongi had been neglected in terms of infrastructure and was not keeping pace. Consequently, there is a now a catching-up movement underway and all sorts of physical improvements: new lamp standards with bright lights spelling out "Roppongi" in the logolike font affixed to the highway walls above Roppongi Crossing; banners that welcome visitors to Roppongi; new sidewalk pavements and curbs; more trees, bushes, and flowers along the line between sidewalks and the big streets; flower boxes; and better signage; among other details. Eyesores and dead spaces are being removed and replaced with brighter landscaping. You can sense the change in ambience and sense too that the improvements are a cooperative effort—the hand of Minato Ward government is there, as are the efforts of citizens, citizen groups, and shopkeepers, as well as those by big business. Consider the example of flower boxes.

There had long been flower boxes along the main streets that emanate from Roppongi Crossing. However, for as long as I can remember the boxes had more spent beer cans, discarded energy drink bottles, and cigarette butts than flowers. But now, there are nice, new flower boxes at the intersection, and inside are newly planted flowers. Also inside the boxes are small signs sticking upright from the soil. They are in Japanese, but I can read the message: *utsutushi machi wo sodateru anata no mana* (Your good manners will make for a beautiful town). There is one more thing on these signs: a new-shaped logo and the words "Tokyo Midtown." That redevelopment project just up the street from the corners of Roppongi Crossing has lots of greenery and promotes itself as being green: now its environmental attention is seen at Roppongi Crossing itself.

Cleanup and Maintenance

There are other examples of everyone pitching in. This week, for instance, I see Japanese-language signs on community bulletin boards around the neighborhood inviting volunteers to gather at a neighborhood center on Saturday morning for some cleanup chores. The invitation is to join a squad of fellow citizens and fan out with brushes and cans of paint to cover over the neighbor-hood's graffiti. It's a monthly event with a score or more of volunteers each time. Volunteers also pick up trash and clean metal surfaces such as the tube railings that run along the side of busier streets. A special solvent is used in this effort to dissolve scuff marks and glue residue from the many advertising stickers that had been posted on those surfaces. The volunteers work efficiently, show-ing their experience at the tasks, and don't complain when I ask if they ever get angry at the condition of the neighborhood that they inherit after a busy Friday night. The red metal mailbox that the thirties-something male to whom I am talking starts to shine as he buffs it during the conversation.

This monthly group is a complement to the more frequent street sweeping by local merchants and residents. Sometimes in the mornings, before they open their stores, members of the local shōtenkai (the same shopkeepers' association introduced earlier with respect to citizen patrols) can be seen in force wearing identifying yellow vests as they methodically sweep streets and sidewalks, bag litter, and wash down vomit from the night before. They look unhappy to be starting days this way, cleaning up someone else's mess, before they can get to work themselves. Once in a rare while I detect a dirty look in my direction, as if I personally were the one responsible for all the empty beer cans and McDonalds' packaging. Quite frequently, the sweepers have to work their way around left-over revelers from the previous night who are passed out amid the mess in a drunken stupor, or deal with inebriated youngsters who are still rowdy and continue to litter as the sweeping progresses. Impressively, they restrain them-selves from swinging a broom in anger; their task is to get the neighborhood clean and orderly before daytime customers and clients arrive. Increasingly, the police have been helping by stirring sleeping drunks and making other morning hangers-on uncomfortable because of stepped-up questioning and searches.

Indecent Fliers

There is one other example of Roppongi cleanup that I want to introduce: col-lection boxes for "indecent fliers." There are several such boxes around the neighborhood, two of them at two of the corners of the Roppongi Crossing intersection. Most people walk by without noticing them or giving a second thought, yet they are fascinating material relics of urban anthropology and Roppongi history. When they finally disappear, I hope that someone will have remembered to save at least one for a museum. They are identified with writ-ing that says "Indecent Flier Collecting Boxes." These rectangular white metal containers are a little more than a meter high and have a narrow slit at the top

FIGURE 5.4 Mori Building Company's notorious "indecent fliers collecting box."

for insertions. On the back panel, there is a metal lock that allows the box-keeper access for removing the contents. Some of the lettering on each box is pink and some is black. The message is more detailed in Japanese, but in pink are the English words "Indecent Fliers Collecting Box," referring to so-called *pinku chirashi* ("pink" fliers or leaflets) that advertise the services of escorts, prostitutes, and various other "fantasy companions." Typically, the leaflets are glossy, multicolored, wallet-sized pieces of paper with photos or drawings of attractive or cute young women and instructions about how to make contact by phone or Internet. They are mass-produced and have a bit of glue on the back, and they are often affixed to utility poles and other surfaces in neighborhoods where hired chirashi distributors think that there might be a larger market for sex.[12] Part of the campaign to clean up Roppongi, literally, is to have passersby pull down the "indecent fliers" as they encounter them and then insert the nasty little things out of harm's way into the slits atop the boxes. This would be a good place for the phrase "Only in Japan," but I think that many readers are already thinking that.

One more thing: who is the inspiration for the Indecent Flier Collecting Boxes? That's what the black text is all about. Most of it is in Japanese and identifies Minato Ward government and the Azabu Police Department as principals, but there, at the very bottom, in English along with the familiar company logo, it says "Mori Building Company," officialdom's powerful partner. Wow! It is the Mori Building Company, the biggest land development company in Japan, the biggest builder of high-rises in Tokyo, the local-born company that changed Minato Ward from fields of rice to forests of ever-taller high-rises (I'm getting a bit hyperbolic here), the developer of the Shanghai World Financial Center–Shanghai Hills complex, what would have been the world's tallest building were it not for the fact that Dubai enjoys faster builders—that Mori Building Company has its name and logo two centimeters above the filthy Roppongi sidewalk in order to claim credit for its invention of the "Indecent Fliers Collecting Box." This is a better spot to write "Only in Japan!" Look one way down the street from the most central collection box, and there is Mori's ARK Hills, a giant high-rise complex that several years ago began heralding the dawn of not just New Roppongi but also of Tokyo's new future. Now look the other way down the same street, and even closer is Roppongi Hills, a more gigantic and glitzier multiple high-rise Mori Building Company redevelopment project that is the company's single greatest pride and joy (Mori Building Company 2007). Just the look of that kingdom says that new days in Roppongi are just about here.

Sign Language

That there is urgency about Roppongi is reflected in various warning signs about crime and public safety that have been posted recently in the neighborhood. There are now many more signs than before, and they seem much more clamant. (There are "dos and don'ts" signs in other parts of Tokyo too, including some with the same messages as in Roppongi.) For a short while, a large electronic billboard looked down on the main meeting corner at Roppongi Crossing and offered advice about crime prevention and instructions for correct behavior in the neighborhood. Its space is now given over completely for commercial advertising, but until that change it beamed these five Roppongi commandments in English:

When you see a suspicious person or object call 110 immediately.

Be alert to the bag snatcher, luggage thief or pickpocket.

Do not leave bicycles or litter cans and bottles.

Please do not stop or park your car near Roppongi Crossing.

Please do not eat, sing or dance along sidewalk.

In the same vein but standing and multiplying in Roppongi are signs of durable plastic and luminous-paint letters. They have elongated vertical dimensions and hang on the various metal poles and thin trees that line the neighborhood's sidewalks. One example shows a pair of watchful eyes and the words "This town does not allow crimes. If you see anything unusual please do not hesitate to call 110—(signed) Azabu Police Department." Other signs, often posted as complementary pairs, have hot red lettering on a dazzlingly bright yellow-chartreuse background and relay warnings from the Azabu police to "be wary of thieves" (*dorobo chui*) and to "be wary of bag-snatchers" (*hitakuri chui*). Similar signs but only in Japanese are affixed to apartment and condominium buildings on the side streets of the neighborhood; they are larger and support more text, and they warn specifically about a growing problem of residential burglaries.

It is interesting to consider which languages are being used to say what in these signs because it seems that ethnic biases abound. Leaving aside the kinds of Japanese-language signs that address, say, parking regulations or the required details about what is going on at construction sites, an overall pattern (or at least a "tendency" that I see becoming a pattern) is that signs printed only in Japanese tell good citizens to be careful in the neighborhood, as in the case of the signs mentioned above about thieves and bag snatchers, while those that are bilingual Japanese-English, in just English, or in multiple languages tend to be more about what to do and what not to do. That was the case with the electronic billboard described above. While I do not want to overstate my case and make too much of what I acknowledge is a rather small topic, it does seem that the choices of which languages are used on public signs that say "no-no" imply that readers of those particular languages are thought to be specifically in need of that particular advice. Let me elaborate.

In some parts of Tokyo, such as the famous electronics district Akihabara, for example, multiple languages are used to attract customers into stores and to inform them about duty-free procedures. In Roppongi, however, multiple-language signs focus only on correcting the behavior of foreigners. Such is the case with yet another vertical sign, black print on a field of caution-yellow like so many other traffic and information signs, and written in Japanese, English, Korean, Chinese, and Farsi (Iranian), in that order. It too hangs on trees and utility poles and reads "This street is equipped with security cameras." The sign is the work of the Azabu Police Department, which does indeed monitor the streets electronically as well as via the patrols already described, and is intended not to miss many possible miscreants with its message. Perhaps a bit too ambitiously, I imagine that for Japanese an implication of that message might be that they may relax because their street is safely under surveillance,

FIGURE 5.5 Multilingual warning that security cameras are in place.

while for foreigners the message might be read more like, "Be careful, we are watching you."

The same blocks also have multiple installations of yet another multilingual sign, one about litter. This one is affixed low, near curb level, near the elevation of litter itself, and has a cartoon drawing of some litter within a red circle and a red slash across it. There is also a cute caricature of a smiling policeman holding up an index finger as a reminder. The text reads "No Littering" in Japanese, English, Korean, Chinese, Spanish, and Portuguese, in that order. If we consider the two multilingual signs together, we could conclude that Iranians are clean and do not throw trash on the streets but need to be surveilled for other reasons, while Spanish- and Portuguese-speaking Latin Americans do not require CCTV monitoring but are hazards instead as potential litterers.[13] Russians must be litterers too, because I have noticed brand new signs (little, cute, hand-made ones) that not long ago appeared alongside a public school. The top line is in Japanese, the English translation "No Littering!" is below, and beneath that is the same written in unpracticed Russian script: "*ne sorit!*"

Likewise, there are hand-made signs in the windows or doorways of shops in Roppongi that say simply "No Shoplifting" or "Shoplifting is a Crime." Similar signs in Japanese or Japanese-English have popped up elsewhere too, as stealing has come to be growing problem throughout Japan, but I note that here, in and near Roppongi, at least some shopkeepers think that it is sufficient to offer this advice to international readers only, without the use of Japanese (I noted only one other antishoplifting warning in both Japanese and English). Another English-only example is a neat, printer-made message affixed on the door of an elevator that leads to, among other floors, an Internet café that is popular among foreigners. It reads "PLEASE DO NOT KICK THE DOOR!!" (This building has since been closed for redevelopment.) And to repeat an example from chapter 4: near a public toilet on a side street dominated by a popular hip-hop club with cheap drinks, an official-looking metal sign screams presciently: "Be quiet! You are disturbing the neighborhood."

Apparently, the Embassy of the Republic of the Philippines is also a source of disturbance in Roppongi. There are new signs (since 2009) along the street outside in English and Japanese (not Filipino) and "signed" by the embassy itself and the local office of Minato Ward government making three numbered points or requests: (1) "Do not hang around the road and street stalls are not allowed in front of the Consular office building"; (2) "Smoking is prohibited around the Consular office building"; and (3) "Any inappropriate behavior may be punished." As a final point, the signs add this: "We appreciate your cooperation to keep the surrounding neighborhood clean and calm." The immediate area around the Philippine Embassy is indeed quiet and upscale, as are the blocks immediately around many other foreign embassies in Tokyo, but this particular embassy is the only one to my knowledge that has such signs.

Perhaps I am making a Mt. Fuji out of a molehill. I would agree except for some "gotcha" examples that prove, to me at least, that sign makers attribute certain behaviors directly to foreigners. First is a variant of the "dorobo chui" (beware of thieves) sign mentioned above. It too is courtesy of the Azabu Police Department but adds the following in English and only English after the Japanese-language warning about thieves:

> WARNING: BURGLARIES ARE ON THE RISE!
>
> KEEP THE LAW
>
> OTHERWISE YOULL [*sic*] BE ARRESTED

Clearly, that addendum is a targeted warning only for foreigners. Driving that point home is a second example of sign-profiling by the Azabu police, this a color ink on paper broadside that was displayed throughout the neighborhood on outdoor information boards. It centered on a caricature cartoon of two strong-looking, armed Japanese policemen successfully subduing a guilty-looking foreign crook with messy stubble on his cheeks, and reported gleefully that a "foreign group of thieves" has been arrested.

I would have stopped here with my discussion of signs, but today, May 25, 2009, a day when I am back in Tokyo and editing the manuscript, is another instance of events in Roppongi not stopping for my convenience. Beginning at about 6:00 p.m., just as the now-tamer Roppongi evening starts to build, I encounter yet another large security operation in Roppongi and an accompanying installation of new behavior-modification signs. This time the security force numbered well over a hundred, including police officers, various private-sector and community-group patrols, and members of various shopkeeper groups and other neighborhood associations (as indentified by arm bands, jacket lettering, and the signs they carried), and was divided into two roughly equal-sized teams that worked opposite sides of the street, affixing with great fanfare and media attention the signs for which many opponents of nighttime Roppongi had been waiting. I had learned that for weeks there had been loudspeaker announcements and printed notices that this day was coming and now it was here: as of this day, there was to be no more stopping potential customers on the street to invite them to a place of business and no more following after them. I walked along and snapped photos in the twilight as the two teams hung a few dozen of these signs around the neighborhood and marveled as each installation, one after the other, was gleefully capped with handshakes and media photos. The demeanor of the two teams was very purposeful and businesslike, but as a whole the group also exuded a sense of happy satisfaction that, at last, the deed was being done.

As this uniformed and business-suited force moved up Gaien-Higashi-dōri from one installation to the next, every newest sign was tested and re-tested by dutiful inspectors who followed on their heels to make sure it was on straight and tight, and then individually photographed by accompanying photographers. They took the photographs even though every sign was exactly like the next. The only difference was that each was individually numbered and tagged, almost microscopically. The text reads the same in English and Japanese:

WARNING

You will be punished if you do any of the following acts against passers-by

To call them to stop as prospective customers;

To block their ways, or keep tagging along with them.

Signed,
Chief of Azabu Police Station
Mayor of Minato City

This is obviously an anti-African streetman measure. It would apply as well to the Chinese and other foreign "massage" specialists who work the streets too, as well as to other touts and entrepreneurs, but it is the Africans who are targeted most directly. It is the Africans about whom there have been the most public complaints and uneasiness, led most prominently by Governor Ishihara and his unsubstantiated pronouncements that Africans in Roppongi steal cars and "engage in who knows what." I managed to follow and photograph the sign hangers with impunity and little notice until the group came upon a street corner with a concentration of strip clubs and a cluster of Africans already at work out front. As I started to discuss the situation with one of them, a long-time friend, other Africans came closer and listened in. At that moment, I saw fingers pointing in my direction from among the security force and observed that I was being pegged as one of "them," on the side of the problems in the neighborhood, rather than whatever they had thought I was, a news photographer or what not. I sensed that my welcome among sign hangers had ended, and I stopped following. Instead, I hung on for a while with my coforeigners on the street who filled me in on the situation.

We agreed that it would probably take a specific, court-ready complaint by an especially annoyed passerby (or an agent of the sign-hanging crowd) to lead to punishment for any miscreant on the street, because without such a complaint, spoken advances by a street tout could be defended as having been welcome. We also wonder what would happen if one were to complain to police about the many Japanese touts who work the streets to entice Japanese consumers (read male office workers after work) into the night spots that they represent. Africans have gotten the attention and bad publicity on the street, followed by foreigner female sex workers, but Roppongi's sidewalks are also lined with young Japanese male street touts and, interestingly, quite a few Japanese hostesses decked out in formal evening gowns and beauty shop hair. In the bad economy of today, hostess clubs are suffering financially, and bosses are sending their staff into the street to find customers. This is common in all Tokyo entertainment zones, but it is only in Roppongi where the chief of Azabu police and the mayor of Minato Ward have posted their new warnings.[14] For the rest of the evening, I observe African streetmen huddled here and there to discuss the evening's events. Those who approached prospective customers did so much more gingerly than before. The Japanese hostesses, however, had more of the sidewalks to themselves this evening and seemed much more visible and aggressive than I remember. (I comment further on these signs in chapter 7.)

Receding Rhythms

A neighborhood of bars, nightclubs, and restaurants is always in flux as establishments come and go depending on shifting consumer tastes, a proprietor's good and bad luck, the vagaries of lease arrangements for space, and countless other factors. Roppongi's mix of establishments especially has not been still, perhaps because of the many competing types of businesses that it has offered over the years and the extraordinarily diversity of the clientele. In my several years in Roppongi, I have seen dozens of establishments in business one day and gone the next, including some favorites that were lost. I have attended at least two "sayonara" nights at places that had announced their closings and least two grand openings of new, hopeful establishments. The changes are apparent with every return to Roppongi: here is a place that's shuttered and under renovation, a new sign and a different business is over there, and an entire building is being demolished somewhere else. Indeed, during a visit near the end of 2008 I was surprised, and then again not so surprised, to see that the large and opulent nightclub with the yakuza-rich grand opening described in chapter 4 is now closed.

Now there is a new business risk with which to contend, the possibility of falling on the wrong side of sanctioned campaigns to clean up the neighborhood. This can happen even if one runs what is apparently a clean business. In addition to the expected periodic closings of establishments that are known for trouble, there are clubs, some of them quite prominent, that have been forced to close despite good reputations, wide popularity among clubgoers, and seemingly genuine efforts to patrol against illegal activity of any sort on their premises. It is hard to imagine a Roppongi without nightclubs, but the picking off of clubs one after the other for forced closure makes it seem that such a scenario is indeed possible. Specific standards are hard to pinpoint, as what is acceptable to the law in one part of the city might not be acceptable any longer in Roppongi, and what is acceptable, for the time being at least, in one club in Roppongi might be unacceptable and a punishable offence in a club next door. The issue seems to turn on the series of 1949 U.S. occupation–generated laws referred to earlier that govern the operation of nightclubs among other activities. The laws are referred to as the *fūzokueigyoho*, translated as "public morals business laws," and comprise an entangled maze of detailed rules and regulations that only a specialist can follow and that police can elect to enforce as they want. Among other details, there are fine points governing the size of dance floors, decibel levels from music, and levels of lighting, as well as the controversial, much publicized, and unevenly enforced rule that confounded me earlier, the one that prohibits dancing in nightclubs after 1:00 a.m.[15]

According to a feature article in Tokyo's *Metropolis* magazine by Maki Nibayashi (1999), the first enforcement of the dancing curfew was sometime in the 1980s after the rape of a woman who had left a popular disco club in Shinjuku named Zenon (there was also a club named Zenon at the time in Roppongi). Afterward, enforcement of this rule also seemed to follow specific bad incidents or a club's general reputation for trouble, with disproportionate targeting of nightclubs taking place in Minato Ward, especially in Roppongi and some neighborhoods nearby. A crackdown began in September 1999 with the closure of Mission, "perhaps Minato Ward's most stylish see-and-be-seen nightclub," and then Luners, another popular club in nearby Azabu Jūban. That was followed by a series of what Nibayashi described as falling dominos: Vivian, 328 (San-Ni-Pa), Breakfast Club, and Yellow. Some disappeared forever while others, such as Yellow, reopened and were then closed for good at a later date.

Sometimes when an especially popular or well-known club goes out of business, the public and press reaction, at least among expatriates, resembles mourning after a death, with the news write-up reading something like an obituary. For example, a 2008 issue of *Metropolis* magazine had a lengthy cover story about the final closing of Yellow, with photos, a "biography" of the club, and, under the heading "memories," comments, reflections, and laments by more than two dozen bereaved fans, DJs, and musicians (Grunebaum 2008, 16–17). The biography recounts the club's critical role over seventeen years as a portal into Japan for new developments in dance music from abroad and explains that the final closing came not as a direct result of the 1:00 a.m. rule, which had accounted for earlier temporary closings, but the demolition of the building in which it leased space. A representative quotation from a devotee, someone named Ken Hidaka and identified as a DJ, states: "I hope that the cool staff of Yellow can open another club shortly so that yellow's spirit will live on, just like our quality-music-loving, hungry spirit lives on" (17). Likewise, there were "obituaries" for Velfarre, once the "largest disco in Asia" (capacity 1,500), which closed its doors with a "Last Dance" party on New Year's Eve 2006. It too had trouble with the police about late-night dancing but succumbed finally, as did Yellow, to urban redevelopment. Velfarre had opened in December 1994 with performances by the girl group from England named Bananarama and the popular Japanese group TRF (Tetsuya Komuro Rave Factory) and then over the next dozen years hosted countless foreign and Japanese performers and live album recordings. Its credits also include the *para para* dance boom in Japan (a synchronized Japanese group dance with specific movements set for each song), for which it was a significant incubator. This club has since reopened.

There are competing explanations for what is going on, none of which seriously attribute the club closings to the official reason, dancing past curfew. No, the dancing issue is an excuse for other agendas: a need to empty a building of tenants so that it can be sold to developers and demolished; getting rid of a nuisance in the neighborhood that has been the source of noise, litter, and drunkenness; punishment for employing foreigners without proper visas or for serving alcohol to minors; or closing a club because it has been associated with illegal drugs. Sometimes, perhaps, a club closes simply because it was a lousy establishment and lacked the volume of business to maintain profitability. Still another range of explanations focuses on the long-lasting poor economy in Japan: there simply is not the money around to support all the clubs of the past. Whatever the reasons, the full story as to why any club closes is hard to pin down: almost always one is told different things by different people about the same establishment; and those in the best position to know the truth, the owners or managers of the establishment, are those who are least willing to be fully honest. As I warned in chapter 1, truth in Roppongi is frustratingly elusive.

The campaign against illicit drugs is probably more important than I have presented thus far, and a strong argument can likely be made that the trouble in "disco city" is most centrally trouble with drugs. This is supported by the specific drugs-related incidents and arrests that were citied earlier for Roppongi, as well as by the almost routine searches by police for illegal drugs in the backpacks, pants and coat pockets, wallets, and private automobiles of people who have been stopped, whether at random or as a result of some sort of profiling. Despite harsh penalties in Japan for possession or use of marijuana, ecstasy, and other banned stimulants, such substances are part and parcel of nightlife in Roppongi, Shibuya, and other parts of Tokyo, perhaps increasingly so. The police campaigns target not just the individual users and those who may have supplied them, but also the places where drugs are used or where they were purchased. That is why there are now many clubs that have placed prominent signs in front in English and Japanese announcing a zero-tolerance policy for narcotics of any kind.

Not long ago, police were searching frantically for the source of some particularly deadly narcotics being sold in Roppongi. The situation was truly serious: there had been at least three deaths, a Canadian, a Brazilian, an American, and maybe one more, plus as many as twelve near-deaths. A rogue drug dealer was said to be responsible, possibly an Iranian who was mixing heroin with the cocaine that victims were buying. Club owners and employees joined with police in the search, asking their own questions, because business had fallen as customers were afraid and stayed away from the neighborhood. Besides, it was the clubs' customers who were dying. In Tokyo, the main users of cocaine, it seems, are young foreigners, males mostly, far from their homes in Western countries and living a fast life in Roppongi. They are well employed at prestigious financial trading companies and other foreign firms nearby with high salaries and huge bonuses, live in lush apartments that come with expat employment packages, and enjoy fully both the chemical and the female temptations of the crazy zoo where life has taken them.[16] It is this category of individual that I referred to earlier as free-spending foreigner-clients in Roppongi's high-end hostess economy.

Nightclub owners and their loyal patrons have protested strenuously against tactics aimed at the clubs, saying that it is unfair to punish them for illegal activity that happens on their premises, particularly so when the clubs have rules against such activity and invest in their own security personnel to patrol against it. They want to stay in business and not be closed down, and much of their business is selling alcohol, a legal stimulant whose sales are in competition with the illegal drug sales that that they have a vested interested in stopping. On the other hand, club owners also know that well-attended drug-fed dance parties mean lots of income from door charges, even if sales levels at bar counters suffer from competition with outside drug sales. What is paramount to them is reputation among customers, not police, and creating an atmosphere of music, light (or lack thereof), and compatible clientele that keeps business going (Malbon 1999). Whatever is lost because customers are fueled by drugs from the outside (or beer bought at convenience stores and imbibed before entering a club) can be made up by the high pressure and aggressive drink selling that many Roppongi bars and clubs employ. For many customers, drinking within measure, whether to stay sober or conserve money, is sometimes nearly impossible, as many establishments provide overly attentive staff to whisk away glasses and bottles even before they are completely empty and then ask impatiently, "What would you like to drink?" On a busy night, there is a waiting line outside of people wanting to enter, and the next person will gladly take the place of someone who is no longer willing to keep paying.

A second overarching explanation for the closings of clubs, in complement to the campaign against illicit drugs, is the overall push for redevelopment in Roppongi—the shaping of a New Roppongi from the old. This is part and parcel of the expansion of Tokyo's overpriced and overcrowded central business district, the ongoing high-rise development of the city previously discussed, and the particular appeal to the Mori Building Company and other developers of

Roppongi and surroundings as just the right place to shape a new, more sophisticated and more upscale look for Tokyo. This is the area near Japan's centers of business and political power, and near as well to where foreign embassies, Japanese offices of foreign companies, and housing complexes for well-paid expatriates are concentrated, and just the place to best present Tokyo to the world, and Japan more generally as well, as a truly international place and hospitable partner in global society. The club life of Roppongi, once accepted as part of Tokyo's wonderful mix of entertainment options, is now vastly different from the relatively innocent times when disco was king, and centers now on activities that Japan's pooh-bahs neither value nor understand. To them, the new music, be it house mix, trance, hip-hop, or even old-time rock and roll, is wrong, the level of clientele is wrong, and there are way too many violations of the law, ranging from visa violations and permits for work to pickpockets, prostitutes, and purse snatchers to the intolerable widespread availability of drugs, a rarity in Japan. It is time to clean house, and if an arcane law about what time of night dancing should end can help, so be it. The next chapter elaborates on the physical remaking of Roppongi.

CHAPTER SIX

Roppongi Remade

Redevelopment Landscapes

I begin with a reminder that remaking Roppongi is not just about the cleanup of a misbehaving nightclub district; the backdrop is also about reforming how people live in Tokyo and setting a new, high standard for Japanese urban life. For those with building in mind and who want to remake in fundamental ways the character of life in Tokyo, it is convenient that Roppongi has been bad: it can more easily be condemned to die, and public opinion will be supportive. With that accomplished, Roppongi's demolition becomes easier and can be followed by the shaping of a new urban form. There will be little political support for the old Roppongi and, conveniently too, little opposition to what is new. "New Roppongi" can come upon the scene without scrutiny, quietly if that is convenient, and with fanfare if fanfare helps. We see that the construction state is not just cement happy, but crafty too.

As established in chapter 2 in setting context for this narrative, Tokyo is a city that never sits still but is always building, rebuilding, and building some more. Because of Minato Ward's centrality and location at the most active advancing edge of Tokyo's central business district, it has been especially dynamic. It is not unusual to see buildings coming down one after the other, even those that seem perfectly functional, and new ones rising in their place. This is Roppongi's story too. Step away from the neighborhood for two or three months, and there will be so many changes by the time you return that you might feel a bit disoriented.

Gaien Higashi-dōri has become gap-toothed, meaning that there are now spaces between buildings that once stood neatly in line like straight teeth. Now buildings are missing, and I wonder who threw the punches that knocked those teeth loose. From across the street, we see that the gap frames perfectly Mori Tower, the glitzy steel and glass centerpiece of Roppongi Hills, the crowning achievement (so far) of the Mori Building Company, changer of Tokyo and collector of indecent fliers. The symbolism is inescapable: the Roppongi Hills version of Tokyo, which is elaborated below, hallmark of New Roppongi, is looming ever larger over the heart of neighborhood, sending it punch after punch until the knockout. I consult my notes and photo archives as to what was on the site before and remember that it was a multistory games arcade and karaoke emporium. I won't miss it, except that it did have a large, multistory, scary-looking metal sculpture of some insectlike monster on its façade and was, therefore, a local landmark. The sculpture was a unique architectural adornment and a nostalgic throwback to some kitsch fad from the past; I hope that someone thought to save the monster. Personally, I'm glad that I had taken photos before it wandered off.

A walk toward a favorite sports bar in another direction from Roppongi Crossing takes me past another, much larger cleared area—in fact, two gaps side by side on either side of a narrow street. I had known that this redevelopment was coming because I had observed at least three years earlier that the various buildings on the sites were being emptied of tenants and then being shuttered. What I did not think of at the time but see now is a street-level sightline between Roppongi Hills in one direction and Tokyo Midtown, the other enormous new redevelopment project in Roppongi that is featured in this chapter, in the other direction. The latter project is by competitors of the Mori Building Company, Mitsui Fudōsan, also a very powerful and influential company, and occupies a footprint nearly as large as that of Roppongi Hills (6.1. million square feet 569,000 square meters versus 7.8 million square feet/724,000 square meters, respectively). Its central tower, Midtown Tower, rises to greater heights (814 feet/248 meters) than the 781 feet (238 meters) of Mori Tower. Aha, I say to myself, the armies of change have established themselves on either side the nightclub district and can now pick off vulnerable block after vulnerable block for redevelopment, until the whole neighborhood is remade.

This particular little district happens to be a yakuza-rich part of Roppongi that was featured in the tour in chapter 4. The centerpiece of what was torn down was nothing less than Hisayuki Machii's TSK-CCC complex (Towa Sogo Kigyo—Celebrities' Choice Clubs), the famous multistory yakuza entertainment complex discussed in chapters 3 and 4. It had gone bankrupt in 1976, in part because of spin-offs from the Lockheed scandal (Kaplan and Dubro 2003, 230–31), and started to deteriorate from that time despite its James Bond–cool porthole windows. There were also a number of nightclubs on these lots, including at least one that was especially popular among European models, at least one very large and famous strip and hostess club known for having especially beautiful women from around the world, and a second hostess club that was managed by a European male friend. I remember it most for sickly red velour upholstery, red velour drapes and privacy curtains, and two floors of wall to wall red carpet. There was also a popular sports bar managed by another friend from a different part of Europe. It had a life-sized faux-gold statue of a lion outside and a small but popular casino in back "for recreation gaming only." I had always remembered this little district as one of the darker and dirtier parts of Roppongi, with dated architecture from the 1970s, and associated it in my mind with leftovers from the days of disco, early Bond girls, and bell-bottom pants. It was not surprising to see that it would not survive into the new Roppongi era. It also follows that most of this strategically sited real estate will be deleted from the rolls of Roppongi's entertainment venues and be remade into multistory office buildings for the white-collar world.

A short block away, after a turn onto Roppongi's main street, is Tokyo Midtown. Across the street is a fraying seven-story, multitenant office building that, like so many other structures in Roppongi, is also being readied for redevelopment. I call attention to this particular building because of who the lead tenant is: the Inagawa-kai, one of the largest of Tokyo's yakuza crime syndicates. They are not the Sumiyoshi-kai or the Yamaguchi-gumi from the mob hit incident discussed in the previous chapter, but a third group, one with 4,800 members and special interests in gambling, including bookmaking, furtive casinos, and offshore gambling tourism. They also deal in real estate and own entertainment companies, bars, restaurants, and hostess clubs (Kaplan and Dubro 2003, 135–41). They have operated quite openly under the name Inagawa Kōgyō (Inagawa Industries) from this particular building for more than thirty-five years, but recently it was reported that they were to be displaced because their lease was ending and the building was to be demolished (*Daily Yomiuri*, December 24, 2008). How this is possible is beyond my reach, as well as beyond the abilities of the newspaper that reported this turn of events, but it might be a spinoff following the death a few months earlier of the gang's aged founder, Kakuji Inagawa, or it might be linked to police action against the gang: in 2007, some 1,235 of the gang's 4,800 members were charged with crimes. Whatever is going on behind the scenes, the displacement (which has now actually been accomplished) is further evidence that Roppongi is being reshaped.

The reconnaissance continues. There are more vacant lots, more construction projects in progress, and more and more of what I call "ghost buildings"— perfectly good structures that were normally engaged one day and then suddenly are out of commission with occupants gone, no lights and no window treatments, and weeds, litter, and accumulations of junk mail all on the rise. Eventually, a barrier fence is erected, signs are affixed to announce oncoming demolition, and the building is shrouded. I go to the southern margins of Roppongi, where the neighborhood approaches Tokyo Tower, and see that the

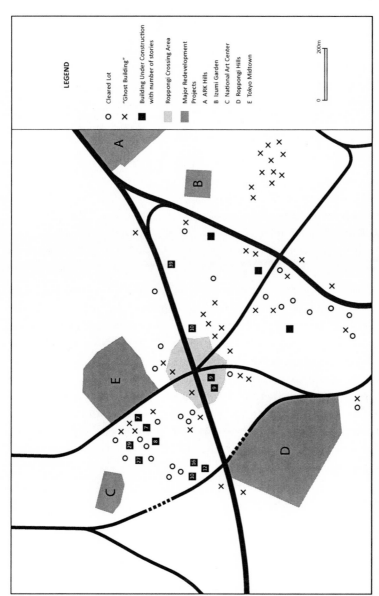

FIGURE 6.1 Redevelopment sites in Roppongi, 2008. The data are from fieldwork and symbols mark approximate locations where there is new construction, where vacant lots await construction, and where there are vacant buildings to be demolished. (Erin McCann cartographer)

LEGEND

○ Cleared Lot

✕ "Ghost Building"

■ Building Under Construction with number of stories

░ Roppongi Crossing Area

▓ Major Redevelopment Projects

A ARK Hills
B Izumi Garden
C National Art Center
D Roppongi Hills
E Tokyo Midtown

0 ___ 200m

substantial cluster of "ghosts" that I had observed months before is now much larger. This is a part of "residential Roppongi" and a next-door neighborhood that spans parts of Azabudai 1-chōme and Toranomon 5-chōme. Until now, it was a pleasant little area of single homes and modest apartment and condominium structures along quiet lanes, but now the lanes are ghostly quiet as most of the buildings are empty. I learn that the Mori Building Company has been buying property after property in this district and is preparing the site for demolition. It seems a waste, as many of the closed buildings look to be perfectly good and expensive. "Ghosts before their time," I think. Clearly, the goal is to amass still another large tract for another landmark redevelopment project.

> A perfectly good building condemned to die young
> Dressed in death shroud, it's being pulled down.
> They truck away parts, its flesh, meat and bone
> 'Till nothing is left, just earth all alone
> Then up comes a big sign, telling what's coming up next
> And to bless the design, a paid priest mumbles prayers from a text.

I start making notes on a map, marking Xs where I see ghosts. The Xs are everywhere, many more than I had imagined. Indeed, there are larger Xs and dense clusters of Xs that bespeak of big projects to come. Again and again, I see Mori Tower framed in the new vacant spaces, not in all of them, of course, but often enough to keep reminding me of what's going on. Other Xs line Roppongi-dōri toward ARK Hills, or cluster in the shadows of Tokyo Midtown where the real estate market is experiencing spin-off effects, and stretch down Imoarai-zaka (potato-washing slope) from Roppongi Crossing toward the residential zone of Roppongi Hills. Patterns emerge, and a new map of Roppongi takes form: big areas with bright new redevelopment projects that are the new present; other areas with clusters of vacant lots and ghost buildings that represent coming change; still other areas where individual buildings are being picked off here and there for new, usually taller buildings on their site; various subdistricts that seem stable, resistant, and safe (figure 6.1).

Two adjacent ghosts on Potato-Washing Slope merit special comment. I discussed both in chapter 3: Gensiro Kawamoto's Marugen 12 and Marugen 22, two side-by-side closed buildings that not only add up to a larger footprint for redevelopment but that also represent quite symbolically the decline in Roppongi of Tokyo's huge and extremely important hostess industry. The sign from Marugen 12, which is still intact, clues us in on what the action had been: there are club names like Candy, Bandana, Cat's Eye, Morning, D.E.E.P., My Baby, Always, and

John Lemon in Roman script, and Purisu (Please), Binokurusu (Binoculars), and Shacho shitsui (The Boss's Office), among others, in Japanese.

I begin to wonder about Tokyo Tower itself, although almost completely without authority. When it opened in 1957, the landmark was a powerful symbol of Japan's rebuilding after the devastation of World War II and the nation's increasing reintegration into the world community via trade and other contact. Tokyo Tower also symbolized the rebirth of optimism among the Japanese public as the postwar economy began to grow. It was featured recently as a half-completed structure in an upbeat film, *Always—3-chōme no Yuhi* (approximately Always—Sunset on 3rd Street) about optimism in Tokyo in the 1950s. While it is far enough away from Roppongi Crossing to be outside my specific geographical purview, it is still a Roppongi landmark in that it is prominently visible down Gaien Higashi-dōri, Roppongi's nightclub spine, and is referred to regularly within Roppongi for orientation about which way to walk. It is beautifully lit at night and complements the multicolored hues of the neon signs along the main commercial street. If rumors are true, Tokyo Tower could become the best example yet of what it means to say that Japan is a construction state. I hesitate to repeat the rumors in writing because by the time this is read the truth will have been revealed, but let me just say that there are stories afloat that the old landmark might be dismantled to make way for more construction of high-rise offices towers, hotels, and upscale shopping centers. Furthermore, it is said that because Tokyo Tower is symbolic and has nostalgic value, it might be reconstructed elsewhere in Tokyo, perhaps at Odaiba, an enormous fantasyland commercial and amusement development on a close-in island reclaimed from Tokyo Bay. If a shōgun once moved a mountain to shape Edo to his personal specifications, why couldn't the construction state that descended from that tradition move a metal tower?

The rumors about Tokyo Tower are fueled by the fact that a new, much more technologically advanced communications tower cum visitor attraction, nearly twice as high, is being developed in another part of the city, Sumida Ward. It has been named Tokyo Sky Tree and is expected to open in 2011, making Tokyo Tower redundant. Furthermore, the land under Tokyo Tower would be extremely valuable in the marketplace, making it difficult to envision an owner sustaining the present tower as it is. What is more, Tokyo Tower is no longer a place for a unique view of the city from up high, as there are now other competitors in the "pay to look" business, most notably the outstanding observation facilities atop Mori Tower. In addition, many visitors have come to regard Tokyo Tower as being somewhat tacky and outmoded in its various displays, galleries, and amusement facilities. When a Japanese newspaper reporter recently asked an official of Nippon Television City, the private company that owns Tokyo Tower, about the tower's future, there was no answer except for the kind of "no comment" that feeds rumors even more: "We have a secret plan, and we are working closely with a famous cultural figure on it."[1]

Encircling Roppongi

If, in fact, the Tokyo Tower site becomes available for upscale redevelopment, it would more or less complete a circle of sorts around the Roppongi of Roppongi Crossing, putting still more pressure on the small but busy district that is the subject of this book. I have already mentioned other critical points on the circle: Roppongi Hills, Tokyo Midtown, and ARK Hills. There is also the National Art Center, discussed below. These four new developments are powerful nodes of planned urban change on their respective surroundings. Each of these projects happens to be located in a different direction along a major avenue that passes through Roppongi Crossing, creating more or less symmetrical distribution of pressure points on the ever-smaller nightclub district in the center (figure 6.2). Moreover, with the exception of the National Art Center, which is a low-slung building, these projects are plainly visible from the core intersection, in some ways even looming over it. Specifically, we see ARK Hills about eight to nine hundred meters to the east of the Roppongi Crossing along our sight line along Roppongi-dōri, Roppongi Hills less than 300 meters to the west along the same street, and Tokyo Midtown just 200 meters to the north along Gaien Higashi-dōri. The National Art Center is in that general direction as well, off a side street. Tokyo Tower is further away, about 1.2 kilometers south along Gaien Higashi-dōri, but looms large in the Roppongi landscape nonetheless because of its size and lighting, and because a turn in the road makes it seem from Roppongi Crossing that the tower is at end of the street itself. Even if the tower stays intact in the future, the south direction will have its big redevelopment project anyway, as that is also the location of Azabudai 1-chōme and Toranomon 5-chōme, described just above as a residential district of newly designated "ghost buildings" that the Mori Building Company has been amassing into a single large development tract.

There are other significant redevelopment projects around Roppongi as well, so many in total that instead of referring to a circle around Roppongi, perhaps the better analogy for what surrounds Roppongi would be either a tight-fitting noose or a bejeweled chocker necklace, depending on one's thinking about the nightclub district. If one prefers the latter analogy, then the other "gems" that encircle Roppongi include ARK Hills, as well as Holland Hills, Atago Green

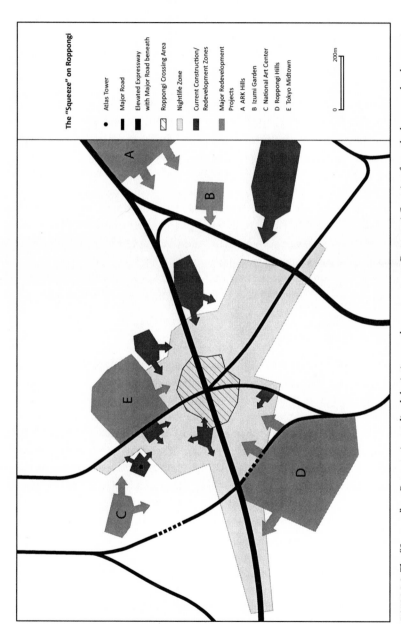

FIGURE 6.2 The "Squeeze" on Roppongi, a stylized depiction on the pressures on Roppongi Crossing from the larger redevelopment projectors that surround it. (Erin McCann cartographer)

The "Squeeze" on Roppongi

- Atlas Tower
- Major Road
- Elevated Expressway with Major Road beneath
- Roppongi Crossing Area
- Nightlife Zone
- Current Construction/ Redevelopment Zones
- Major Redevelopment Projects
  - A ARK Hills
  - B Izumi Garden
  - C National Art Center
  - D Roppongi Hills
  - E Tokyo Midtown

0   200m

Hills, Moto-Azabu Hills, Shiroyama Hills, all of them Mori Building projects, and the Izumi Garden complex, a project by competitors. They too are high-rise projects and combine residential and commercial components in varying percentages, always for an upscale, high-rent market. There is also Moto-Azabu Hills, a mostly residential tower mentioned in chapter 2. It is particularly distinctive in form and is a prominent local landmark because of shape that suggests an upright ice cream cone.

In the pages below I examine in closer detail the three biggest of the new redevelopment projects in Roppongi: Roppongi Hills, Tokyo Midtown, and the National Art Center. I also introduce still one more geometric shape associated with New Roppongi, the "Roppongi Art Triangle," a concept derived from the new, prestige art galleries and museums that have been opened at each of these three places. First it would be appropriate to fill in some details about the Mori Building Company, which is mentioned many times in the previous pages as an extraordinarily key player in Roppongi's transformations. This huge privately owned company was born of small beginnings not far from the Roppongi neighborhood, has had a great deal to do with the high-rising of Minato Ward in the first place, and, in the persons of both its founder and his son, the CEO successor, has long been involved in remaking Roppongi in a new image.

The Mori Building Company

The Web site of the Mori Building Company (http://www.mori.co.jp/en/) provides a handy and presumably accurate profile of the company and its history, although I suspect that by now there is public relations spin mixed with routine historical facts, and the exact truth about the company's birth is starting to be romanticized. It all began in 1955 in the wasteland of war-destroyed Tokyo "with a relatively minor event, the construction of a single building." That structure was built by Taikichirō Mori (1904–93), the founder of Mori Fudōsan, as the company was originally called, and was an office building, the first of many "new buildings on charred ruins" that Mori said he would erect. His goal was to rebuild Japan, or at least its capital city, after the war and prepare it for business with the world. Indeed, many of his first tenants were foreign companies, drawn to him because Mori was rare in Japan in providing office space at Western standards. He began in Toranomon, a part of Minato Ward just east of Roppongi, where his ancestors had once grown rice and where his father was a rice merchant and small-time landlord. He is quoted as saying at one point that to succeed in the emerging global economy, Japan would need to grow office buildings instead of rice. That first building occupied a small plot and may have been just over four stories in height, as illustrated in a black and white photograph that is shown on the company's Web site, or it may have been ten stories high, in counterpoint to the "rabbit-hutch houses" (Mori's words) that his neighbors were throwing up, as an aging Mori may have told a writer who interviewed him for a book (Popham 1985, 78). Regardless of height, that first "concrete baby" (Popham's words) was called Mori Biru 1 (Mori Building 1), the first of many buildings that Mori numbered in sequence as they were built.

I discuss the book by Popham in chapter 4, in connection with its descriptions of slender and tall "bar buildings." However, the most significant contribution of this little-known and now lamentably scarce volume is its account of that interview with Taikichirō Mori. The interview was a coup, because the elder Mori was publicity shy and did not speak in public as often as his son, the present CEO of the Mori Building Company, Minoru Mori (1934–). Mori the father gave Popham some truly rare personal insights into the giant company that he founded, its methods, and its objectives. More than twenty years after that conversation took place, it is still interesting to reflect on the founder's assessment of Tokyo at the time and what it needed to prosper, and on the sense of mission that he had in building his business, a sense that not only survives but thrives within the company today. It was important to Mori to build right there, in his own neighborhood, among the people he knew best, because change begins at home. It is among his own people, where he was known and trusted, that he could best advocate his vision for the future. Thus, in a city where land characteristically stays in the same family for generations, Mori was able to work a sort of magic, not wresting property from owners, but reasoning it away, convincing his own people that "the ordinary Japan could not survive, [as] it would be defeated by the advanced nations" (Popham 1985, 79, 82; quotation on 82). One of Mori's assistants then added that "the secret is to establish close relations with the local people. We go on holiday with them, for example. We take part in festivals—even helping to carry the portable shrine" (82).

Popham relates this with bite, as I think he should. Here, in Toranomon, Mori's own neighborhood where people had survived fires, war, earthquakes, and other calamities, when "confronted with Taikichirō Mori they appeared helpless to resist. Meekly they packed up their things and stole away" (78), thereby allowing their neighborhood to be made into Mori Biru after Mori Biru. If one looks almost anywhere in the air in that part of town, there will be the Mori logo and a number. From Mori Biru 1 in 1955, the number had grown to 25 by 1973 and capped at 37 in 1981 with a building in Toranomon. Mori explained to Popham that the numbering of buildings in sequence of construction was because each was an element of a next generation that represented Japan's

future: "I look on my buildings as if they were my children" he told his inter-
viewer, "and like children I give them names. 'Mori' is the family name, then
I give them numbers, just as Japanese forenames—Ichiro, Jiro, Saburo, and so
on—often contain numbers, to indicate the child's place in the sequence. That's
the reason" (74). After Mori Building Number 37, the naming system changed,
as did the kinds of developments that the company took on, and the "Hills" era
of Mori construction was born (table 6.1).

Mori was aided in his quest for property not just by an ability to "reason"
with owner-neighbors but also by being patient, because he typically had to wait
years to acquire all the small lots that were needed for any given redevelopment
site. He was further aided by the *koteishisan*, the property tax that owners pay on
the land they own. There are reassessments every three years, resulting in higher
and higher taxes on the higher-valued land that Mori and other office building
entrepreneurs had been converting from residential to commercial uses, which
in turn caused homeowners to sell the land where they had lived. Furthermore,
there is a steep inheritance tax that is tied to the value of the land, which all
but guaranteed that the children of an old-aged homeowner who passed away
would be forced to sell the land to raise money for the tax. It is through such
vehicles that Toranomon and other formerly residential districts pressing on
Roppongi were "evacuated" of inhabitants and turned into "glassy ghost towns"
(Popham 1985, 78), and that Taikichirō Mori was able to become extraordinarily
wealthy. He was said to be the world's richest man in the bubble years 1991 and
1992. Popham's account also includes the fascinating detail that Taikichiro Mori
was baptized a Christian at age sixteen, "graduated from Christianity" at a later
age, and then, sixty-four years after the baptism, bought and demolished the
church where he had been baptized (84).

The Mori Building Company is now capitalized at 65 billion yen ($680 mil-
lion), has more than 1,200 employees, leases 107 buildings (as of April 2008)
totaling approximately 1,160,000 square meters, and is landlord to some 2,212
commercial tenants. Its headquarters is in Mori Tower, its own building in the
Roppongi Hills complex, and the president and CEO is now Minoru Mori, the
elder son. (Taikichirō Mori passed away in 1993.) Another son, Akira Mori, is
the president and CEO of Mori Trust Company, another real estate empire. In
1983, the Mori Building Company started construction of the ARK Hills complex, named for where Akasaka, Roppongi, and Kasumigaseki come together
(see chapter 2), which it completed in 1986. It was the first of many "Hills"
projects that were to come, the new theme in Mori branding that replaced the
numbering of buildings. The name derives from the "hills" aspects of *yamanote*,

TABLE 6.1 Landmarks in Mori Building Company history

1955 (August)	Established Mori Fudosan
1956 (April)	Completion of Nishi-Shimbashi 2 Mori Building
1957 (November)	Completion of Nishi-Shimbashi 1 Mori Building
1959 (June)	Established Mori Building Company, Ltd.
1959 (July)	Completion of Nishi-shimbashi 3 Mori Building
1973 (August)	Completion of Roppongi 25 Mori Building
1978 (October)	Opened LaForet Harajuku
1981 (September)	Completion of Toranomon 37 Mori Building
1983 (November)	Started construction of ARK Hills
1986 (March)	Completion of ARK Hills
1993 (October)	Completion of Roppongi First Building
1996 (October)	Completion of Senmao Building (Dalian, China)
1998 (April)	Completion of Senmao Building (currently HSBC Tower) (Shanghai)
1999 (January)	Published "Urban New Deal Policy"
1999 (July)	Opened Palette Town Sun Walk (currently Venus Fort Family)
1999 (August)	Opened Palette Town Venus Fort
2000 (March)	Completion of Koraku Mori Building
2000 (April)	Started construction of Roppongi Hills
2000 (September)	Completion of Akasaka Tameike Tower and Residence
2001 (June)	Completion of ARK Yagi Hills
2001 (July)	Completion of Atago Green Hills Mori Tower
2001 (October)	Completion of Atago Green Hills Forest Tower
2002 (May)	Completion of Moto-Azabu Hills Phase I
2002 (September)	Completion of Moto-Azabu Hills Phase II
2002 (November)	Completion of Prudential Tower
2003 (April)	Completion of Roppongi Hills
2003 (October)	Opened Mori Art Museum
2004 (October)	Completion of high-rise portion of Holland Hills Mori Tower
2005 (February)	Total Completion of Holland Hills Mori Tower
2006 (February)	Completion of Omotesando Hills
2008	Completion of the Shanghai World Financial Center

Source: Mori Building Company.

the green and undulant side of Tokyo that since the start of the city has been tied to power and prestige, and is applied especially to the company's multibuilding projects. ARK Hills is a unified cluster of office buildings, hotels, residences, and cultural facilities, all set apart by distinctive design from the immediate surroundings. Other "hills" projects in and near Roppongi are Atago Green Hills in 2001 and Moto-Azabu Hills in 2002, as well as Holland Hills in 2004, an office and residential complex near the Netherlands Embassy (yes, there are no hills to speak of in the Netherlands; the reference is to the embassy, which is on a nearby slope). There is also the controversial shopping mall (controversial because of the historic residential district with funky galleries and boutiques that it displaced) Omotesando Hills in 2005 (Devlin 2005), as well as Roppongi Hills.

The center of gravity of operations for the Mori Building Company is still in Minato Ward, not far from its birthplace in the ward's Toranomon district, with the prime showpiece being Roppongi Hills, which opened in 2003. Figure 6.3 shows the distribution of Mori buildings in central Tokyo, particularly within Minato Ward. However, the company is now no longer local only, as under the leadership of Minoru Mori, the Mori Building Company has branched out from home territory and developed projects in other parts of Tokyo, in other parts of Japan, and even abroad. Most significantly, and quite famously too, the company has entered China, first completing a modest office building called Senmao Building in 1996 in Dalian, then the soaring HSBC Tower in Shanghai's Pudong in 1998, and going for gold with the Shanghai World Financial Center (WFC) that opened in 2008, also in Pudong.[2]

Truth and Accuracy in New Roppongi

In chapter 1, I discussed Roppongi as a place where truth is hard to find, noting that research in the murky world of nightclubs, hostess bars, illegal immigrants, and fast-buck operators requires a superior BS detector. Now, I add that a sensitive BS detector is needed as well in the "New Roppongi." In the stage-managed world of slick-and-glossy publications, commissioned books, and self-serving Web sites, truth is not just shaded, as it is on the streets, but is also created and recreated by big companies' publicity machines. It is just as hard if not harder to get to the bottom of the business decisions of the Mori Building Company or Mitsui Fudōsan (Tokyo Midtown) as it is to get proprietary information from businessmen and -women, formal sector and not, in the competitive entrepreneurial environment of Roppongi. Recall the small-time Russian businessman who yelled at me for asking about how he earned a living. At least here I could

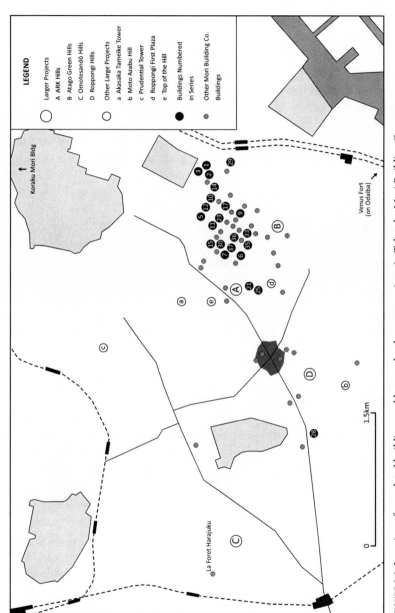

FIGURE 6.3 Location of completed buildings and large redevelopment projects in Tokyo by Mori Building Company, 2007. (Source: Mori Building Company; Erin McCann cartographer)

LEGEND

Larger Projects
A ARK Hills
B Atago Green Hills
C Omotesandō Hills
D Roppongi Hills

Other Large Projects
a Akasaka Tameike Tower
b Moto Azabu Hill
c Prudential Tower
d Roppongi First Plaza
e Top of the Hill

Buildings Numbered in Series

Other Mori Building Co. Buildings

build a personal relationship, and he told me eventually what he was up to: importing cheap cats from Siberia for resale at huge markups to Japanese pet lovers. I did not get this information until after his sweet ride had ended with the arrival of competitors and wiser consumers, but at least I got the information. With respect to studying Roppongi Hills, however, the distance between researcher and truth is even greater, and the road between the two is lined with all manner of gatekeepers and spinmeisters, as well as a very well-oiled Mori (and Midtown) publicity machine. I do my best to learn from what is presented about the New Roppongi by its activist advocates, listen as well to the independent voices, and in the end make my own judgments from what I see and the processing power of my own personal, well-practiced BS detector.

Deconstructing Roppongi Hills

There is an entire book to be written about Roppongi Hills. The first chapter might be about how you need to climb to get to the heart of the project or to surpass other obstacles. Even the base of Mori Tower, the project's soaring centerpiece, is above street level, and from whichever direction one approaches, one needs to ascend just get to the lobby. From Roppongi-dōri there are escalators that help one reach the base level, although they are so narrow that people can ride only in single file. Perhaps that prevents invasions. The same is true at the elevation precipice with Keyakizaka-dōri on the opposite side of Roppongi Hills, as well as at other approaches. At the approach to the Grand Hyatt Hotel there is even a symbolic mountain that has to be circumvented from outside the complex before the reaching the taxi stop in front. There used to be running water and steam vents in the mountain, I suppose like in the mountains outside Tokyo, but they seem to have been turned off, perhaps because the steam was obscuring traffic. From still another direction, the "keep" of Roppongi Hills seems to lie behind a high fortress wall. It reminds me of the Wailing Wall. There are lookout points at the top from which one can be observed as one approaches to climb a difficult, winding staircase. And, of course, everywhere there are cameras, big ones, forbidding and prominent, to remind everyone that eyes are watching as they enter the premises and that they are not in their own place.

It is Minoru Mori's place. He loves the project and promotes it with unrestrained enthusiasm (figure 6.4). About a year before the project opened, he described Roppongi Hills as follows, with no trace of characteristic Japanese modesty: "People will feel they can't die without having visited here once. It will be the ultimate destination for people all over the world."[3] His company's

FIGURE 6.4 Minoru Mori standing proudly with a model of his Roppongi Hills development. The tallest structure is Mori Tower where the Mori Company's offices are located, while the other tall buildings (under Mori's right elbow) are high-priced residential towers. The photograph is from the archives of the Associated Press and comes with a caption that explains that Roppongi Hills will clean the nearby nightlife of "prostitution and shady foreigners." The text seems to be from the same slanted interview that we discussed in Chapter 5 under the heading "Japanese Voices." (Photo courtesy of Associated Press, Shizuo Kambayashi photographer, dated 12/05/2002)

advertising for the project has been no less restrained: an early publicity piece carries the title "Roppongi Hills: The City Where New Ideas Are Born," and a cover photograph taken from the air of the shining new development positioned in Tokyo's center and Mt. Fuji in the background, providing the project with the nation's imprimatur. A curious new term appears in the Roppongi Hills lexicon: "Artelligent City," which refers to "the fusion of art and intelligence in an urban setting" ("Artelligent City" 2004). More specifically, the term is meant to focus (I think) on the project's attention to the arts, its plethora of public art, and its high-technology, "intelligent" buildings that are programmed for energy savings, earthquake countermovements, and other sustainability features. The word reminds me of "Hoterukan," the awkward place with the awkward name blending *hotel* and *kan*, the Japanese word for inn that was built in 1868 at Tokyo's waterfront to contain the first wave of foreigner arrivals (see chapter 2).

"Artelligent City" might also refer to still another distinguishing feature of Roppongi Hills, Academyhills. This is a members-only zone on the fortieth and forty-ninth floors of Mori Tower where, we are told, "new connections germinate and prosper" and insider literati enjoy a library and educational seminars (Mori Building Company 2007, 34). The Mori Web site describes Academyhills as "the intelligence center of Roppongi Hills" (Mori Building Company 2008). A leaflet that is available at the entrance to the library (I am not a member and have not been inside) has a photo of a well-stocked bookshelf and the following text in Japanese and English: "Welcome to Roppongi Hills, a paradise of 'knowledge'. High in the sky on the 49th floor of Roppongi Hills More Tower lies a stylish space where people and knowledge intersect. Here, members leave behind their corporate and academic badges to build network. This is 'Academyhills Roppongi Library'" (reprinted unchanged from original). To my delight, on one shelf of books below the last of those words, in a section of the stacks marked "Books on Japan," directly beneath the *s* in Academyhills, the photo shows what appears to be the spine of my 1998 book about Tokyo. What is more, on another shelf just to the right, appears, without question, the unmistakable image, readable with a magnifying glass, of the spine of my 1997 reference book about Tokyo. Hooray!

Indeed, Roppongi Hills seems to be built on hype and branding, new terms, and catchy slogans. Such is the case, too, with many new products, I believe. Thus, we see another promotion of Roppongi Hills in the form of crafty backlit posters along the underground concourse of the Roppongi subway station that show a nightscape of the tallest buildings of Roppongi Hills and the English-language message "Welcome to Tokyo's Finest Neighborhood." We also see (and read) prominent mention and nonstop praise of Roppongi Hills in Tokyo's various "what's going on in town" and "where to eat" magazine-type publications, of which there are many.[4] There are also already several books about Roppongi Hills, none critical, all or most of them available for sale in the Roppongi Hills gift shop. The list includes: (1) a collection of photographs of Roppongi Hills by Kishin Shinoyama called *Roppongi Hills X Kishin Shinoyama* (2006); (2) a collection of photographs of the Roppongi Hills site taken between 1992 and 2000, before the project's construction started (Ito 2003); (3) a collection of photographs by Chotoku Tanaka of Roppongi Hills with special emphasis on Mori Tower shot from all angles (2004); (4) a slick and glossy bilingual guide to public art in Roppongi Hills that was published by the Mori Art Museum (Nanjo, Ogita, and Machino 2004); and (5) a book produced by Minoru Mori called *The Global City* (Mori 2003). That too is a slick and glossy volume, the souvenir book of the opening exhibition that was held at the Mori Art Museum (April 25–September 21, 2003).[5] The gift shop also sells an array of Roppongi Hills postcards, art prints, souvenir key chains, pens, paperweights, boxed chocolates, crackers, and other logo-imbued snacks.

Roppongi Hills Highlights

The most straightforward way to summarize Roppongi Hills is to say that it is an ambitious and very self-conscious "new town in town," set on its own large footprint, distinct, separate, and even aloof from the fabric of neighborhoods across the streets and other edges. It measures 7.8 million square feet (724,000 square meters) and consists of a more-or-less integrated patchwork of high-rise buildings, mid-rise buildings, parking garages, plazas, and green spaces that Mori has said contains "everything you need for daily life" (Bremner 2002). The paragraphs below will provide my own tour of this new world. A complementary reading, one that is in both English and Japanese and profusely illustrated with superb photographs and detailed architectural drawings, is the special issue of the periodical *Visual Architecture* entitled "Artelligent City" (2004).

What used to be on the site before was also a mixed-use neighborhood, but one that the Mori Company succeeded in having officials in Tokyo government and in the government of Minato Ward designate in 1986 as a "Redevelopment Inducement Area." Capitalizing on the need in urban Japan to mitigate hazards from earthquakes, the whole of Roppongi 6-chōme was marked as a "red zone" and fast-tracked for urban renewal clearance because of crowding, fire-prone construction, and other deficiencies. That a great many other neighborhoods in Tokyo seem even "redder" is beside the point; they were in other parts of the city and were not coveted by the city's largest building and development company. Using all of its resources, the Mori Building Company devised a detailed plan for the sequence of demolitions and new arrangements for displacees, and then for the new shape of the site. That plan was called the "66 PLAN" (pronounced *roku-roku puranu*) in reference to the "six" in the word Roppongi (see chapter 1) and the specific address of the site as Roppongi 6-chōme.

A major occupant of Roppongi 6-chōme, accounting for nearly one-quarter of the land, was the studios of TV Asahi. The owners agreed to move the facility to Mori's nearby ARK Hills, where they were offered new and better accommodations, presumably on favorable terms. Other landowners and tenants, including some industrial land uses, retail businesses, and approximately six hundred resident families were also displaced. Some of the residents were renters in an old-fashioned apartment complex that was erected in 1958 by the Housing Corporation as part of the postwar rebuilding of Tokyo and assistance to people who were poor, while other residences were mostly low-rise, densely built owner-occupied structures. Displacees were compensated for their losses. Many did not go far, as beginning in 1998 the Mori Building Company constructed replacement housing in mid-rise structures on land that it had acquired on nearby streets for those who had once lived in Roppongi 6-chōme. According to ongoing research by a colleague from Philadelphia, Stéphanie Feldman, not yet published, about four hundred of the six hundred families remain in Roppongi Hills as either "partners" or property rights owners and either own an apartment in the development or rent other preferred space (Feldman n.d.). TV Asahi managed to return to its old site after a short stay in ARK Hills and is now in a glamorous facility that counts as one of the attractions in Roppongi Hills.

The centerpiece of Roppongi Hills is Mori Tower, a fifty-four-story (781 feet; 238.1 meters) postmodern icon of steel, glass, and gleaming light that rises self-assuredly above the surroundings (see figure 6.4). It is Tokyo's fifth-tallest building and home not just to the Mori Building Company but also to such enterprises as Ferrari Japan, Goldman Sachs, and many other foreign and Japanese companies. It also houses the ghosts of Lehman Brothers and other former occupants (see below). The top floors house the Mori Art Museum, a top-flight facility with an ever-changing program of magnificent exhibits from both Japan and around the globe. It is certainly the world's highest art. As I write this, the museum is showcasing an exhibit called "A New Era of Indian Art." Other exhibits have included the Global City gala mentioned above, a retrospective on the cultures of Tokyo and Berlin, "China: The Crossroads of Culture," an exhibit about modernist-icon architect Le Corbusier, a walk through ordinary objects made into art by French artist Annette Messager, and an encounter with the astonishing video art of American artist Bill Viola. There is also a fine glass-enclosed and photographer-friendly observation deck (not free) on the level above the museum and, under favorable weather conditions, opportunity to see the city from the edges of helicopter deck on the roof.

> Mori Tower rising high
> Manly piercing the Roppongi sky
> A steel-sheathed beacon against the night
> And postmodern standard setting Roppongi right.

Surrounding the centerpiece are the other land uses of Roppongi Hills. The model in figure 6.4 shows a bit of the layout. In one direction from Mori Tower is the Grand Hyatt Hotel with its better eateries and pubs, meeting rooms and banquet facilitates, and, quite regularly, global celebrity residents. Its front drive has a faux mountain landscape with a running waterfalls and Japan-like steam vents, but the plumbing seems to have encountered problems, and the attraction is only rarely turned on. Perhaps the issue was a having a steam-sodden hotel entryway. Other passages of Roppongi Hills lead through various levels of shopping mall beside and beneath Mori Tower, some completely indoors and others with stores that open to the outdoors. There are more shops in a separate building called Hollywood Plaza (spelled "Holleywood" on the illustration but "Hollywood" elsewhere in Roppongi Hills), and more still along Keyakizaka-dōri (zelkova tree slope street), a busy new thoroughfare that cuts through the development and marks the line between its main commercial zones and the residential parts. There are several glitzy designer emporia along the length of this street (e.g., those of Diane von Furstenberg, Louis Vuitton, Christian Lacroix), and at the end opposite the hotel there is a large book and magazine emporium with a built-in Starbucks and an equally large DVD and CD department on the floor above. For many foreigners and Japanese alike, these particular premises have evolved into a popular singles zone, perhaps an alternative to the Roppongi bar scene, where literate people can pass time and meet others.

Other commercial-use parts of Roppongi Hills include a nine-screen movie theater, the discrete building for the offices and studios of TV Asahi, and a strategically sited singles bar named Heartland near one of the approaches to Mori Tower that is especially popular among the postwork office crowd.[6] There are also lots and lots of restaurants in the complex ranging from some of Tokyo's best and priciest to a "food court" zone near the subway access. All together, Roppongi Hills has almost exactly 115 retail stores of various kinds, plus 99 restaurants, cafés, and bars, and 37 businesses providing various services such

TABLE 6.2 Businesses in Roppongi Hills by type, 2003, 2006, and 2010

CATEGORY OF BUSINESS	NUMBER IN 2003	NUMBER IN 2006	NUMBER IN 2010
Fashion wear	57	45	46
Fashion accessories	12	38	36
Household items	8	11	16
Food stores	6	5	5
Others	16	13	12
TOTAL RETAIL STORES	99	112	115
Hair, beauty, fitness services	7	14	12
Clinics	6	5	5
ATM	4	5	5
Banks	3	4	3
Post offices	1	1	1
Others	11	10	11
TOTAL SERVICE ESTABLISHMENTS	32	39	37
Restaurants	59	56	63
Bakeries/Cafés	6	5	5
Coffee shops	15	17	18
Bars	8	8	8
Food take-out	9	6	5
TOTAL FOOD/DRINK	97	92	99
TOTAL ALL CATEGORIES	228	243	251

Source: Compiled from "Roppongi Hills Floor Guide," 2003, July 2008, and April 2010, Mori Building Company, http://www.roppongihills.com/en/guide/floor_guide/.

as beauty shops, dry cleaning, or medical care—a total of 251 establishments. Although there has been some sifting and sorting since opening day, the mix of business in Roppongi Hills has remained quite stable over the three periods in which I took inventories (table 6.2).

The residential zone of Roppongi Hills consists of six mid- to high-rise buildings on the far side of Keyakizaka-dōri from the main part of the development. There are four buildings known collectively as Roppongi Hills Residences and individually as Buildings A, B, C, and D. They total 793 units, 473 for lease and 350 for sale, and have 640 indoor parking spaces. Buildings B and C have 43 stories each and stand out in the landscape along with big brother Mori Tower, while A and D are 6 and 18 stories high, respectively. Behind these four buildings is Roppongi Sakurazaka Residence (cherry street slope) with 22 residences on 11 floors and 24 parking spaces, while near the book and Starbucks emporium is Roppongi Gate Tower Residence, 44 residences (mostly leased), 15 stories, and parking for 49 vehicles. There is also a supermarket in this building. Not counting the hotel, I estimate that Roppongi Hills has a total residential population of more than 2,000 inhabitants in its 859 apartment and condominium (*manshon*) units.[7] It is these buildings and these 2,000-plus people that Mori advertising promotes as "Tokyo's Finest Neighborhood." The cachet comes at a steep price: according to Mori Building Company rental information, one-bedroom units rent for 550,000 to 570,000 yen per month ($6,000 in round numbers), while a family-sized four-bedroom unit rents for a mere 2,530,000 yen (approximately $28,000) per month. Purchase prices for condominium residences are correspondingly high.

A minimum of six major architectural firms from various nations divided specific parts of the Roppongi Hills design. It was the wish of the Mori Building Company to have different looks or textures in the complex, which the company would strive to integrate, as well as to have an impressive array of "signature" designers whose cachet would, in turn, attract "signature" shops and office tenants. The six architects for Roppongi Hills and their responsibilities are listed in table 6.3.

The designers of Roppongi Hills have gone to extraordinary lengths to maximize the project's greenery and soften the harsh features that are normally part of high-rise environments. The Mori Building Company has been the first and loudest to say as much and has spelled out at every opportunity considerable detail about the landscaping and its declared advantages. For example, the 2007 public relations brochure boasts that Roppongi Hills today has substantially more greenery than the site had before redevelopment (2.56 hectares versus the earlier 1.65 hectares), that it has planted an astonishing 68,000 trees and shrubs, and that the urban heat island in the vicinity of Roppongi Hills has been significantly mitigated. Indeed, a thermograph map of central Tokyo in summer now shows the area around Roppongi Hills as a relatively cool zone in comparison to its stifling surroundings (Mori Building Company 2007, 21). Furthermore, the brochure states (and I have seen this myself on a commercial tour) that there is a rooftop garden in Roppongi Hills with rice paddies. It is atop the Virgin Cinemas complex and measures about 1,300 square meters. The part that is rice covers 130 square meters, enough for an annual harvest of about 60 kilograms (approximately 130 pounds). In what has become an annual routine intended to educate children about time-honored rhythms of

TABLE 6.3 Roppongi Hills architects

ARCHITECTURAL FIRM	MAIN OFFICE	ROPPONGI HILLS RESPONSIBILITIES
Kohn Pedersen Fox	New York & London	Mori Tower
		Grand Hyatt Tokyo
		Keyakizaka Complex
Fumihiko Maki	Tokyo	TV Asahi new building
Conran & Partners	London	Roppongi Hills Residences A-D
		Roppongi Hills Gate Tower
Jerde Partnership	Venice, California	place-making within Roppongi Hills
		Metro Hat
		Hollywood Beauty Plaza
		Virgin Cinemas
		Hillside
Gluckman Mayner	New York	Mori Art Museum
		Museum Cone
Kengo Kuma	Tokyo	Roppongi Academyhills

Source: Mori Building Company.

nature and farm work in Japan, the rice is planted by children on May 5 each year, a national holiday called Children's Day, and then harvested by children in September (Kamiya 2003; "Kids Harvest" 2005). Minoru Mori has said in an interview that the objective of the *tanbo* (paddy field) is to teach city children about elemental Japanese traditions. The idea of that garden, as well as thirteen English and other style gardens on the roofs of other buildings in the complex, is to create a diverse, rooftop biotope complete with birds and insects (Kamiya 2003). As expressed in the Mori Building Company's 2007 brochure, "We [the Mori Building Company] do not simply plant vegetation, but aim to bring the feeling of changing seasons in cities" (20).

The largest and best known of the green zones in Roppongi Hills is a traditional Japanese garden called Mohri Garden. Named after an Edo Period family that once had an estate and garden on the same site ("Mohri" and "Mori" are different names) and designed by either Shoji Ogata and Hachiro Sakakibara (Matsuba 2004, 33) or noted English garden designer Dan Pearson, its 4,300 square meters offer a lovely place for strolling and relaxation in a parklike set-

FIGURE 6.5 Mori Tower and the celebrated *Maman* spider sculpture that is a landmark and designated meeting place near the main entrance.

ting.[8] The garden can also be viewed from above from several vantage points near the base of Mori Tower and enjoyed as a snapshot landscape. There is a small pond, an artificial stream with waterfalls and rapids, areas of exposed rock, winding paths, and a wide mix of trees, shrubs, grasses, and flowers that do indeed introduce the feeling of the four seasons to an urban environment. In the spring visitors can walk among cherry and plum blossoms, and in fall they can enjoy the changing colors of foliage. On a good-weather Sunday, photographers are everywhere.

There are other pleasant public spaces in Roppongi Hills. Roku-Roku Puraza (Six-Six Plaza) sits in the heart of the complex, between the main doorways to Mori Tower and its corridors to shopping malls, movie theaters, and high art on the one side, and the main access to subways below on the other side. There, a long, four-lane escalator cuts through a curious hat-shaped structure called Metro Hat as it connects the subterranean corridors with the lofty level of the plaza. That's where Louise Bourgeois's giant metal sculpture of an egg-carrying spider named Maman stands as a conspicuous centerpiece.[9] It is a landmark that everyone can find and that might soon replace Roppongi Crossing's "Almond" as the neighborhood's principle waiting and meeting spot. Just like "Artelligent City" or "Roppongi Art Walk" seem destined to supplant "Roppongi High-Touch Town" as a neighborhood motto, "Meet you at the spider" or "Meet you at Maman" could well replace "Meet you at Almond" as Roppongi's most familiar apothegm.

From a precipice edge of 66 Plaza, we look down to see Mohri Garden as a whole, which is at street level, and see as well the garden's co-elevationist neighbor, Roppongi Hills Arena. This is still another prominent outdoor public space with memorable design, this one intended for public music performances and other staged events. Its giant speakers, however, thundered down a cleavage between Roppongi Hills erections into the Roppongi neighborhood beyond, violating a basic rule of Japanese neighborliness to be quiet. The result was that the nature and timing of programming in Roppongi Hills Arena has had to be significantly cut back. Too bad, I think, because there were some terrific free concerts the first months after Roppongi Hills opened that now seem to be an "artelligent" idea of the past.

International Roppongi Hills

Roppongi Hills is international, very self-consciously so, like the Roppongi of old. There are foreigners everywhere, even more than it appears to the eye because many foreigners in Japan blend comfortably with the look of the Japanese

TABLE 6.4 Designers of public art in Roppongi Hills by place of birth

MAJOR INSTALLATIONS

ARTIST	NAME OF WORK	PLACE OF BIRTH
Louise Bourgeois	Maman	France
Isa Genzken	Rose	Germany
Choi Jeong Hwa	roboroborobo	Korea
Martin Puryear	Guardian Stone	United States
Sol LeWitt	Bands of Color	United States
Miyajima Tatsuo	COUNTER VOID	Japan
Miura Keiko	True Love	Japan
Mori Mariko	Plant Opal	Japan
Cai Guo-Qiang	High Mountain–Flowing Water	China

STREET FURNITURE

ARTIST	PLACE OF BIRTH
Droog Design	Netherlands
Jasper Morrison	United Kingdom
Hibino Katsuhiko	Japan
Uchida Shigeru	Japan
Andrea Branzi	Italy
Ito Toyo	Japan
Ettore Sottsass	Austria
Yoshioka Tokujin	Japan
Ron Ard	United Kingdom
Thomas Sandell	Sweden
Karim Rashid	Egypt

Source: Mori Building Company and Mori Art Museum, 2004.

population and do not stand out. But the international aspects are clearly on the terms of the Mori Building Company. The company's choice of six architectural firms from different parts of the world to design Roppongi Hills included two firms from Japan, two from the United States, one from the U.K., and one with U.K. and U.S. main offices, and there is an international mix of other invited architects and designers—those who created the public art for the project and those responsible for street furniture (table 6.4). Likewise, we see international

FIGURE 6.6 Entry to Mori Art Museum in Roppongi Hills.

faces in the various institutions and businesses that are part of Roppongi Hills, in what is playing at the movies in the rice-growing nine-screen multiplex theater, in the mix of special exhibits on display at the Mori Art Museum, the origins of goods and fashions in the hundred or so retail stores in the shopping malls of Roppongi Hills, the range of music and chanson that we hear in mall's corridors and on elevators, and in the international mix of cuisines in Roppongi Hills restaurants.

I have hard data on these topics. Consider, for example, that among the 56 restaurants in the complex, 19 are identified as "Japanese" in the 2006 "Floor Guide" brochure, 10 as Chinese, 6 Italian, 4 French, 4 "Western," 2 Indian, and 1 Indonesian. In addition, 8 other restaurants are classified as multinational. Similarly, a review of the historical record of the exhibits that have been held at the Mori Art Museum in 2004–8 (inclusive) reveals the following mix of art origins or featured artists' ethnicities: 8 Japanese, 2 Chinese, 2 Dutch, 2 U.K., and 1 each French, German (a Berlin-Tokyo show), Korean, Russian, and U.S. There were also the works of an artist who was born in Argentina but who has lived for a long time in the United States, an exhibit of works from various parts of Africa, as well as three exhibits described as "Asian mix" and four as "global mix." Other "international" indicators are the mix of ethnicities or national origins of residents in the new Roppongi Hills housing units,[10] the array of origins and languages of books and magazines in the complex's large bookstore—social cruising grounds, the origins and languages of movies available for rent in the neighboring DVD shop, and the mix of corporate and institutional office tenants of Mori Tower. A perusal of the building's directory in the lobby shows American, British, Italian, French, and German firms, in addition to those, like the Mori Building Company, that are Japanese.

Roppongi Hills has also become an increasingly popular venue for the staging of international events such as Japan or Asia premiers of major Hollywood movies, international film festivals, banquet hall celebrations of individual countries' national days, and conferences related to global business or Japan's international trade, among other events. It is also where celebrities from foreign countries sometimes choose to be photographed for publicity during their Japan visits. For example, as a complement to earlier discussion about Russians in Roppongi, I add that Vladimir Putin, then the president of Russia, was photographed in Roppongi Hills in November 2005 in connection with a meeting of a Japan-Russia friendship association to discuss trade between the two nations, as well as in connection with his well-known personal passion for judo. Likewise, the development seems to be emerging as a place where foreigners with an international relations or international affairs agenda choose to gather to seek publicity for their specific causes. One example is a protest march and demonstration by ethnic Uyghurs and their supporters on behalf of independence from China for East Turkestan that I witnessed on the street outside Roppongi Hills (the development is very near the Embassy of the People's Republic of China); while a second example is the April 12, 2010, protest by the Japanese widow of Awudu Samad Abubakar (known locally as Mac Barry and described in news reports as a prince from Ghana) and his many African friends to demand a Japanese government investigation into his death, which took place some three weeks earlier at Narita Airport while he was in the custody of Japanese immigration authorities who were about to deport him.[11]

Roppongi Hills' Reputation

Just what kind of place is Roppongi Hills and what have we gained from its presence? It is important to address these questions because, from the outset, we have seen Roppongi Hills as emblematic of a new chapter in urban living that is being promoted for Tokyo with the greatest energy. I put aside the official Roppongi Hills presentation about Roppongi Hills, which is biased and self-serving, and try to work independently, with any and all available data that do not come from the company itself. That is still another large research project, but I have a start in that direction that I can share. I choose to organize my thoughts under the heading "Roppongi Hills' Reputation" because it was under a similar heading in chapter 5, "Roppongi's Reputation," that I reviewed official-dom's and Mori's case for reclaiming the nightclub district.

I begin the assessment of the New Roppongi world with a critical reading of an official Roppongi Building Company text and an unwonted story about the pond in Mohri Garden. Mohri Pond, it seems, has been stocked with fish from space. That happened on July 25, 2003, when Japanese astronaut Mamoru Mohri (same family name as the park and pond; no relation) presided over a ceremony to introduce some ten thousand *medaka* (killifish) that were direct descendants of the killifish that had orbited the earth in 1994 aboard the space shuttle *Columbia* with Japanese astronaut Dr. Chiaki Mukai. It was some sort of scientific experiment to take the fish into space. With more than a thousand schoolchildren listening in at the pondside gathering, Minoru Mori explained why he was assigning the offspring fish to a life in Roppongi Hills:

> With Roppongi Hills welcoming visitors from around the world, it is very appropriate that we also have created a home for fish that traveled around the world. . . . This pond has been a relaxing refuge for more than 400 years, and now is in the center of one of the most exciting urban complexes ever built. These fish will make us remember that even in the middle of Tokyo we can have intimate contact with nature and animals. I hope that they inspire the curiosity of children who come to Roppongi to see the fish. ("10,000 Descendents" 2003)

Let me catch my breath. Space fish indeed! Fish that have traveled around the globe as a natural complement to Roppongi Hills' human visitors from around the globe? Alien fish in an artificial pond as intimate contact with nature and animals? What's that about? I smell a fishy story. Besides, I heard rumors that the fish may have died; that they did not like Mohri Pond.[12]

I look askance as well at the rice on the roof of the movies complex, the art in the sky, and micro-managed globalism. All of these things are nice (maybe), and maybe even educational or inspiring for children, as the claims decree. They might also be wonderful improvements to Tokyo's cultural life and physical environment. However, what the BS detector keeps sniffing is the plain and simple fact that the Mori publicity machine never puts on the table: Roppongi Hills is first and foremost a huge business. The complex may be a social and architectural experiment too, but business for profit is the bottom line. Whatever great ideas about urban life and design that the project puts forth, one can't forget that there were once thousands of people in Roppongi 6-chōme who were in charge of their own lives and their own businesses on their own land, and now that same space is the purview of one very rich man and one giant, privately owned, for-profit corporation. For Mori and his company, the best idea of all is money. The BS detector will keep flashing until that is acknowledged and all the Mori stories about rice and fish and high-rise heaven are reconciled with that fact.

Is Roppongi Hills "one of the most exciting urban complexes ever built," as Mr. Mori claims again and again? Is it the "ultimate destination for people all over the world," a place that "people will feel that they can't die without having visited" as the boss has been quoted as saying? Is it as widely appreciated around the world, even more than in Japan, as Mr. Mori's Web site message to the world claims? (Mori Building Company n.d.). The answers to all the questions are, of course, "no" across the board: there are lots of clever-looking tall buildings with attached shopping malls, pricy hotels, green gardens, and foreign-looking people all over the globe. A lot of Singapore is that way, and so, too, is a lot of Dubai. The Petronas complex in Kuala Lumpur is that way as well, as is much of Pudong, much of La Defense, London's Docklands and Canary Wharf, Sydney Down Under, the new waterfront area of Yokohama that is visible on a clear day from atop Mori Tower, and, oh yes, Mori's own competitor just a five-minute walk away, Tokyo Midtown. We also have nice, tall buildings with attached shopping malls, green spaces, public art, and rich people even in Philadelphia, where I have lived longest, and in Kyiv, where I live now, not to mention Manhattan, Los Angeles, Chicago, and San Francisco, among other cities. And I won't even get into Babylon, the Forbidden City, Tenochtitlan, Angkor, Mughal Lahore, pre-Golden Horde Kyiv, the Acropolis, the Roman Forum, and Venice, among other "exciting urban complexes ever built." Surely, Mr. Mori's 140-acre shopping mall with art in the sky and rich people next door is not superior to all these great places!

Thus, despite what we are told by the publicity machine, Roppongi Hills is actually something that exists already in various forms in many cities around the world, even to some degree elsewhere in Japan. What is more, some of the very same architects who contributed to Roppongi Hills shaped its older and younger cousins in other countries. Roppongi Hills is, therefore, unique only in specific detail and level of hype, and it is greatly overblown. And because it is continually being overblown by company practice, Roppongi Hills has come to be an easy target for critics who find fault with virtually everything. The blogosphere is alive with assessments that the complex is a confusing mix of designs, motifs, and elevation levels, that it is sterile and overmanaged, that it's a world for the rich with stores and restaurants that are overpriced, that it is exclusivist and undemocratic, that it is arrogant for making claims to having superior arts and intelligence, and even that it looks silly and pretentious.

There is a basic geographical fact to remember about how the Mori Company is reshaping Tokyo: it prefers working on the good side of Tokyo only. That is, Roppongi Hills could have been built in any of the many much needier places in the city, as there are plenty of older neighborhoods in less prestigious wards with overcrowded and outmoded housing, little greenery, inferior community services and facilities, and no "artelligence" whatsoever. Land there could have been gotten much cheaper. But Roppongi Hills was not built in any of these places; it was built instead, by choice, at the hottest edge of Tokyo prestige and real estate. The same is true for every other Mori Building Company project in the city, from the time of the company's founding in 1955 to the present. Roppongi Hills is, therefore, less a benefit for the needy side of Tokyo and more a calculated upgrading of what was already lofty. The children of Arakawa or Katsushika Wards, to name two places on the blue-collar side of town, might have wanted to see space fish and rooftop tanbo too, but such is not to be. Mori does not work there.

Roppongi Hills Lowlights

There are people who say that Roppongi Hills is cursed. I am not a believer in that kind of language, but I do think that it is interesting that there are, apparently, quite a few such people, and that the blogosphere is alive with their theories. One view, attributed to an unnamed feng shui master, claims that the bad luck problem applies to all of Roppongi, Hills and not, and stems from the destruction long ago of ancient temples to make way for Tokyo urbanization. The same thinker also blames Roppongi's long history with a foreigner population for a curse, because "foreigners worship their own deities."[13] Another observer has blamed the unlucky number 13, pointing out that this is the number of the stairway exit from Tameike Sanno subway station that leads most directly to Roppongi, ignoring the fact that no one uses Tameike Sanno station to go to Roppongi because it is far ("Curse" 2008). And then there is a blogger named Mari who entered the following on September 30, 2008, in her blog "Watashi to Tōkyō" (Me and Tokyo). She is dead wrong with her facts, but her earnestness is palpable:

> As a person who works in Roppongi Hills every day, I must tell you it's not so
> great. . . . I just feel that there is something wrong there (trust me!!). Also, I must

tell you one more thing. In Roppongi Hills, there is a small Japanese garden called Mohri Garden. The owner of Roppongi Hills (Mori building) left the garden in fact and didn't build anything in that area on purpose. Because it was the place where the Forty-seven Ronin . . . committed hara-kiri. Yes, here is a new urban legend! (Kanazawa 2008; minor spelling and punctuation mistakes corrected)

The reason that people think that Roppongi Hills is on the wrong side of the supernatural is because of its constant, chronic, and now characteristic run of bad luck since the opening. There is never any lack of new examples. On December 31, 2008, I was back in Tokyo to celebrate the coming of the New Year with my special someone, and I went to Roppongi early in the morning with my laptop to fill in some details in the manuscript. It was a moderately windy winter day, blustery and cold. I saw 66 Plaza roped off from all directions with yellow "caution" tape and uniformed guards in position several feet apart at all sides to make sure that no one crossed the plaza. "What happened?" I asked, expecting an answer about the notorious wind tunnel hazards in Roppongi Hills. Just then a worker with a cart of empty cardboard boxes appeared on the plaza, and the wind took hold of his cargo, blowing it directly at me and the security guard I was questioning. We both had a laugh as we tried to help the worker retrieve his load, but the boxes kept tumbling further and further into forbidden territory. I was forbidden to cross the line to help. For me, the scene of caution tape tied to the legs of Maman the giant spider and then running to the very famous front door of Mori Tower was worth the price of being bonked by a bouncing box.

But no, the caution tape and security guards were not there because of the wind, I learned. The scene was a crime scene, and the security personnel were waiting for the police investigators to arrive. I returned again at 10:00 a.m., as I was advised, and observed as more than two dozen uniformed police officers in blue and gold with "Police Investigation" written across their backs combed through 66 Plaza, taking measurements and searching for a spent bullet. There had been a crime incident the previous night on the plaza precisely between Maman the spider and the main door to Mori Tower, and this was the investigation. There had been a man with a knife, and a police officer had fired a shot into the air to get him to lay down his weapon ("Man Arrested" 2009). After some time, the largest numbers of police were gathered amid the shrubbery at the base of Isa Genzken's "Rose," which I thought was a poignant scene. I took several photographs, but the harsh light of the bright winter morning prevented any of my snaps from being keepers.

That same morning was my first time to see that the stone address marker outside Mori Tower that announced the American financial services firm

Lehman Brothers as a prominent tenant was gone, replaced by a planter. That was another bit of bad news for Roppongi Hills, the shocking announcement heard more or less around the world on September 15, 2008, that this global company had gone bankrupt. Employees lost their jobs, not just in the head-quarters in New York, but also the regional headquarters in London and in Mori Tower, and in other Lehman offices around the world. For Mori Tower, that meant very prominent empty floor space and a painful loss of rental income, although the Mori Company was making face-saving claims already that there was a Plan B for the space and interested new tenants. There were losses as well for the Roppongi Hills residences where many Lehman employees had lived, and a ripple effect to local restaurants, bars, shops, and cultural venues that had counted Lehman employees among the clientele.

What happened to Lehman Brothers happens, of course, from time to time to once-solid businesses around the world. Bad luck, bad business decisions, a weak economy, and bang, even the giants can tumble. What is unusual in this case though, is that for Roppongi Hills this has all happened before—a number of times, as over the short life of Roppongi Hills the Mori Building Company has had bad luck with headliner tenant after headliner tenant. Before Lehman Brothers, the biggest demise was that of Livedoor, an Internet provider and Web portal company that had grown spectacularly from nothing in 1995 to become the darling of Japanese start-ups and the symbol of Japan's turn to a new economy based on information services. The founder, Takafumi Horie, nicknamed Horiemon in Japan, was a rising star and looked comfortable in a new role as one of the wealthiest businessmen in Japan. However, it wasn't to last. On January 16, 2006, the Livedoor offices on the thirty-eighth floor of Mori Tower were raided by authorities who suspected violations of securities laws. Exactly one year and two months later, March 16, 2007, Horiemon was convicted of securities and accounting fraud and was sentenced to two and a half years in prison, and Livedoor was gone. So too, there were scandals at other Roppongi Hills companies: for example, the founder of the asset manage-ment firm Murakami Fund, Yoshiaki Murakami, an associate and neighbor of Horiemon, was arrested June 6, 2006, for a brazen case of insider trading, while another company in the same building, ironically named the Goodwill Group, was implicated in a scandal in its temporary worker division exactly one year later, resulting in the arrests of several company officials and the loss of some 2,400 full-time jobs (Takahara 2008).

This series of company mishaps has people talking about there being a "Hills Tribe" of corporations, a certain type of aggressive, risk-taking, profits-hungry company that seems drawn to having Roppongi Hills Mori Tower as an address. That, in turn, is bad publicity for the remaining companies who want to distance themselves from the bad image. In this regard, as far back as December 31, 2005, the leadership of Yahoo!Japan expressed concern in the *Mainichi Daily News* that their being in Roppongi Hills was a public relations problem and announced plans to move to Mori's competitor, Tokyo Midtown, which they did. The travel company Rakuten left as well before the complex turned five years old, settling in instead at much lower rent in Shinagawa. I have heard that Goldman Sachs, the largest non-Mori tenant in Mori Tower, was able to negotiate a cheaper rent as a result of the buildings' problems.

Other bad publicity has come not from the office tenants but from the Roppongi Hills buildings themselves and from incidents that have happened on the Roppongi Hills grounds. The knife wielder and police warning shot are but one example. Other bits and pieces gleaned from the news are as follows. I arrange them in bullet point format, just as I present bad news from the nightclub sections of Roppongi in chapter 5 to emphasize the parallelism. Both Roppongi and "New Roppongi" seem to be full of bad news and bad publicity, with each relishing in the other's misfortune. Maybe one day the U.S. Embassy in Tokyo will issue warnings to citizens about the dangers of Roppongi Hills, as we saw in the case of warnings about the Roppongi nightclub district. That won't happen, I'm sure, but it is an interesting thought. Here are some Roppongi Hills newspaper headlines:

"Fetus in Bottle Found in Roppongi Hills" (*Mainichi Daily News*, February 21, 2005)

"Nippon Otis Elevator Co ordered checks on some 56,000 lifts nationwide after one of its elevators began shooting sparks in Roppongi Hills" (*Metropolis*, no. 686, May 18, 2007, p. 06).

"Niigata earthquake snapped cable in Roppongi Hills elevator" (*Mainichi Daily News*, August 31, 2005).[14]

"TV Asahi punishes 13 for bill-padding, hiding ¥137 million" (*Japan Times*, September 29, 2006, p. 1)

"2 hid 750 mil. yen in income: Metal-Recycling Roppongi Hills residents accused of tax evasion" (*Daily Yomiuri*, April 2, 2009).

As I edit this page more than a year after writing it, I have today's issue of the *Japan Times* before me and read about the death of a thirty-year-old Japanese woman, apparently a hostess, in the upscale Roppongi Hills Residences B apartment of popular actor and pop singer Manabu Oshio. Both the woman (her name was not given in the news account) and Oshio had been consuming the synthetic drug MDMA (ecstasy). She apparently overdosed; he is under arrest (*Japan Times*, August 7, 2009, p. 2). The bad news keeps coming.

Receding Rhythms in Roppongi Hills

At the end of chapter 5, I wrote about "receding rhythms" in Roppongi's night-club district in the face of all the pressures on the area. I can now write about receding rhythms in Roppongi Hills because of its own problems: the national economy in general remains weak; shoppers and diners spend less; and tenants in Roppongi Hills break their leases and move out either because of bankruptcy or troubles with the law. These problems come together quite visibly as Heartland, the "strategically sited singles bar" just outside Mori Tower, where, from opening day in 2003, the nightly rhythm was a post–working hours "mate market." It was quite a famous establishment and was known especially as a place where highly paid foreign business executives and employees with expat benefits drank beer and cocktails in the company of single Japanese women who had come not just from Roppongi Hills to meet them but indeed from all over the Tokyo metropolis. It was a sizable establishment, much larger that the vast majority of Roppongi's bars, and was very well decorated. When things were going well, the place was packed every evening, particularly right after work as opposed to late at night when it was time to dance elsewhere—so packed, in fact, that the crowds literally spilled outside the establishment into the world of the Roppongi Hills plazas and narrow escalators. Guards had to be hired to contain the drinkers within a certain perimeter and to prevent outdoor Roppongi Hills from becoming a cocktail zone, ironically something like the bad streets of Roppongi.

All of that is now changing, as Heartland has become a victim of not just Roppongi's hard times but more specifically the hard times of Roppongi Hills. The opening text of a recent feature article about the bar in the *Times* of London states, "The party is over for the cash-flashing traders who once propped up Tokyo's Heartland bar—and for the Japanese women hoping to bag themselves a banker" (Lewis 2008). Incomes are down, bonuses are cut or canceled, and a great many jobs have been lost altogether. In fact, quite a few of the "Western playboys," as the article refers to them, have left Japan and gone home. Heartland has fallen quiet, and the young Japanese women who were interviewed for the news article say that their commute to Roppongi was a waste of time and that next time they will "shop" closer to home. Pawn shops and "recycle shops" near Roppongi are now stocked with "trinkets bought in the boom," as both "playboys" and their former girlfriends trade jewelry and designer accessories for needed cash, much like the hostesses from Roppongi who have supplemented incomes by selling the gifts they receive from clients.

"Please Lead Children by the Hand"

Readers who already know Roppongi know that I have been holding back with the worst story of all from Roppongi Hills. The context is a spate of bad designs in Roppongi Hills—architectural and engineering flaws that invite accidents and make the glitzy complex unsafe. There are examples galore: outdoor pavements that are slippery when wet, covered walkways and sitting areas that leak rain, stairways with varying and unpredictable step heights, widths, and depths, even between adjacent steps, escalators that are so narrow that they can be ridden only single file, causing backups of people waiting to board. Visitors complain as well about the wind tunnel effect in open spaces and about the project's maze of walkways and elevations that make orientation difficult. The fix has been to pepper Roppongi Hills with directional signs and maps, with warning signs about accident hazards and, incredibly, with yellow caution tape. The tape is on every stairway, it seems, as an after-the-fact add-on to every single step, signaling that everyone who passes should be careful. There is also duct tape, lots of it. It used on the escalators to span what are apparently poorly joined slats of steel on either side of the movable stairs. The escalators are shiny as can be, being cleaned and polished repeatedly during the course of every day, but as one rides up or down, there is duct tape at the base on both sides every few feet. Duct tape! Unbelievable! All the money that was spent on building an "artelligent" paradise, but the complex depends on caution tape, duct tape, and an extraordinary empire of warning signs (see "Empire of Signs" below) to be habitable.

That brings me to the dangerous, nay deadly, doors in Roppongi Hills, most particularly the famous main door to Mori Tower that killed little Ryo Mizokawa, age six. Ryo and his mother were visiting Roppongi Hills from Osaka Prefecture, and he had run a few steps ahead of her to enter the building first. The sensors failed to detect someone his size in the revolving door, which continued to turn as if there was no obstruction, crushing his head between the moving part of the door and the door jamb. The tragedy happened at 11:30 a.m. on Friday, March 26, 2004, in the presence of his mother and other terrified and helpless onlookers; two hours later in a hospital little Ryo was gone. It should not have happened, because there had been many complaints in the past about the mechanisms of doors at Roppongi Hills, and there

FIGURE 6.7 One of the great many clusters of warning signs of all kinds that are seemingly everywhere in Roppongi Hills. This group of dos and don'ts is about escalator use. The words "Watch Your Step" are posted widely in Roppongi Hills, suggesting that they apply not just to the placement of one's feet but also to a wider meaning of the term.

were reports of at least thirty-two incidents on record where people had been struck. There were also records of at least two cases of injuries to children from Mori's revolving doors. Yet, nothing was done until after young Ryo died. And what happened then was public finger-pointing back and forth between the developer, the door's manufacturer, and engineers—everyone blaming the next person to draw attention away from themselves. In the end, three executives in charge of the operations of Mori Tower were convicted of negligence and sentenced to prison terms, and all the doors in the complex (and in many other buildings in Japan) were changed to a different design. Also, yellow caution signs were pasted on the glass surface of every new door in Roppongi Hills with the following admonition: "Please lead children by the hand" (figure 6.8).

There is now an engraved steel plaque affixed to an exterior wall of Mori Tower near the spot where Ryo Mizokawa was crushed. It does not mention his name, nor is there an apology. It simply says that as a result of the accident there has been a "scientific investigation" of the doors in Roppongi Hills and that all

FIGURE 6.8 "Please lead children by the hand"—one of a great many instructional signs at Roppongi Hills. This one appeared after a tragic incident.

the doors have been changed. My translation of the full text on the plaque reads as follows:

REGARDING THE REVOLVING DOOR ACCIDENT AND THE STORAGE OF THE DOOR THAT CAUSED THE ACCIDENT

On March 26, Heisei 16, a child lost his precious life at the big automatic revolving door located at the main entrance of Roppongi Hills.

The cause of the accident has become clear under the scientific investigation of the safety of the revolving door conducted by "Door Project" (representative: Prof. Yotaro Hatamura of Kogakuin University). Besides removing all revolving doors from Roppongi Hills, in order to remember the lesson of this accident, together with the seller of the revolving doors—Miwa Tajima, Inc., we have stored the doors in its factory in Irima County, Saitama Prefecture.

We are aiming to create a safer and more worry-free town.

—March, Heisei 18, Mori Building Company

The Number of the Beast

Oh, what the heck! This is the sixth part of chapter 6; I've mentioned sixes throughout this book, and I might as well put this bit of silliness on the table, just for the record. Let's have some fun with the number 666. For those readers from cultural traditions that might not be aware, the fact is that among some people in the Western or Christian worlds, this particular combination of numbers is, let's say, bad feng shui. It is referred to as the Number of the Beast and derives from the Book of Revelation in the New Testament of the Christian Bible, where there is a vague apocalyptic but often-repeated warning about some unspeakable, underlying evil associated with this combination of digits. It has been linked by various interpretations to all of the following, plus others: the bad Roman emperor Nero; the concept of the antichrist; the supposed dangers of one-world government; microchips, bar codes, and credit cards; and even the tonsured haircut that Protestant Reformationist Martin Luther disliked about Roman Catholic priests. Knowing this, how could I not divulge the many links between Roppongi Hills and that ominous number?

I begin with a reminder that the word *Roppongi* means "six trees." I add that the address of Roppongi Hills is number 6-chōme of Roppongi machi. Then I note that the main public plaza of Roppongi Hills would have as its address the number 6 subdistrict (*banchi*) of number 6-chōme, as that space had before the coming of the big footprint. That's 666. That plaza is called Roku-Roku Puraza (66 Plaza), and it's in "Six Trees." That's 666 too. In that plaza just outside the main doors to Mori Tower is the large eight-legged spider sculpture named Maman; two of its legs are planted in transplanted earth, while six encroach on the paved surface of 66 Plaza. That's 666 again. Moreover, Roppongi Hills was designed by not one and not five major architectural firms, nor by seven, but by exactly six. That means that this neighborhood, one that takes its name from six samurai in history whose family names happened to be six different types of trees, is now being remade by six global (read "one-world") architectural firms in the employ of Mr. Mori, an imperious man whose name, like that of Nero, has four letters, and that as a clincher happens to be the Japanese word for *forest* (more than six trees). I think that we have the makings of an urban legend here!

Tokyo Midtown (Burberry and Bamboo)

In comparison to Roppongi Hills, Midtown has a taller office tower, a larger Japanese garden, a superior shopping mall, and a footprint almost as large that

FIGURE 6.9 Tokyo Midtown as seen from Mori Tower, 2007.

was acquired with less pain and controversy. That must rile the Mori Building Company, although I've never seen it written or heard anyone in authority say it. It is clear that the two are sharp competitors, the Mori Building Company on the one side and Mitsui Fudōsan, the developer of Tokyo Midtown, on the other. One can pore through the various brochures, commissioned books, and other publicity materials that both companies have issued, and only rarely does one company mention the other company's nearby project. Furthermore, the

FIGURE 6.10 "Burberry and bamboo" in the Tokyo Midtown shopping mall.

great many photographs that both companies have published to show off their Roppongi projects almost always seem to be taken from angles that do not show the other's sky-piercer. Yet, the distance between the Mori Tower and Midtown Tower is only 555 meters as the Roppongi crow flies, and the sightlines from one project to the other are plentiful, as are prospects where both developments can

be seen at once. The Mori side seems to be especially reticent about acknowl-
edging its near neighbor.

Tokyo Midtown was opened in March 2007. The site measures 6.1 million
square feet (569,000 square meters) and was not a challenge to assemble because the land was once the main offices of Japan's National Defense Agency
and became available as a single unit when "Japan's Pentagon" moved to another
part of the city. There is probably a fascinating inside story to be told about
how the decision was made in the Japanese government to vacate Roppongi
and build new facilities in Ichigaya in Shinjuku Ward. Without doubt, the high
price that the Roppongi land would command in the marketplace was part of
the Defense Agency's motivation for moving, as was perhaps a desire to dis-
associate from the rowdy neighborhood that it had found itself in (Asakura
2000). A second fascinating story would be about how Mitsui Fudōsan and
partners came to own the property instead of Mori and or likely competitors, as less than a full year elapsed between the official announcement in
April 2001 that the land would become available for redevelopment, the
commencement of competitive bidding, and the transfer of title to the new
owners. It was a six-company consortium (there's that number again!) that
actually won the bid and developed the concept. The term *Midtown* comes
directly from Manhattan, New York City, a place that the developers said is
"cherished as a venue of recreation and relaxation awash in creativity and
communication."[15]

Midtown Tower is Tokyo's tallest building, measuring 248 meters (814 feet),
and is the fourth-tallest building in Japan (the tallest is Landmark Tower in
Yokohama). In contrast to Mori Tower, which has a curved look, this building
is blocky. The rest of the Midtown complex is also rectangular, in contrast again
to Roppongi Hills, which has considerable architectural detail that is rounded,
conical, or otherwise curved. In fact, the straight-line geometry and right angles
of the Midtown complex are so pronounced that I am reminded of the popular
designer line from the United Kingdom, Burberry. The colors fit too, as Midtown
is mostly a blend of brown, beige, black, and white tones, like the most famous
of the Burberry patterns, the one called "haymarket check" or "Burberry classic
check."[16] The Midtown grid is very nicely softened by abundant use of greenery, particularly young, light, and tall bamboo. In outdoor spaces such as the
main plaza, the bamboo's motion in the wind is an added architectural success.
Like Roppongi Hills, the plaza and other spaces use falling water to muffle city
noises and create architectural barriers. However, Midtown has no giant spider.
Instead of Maman, we find stylized "donut" sculptures: on the main plaza is one
in glistening black by Kan Yasuda and called *Key to a Dream*, while another, by

the same artist, sits under a glass roof a floor below, is of white marble, and is called *Shape of Mind*.

The leading office tenants of Tokyo Midtown are some well-known companies: Fujifilm, Fuji Xerox, Yahoo!Japan, and Konami, a top maker of video and arcade games, slot machines, anime toys, and publications, and other contemporary icons of Japan's playful side. The complex also has a section of residential high-rise buildings, a luxury 250-room Ritz-Carlton Hotel, and a multilevel shopping mall with the copycat name Galleria. There are about fifty shops and fifty bars and restaurants of various kinds and various international flavors. Some of the most famous establishments include the first Terence Conran restaurants in Japan, Dean & DeLuca, and the interior design store Muji. There is no art in the sky, but the complex has a fine art museum nonetheless, the Suntory Museum on the third floor, relocated from a previous location in Tokyo's central business district. There is also an exhibition building conceived by fashion designer Issey Miyake and architect Tadao Ando that is dedicated to promoting new design ideas, a photography gallery in the Fujifilm part of the complex, and a very fine venue for concerts and other stage performances called Tokyo Billboard Live.

Like Roppongi Hills, the Midtown project boasts of design details that contribute to Tokyo greening. The 40,000-square-meter (ten-acre) Midtown Garden is the highlight. It combines a new green space with an existing park called Hinokichō Park to make a beautiful and diverse zone of open lawn, fountains, sculpture, places for sport and children's play, and an appealing Japanese garden with a pond, steam, waterfalls, and superbly arranged combinations of rock and vegetation. Other greenery is on rooftops. The panorama from the garden is the future of Tokyo: new tall buildings for Japanese and foreign companies of the global economy; construction cranes heralding more and taller buildings to come; and blocking any view of Mori Tower, the glistening and grilled giant edifice of Midtown Tower itself.

Also as in Roppongi Hills, rhythms abound in New Roppongi. On workdays there are office workers in business suits scurrying back and forth, lunch-time and after-work gatherings and relaxation in the project's restaurants and public spaces, and tidy groups of housewife friends from the suburbs who gather during the day while their husbands are at work and children in school. They refresh friendships as they shop, visit art galleries, and linger over tea or coffee. In the evenings, many of the office workers extend their workdays to discuss business over dinner and beer, and sometimes linger into the night as groups and become tipsy.[17] Some of them migrate in the course of the evening from the more formal environs of Midtown (or Roppongi Hills, as the case may be) to explore the shadier side of Roppongi. They become favored targets for African streetmen and other touts, as such salarymen groups are often new to the old Roppongi, somewhat naive, already a bit inebriated, and more susceptible to enticing sales pitches. The New Roppongi also has lots of couples on evening dates—nicely dressed young men and women who meet after their respective workdays have ended and spend their time together exploring the new environs and selecting where to dine. Many of them shop as well and come to dinner with crisp shopping bags from popular stores in the mall. Weekends and holidays are also times for couples to see Midtown (and Roppongi Hills), as well as for mom, pop, and the kids, older people, and various other combinations of Tokyo demography. There are tourists too, Japanese and foreigners, sometimes visiting independently, sometimes as part of guided tours. Cameras abound, even among couples on dates and housewife reunions, although there are signs posted widely that photography is not allowed.

The National Art Center and the Roppongi Art Triangle

A third glistening addition to New Roppongi is the National Art Center, a 14,000-square-meter taxpayer-funded art museum and exhibition facility that opened January 21, 2007, on a site that had formerly housed a research facility of the University of Tokyo. It is the Japanese government's fifth art museum, after two others in Tokyo and one each in Kyoto and Osaka. It has no holdings of its own but specializes in traveling art. Exhibitions that I have seen myself include one centered on Vermeer and his "Milkmaid," another on Modigliani, one on Monet, Avant-Garde China, a collection of Picassos, and the museum's opening show, featuring the works of metabolist architect Kisho Kurokawa. The new building is spectacular. It was designed by Kurokawa and is a wonder of glass and steel and waves and cones, as well as other shapes and materials. According to an interview with Kurokawa for the periodical *Architecture Week*, the intent was for the building to be ambiguous and confusing, as good art is supposed to take people into a maze and make them think. In the architect's own words: "One of my intentions with the design was to be fuzzy. . . . Great art and architecture should be fuzzy. If it is easy to understand, it is functional like a factory" (Liddell 2007). The National Art Center is certainly not like a factory, I agree, but "fuzzy"? That's not the word I would have chosen. A recently published assessment by two Tokyo-based foreign architects seems more on target: they describe the National Art Center as being a "mature, fully grown building" that is "in sync with mainstream appetites," and that is "national" because it is "in accord with the establishment" (Worrall and Solomon 2010, 146).

FIGURE 6.11 National Art Center as seen from Mori Tower.

The three new art facilities combined—the National Art Center, the Mori Art Museum, and the new facility for the Suntory Museum of Art—are intended to make Roppongi a significant venue for seeing great, world-class art. The combination is being referred to as the "Roppongi Art Triangle" or the main destination points of a "Roppongi Art Walk." I've also seen the term "Roppongi Mile" applied to the museums complex. Whatever it is called, it is a truly central focus of the New Roppongi: it is daytime-oriented, sophisticated and high in culture and refined taste, and geared to a new class of people who will be the next Roppongi-zoku (Roppongi tribe). Instead of mingling with forgettable foreigners in the netherworlds of disco and hip-hop, the next Japanese clientele will come to Roppongi to be enriched by the artistic and material treasures of the wealthy countries of the world and by the foreigners who represent them. These Japanese will be more genuinely international, as their global experiences will be higher, deeper, and richer, and their foreign contacts will be wealthier, better dressed, and certainly better behaved. Figure 6.13 shows a next-generation Japanese couple in Roppongi getting oriented to the new neighborhood and its ways.

Indeed, it might be that the next generation of Roppongi consumers will

FIGURE 6.12 Inside the National Art Center.

eventually reclaim the Roppongi night as well as the day. Perhaps as an experiment, arts promoters in the neighborhood are now advertising the advent of a Roppongi Art Night, scheduled from sundown (5:59 p.m.), March 28, to sunrise (5:32 a.m.), March 29, 2009. It is to feature arts all night long at various New Roppongi venues, including a promised "giant fire-breathing robot" that will light the night with flames. If the party is good and the crowds stay until the end, it will be the first opportunity for Roppongi's morning crows to savor tastes of a vastly different sort.

Is It Gentrification?

Yes, of course it is gentrification, without a doubt! Not only that, it is planned gentrification, stage-managed gentrification, gentrification that the Mori Building Company, Mitsui Fudōsan, Governor Ishihara, and other critics of the recent Roppongi have been working, directly and indirectly, to achieve. My understanding of the word is a change in an urban setting in which wealthier or more privileged "gentry" replace poorer residents and business makers, or when the physical fabric of that part of the city (that is, the housing, shopping, and

FIGURE 6.13 A new generation of Roppongi-zoku getting oriented to the redevelopment landscape. The photo was taken near the National Art Center.

entertainment facilities) is upgraded or redeveloped to fit not primarily those people who had been there all along, but the specific tastes and deeper pockets of gentry-class newcomers (Smith and Williams 1986). So, yes, of course it's gentrification when we read about "a much needed facelift" for Roppongi that will come with the arrival of "the top-crust of foreigner population," as an alternative to "the lowlife loitering around today," to repeat quotations from an article discussed in chapter 5. The title of that article confirms gentrification as well: "Tokyo Complex Targeting Rich" (Kageyama 2002).

As I look around Roppongi, I see that almost all the new apartment-condominium buildings are luxury units that cost far beyond the means of the vast majority of Tokyo's population. That will almost certainly be the case for Atlas Tower Roppongi, a twenty-nine-story residential structure that is being built near the center of that triangle formed by Midtown Tower, Mori Tower, and the National Art Center; the developers promise potential investors an extra measure of status and exclusivity, central location, and great views. It is also the case with the many "serviced apartments" that have been built recently in Roppongi and adjacent neighborhoods. This is a fairly new type of housing arrangement, common as well in many other cities around the world, that caters especially to a highly mobile population of business travelers and others who require stays longer than what is typical for a hotel but shorter than the usual minimum for apartment rentals. Individual apartments are attractively furnished and include all kitchen needs, linens, towels, and so on, as well as Internet services, security, laundry and cleaning services, access to a fitness center, and many other amenities. The usual stays range from a week or two to several months. In Japan, such units are upscale variants of what have been called "weekly mansions," also short-term, furnished rental units, but typically quite small and below international standards in services and amenities. Increasingly, foreign and Japanese companies provide serviced apartments for expatriate employees on short contracts, as well as for Japanese workers who might be in town on period assignments.

In Roppongi, the buildings with serviced apartments are all new (as opposed to remodeled) and, in most cases, have replaced older, cheaper apartment buildings. There are now quite a few such structures in the neighborhood, largely because of its nearness to the offices of international companies, with several providers, including chains named Somerset, Oakwood, Asahi Homes, and the Mori Building Company's own Mori Living, having multiple buildings. That such housing targets "top-crust" foreigners is seen in Somerset's Web site advertisements and in the promotional posters that it has hung in Roppongi. We see only model-like Caucasian men and women in these photographs, relaxing with exaggerated smiles in spacious apartments, toasting one another with wine glasses in front of a backdrop with Tokyo Tower, and working out together in a fitness center ("Somerset Roppongi" n.d.). Mori Living's advertising text about its own serviced housing units sets the context:

> Roppongi Hills is a neighborhood where an international atmosphere permeates the air and people from all over the world meet and mingle. Here is the cultural heart of Tokyo, including the Mori Arts Center, shopping that ranges from luxury brands to casual cafes, a TV network headquarters, a 9-screen premier cinema complex, and a luxury, five-star hotel. Plus, a clinic and childcare center, banks, and a post office—everything you need is close at hand. Roppongi Hills is a space that sets new standards for life in the city, designed with top priority given to the comfort and enjoyment of the people who live here. It sets the standard for a relaxing new lifestyle. (Mori Living n.d.)

We pass an office building under construction on Gaien Higashi-dōri, the main commercial street through the neighborhood. It is to be called Axall Roppongi (who knows where these names come from?), the builder is Shimizu

Construction Company, another giant of the construction state, and the site is directly across the street from the main entrance of Tokyo Midtown. An artist's rendering on the protective fence at the construction site shows a handsome glass-skinned building with attractive postmodern form, as well as a collection of sample people out front, all of whom appear to be in their happy twenties. There are some Japanese, including a woman wearing one of those antiallergy, antiflu face masks that are so common in Japan, but at least six of the twelve individuals drawn are clearly foreigners. Interestingly, among them is a disproportionate number of beautiful blonde females. They wear miniskirts, while the equally attractive young Japanese women who are shown are more modestly dressed. I have long considered such artwork, as well as other aspects of publicity documents about construction and redevelopment, as cultural texts that give insights to the biases of the bosses and the future that is to come (Cybriwsky 1986; Perin 1977).

Normally, the turnover of residents and businesses in a gentrifying neighborhood is not totally complete, as various old-timers find ways to stay, usually as a minority presence. Such is the case even within the controlled confinements of a place like Roppongi Hills. Because both law and custom in Japan provide tenants with secure rights vis-à-vis landowners, the Mori Building Company had made accommodations for quite a few of the long-standing residents from the old houses in Roppongi 6-chōme to live in the high-rise building that replaced them. Likewise, some of the privately owned businesses continue in new structures in the new surroundings. But in Roppongi Hills and not far outside its boundaries, it is all very much according to plan: new structures, high rents, upscale businesses and cultural programming, and a superior assortment of new, upscale residents in the apartments and new, upscale business folk in the malls. I reflect on this every time I pass Keyakizaka intersection at one of the formal edges of Roppongi Hills: there, across the street from the Roppongi Hills residential zone and the local, quite upscale supermarket is your local, conveniently located, new-in-the-neighborhood dealership of Bentleys and Rolls Royces, while on Gaien Higashi dōri, almost midway between Roppongi Crossing and Tokyo Tower, is where you can go to make a choice between buying a Porsche or a Lamborghini.

Although I did not have direct access to smoking gun information about the process in Roppongi, I can imagine that the pressure on its last pockets of single homes must be extraordinarily high. For decades now, in all the hot, high-rising neighborhoods in central Tokyo, gangsterish "land turners" called *jiageya* push hard at owners to sell. They are paid as bounty hunters with packets of cash on delivery of signed contracts from homeowners and shop owners to sell their land by developers and their trough-feeding intermediaries. They have been known to use every trick possible to undermine community solidarity, intimidate nonmovers, and change reluctant minds. When it really matters, there is even violence (Kaplan and Dubro 2003, 178–80). Occasionally, homeowners who have had enough of the pressure and feel brave post signs that their property is not for sale. The gap between what rents are today in ordinary buildings with great locations and what they would be from that square of ground in a much taller building designed to luxury standards is almost certainly so large that some of the worst jiageya practices are almost certainly employed in Roppongi against uncooperative landowners. The end result for a neighborhood being targeted for such remaking is, almost certainly, its gentrification.

It is interesting to go back full circle in the history of Roppongi and recall that in the early days, in Edo time, this was yamanote, the rarified higher lands of the city where samurai had their estates. At least six of them happened to have "tree names," which led somewhere along the line to a derivative name for the neighborhood itself. Now, the "elite hills" have returned thanks to Mr. Mori ("Mr. Forest") and his competitors in places like Roppongi Hills, Moto-Azabu Hills, Atago Green Hills, Holland Hills, and Omotesando Hills, and in Tokyo Midtown. Perhaps we can apply the words "foreigner hills" to the setting. Or, maybe instead of saying that Roppongi is being gentrified, we should take a longer-term perspective and say that it is actually "re-gentrification" that is taking place.

CHAPTER SEVEN

Roppongi Reflections

Empire of Signs

In 1970, the Five Man Electrical Band wrote a song called "Signs" in which the lyrics complained that everywhere one looked, there were posted signs about what to do and what not to do in a particular area. Their words were quite prescient about how social control would evolve in the surveillance of closed-circuit television (CCTV) and the overtly privatized urban spaces of cities everywhere about a generation later and would apply quite comfortably to the New Roppongi of today, a landscape in which posted signs abound to let one know who is welcome and who is not and to teach the neighborhood's new rules. I return to the topic initiated in chapter 5 under the heading "Sign Language," as the neighborhood has become, like the title of the famously impenetrable book about Japan by linguist-anthropologist Roland Barthes (1982), a veritable *Empire of Signs*. Especially in Roppongi Hills and Midtown, but also in the heart of the leftover nightclub district, there are signs everywhere, saying, just like the band sang, that we should do this, we should not do that, and that the sign owners will do the thinking for us. Some of the signs are pedestrian, as in routine "No Smoking" and "No Parking" signs, but other signage is over the top and obsessive. In Roppongi Hills, for instance, in addition to the routine signs, there are fully eight posted commandments for escalator use (e.g., "Do Not Run Walk" and "Please Stand within the Yellow Lines"), five strong admonitions on the helicopter pad at the top of Mori Tower (e.g., "Remain on Wooden Deck," "Beware Strong Wind," and "Keep Hold of Children") and no less than sixteen posted commandments of behavior in Mohri Garden (including "Treat the Trees with Care," "Do Not Touch the Medaka," and "Do Not Throw Coins or Stones into the Pond").

The same spirit marks Tokyo Midtown. One sign, on a device with an emergency call button to the police, informs that the area is under camera surveillance and then adds in Japanese and English: "Please do not get into mischief." Other directives posted on the property say that pets must be placed in a "cage" before entry into the buildings and that photography is forbidden. It is interesting, I think: here in New Roppongi, in the heart of a photo-taking nation, in an attractive place where good people are being encouraged to go for clean fun, in a complex that houses offices of a giant film and photography company (Fuji), and where there is a very fine photography museum, the sign says, "Do Not Take Photographs." Maybe their concerns are with architectural photography, which is always difficult to do well and often proprietary, instead of with people photographing themselves, but the signs make no distinctions.

New Roppongi is an Orwellian world, at least proto-Orwellian. Not only are there police and security guards seemingly everywhere, but there are also CCTV security cameras in every corner of this emerging terrain, and the leaders' agents are watching. One doesn't know where the peering eyes are nor how many pairs there are, but the cameras are visible on all sides, and one is aware of being followed and filmed. Perhaps there are big rooms with TV monitors somewhere in the bowels of Mori Tower and Tokyo Midtown filled with sharp-eyed technicians manipulating cameras, scanning left and right, and zooming in for details whenever they like. Beware! It was freer in the nightclub district, I think, even with all the warnings about crime. But here on the private, corporate-owned properties of Roppongi Hills and Tokyo Midtown, one is told directly, again and again, what to do and what not to do, and one is continually being watched. It is a litany of safety tips, because it would be inconvenient if we should get hurt on the property (poor Ryo Mizokawa), as well as rule after rule after rule, all set unilaterally, everything from skateboards and open flames to unauthorized gatherings and photography. Maybe next there will be requirements about how to dress (various business establishments already do this) and about being physically fit and good looking ("modelish" nightclubs do this already). Hmm . . . New Roppongi spins from the old.

These thoughts remind me of the "Big Brother is watching us" presentation that author Mike Davis made some years ago in his famous eye-opening account of newly renewed, neoliberal, nonliberal Los Angeles (Davis 1992). They also connect to a detailed story about surveillance and control of public space in Japan specifically that was published in a recent issue of the periodical *Urban Studies* by David Murakami Wood, David Lyon, and Kiyoshi Abe (2007). That article takes a very interesting long view, ranging from the times of the shōguns to today's era of high-tech security operations, to demonstrate that surveillance of citizens to support the interests of property owners and an insecure state has been a long-established practice in the country. That argument, in turn, provides historical context for understanding still another posted sign in

FIGURE 7.1 Chaos and craziness along Gaien Higashi-dōri, nighttime Roppongi.

Roppongi Hills, one prohibiting all "acts that impede in any way the operation of Roppongi Hills."

Let me return to Tokyo Midtown and its rule against taking photographs. At every entry to the complex we see the admonition "Do not take photographs" and a drawing of a camera within a red circle across which is the characteristic red slash. Too bad, because there is something I want to show you. Aha, I think, I can read their sign literally, take none of their photographs, leaving them precisely wherever they have left them, and instead can snap a few of my own. I did just that and got away with it. Now I can compare two photos, one from New Roppongi taken during the day in Tokyo Midtown and one from Roppongi, taken late at night on Gaien Higashi-dōri.

What do readers think? The night photo is chaos: people everywhere, one on top the other literally, not all of them sober, and all sorts of faces and races. It might even show incipient miscegenation. I took the picture from a second-floor window of a bar during the nighttime rush hour on one of the main blocks of Roppongi. It did not seem to be against any rules to shoot the photo, and no one complained. The other photo is from a Sunday afternoon in Midtown and may have broken rules. We see that everyone is neatly distributed polite dis-

FIGURE 7.2 Order and composure in Tokyo Midtown, daytime New Roppongi.

tances apart, paired off or in manageable small groups, sober and well behaved, and maybe even in discrete groups by ethnicity. I call that an "everything in its place" scene, after a brilliant book by Constance Perin, an anthropologist who studied, of all things, the social meaning of zoning rules in the United States (1977). Perhaps the two photos together summarize some of the major threads of this book, Roppongi Crossing, conflict and change, chaos and order, spontaneous fun and fun doled out.

Roppongi Crossing as Art Exhibit

The name *Roppongi Crossing* is still best known in Tokyo with reference to a wild, international nighttime pleasure district, and its coffee shop Almond is still remembered as a landmark for meeting before going out. However, the term *Roppongi Crossing* has now been borrowed by the Mori Building Company as the catchy title for a series of art exhibitions in the Mori Art Museum, Almond has been moved aside at least temporarily, and in Roppongi Hills a new landmark for meeting is being promoted to supplant the Roppongi Crossing icon—Maman, the eight-legged spider in front of Mori Tower. It might be that eventually the Mori art exhibit usage of the term *Roppongi Crossing* will supplant the original meaning and that "meet you at Maman" will supplant "meet you at Almond" as Roppongi vernacular. That would fit the Mori agenda of reshaping Roppongi in a way that makes Roppongi Hills the focus of the district. Place making, as we have seen, is a campaign that is waged on many fronts: police action, real estate development, public education via signage, and obsessive community spruce-up and cleanup, among others. Now we see that the campaign also employs appropriation of geographical toponymy and substitution of architectural landmarks. (The Midtown complex has its own parallel story: "Meet you at the donut in front of Midtown" [referring to sleek sculpture by Kan Yasuda at the street-level front of the complex] has probably already entered the local vocabulary).

There have now been three Roppongi Crossing art exhibits at the Mori Art Museum in 2004, 2007, and 2010, with works by 57, 36, and 20 artists, respectively. By design, all of the artists are Japanese, mostly younger ones but also some "veterans," as the publicity words it, and the intent is to showcase Japanese talent as well as to explore the "essence and potential of Japanese art." Media include photography, sculpture, installations, video, and performance, and the works are typically large, often with a single piece occupying an entire room, and shocking, puzzling, amusing, and otherwise enjoyable.[1] It is an exciting event (I attended all three) and speaks well for the artists and the juries that selected them, for the Mori Art Museum, and for Roppongi Hills. The exhibits seem to be well attended, and there are said to be quite a few visitors who do not normally go to art museums but who find this world opened to them as they explore the New Roppongi exhibits. It's a greatly positive story. I just find it ironic that the search for what defines contemporary Japanese art takes place in a development that is placeless by design and devoid of Japaneseness. Roppongi Hills is exactly what I have in mind when I caution about "the possible end of Japan."

Parallels: New Roppongi and Old

It is interesting to compare the two Roppongis side by side and ponder the parallels. Both aspects of the neighborhood, for instance, are consumer oriented, with the old Roppongi offering nightclubs and other entertainment spots, while the new offers high art, brand-name shopping, and upscale restaurants and cocktail bars. Both work hard to snare customers, old Roppongi with street touts, promotional leaflets, and bright, bright street signage, while New Roppongi employs printed guides, maps, and leaflets in multiple languages, information booths staffed with pretty girls, and the publicity that is available in glossy "what's happening in Tokyo" magazines. Likewise, both are international, certainly in the mix of customers on any day or evening and, I think, in the mix of people who work in them. The specific list of countries might differ between old Roppongi and New Roppongi, as might income levels and other indicators of socioeconomic standing, but both aspects of the neighborhood, old and new, rank very high as "foreigner OK" zones in Japan. It would be interesting to compare ethnic patterns in detail. Who works in the kitchens of Roppongi Hills and Midtown? Who changes sheets in the Grand Hyatt and the Ritz-Carlton? What differences are there between service workers in the formal economy of New Roppongi and those in both the formal and informal aspects of nighttime Roppongi?

Both nighttime Roppongi and New Roppongi are popular among different clientele, each depending on its own respective customer base and each having its own loyal regulars. Both also have critics and haters. This is certainly true for the nightclub district, which has many aspects to despise and many dangers and is, perhaps in the opinions of a majority of Tokyoites, a place to avoid. Unexpectedly, the "critics and haters" aspect turns out to apply as well to Roppongi Hills and perhaps to Midtown too. Some people are spooked by the bad luck. Still others complain about stumbling on steps, getting lost in the maze of commerce, or following orders in the environment of rules. There are also those who resent the new landscapes on principle, calling them elitist, planned gentrification, and private spaces masquerading as public. My dog-loving someone special vows never to return to Tokyo Midtown after being scolded about walking our two tiny dogs on a pathway through the "public" gardens. Other critics are simply ambivalent: "What's the big deal about these places? There are shiny new commercial complexes like these in every city. Over-hype deserves a boycott."

And then, of course, there is the parallelism between two deaths, that of Lucie Blackman from the nighttime Roppongi and Ryo Mizokawa in the family-friendly daylight of Roppongi Hills. Yes, the two are very different stories and not connected, but they need to be linked on the same page nonetheless. Both deaths could and should have been avoided. In the case of Lucie, it was known that Joji Obara was a dangerous man with a taste for pretty Western girls and was trolling Roppongi's hostess clubs. He could do so because he was regarded as a favored, free-spending customer. In the case of Ryo's death, there had been warnings that doors in Roppongi Hills were malfunctioning and that people were getting hurt, but nothing was done until it was too late. The similarity between the two tragedies is that both took place in a context where immediate goals for maximizing private business took precedence over the need to do something about dangers that lurked.

The Pace of Change

Roppongi changes faster than I can type. Every return to Tokyo, even if it's only for personal reasons and not directly for this book, and almost every walk through the neighborhood yield another bit of news, a new incident, or another something that needs to be corrected because what I had already written is now out of date. This time it's the building right at the corner of Roppongi Crossing, a narrow nine-story structure named the Amagi Building. It has emptied of all but one of its tenants, including an Internet café that I used to frequent, and will soon be a "ghost building," a seemingly fine and functional structure being readied for dismantlement. The last occupant was Almond, the iconic coffee shop with pink and white awnings that Roppongi-goers not so much enter as use for a meeting place. Indeed, I have long sensed that Almond did not much care for the people who gathered outside and their shenanigans and drew much of its clientele instead from other, let's say more conservative, slices of Roppongi whose origins in the neighborhood predate its history of partying. On January 6, 2009, I watched Almond's moving day for a few minutes, observing workers removing furniture and other fixtures and the shocked reactions of passersby who were learning of the change for the first time. Now, the vernacular "Meet you at Almond" will truly be on the way out, and a next generation of Roppongi visitors will not even know the meaning of the phrase. That is, unless, of course, Almond returns, as I was told it would, after two years to its rightful spot, but in a new building. By that time, surely the street corner scene at Roppongi Crossing will have been cleansed and sanitized. But with this famous symbol of Roppongi in transition for now, it is indeed truly the case that my writing speed has not kept up with Roppongi's motions, and I need to finish this project tout de suite.

Another landmark is gone more firmly, also bidding farewell to the pre-Mori era. Down Imoarai-zaka from Almond, at the bottom of the hill at the Keyakizaka-dōri entrance to Roppongi Hills, are the large Starbucks-with-bookstore singles cruising grounds described earlier and my favorite Bentley and Rolls Royce dealership (now closed). A side street from there in the direction away from Roppongi Hills is the main street through Azabu Jūban, the close-in, upscale, and close-knit neighborhood where I lived when this research started. It's still a great place, mixing apartments and single homes, Japanese neighbors and residents from all over the world, and has the best of neighborhood shopping streets. Unlike almost everywhere else in Tokyo, here the telephone and power lines are buried underground, sparing the neighborhood the typical overhead clutter that is typical of Tokyo and producing a fresh charm that helps makes Azabu Jūban truly popular. I occasionally see the neighborhood on TV and in the movies as backdrop for stories set on the upscale side of Tokyo. The very center of that little urban paradise had a *sentō*, a traditional neighborhood public bath. Before the days of showers and bathtubs in every private dwelling, Japanese used to bathe communally in such structures, men on one side of a divide, women on the other. Where nature provided, the source of hot water was geothermal heat, plentiful throughout Japan. Elsewhere, wood was burned. Hence, sentō were often marked in the landscape with tall smokestacks that pierced neighborhood skies. Whenever there was black smoke, neighbors knew that the water was hot and that it was time to get together for the evening washing.

The Azabu Jūban sentō is now history. It was demolished some months ago, and a tall building is going up on its bigger footprint site. Public baths are fast disappearing all over Tokyo; there were once thousands, but now they number only in the handfuls and are left only in the most remote and unchanged neighborhoods (Kami 1992; Kiritani 1995). This one was special because Azabu Jūban and Minato Ward have long been upscale, and the presence of this bath symbolized the persistence of things Japanese amid urban change and international population. I had always thought it interesting to look in the back lot at the wood supply. In my time, it was never logs from the forests, but always the wooden beams from people's demolished homes. Yes, as the city modernized and old wooden houses gave way to taller and taller new buildings, the wood that supported the past was used to heat the baths. Its ash then rained over the remaining low neighborhoods.

There is now an eye-catching poster with great urban interest that hangs among the many commercial advertising posters along the subway concourses in Roppongi and other stations. It is one of those posters that are neatly set in a frame and backlit, and it must have been designed by a very talented graphic artist or team. The poster is yet another self-promotion by the Mori Building Company and its vision. There is very little text: what there is states that on the ground, above the ground, and below, the Mori Building Company brings change and a new way to live in cities. The brightly colored art covers almost all the surface and speaks for itself. There are a hundred or more cartoonlike people in a verdant, hilly setting with trails and waterfalls, all engaged in any of a number of wholesome activities amid buildings that look like those of Roppongi Hills: riding bikes, skateboarding, flying kites, milking cows, and performing

FIGURE 7.3 Vision of urban life as presented by the Mori Building Company.

tai-chi, while on the roof of one of the buildings are youngsters engaged in growing rice and raising lobsters. An open cross-section of the main building (read Mori Tower) reveals a symphony orchestra in action and a diva at the microphone, a cooking school, a crowd of people watching a big-screen movie, a fitness class, people shopping, and people reading. There's an occasional admonition too, as when a good-citizen pedestrian wearing earphones signals "stop" with his hand to a facing youth shouldering an oversized boom box in the shopping mall. Down below the entire scene is the subway and people getting on and off, and deeper still (and smaller) is some car and truck traffic, well out of the way.

Norman Rockwell could not have done better! One can't argue with the poster's sentiments. On the other hand, it might be interesting to wonder why, when the hundred-plus people come in all shapes and sizes and all colors of hair, there is not one at all who looks Japanese, nor one face or style of hair that might look like someone from Africa or South Asia or the Andes or the Middle East—or anywhere actually. With the exception of the lone tai-chi coach leading his class, who is obviously an old Chinese with a kung-fu moustache, and one Indian snake charmer (still another stereotype), everyone else is ethnically and racially bland. It looks like the era when Japanese were learning ballroom dancing at the Rokumeikan (see chapter 2). Furthermore, there is nothing shown in all the dozens of little scenes and activities that says "this is Japan." Not one thing. With that, I return once more to the kibitz-rich topic heading in chapter 1, "The Possible End of Japan," and see that here is an artist's rendition!

It's ironic that the New Roppongi has so little that is Japanese. Roppongi Hills, Midtown, and all the other new construction projects are international or global in style, designed without cultural or geographical context. It is, in fact, Japan that is disappearing in the face of this construction; lamentably, the New Japan that rises as a result of the construction is the Japan of nowhere—a country of concrete and everyone's architecture and the same chain stores, convenience stores, comfortable coffee shops, and ultrafamiliar fast-food outlets that are found in most every country where there are incomes to spend. (The poster described above has a caricature of a hamburger and the posted sign "Do not think. Eat!") The beautiful Japanese gardens that have been added to the new developments don't really count; there are beautiful Japanese gardens all over the world. We have one in a park in Philadelphia. Had Alan Booth lived to see the "New Japan" in the New Roppongi (had he cared to go there), he would have had makings for another fine chapter for his wonderful book *Looking for the Lost: Journeys through a Vanishing Japan* (1995).

On the other hand, I acknowledge that Roppongi has actually not been "Japan" for a long time. While New Roppongi is simultaneously "no place" and every place," nightclub Roppongi was never particularly Japanese either unless considered as a foreigner-flavored variant of Japan's traditional nighttime urban amusement zones. Indeed, from the 1868 start of the Meiji restoration onward, it has been the role of Tokyo in general to put aside its Japaneseness and take on new trappings from abroad in order to keep Japan current in fashion, technology, and trend and to moderate new ways from abroad as they enter Japan. All this has helped to keep what is Japanese more firmly intact in the rest of Japan. As a result of its assigned task, Tokyo changed dramatically in the post-shōgun decades, especially in the core districts, leaving tradition mostly for holidays and for some neighborhoods in the city's corners.

Why should there be surprise that the hot piece of real estate that is Roppongi has put on the newest garb of globalization? In fact, it is exactly what we should have expected, given certain details that we now know about urban redevelopment trends in cities around the world. As far back as 1992, we were alerted to what was going on globally by architect and writer Michael Sorkin in his introduction to one of the earliest intelligent commentaries about the new urban form, the popular collection of essays titled *Variations on a Theme Park* (1992). Writing about New York, Los Angeles, and other American cities, Sorkin observed "three salient characteristics," the first of which was "dissipation of all stable relations to local physical and cultural geography [and] the loosening of ties to any specific place." The new city, Sorkin continued, is "inward-looking . . . [and] fully ageographic: it can be inserted equally in an open field or in the heart of town" (xiii).[2] It can also be inserted to replace Roppongi 6-chōme and to lord over its neighboring nightclub district.

Let me add this: I am reminded now of the section in chapter 3 about "Recreation and Amusement Associations," that very sad story from 1945 in which (male) Japanese officials thought that they would protect Japanese culture and save the virtue of proper Japanese women by opening "comfort stations" and staffing them with young Japanese women from the lower classes who were instructed to pleasure the male foreigners who arrived with the occupation. With respect to the central topic in this book, I see irony upon irony: to rid old Roppongi of its unsanctioned whoring, a new patriarchal officialdom creates Roppongi Hills and designates it "whore in chief," charging it with the task of playing with the foreigners and moderating their wider impact. The New Roppongi, then, gets all the work and attention and deflects notice from Japan's provinces and Tokyo's corners. As a plus, it is to make money for the men in tailored suits who are in charge. However, with all the bad luck the complex has had, its characteristic secretiveness about business details, and its history of overblown hype, we are likely to never know for sure just how much money was or was not made. Roppongi Hills as whore? That's just a theory, of course, but an interesting one, I think, with at least a modicum of solid footing.

Roppongi and Rome

As I wind up this book, I reflect on my own personal relationships with Roppongi and how they have changed. I end up thinking of Rome. Ideally, one would expect that a researcher-author who gets to know a study area very well will develop a close, personal, and fond relationship with that place and its people. That was the case for me long ago with my doctoral dissertation neighborhood in Philadelphia, Fairmount, as well as for those social science scholars whose neighborhood studies influenced me then or have influenced me since: my "dissertation buddy" David Ley in another part of Philadelphia (1974); William F. Whyte (1943) and Herbert Gans (1962) and their studies of the North End and West End of Boston, respectively; Gerald Suttles in the Addams area of Chicago (1968); John Western in Cape Town under apartheid and among immigrants in London (1982 and 1992, respectively); Ted Bestor in Tokyo's "Miyamotochō" and Tsukiji (1989 and 2004, respectively); Louise Brown in Lahore (2005); and the ethnographies of African American men in inner-city Philadelphia by sociologist Elijah Anderson (1990, 2003), among others. But it has not been exactly so for me in Roppongi. My thinking about the neighborhood has been all over the map, has changed again and again with time and perhaps with different levels of understanding, and has now moved in the eleventh hour of this project to one that is, I am sorry to say, decidedly negative. It hurts me to say that because my relationship with the neighborhood is indeed still close and personal: it's only the "fond" that is missing.

There were times when I was, in fact, fond of Roppongi. When I started to spend time in the neighborhood in 2001, again initially simply because it was near where I lived and worked, I found it to be fascinating intellectually and exciting for its energy and, for me, new activities. I had never been a club person, even when I was young, so when happenstance brought me to Roppongi, I was intrigued. Here was a place of a type that I had missed in my youth but that was accessible to me now. It started with occasional dinners and simple relaxation after work. I then began to meet people and soon enough was being escorted into places such as dance clubs and singles bars that I would not normally have entered on my own. It was interesting to observe unfamiliar social worlds and anthropologically rich routines and to graduate over the ensuing years from one level of this schooling to other levels and other "majors." I admit, too, that it was more than a little interesting to meet people from all over the world who had come to play or to work in this neighborhood, particularly the many young women and men from Russia, Belarus, and Ukraine who continue to be my main community of friends in Tokyo. They helped me to connect Roppongi with the wider world and to think of my setting as an untapped microcosm for studying social interactions in globalizing Japan. It was at that point, when I began to apply my social science interests to my nighttime experiences and to the lives of new networks of friends and acquaintances, when the idea of writing a book came to the fore.

But as already mentioned, there were many things in Roppongi that I could not like: the drug scene; sex shows and prostitution; excessive drunkenness and vomiting; the exploitation by wealthy men with expense accounts of young women from poor countries; the parallel exploitation by shrewd, hot-looking women from poor and rich countries alike of lonely and naive Japanese men; and the slovenly youth scene, Japanese and foreigners both, whom I associate, fairly or not, with hip-hop and its cousins. There were other peeves too. I could deal with such dislikes when I thought of them as subjects for observation and study, but I was angered by them, sometimes overtly, whenever they crossed too heavily into "my Roppongi." Because the relationship became close and personal, it was always a struggle to maintain professional detachment in this place where so many things are so wrong.

As indicated as a central theme in this book, a "New Roppongi" has emerged. It is centered on the megaprojects of Roppongi Hills and Tokyo Midtown, and it is being built in tandem by gigantic and powerful corporations and by architects and developers with the highest credentials. Instead of nightlife, the new Roppongi focuses on upscale international lifestyles, brand-name shopping emporia, stages for some of the best of the world's live concerts and other performances, and some truly fine new art museums. I have especially enjoyed the art, long a passion of mine, many memorable concerts (hooray for Keri Noble and hooray, too, for my cousin, the Munich-based pianist Oresta Cybriwsky), international film festivals, and the openings of several Hollywood movies thanks to my Hollywood daughter Mary Cybriwsky. With *Batman Begins*, I make claims to an evening I had in Roppongi with Katie Holmes, overlooking the fact that there were many other people at the premiere too and that Ms. Holmes never once looked in my direction. But even with these wonderful memories and beautiful venues and my own personal history as an art museum lizard, I think of New Roppongi as corporate gentrification and do not much like it.

So, Roppongi changes for the better, but my opinions of it decline. What is more, there is always a turnover of people in Roppongi, meaning fondnesses that were there at one time may no longer be around. Some of my best Roppongi friends have now moved on and have new, different kinds of work in places like St. Petersburg (Russia, not Florida), New York, and even Mariupil (Ukraine). I have left Japan as well and am doing better too, in my case in Philadelphia and, more recently, in Kyiv, Ukraine. I still have lots of friends and acquaintances in Roppongi and enjoy their company during frequent return visits, but the neighborhood is changing all around and directly beneath. In one direction, it's the same gentrified urban landscape that has been imposed on us all in New York and Moscow and London, taking away from the uniqueness and authenticity of the place where we had met. The other aspect is worse; it's new poor people, hungrier than we ever were and greedy, seemingly grabbing for every last buck before nighttime Roppongi closes altogether. There are more gangster types, more drugs, more aggressive prostitution, and, sorry to say so, more creepy-looking Japanese clients of the kind who possibly kill. Chapters 4 and 5 look at these problems and the conflict between the two sides of Roppongi. My Roppongi has become something like decadent Rome, a world of sins and excesses, a nighttime civilization in decline. Over and over again, I hear the neighborhood being described in perfectly plain and simple English: "It's getting really bad." My own description uses Roman terminology: it's the fall of the Roppongi Empire.

When Rome burned, it's said that Nero fiddled.
Now that Roppongi's turned, I imagine that Mr. Mori's giggled.

The Next Roppongi

Yes, the Roppongi nightclub district is receding, and the neoliberal lifestyles and landscapes represented by Roppongi Hills are on the rise. The two still coexist and might be able to do so with a tamed nightclub zone for quite a while, because one operates at night and the other takes over during the day. But the long-term trend seems pretty clear: the nature and geography of night-life will continue to shift in Tokyo, as it has since Edo times (see chapter 2), and will move away or be pushed away from Roppongi; Roppongi has changed from "High-Touch Town," whatever that meant, to "artelligence," whatever that means; and consumers will come to the neighborhood more for the Roppongi Art Walk than for Roppongi Night Talk, the latter being a rhyming reference to the banal conversations of the world of hostess clubs.

Despite an amazing string of bad luck since its opening on April 23, 2003, Roppongi Hills will win the war, and at most, only a small relic of relative-ly tame nighttime establishments will remain down the road near Roppongi Crossing. There will be places to eat, but not so many because Roppongi Hills and Midtown have their own everything-under-one-roof selections of restau-rants, and some places to drink and unwind for the office tower crowd, but not much more than that. I suspect that a disproportionate number of the few businesses that survive will be postwork cruising spots with international flavor for office workers in global-economy companies who prowl for companionship, and group-oriented eating and drinking establishments for Japanese office co-workers who are not quite finished working after the office closes.

There is no reason to lament the lost Roppongi, at least not for me. The neigh-borhood had a half century or so of interesting history as a party place and, I am sure, is the source of many fond memories of wild nights by Roppongi-zoku of the past. But there are no rich traditions to cherish, nor is there anything for us to keep from the neighborhood that might make Japan proud. Roppongi is in the new, upscale, and leading-edge side of town: therefore, it never sits still and is not expected to. It's supposed to change, to put on new faces, to get better. What I am sorry about is that so much of what is new in Roppongi, particularly on the Roppongi Hills side, is not really new—only pretentious. I have seen that places like Roppongi Hills are quite common around the world. Most of the keepsakes in Tokyo are on the other side of the city, in the old "low" neighborhoods where history matters and losses of historic structures and traditions can be heartfelt. Asakusa, for example, still stands from the early years of the city, still functions as it always did as a place of combined religious pilgrimage and merrymaking, and even tries actively, with considerable public support, to recapture details that had slipped away over the years. Conversely, there will be no pressure from anyone anywhere to recapture Roppongi's recent past.

And what of the Roppongi proletariat, particularly the foreigners? That is a very interesting and very small specialist slice of Japan's social and labor history that will probably pass too. Japan has a long way to go before it becomes international in its population makeup, even in Tokyo. The unique arrangement that we saw in Roppongi in which a great many foreigners from all over the world gather as consumers alongside roughly equal numbers of Japanese, to be served in their consumption by service worker foreigners also from around the world (but not from the same countries in the same proportions as the consumers), as well as by Japanese workers, was just that—unique. It is a pattern that is still there and might hang on into the future in diminished numbers, but it certainly won't grow and flourish in Roppongi. Foreign immigration to Japan will grow faster elsewhere, such as in industrial districts where immigrant labor is already needed, and most of those foreigners—the proletariat foreigners—will live elsewhere too. As for the upper crust of foreigners, Mr. Mori's own choice of words to describe those who are most welcome to his hills, they might remain and even grow in numbers with Tokyo's return to global supremacy. But my book is not about them; I'm happier to have made a contribution instead, however small, to readers' understanding of the roles that people from poor countries play behind the scenes in a place like Roppongi. They have come from poverty, are far from home, are often lonely, do not feel especially welcome in Japan, and work hard without complaint to build lives for themselves and for those they love. Japan will someday learn to appreciate and admire these people.

Roppongi Resistance

I think that it is an act of resistance and that if Mr. Mori knows about it, he is probably more upset than amused. Personally, I'm amused. I am not sure how long the sign has been there, but I saw it only just now, at the end point of this writing, and I immediately thought of it as evidence of resistance. The sign is about two feet by three in size, and like so many others of the dozens of similar signs on its block, it is a backlit announcement saying that here, in this very building, is such and such place of business. At night, all the signs together add up to a "neon landscape" for the nightclubs district, even though there is actually no neon—just lightbulbs behind colored plastic. This particular piece of plastic is yellow, and the words, in Japanese and English, are in red. It is affixed low, right at sidewalk level, its top being about belt high, but it advertises a business that is on the ninth floor. Just go through this door and up the elevator is the message.

I had walked past the spot hundreds of times, but somehow I never saw the sign before. I could have missed it in the clutter, as this is Gaien Higashi-dōri, Roppongi's densest concentration of clubs and clubgoers and that same block where I had photographed chaos (see figure 7.1). Distractions abound. But no, I had been here hundreds of times even when Roppongi was quiet, and I still did not see it. What is more, there is no record of it in my building-by-building inventory of the neighborhood, either in the written notes format or in my photo files. No, it must be a new business that has opened there on the ninth floor and that is paying a premium for sign space at street level. Or, at minimum, it is a new sign in a new spot for a preexisting business that I never noticed. Regardless, the business is a massage parlor, the bane of Roppongi according to the conservative voices that we have heard in this book.

Mr. Mori would hate to be told that yet another massage parlor has opened in this district that he is trying to reform. But even more than the massage parlor itself, it is the name of the establishment that would get him especially hot under the collar and that I instantly thought of as working people's resistance: this particular massage parlor, advertised in the national colors of the People's Republic of China, is called "Massage Hills." Wow! As the expression has it, you can't make this stuff up. Even more, a visit to Roppongi at the end of 2009 reveals that the clever name of this establishment has changed, maybe because of someone's unhappiness about use of the trademark word *hills*. Instead of *hills* we now have *mori*, the Japanese word for "forest," such that the red and gold sign now reads "Massage Mori." How about that? If the Mori Building Company can appropriate "Roppongi Crossing" as the name for its Japanese-only art shows, why shouldn't a nighttime massage parlor appropriate vocabulary from New Roppongi?

What I see about other new signs in Roppongi might also reflect a sign of resistance. Some six months after that ceremonious hanging of the anti–African streetman signs that I describe near the end of chapter 6, I see that many fewer of those signs still hang where they were affixed and that those that remain now carry a glued-on additional warning: "Damaging this signboard shall be

FIGURE 7.4 Vandalized sign warning against aggressive touting on Roppongi streets and against damaging the sign.

punished by the law." Need I add that the added warning is in English only? Recently, I snapped a photograph of the sign nearest to Roppongi Crossing: it had obviously been kicked again and again, had a gaping hole in the center, and was still hanging only because the sign-hangers had fastened it in place so meticulously with so many individual bindings.

Akira Yamaguchi Paints Roppongi

Akira Yamaguchi (1969–) is one of Japan's most popular contemporary artists, known especially for his detailed paintings of landscape scenes and significant personalities from Japan's history, cultural life, and transitions. He is brilliant. I first learned about him in Roppongi Hills, actually in the Roppongi Hills gift and souvenir shop, which was selling signed prints of two of his pen and watercolor paintings, *Tokei [Tokyo]: Hiroo and Roppongi* and *Tokei [Tokyo]: Roppongi Hills*," both from 2002. I was dazzled but could not possibly afford the prices. Thankfully, there were also postcard versions and other inexpensive reproductions that I could take home. Later, I bought his book: *The Art of Akira Yamaguchi* (2004), which comes with an enclosed plastic magnifying glass for help with the thousands of tiny details in various works. I can't reproduce his art because it is copyrighted and almost certainly very expensive to reproduce in detail, but there are Web sites that sell prints and provide illustrations, as well as wide public distribution of the very beautiful and affordable book.

Yamaguchi's urban scenes show many topics: the insides of Japanese department stores in cross-section; landscape details in Osaka from the sky above; scenes of happy Japanese in an urban amusement district; and the aforementioned views of Roppongi Hills. His style reminds me of Canaletto (Giovanni Antonio Canal; 1697–1768), a long-time favorite painter famous for his vivid *vedute* (views) of Venice. Yet, Yamaguchi's style is profoundly Japanese as well, derived directly from classical Yamato-e painting, a centuries-old art form inspired by Tang Dynasty painting that was developed in the Heian Period (794–1185). Typically, such paintings were either folding screens or hand scrolls read right to left. They illustrated narrative themes and recorded history, represented the beauty of nature, and honored earthly authority. Landscapes were often profuse with puffy clouds, often golden yellow. While much of Yamaguchi's work has that distinctive Yamato-e look combined with Canaletto-like faithful detail, the content is totally contemporary. His landscapes are especially thought-provoking, ironic, and frequently funny. They might be political too, with commentary about trends in Japanese society, new technologies, and other timely issues, although different viewers might have different interpretations (McGee 2003).

I leave readers with Yamaguchi's paintings of Roppongi Hills because of what they seem to say about the place. When I first saw the prints from a distance, I thought I was seeing Edo Castle or some other center of feudal-era Japanese warrior power, but no, the soaring tower in the center was Mori Tower. That's what caught my attention: the iconic Japanese *jōka machi* (castle town) had been turned into Mori's town. Instead of the iconic donjon and its soaring gabled roofs, there was Mori Tower rising from within its own fortified *honmaru* (central bailey), exerting confident authority over the crowded and sprawling town below. And instead of the slate-roofed wooden houses and narrow lanes of historic urban Japan, Yamaguchi has painted the vernacular of today's city: multistoried apartment and condominium buildings, shops, highways and traffic, underpasses, overpasses, rooftop gardens and rooftop air conditioning units, construction cranes, power lines and utility poles, and lots and lots of little tiny people doing what people do outdoors in city, among so many other details. There are also representations of Japan's past with traditional temple buildings, bits and pieces of architecture from Japan's initial modernization, and other records of national transition.

None of this seems fixed in place. Yes, the old castle is gone and a new tower has risen in its place, and yes, there is no nightclub district at its feet. And everywhere is change, change still underway, quickened change. The great Edo Castle of Tokugawa Ieyasu lasted but a few years; the castles of today are ephemeral too. That is how I interpret this engaging work: Akira Yamaguchi has painted New Roppongi and made it the center of an ever-building, ever-changing construction state Japan.

NOTES

CHAPTER ONE *Roppongi and the New Tokyo*

1. It turns out that "Roppongi Crossing" is also the title of a periodic art exhibit that is held in the Mori Art Museum, one of the premier venues of the New Roppongi, further described in chapter 7.

2. Almond is a chain of coffee shops. Even though there other Almonds in Tokyo, the Roppongi Almond is best known.

3. In 2004 "High-Touch Town" was singled out for the year's Nonsense Award in the "Surprising English" competition conducted by the English Speaking Union of Japan. For more about this sign see chapter 2.

4. The Almond coffee shop is gone too, but only temporarily. This problem exists throughout the book—landscape changes faster than I can write. Its building was a bad one for this strategic corner and has been pulled down for redevelopment. The coffee shop is a Tokyo institution on the right side of power and influence, and at this writing it is just a block away in temporary quarters while the new building is being constructed. The changing Roppongi routines and landscape continue to be a problem, as it is difficult for me to keep current.

5. According to data provided by the Japan Tourism Marketing Co., in the first eleven months of 2008 the number of foreign visitors entering Japan was 8,392,000, whereas the number of Japanese tourists traveling abroad was 14,695,000. In rank order, the top five countries for short-term visitors to Japan during this period were Korea (ROK), Taiwan (ROC), China (PRC), the United States, and Hong Kong ("Japanese Economic Trend," http://www.tourism.jp/english/statistics/market.php).

6. I am speaking here primarily about foreigners who are easily recognized to the eye as foreigners, as opposed to the many Chinese and Koreans, as well as Chinese Americans, Japanese Americans, Japanese Brazilians, etc., who are less distinguishable from Japan's majority population.

7. The contours of work by today's immigrants in the night economy of other cities in other countries is also just now coming to be studied (e.g., Takenaka and Osirim 2010; Talani 2009, and Wills et al. 2009).

8. Until its recent economic halt, the United Arab Emirates (Dubai) was probably catching up fast.

9. A similar construction-driven assault occurred in the same year against the famous bridge at Nihombashi, "Japan Bridge," some five kilometers away. There, one of Japan's

most important historical landmarks was plunged into its own darkness by the same highway, creating what was identified as "the biggest eyesore in Japan" (Lewis 2005) in a serious government report commissioned by the prime minister.

10. I refer readers interested in learning about academic geography to two exciting books by the late Peter R. Gould, *Geographer at Work* (London: Routledge & Kegan Paul Books, 1985) and *Becoming a Geographer* (Syracuse: Syracuse University Press, 1999).

11. *Seinfeld*, episode 137, "The Bizarro Jerry," season 8, number 3, broadcast date October 3, 1996.

12. Some key examples are the now-classic collection of essays about New York, Los Angeles, and other "New American Cities" edited by Michael Sorkin (1992); the essays about Berlin, Washington, and New York City in the book edited by Paul Knox (1993); Neil Smith's book (1996) about reshaping the social geography of New York City; the highly regarded reader about the emergence of new spatial order in a broad range of cities around the globe edited by Peter Marcuse and Ronald van Kempen (2000), work by Kris Olds (1995) on the megastructures phenomenon in cities around the Pacific Rim; and journal articles about the intersection of new urban form and new urban lifestyles in Singapore (Chang, Huang, and Savage 2004), Shanghai (Wu 2000), Amsterdam (Nijman 1999), Toronto (Kern 2007), and London (Davidson and Lees 2005). The Marcuse and van Kempen reader includes an article about the conflict between tradition and urban change in Tokyo by Paul Waley (2000). I might also mention here my own 1999 article comparing public space characteristics in newly built development and redevelopment zones in Tokyo and New York City.

13. See "*Gaijin Hanzai* Magazine and Hate Speech in Japan: The Newfound Power of Japan's International Residents," *The Asia-Pacific Journal: Japan Focus*, the article by Debito Arudou at http://www.japanfocus.org/-Arudou-Debito/2386. I did, in fact, originally plan to include quite a few exposé type of photographs in this book but made my decision to the contrary as I was shooting pictures of street life from inside a second-story bar and was made to reflect a bit more deeply by Sting's words in the song that started to play, "Every Breath You Take" by the Police, which talks of obsessively stalking a loved one. It's possible that the DJ was sending me a message.

14. Anthropology of Japan in Japan Fall Workshop, Meiji Gakuin University, Tokyo, October 29, 2006.

CHAPTER TWO *Roppongi Context*

1. I wrote about multinodal Tokyo in an earlier book (Cybriwsky 1998). Also see Sorensen 2001.

2. While it is only a nine-minute ride between the Ōedo Line's Roppongi Station and Shinjuku, the total trip time is actually considerably longer. At both places the tracks are deep below ground, and it takes time to negotiate the maze of escalators, elevators, and stairs that are required for access. Almost always there are crowds that slow movement, so the much-touted nine minutes is actually closer to thirty minutes.

3. Ginza is an exception and a different story. It is an expensive and high-fashion shopping district but in the opposite direction in what was once shitamachi.

4. The term is not mine. I heard it at an academic conference in, I think, Tokyo in about 2004 and adopted it immediately. Unfortunately, I can't remember who used the term in his or her paper, nor can I remember exactly which conference this was.

5. In one of many fascinating details about Japan, its enormous sex industry, its often awkward relations with foreign people, and its frequent adaptation of foreign loan words, it is interesting to learn the history of the odd word *soapland* (*sōpurando*). The word was added to the Japanese vocabulary in the mid-1980s following a national contest for a new term to replace the previous *toruko-buro*, a Japanese corruption of "Turkish bath." That latter appellation had offended a Turkish resident of Japan who carried out a successful public relations campaign to force a change (Richie 1999, 100–101). He argued that what was going on in toruko-buro was not Turkish bathing and an insult to Turkey. I am personally pleased that one of the other contender words in the contest was not chosen: *roman-buro*. Otherwise, it is I who would have had to complain.

6. There is an endless bibliography of Japanese sources about Asakusa history, customs, events, and personalities, including fiction and nonfiction, plus a selection of best works in translation. I recommend the novel *The Scarlet Gang of Asakusa* (1968) by Nobel Prize–winning author Yasunari Kawabata and translated into English by Alisa Freedman. It was originally serialized in 1929 and 1930 in a Tokyo daily newspaper and tells the engaging stories of Asakusa's characters and entertainers during the exciting 1920s.

7. Telekura stations are "telephone club" establishments that facilitate "dating" by providing men with the phone numbers (at a cost) of young women that they select from photo-filled catalogues.

8. I also recommend the ethnographic work by Mary Reisel about schoolgirl sex workers in Shibuya and Kyle Cleveland's research on Shibuya's hip-hop culture. Both scholars have been colleagues of mine in academe and are still close friends. They have spoken brilliantly about their work at various academic conferences in Tokyo, but their published papers, or better yet books that we all await from them, are still "under construction."

9. I see parallels between the history of decline of Yoshiwara and the decline of the nightclub side of Roppongi today, particularly in terms of the cheapening of sex, the availability of commercial sex at discount rates, and declining standards for music and other entertainment.

10. *Hallucination*," directed by Elena Shpak, Fedotova Productions, 2008.

11. "So You Want to Be a Hostess?," n.d., http://akasenkuiki.homestead.com/files/hostess.html. Another good source is the article "Women's Work and Japan's Hostess Culture" in the *New York Times*, August 12, 2009, and the follow-up blog: http://roomfordebate.blogs.nytimes.com/2009/08/11/womens-work-and-japans-hostess-culture/?ref=world.

12. *The Stratosphere Girl*, directed by M. X. Oberg, TLA Releasing, 2005; *Tokyo Girls*,

directed by Penelope Buitenhuis, National Film Board of Canada, 2000; and *Posledniy poezd so stancii Roppongi* (Last Train from Roppongi Station), directed by Vera Svechina, 2008 (in Russian).

13. For a study of the geographic distribution of foreigner population in Tokyo by nationality, occupation categories, and other characteristics see Machimura 2000.

14. The Shimizu company actually dates its own founding to 1804.

15. The Normanton Incident refers to the accidental sinking of a British ship of that name off Japan's coast on October 26, 1886. The captain and his British crew all managed to save themselves while all twenty-five Japanese passengers were abandoned and drowned.

16. I do not mean any injustice to the many foreigners with enormous talents who also work in Japan.

CHAPTER THREE *Roppongi Rises*

1. In addition to the works by Jinnai (1988, 1995), I am indebted for this insight on patterns to Yoshinobu Ashihara (1989) and to a most memorable walk through a different section of Tokyo on a Saturday in 1985 with urban-historical geographers Noriyuki Sugiura and Paul Waley. I was new to the city at the time, and they both told me that I needed to learn how to look closely at Tokyo, and that I would then see the patterns of Edo-Tokyo evolution.

2. My informant had been an actor in wartime Japan, always portraying the evil American in propaganda films. He very soon became a translator for the Americans and then served the occupation forces and later the U.S. Embassy in Japan in other significant ways. He is well known in central Tokyo and beloved for more than a half-century of good works. The Russian American soldier and my Russian-in-Japan informant went off together soon after their meeting on the tarmac for prayers and a candle lighting at Nikolaidō, St. Nicholas Russian Orthodox Cathedral in Tokyo. Some other details about his interesting life that he had also shared with me were published online in Mongolian by the Mongol News Group in 2005 (Zhargalant 2005).

3. Most of the data about changing U.S. troop levels in Japan and Korea in this paragraph are from Kane (2006). The exception is the figure 600,000, which is a commonly cited number for the maximum population of American personnel in Japan at the peak of the occupation.

4. For those personnel who were married, the option of having their spouses join them in Japan was not available until 1948, and even then, relatively few spouses and dependent children came. The now-familiar phenomenon of U.S. military families in Japan did not really begin until the late 1950s or even the 1960s. Consequently, the occupation was mostly that by single men and by men who were physically separated at the time from wives and girlfriends.

5. The story about these mobsters and the restaurant is, again, Whiting's, and I refer readers to his entertaining 1999 book for details. There is even more juicy detail about

Machii and Kodama in the longer and scholarly tome by Kaplan and Dubro (2003). It too is highly readable.

6. There is a Nicola's restaurant near where the original eatery stood. The connection to the original is uncertain despite claims to the contrary.

7. The branch of the Almond coffee shop where the hand towel was said to have originated was founded in Ginza in 1946.

8. The *maru* part of *Marugen* is the Japanese word for "circle," while *gen* comes from Kawamoto's given name, Gensiro.

9. Some of the details about Kawamoto and Marugen are from the JREF (Japan Reference) website at http://www.jref.com/forum/showthread.php?t=2681, particularly from a posting by someone who signed her name as Satori. Kawamoto's given name also appears as "Genshiro" in English sources. There is considerable recent reference to him on the Internet with regard to controversies about the impact of his real estate businesses in Hawaii and California on low-income households. Examples from the *Los Angeles Times* are at http://articles.latimes.com/keyword/gensiro-kawamoto.

10. The quest for acceptance and preferred status is, of course, still a characteristic of many clubgoers in any setting, even well past the original disco era, as is fear of rejection by judging doormen (Malbon 1999).

11. There is a whole chapter of the book (pp. 55–62) with that title, a chapter that begins with a quotation from the late Jim Morrison: "I am the Lizard King . . . I can do anything."

12. I do not recognize the name of the restaurant, Il Quale, that Gerster provided at the top of the essay, but some details ring familiar.

13. That concern was fueled in part by incidents that resulted in school closings in 1999 in Dusseldorf as a result of trouble related to a Germany-Netherlands soccer match (Gordenker 2002).

14. "Prison Ships," Soccerphile, 2002 archives, http://www.soccerphile.com/soccerphile/archives/wc2002/ne/hrgps.html.

CHAPTER FOUR *Roppongi Rhythms, Recently*

1. Talking about foreigners in Roppongi or other settings in Japan is always tricky. Please see the discussion about "visible foreigners" in chapter 1.

2. I had said I was not going to identify places that are not already Roppongi landmarks. CCCP Girls is an exception because you can't get inside.

3. I had to use my own coin flip as to whether a particular establishment should be counted as primarily an eating establishment or primarily a drinking establishment.

4. In order to be consistent with how other national or ethnic identities were counted, the category "Japanese" reflects only those places that overtly call themselves "Japanese" or that display other symbols such as the national flag. Without such added information, restaurants that serve traditional Japanese cuisine were not counted as Japanese.

5. The number of pachinko establishments is from the National Police Agency as reported in the *Japan Times*, September 25, 2007.

6. A fascinating and highly original scholarly study of women working out in Tokyo's fitness club is the book *Working Out in Japan: Shaping the Body in Tokyo Fitness Clubs* (2003) by anthropologist Laura Spielvogel.

7. These points, of course, touch on universal themes about the sexual chase and are amplified with examples from various places around the world and all periods of history. As I edit these pages, I happen to be reading a pertinent novel, Paulo Coelho's *Eleven Minutes* (2003), about Maria, a young woman from the interior of Brazil who becomes a sex worker in Geneva, Switzerland.

8. Studies about the sociology of work in contemporary Japan include the following: Ballon 1969; Fowler 1996, Kumazawa 1996; and Woronoff 1983.

9. I recently presented a very personal paper about this topic at the Race, Ethnicity and Place Conference in Miami, Florida (November 4–6, 2008), sharing both my findings and my nervousness about methodology. I found an understanding and supportive audience that encouraged me to go ahead with this eleventh-hour insertion to a chapter that I had already thought was finished.

10. A related term in use in Japan is NEET, introduced from Great Britain and standing for "not in education, employment or training" (Kosugi 2006).

11. There are men who work in Tokyo as hosts, strippers, and dancers, too, but not in Roppongi to my knowledge. The existence of transgendered people and cross-dressers is still another topic. Roppongi has had establishments that cater specifically to such people at least since the mid-1970s, as well as places that employ them as a central attraction (McLelland, Suganuma, and Welker 2007, 160–63).

12. I learned the term *bachelor sojourners* from the sympathetic portrait of male traders from Africa in Guangzhou, China, that was published in a recent issue of the *New Yorker* (Osnos 2009).

13. As mentioned in chapter 1, there are no genuine "Roppongi Royals" except for the self-enthroned, as the neighborhood centers on no one person, no one place, and no one type of activity. My assortment of insider-informants is wide and diverse and purposefully steers cautiously around individuals who would most want to be a leading character a book such as this. Their stories have been trumpeted quite widely already.

14. Such activities are also common among Filipino domestic workers in Hong Kong, Singapore, and other prosperous business centers. Whether they are domestic servants, health care workers, bartenders, dancers, or construction workers (men), most Filipinos in Japan support family members back home, contributing remittance income to the country that depends more on remittances than any country in the world (Ballescas 1992).

15. Toyo Eiwa Jogakuin Christian Education, n.d., http://www.toyoeiwa.ac.jp/english/engtop.html.

16. Gonpachi is where the Crazy 88 scene of the Quentin Tarantino film *Kill Bill 1* was supposedly staged, along with the Bride's sword fights against nemesis O-Ren Ishii and

her evil seventeen-year-old schoolgirl bodyguard Gogo Yubari. However, it might just be that another version of the story is true, that the restaurant inspired Tarantino to build a set that looks like it and that the filming actually took place in China. For sure, though, Gonpachi is where, on separate occasions, U.S. presidents Bill Clinton and George W. Bush have famously eaten. The 1992 incident in which George H. W. Bush vomited on Japanese prime minister Kiichi Miyazawa took place elsewhere in Tokyo.

17. Kingyo Club, http://www.kingyo.co.jp/en/shp01.html. For a fine article about the Kingyo Club see Otake 2005.

CHAPTER FIVE *Roppongi Troubles*

1. Embassy of the United States: Japan, http://tokyo.usembassy.gov/.

2. Tokyo also happens to be the first place (but no longer the only city) where I personally saw a murder victim. It was even before the police arrived on the scene. It was in the mid-1980s and not in Roppongi but in Shinjuku's Kabukichō, that other dangerous nightlife district of Tokyo. I saw rainwater flowing past me turn pink and then darker red, and I rounded the corner to look for the source of the color. There, I spied a dead man at my feet disgorging blood from multiple stab wounds. For a long few seconds until others who did not flee instantly happened upon the scene, it was just me and the victim, in a gentle rain and a fresh red river, all bathed in the rainbow hues of Kabukichō's nasty world of neon. The victim looked like he belonged in Kabukichō, a young punch-permed Japanese or Zainichi-Korean hood, and I felt as if I had been transported into a detective novel.

3. There are hundreds of news items available about the Lucie Blackman story. Simply enter the name "Lucie Blackman" in a search engine, and a plethora of leads appears. The best writing by far and a key source for me in this section of the chapter is the news article by Evan Alan Wright, "Death of a Hostess," (2001). I am also indebted to and recommend the article by Justin Norrie, "A Tale of Rape, Murder and a Japanese Playboy" (2007). There is an excellent chapter with firsthand details about the case from the view of a reporter on the beat in the recent book about Tokyo's underside by Jake Adelstein (2009). A second "exposé" book recently came out about the subject as well (Campbell 2009).

4. Laura Fumiko Keehn, "As Lucie Blackman Murder Verdict Approaches, Foreign Hostesses Remain Vulnerable, *Japan Times*, April 13, 2007, http://archive.japantoday .com/jp/feature/1219 (story is no longer accessible).

5. Jōji Obara represents a dark side of Japan that Japan needs to know better. He is one of theirs, a Japanese success story gone weird. Born Kim Sung Jong in the ruins of postwar Osaka to a poor Korean family, his world of opportunities and comforts grew as his father successfully climbed Japan's economic ladder, eventually becoming owner of a fleet of taxis and a chain of pachinko parlors, as well as valuable real estate that was bought before the Japanese bubble. He entered a top high school near Tokyo and then Keiō University, one of the nation's most prestigious institutions. After his father's death,

he eventually took over the family's extensive real estate holdings. Like many of Japan's Koreans who want to escape discrimination, at age twenty-one he changed his name to one that was Japanese and took on Japanese nationality. He was wealthy, the boss of many employees, the owner of homes in the best districts of Tokyo and at the beach. Then the bubble broke, real estate fortunes fell apart, and a sick man became sicker and began doing unspeakable things to hundreds of victims. Japan looked the other way. Even though the chopped-up body of a young foreign woman was found in a beach cave just outside Obara's beachfront apartment, and her DNA was found in his apartment, along with photo images of her in this apartment, and he been seen by police officers with cement on his hands the day her severed head was encased in cement, and there were as many as four hundred self-made videotapes of him as a date-rapist Zorro, and he gave Tim Blackman £450,000 in "sorry money," the Japanese justice system said he was "not guilty" of murder.

6. The description of this publication and the translations from Japanese are from Debito Arudou (2007). I have many of my own photographs of a type like that in figure 5.4, but as discussed in chapter 1, I decided not to publicize them.

7. "Consider a building with a few broken windows. If the windows are not repaired, the tendency is for vandals to break a few more windows. Eventually, they may even break into the building, and if it's unoccupied, perhaps become squatters or light fires inside." See Wilson and Kelling (1982) and Kelling and Coles (1996).

8. I remember being in a police-targeted dance club late one night (after the 1:00 a.m. dance curfew) and being cautioned by staff to stop moving my feet as I stood near the bar with a drink in my hand, responding with what I thought were unobtrusive body movements to the rhythm of the music (to the extent that I am capable of such). It was my own personal *Footloose* moment, referring to the 1984 film about moralistic small-town America starring Kevin Bacon, the son of Philadelphia city planner Edmund Bacon. Thankfully, I have never experienced a police raid personally and did manage to successfully leave the raided establishment along with many others that night shortly before police arrived because word was spreading that a raid was imminent. It turned out to be a check of foreigners for work permits and proper visas. An informant said that police simultaneously blocked all exits, let Japanese customers leave on sight, and then excused foreigners one by one as they presented valid documentation. A young, possibly underage, Romanian woman whom I had met in a different setting several weeks earlier was working that night as bar waitress; I never saw her again and assume that she was arrested and deported along with other illegal workers who were caught that night.

9. *Metropolis* 741 (June 6, 2008): 03.

10. The only time I was stopped by police in Japan I was speeding on a bicycle with hopes of reaching home before the start of a coming rainstorm. My hopes were drowned. The police officer and I stood in the downpour that started just then, both of us becoming drenched, until he was able to confirm by radio that the bike was indeed mine.

11. See Guardian Angels Japan, www.guardianangels.or.jp. There is an English-language section. Why the Guardian Angels came at all to Japan, how they were greeted,

and how they evolved to fit the special circumstances of Japanese society is a separate story, not directly relevant to my Roppongi narrative, but one that I think would be interesting to write about.

12. Until they all but disappeared with the advent of cell phones, chirashi used to almost literally cover many of Tokyo's telephone booths, inside and out. As I look into a rare telephone booth that still stands in Roppongi, I see several "pink chirashi" on the glass walls and on the phone itself. I also note the signs inside in Japanese, English, Chinese, and Korean that were put up by the NTT telephone company. They read: "Entry strictly limited to using the public phone" and "Bill posting/distribution prohibited. Violators will be punished by law."

13. The majority of Roppongi's Spanish speakers are from Central and South America, most notably Mexico, Colombia, and Peru, while most Portuguese-speakers are from Brazil.

14. In the electronics district of Akihabara there are dozens of young Japanese women, some of whom still look to be in high school, who work the streets without any evident official disapproval dressed as maids to entice male customers into "maid cafés."

15. The law originally called for an end to dancing at midnight à la Cinderella, but a reprieve was allowed for an extra hour beginning in 2006.

16. "The Roppongi Hills Are Alive," http://jlowsjunk.blogspot.com/2008/06/roppongi.html. Also see the article "The Ultimate Party Pooper: Drug Overdoses and Deaths in Roppongi," in the *Asahi Shimbun*, August 3, 2004.

CHAPTER SIX *Roppongi Remade*

1. Yasukazu Akada, "Shadows Look over Tokyo Tower," http://www.asahi.com/english/Herald-asahi/TKY200803010051.html03/01/2008. In the course of my own inquiries, I received a written reply from an information officer for Minato Ward who assured me that while the tower is a private business concern that is entitled to keep its business plans private, there is no knowledge of any plans to remove it. In fact, I was informed that Tokyo Tower will continue to provide communication services as a complement to those that are expected from the new facility. Time will tell.

2. At 101 floors and 492 meters (1614.2 feet), Shanghai WFC is one of the two tallest buildings in the world, and a major new landmark in a city known for gaudy landmarks. It was at first referred to as Shanghai Hills, but the brand moniker did not fit the Yangtze-Huangpu lowlands, and the name was changed. Also changed was the building's appearance. In addition to its spectacular height, the building is distinguished by a large rectangular opening at the uppermost portion of the building, an opening that the Mori Building Company website describes as symbolizing China's "new window on the world." The original design called for a large circular opening instead of the quadrilateral; it was nixed by Chinese authorities and widely declaimed in China as a sneaky representation of the Japanese flag. Not only would it be seen high in the skyline, but there was also an accusation that it would cast a flaglike shadow on Chinese soil. Despite

explanations by the architectural firm in charge of the design, Kohn Pedersen Fox, that the circle was actually a traditional Chinese way to represent sky (and that it also represented a Chinese moon), construction of the Shanghai World Financial Center was not allowed to proceed smoothly until the switch was made to a quadrilateral. Now, funsters like to point out that the building looks like a long and sleek bottle opener.

3. Quoted in the *Honolulu Advertiser*, December 24, 2002. This is the same article by Yuri Kageyama (2002) that I describe in chapter 5.

4. Two of the most detailed and best illustrated publications in this genre about the new face of Roppongi, useful even for people with little or no reading knowledge in Japanese are PIA Roppongi Convenient Book published June 10, 2003; and a special issue of the periodical *Machi-Gurashi* (vol. 27, dated December 1, 2006), entitled "Next Tokyo" and focusing on what's new in Roppongi and its next-door neighbors Nogizaka and Akasaka.

5. That exhibit featured fantastic room-sized models of Tokyo's desired peer cities: Paris, London, Frankfurt, Berlin, Chicago, New York City, and Shanghai. There were also maps of these cities, posters, photographs, and other displays. As the climax, under the heading "Tokyo Rising," the best project of all was introduced, Roppongi Hills.

6. I identify this establishment by name base because it is mentioned below in the context of a *Times* (London) newspaper article about it in which it is clearly identified.

7. There are discrepancies between the population estimates given here and the population numbers given in table 1.2 in chapter 1. The numbers that I gave earlier are from official statistics. However, many people choose to be counted by the census not where they live in the city but in their old hometowns instead or in other places where they might have a residence.

8. There is conflicting information about the design of the garden in Mori Building Company sources. The garden is attributed to Pearson in "Gardens," Mori Living, Mori Building Company, http://www.moriliving.com/en/estate/services/gardens.html.

9. There are other Maman sculptures by the same artist, the most prominent of which stands outside the National Gallery of Canada in Ottawa.

10. I do not know of any specific data or count that has been made along these lines. However, that there is a mix of ethnic groups living among the Japanese-majority population in the six buildings of the Roppongi Hills residential zone, becomes quickly evident with casual observation in the field.

11. The cause of death remains unexplained. However, there is no connection between the death of Mac Barry and Roppongi Hills, as far as I know, and the demonstration was at Roppongi Hills only because of the project's visibility.

12. I did not see any fish in the pond when I tried to track this down on a December day but was told at an information kiosk that the space fish were not dead, only asleep for the winter.

13. *Metropolis* 641 (July 7, 2006): 03.

14. Six elevators stopped running because of the earthquake centered two hundred kilometers away in Niigata, with passengers being in trapped in two of them.

Other elevators in city also reported problems, but only these elevators became headline news.

15. I love reading this kind of text; it's fun. The quotation is from Tokyo Midtown's website: "About Tokyo Midtown," http://www.tokyo-midtown.com/en/about/index .html.

16. Burberry is so popular in Japan as a design for handbags, scarves, jackets, women's skirts, and so many other clothing items and accessories that, I suppose, it makes sense that Japanese capital's largest single commercial complex should have the Burberry look. I've never actually heard this subject discussed or read about in print, but I doubt that I am the only person who has had such thoughts.

17. I have no information that the "Heartlands" in Tokyo Midtown has fallen on hard times, as has the one in Roppongi Hills, except for a personal sense that those places seem a bit quieter than they used to be.

CHAPTER SEVEN *Roppongi Reflections*

1. There are numerous reviews in various newspapers and magazines and online. For a start, see Eubank 2010.

2. The other two characteristics of the new city as expressed by Sorkin were "obsession with security" and an architecture of "simulations." As mentioned in chapter 6, both are also characteristic of the New Roppongi.

GLOSSARY OF JAPANESE TERMS

afta-no-machi   The "city of after," referring to Roppongi picking up business late at night after bars and restaurants have closed in other entertainment districts

bakufu   The shōgun's government

banchi   A subdistrict of a chōme

bōryokudan   The official Japanese term for organized crime groups, the *yakuza*

bōtaiho   Short form for the name the laws that have been enacted to control the activities of the *bōryokudan*

chirashi   Advertising leaflets, sometimes handed out, sometimes affixed to surfaces; see *pinku chirashi* below

chōme   A district of a city, part of a ward

daimyō   Feudal or territorial lords in Edo whose estates in the city were in the *yamanote* district, including in what is now Roppongi

dohan   A compensated date between a hostess and a client, often for dinner; afterward they both go to the club where the hostess works

dokken kokka   Japanese term for what is referred to here as the Japanese construction state

dōri   Street or avenue

Edo   The historic name of Tokyo until 1868

freeter (also *furita*)   Free-roaming part-time worker

fūzoku   Term referring to the prostitution and sex industry of Japan

279

fūzokueigyoho	Laws that govern "public morals" with respect to business activities
gaijin	Foreigner; a casual-language word, perhaps a bit impolite
gaikokujin	A more polite version of *gaijin*; a person from a foreign country
geisha	A category of professional female entertainers in Japan with skills in traditional Japanese arts such as classic music and dance
ginbura	Strolling in Ginza on the part of *mo-bo* and *mo-ga*
hanamachi	A word meaning "flower towns"; it refers to the traditional spatial and occupational organization of the world of Japanese geishas
heitai machi	"Soldiers' town"
izakaya	A type of Japanese food and drinking establishment that is especially popular for after-work gatherings
jiageya	A shady person who assembles land parcels for developers, often through intimidation of reluctant sellers
jō	Castle, as in *Edojō*, which means Edo Castle
jōka machi	A castle town
kanbu	A "director" in Japan's *yakuza*
karaoke	Popular recreational activity involving singing along with friends into a microphone to prerecorded music and accompanying video; Roppongi has many *karaoke* establishments for nighttime enjoyment
kissaten	A Japanese-style coffee shop; such establishments typically also serve food, especially breakfast for commuters on their way to work
kōsaten	Street intersection or crossing
koteishisan	Tax on land ownings
ku	Ward

kuromaku	Behind-the-scenes power broker
machi	A town or district
manshon	A condominium apartment, from the word *mansion*
meishi	Business card or calling card
mizu shobai	Translated as "water trade," a euphemism for the night-time pleasures industry
mo-bo	Fashion-conscious "modern boys" who were seen in Ginza in the Meiji Period
mo-ga	Fashion-conscious "modern girls" who were seen in Ginza in the Meiji Period
pan-pan girls	A term that U.S. soldiers used during the occupation to refer to Japanese prostitutes
pinku chirashi	Small stickers affixed to telephone booths, utility poles, and other surfaces that advertise "pink" (i.e., sexual) commercial services
Roppongi zoku	The "Roppongi tribe"; people who hang out in Roppongi
sakariba	Nightlife district; a place with many bars and restaurants for after-work enjoyment
sake	An alcoholic beverage made from rice
sangokujin	Person or persons from a "third country," a derogatory term for Chinese and Koreans in Japan
sentō	A public bath
shitamachi	The "low city"; the historic plebian neighborhoods at low elevation near Tokyo Bay and Tokyo's rivers
shōgun	Supreme ruler of Japan in historic times
shōtenkai	Shopkeepers' or merchants' association
shōchū	A type of Japanese distilled alcoholic beverage
sumō	A traditional Japanese sport sometimes referred to as Japanese wrestling

tanbo	Paddy rice field
Tōkyō-to	Tokyo Prefecture or Tokyo Metropolis, the administrative unit that is Tokyo and that contains what was once the City of Tokyo
yakuza	Japanese gangsters
yamanote	The "high city"; higher-status neighborhoods on hillier terrain to the north and west of Edo Castle; also the name of a prominent commuter rail line that loops around the center of Tokyo.

REFERENCES

Adelstein, Jake. 2009. *Tokyo Vice: An American Reporter on the Police Beat in Japan.* New York: Pantheon.

Allinson, G. D. 1979. *Suburban Tokyo: A Comparative Study in Politics and Social Change.* Berkeley: University of California Press.

———. 1984. "Japanese Urban Society in Its Cultural Context." In *The City in Cultural Context*, ed. J. A. Agnew, J. Mercer, and D. E. Sopher, 163–85. Boston: Allen and Unwin.

Allison, Anne. 1994. *Nightwork: Sexuality, Pleasure and Corporate Masculinity in a Tokyo Hostess Club.* Chicago: University of Chicago Press.

Anderson, Elijah. 1990. *Streetwise: Race, Class, and Change in an Urban Community.* Chicago: University of Chicago Press.

———. 2003. *A Place on the Corner: A Study of Black Street Corner Men.* 2nd ed. Chicago: University of Chicago Press.

"Artelligent City." 2004 (March). Special issue, *Visual Architecture* 40 (305).

Arudou, Debito. 2004. *Japanese Only: The Otaru Hot Springs Case and Racial Discrimination in Japan.* Tokyo: Akashi Shoten.

———. 2007. "*Gaijin Hanzai* Magazine and Hate Speech in Japan: The Newfound Power of Japan's International Residents. *Asia-Pacific Journal: Japan Focus.* http://www.japanfocus.org/-Arudou-Debito/2386.

Arudou, Debito, and Akira Higuchi. 2008. *Handbook for Newcomers, Immigrants and Migrants to Japan.* Tokyo: Akashi Shoten.

Asakura, Takuya. 2000. "Defense Agency Undertakes Move to Ichigaya Site Today." *Japan Times*, April 26.

Ashihara, Yoshinobu. 1989. *The Hidden Order: Tokyo through the Twentieth Century.* Tokyo: Kodansha.

Ballescas, R. P. 1992. *Filipino Entertainers in Japan: An Introduction.* Quezon City: Foundation for Nationalist Studies.

Ballon, Robert J. 1969. *The Japanese Employee.* Tokyo: Sophia University.

Barthes, Roland. 1982. *Empire of Signs.* London: Jonathan Cape.

Berman, Marshall. 2009. *On the Town: One Hundred Years of Spectacle on Times Square.* London: Verso.

Bestor, Theodore C. 1989. *Neighborhood Tokyo.* Stanford: Stanford University Press.

———. 2004. *Tsukiji: The Fish Market at the Center of the World.* Berkeley: University of California Press.

Booth, Alan. 1995. *Looking for the Lost: Journeys through a Vanishing Japan*. New York: Kodansha International.

Bornoff, Nicholas. 1991. *Pink Samurai: Love, Marriage and Sex in Contemporary Japan*. New York: Pocket Books.

Borovoy, Amy Beth. 2005. *The Too-Good Wife: Alcohol, Codependency and the Politics of Nurturance in Postwar Japan*. Berkeley: University of California Press.

Brasor, Philip. 2007. "'Africans in Japan' . . . Not from the Quill of Ishihara, Thank God." *Japan Times*, February 18.

Bremner, Brian. 2002. "Rethinking Tokyo: Can Minoru Mori Make It More Livable?" *Business Week*, November 4. http://www.businessweek.com/magazine/content/02_44/b3806076.htm.

Broadbent, Jeffrey. 2002. "Comment: The Institutional Roots of the Japanese Construction State." *Asien* 84 (July): 43–46.

Brown, Louise. 2005. *The Dancing Girls of Lahore: Selling Love and Saving Dreams in Pakistan's Pleasure District*. New York: Harper Perennial.

Bull, Brett. 2008. "Last Call for Kabukicho." *Metropolis* 769 (December 19):14, 15, 17.

Campbell, Clare. 2009. *Tokyo Hostess: Inside the Shocking World of Tokyo Nightclub Hostessing*. London: Little, Brown.

Chang, T. C., Shirlene Huang, and Victor R. Savage. 2004. "On the Waterfront: Globalization and Urbanization in Singapore." *Urban Geography* 25 (5):413–36.

Chaplin, Sarah. 2007. *Japanese Love Hotels: A Cultural History*. London: Routledge.

Chatterton, Paul, and Robert Hollands. 2003. *Urban Nightscapes: Youth Cultures, Pleasure Spaces and Corporate Power*. London: Routledge.

Clammer, John. 1997. *Contemporary Urban Japan: A Sociology of Consumption*. Oxford: Blackwell.

Coaldrake, William. 1996. *Architecture and Authority in Japan*. New York: Routledge, 1996).

Coelho, Paulo. 2003. *Eleven Minutes*. London: HarperCollins.

Cohen, Theodore. 1987. *Remaking Japan: The American Occupation as New Deal*. New York: Free Press.

Culp, Samantha. 2006. "Being a Hostess." *Asia Sentinel*, December 22, 9 pp. http://samanthaculp.com/2006/12/being-a-hostess-asia-sentinel-dec-2006.

"The Curse of Roppongi Hills." 2008. *Japan Probe*, October 1. http://www.japanprobe.com/?p=6420.

Curtis, William, J. R. 1986. *Le Corbusier: Ideas and Forms*. New York: Rizzoli International.

Cybriwsky, Roman. 1986. "The Fashioning of Gentrification in Philadelphia." *Urban Resources* 3 (3): 27–32, 53.

———. 1988. "Shibuya Center, Tokyo." *Geographical Review* 78 (1): 48–61.

———. 1998. *Tokyo: The Shogun's City at the Twenty-First Century*. Chichester, U.K.: Wiley.

———. 1999. "Changing Patterns of Urban Public Space: Observations and

Assessments from the Tokyo and New York Metropolitan Areas." *Cities: The International Journal of Urban Policy and Planning* 16 (4): 223–31.

Cybriwsky, Roman, David F. Ley, and John C. Western. 1986. "The Political and Social Construction of Revitalized Neighborhoods: Society Hill, Philadelphia and False Creek, Vancouver." In *Gentrification of the City*, ed. N. Smith and P. Williams, 92–120. London: George Allen and Unwin.

Dalby, Liza. 1983. *Geisha*. Berkeley: University of California Press.

Darling-Wolf, Fabienne. 2003. "Surviving Soccer Fever: 2002 World Cup Coverage and the (Re)Definition of Japanese Cultural Identity." Paper presented at the annual meeting of the International Communication Association, San Diego, Calif., May 27. Summary available at http://www.allacademic.com/meta/p111373_index.html.

Davidson, M., and L. Lees. 2005. "New-Built Gentrification and London's Riverside Renaissance." *Environment and Planning A* 37:1165–90.

Davis, Mike. 1992. *City of Quartz: Excavating the Future in Los Angeles*. New York: Vintage.

Davis, Mike, and Daniel Bertrand Monk, eds. 2007. *Evil Paradises: Dreamworlds of Neoliberlism*. New York: New Press, 2007.

De Becker, J. E. 2000. *The Nightless City; or, The History of the Yoshiwara Yūkwaku*. New York: ICG Muse (Orig. pub. 1899.)

Devlin, Mark. 2005. "The Wailing Wall: Mori and Ando Scar Omotesando." *Metropolis* 604 (October 21). http://archive.metropolis.co.jp/tokyo/604/lastword.asp.

Dong, Stella. 2000. *Shanghai: The Rise and Fall of a Decadent City*. New York: Perennial.

Dore, R. P. 1958. *City Life in Japan: A Study of a Tokyo Ward*. Berkeley: University of California Press.

Dougill, John. 2006. *Kyoto: A Cultural History* (Oxford, Oxford University Press.

Dower, John W. 1999. *Embracing Defeat: Japan in the Wake of World War II*. New York: Norton.

Duncan, James S. 2004. *The City as Text: The Politics of Landscape Interpretation in the Kandyan Kingdom*. Cambridge: Cambridge University Press.

Eliot, Marc. 2001. *Down 42nd Street: Sex, Money, Culture, and Politics at the Crossroads of the World*. New York. Warner Books.

Emerson, Ivy. 2007. "Confessions of a Hostess." *Japan Times*, May 8.

Enbutsu, Sumiko. 1993. *Old Tokyo: Walks in the City of the Shogun*. Rutland, Vt.: Charles E. Tuttle.

English, T. J. 2007. *Havana Nocturne: How the Mob Owned Cuba . . . and Then Lost It to the Revolution*. New York: Harper.

Eubank, Donald. 2010. "'Roppongi Crossing' May Be Better When Crowded." *Japan Times*, April 9.

Feldman, Stéphanie C. n.d. "Roppongi Hills: Globalization of the New Tokyo Landscape." Unpublished draft of research in progress (approximately 2006).

"Fetus in Bottle Found in Roppongi Hills." 2005. *Mainichi Daily News*, February 21.

Field, Andrew David. 2010. *Shanghai's Dancing World: Cabaret Culture and Urban Politics, 1919–1954.* Hong Kong: Chinese University Press.

Fishman, Robert. 1977. *Urban Utopias in the Twentieth Century.* Cambridge, Mass.: MIT Press.

Ford, Larry, R. 1994. *Cities and Buildings: Skyscrapers, Skid Rows, and Suburbs.* Baltimore: Johns Hopkins University Press.

"Foreigner Crime File." 2007. Flickr, February 13. http://www.flickr.com/photos/ultraneo/sets/72157594531953574/.

"Foreigner Injured by Sword in Roppongi Fight." Crisscross News Japan, September 8, 2005. http://www.crisscross.com.jp/news/348439.

Fowler, Edward. 1996. *San'ya Blues: Laboring Life in Contemporary Tokyo.* Ithaca: Cornell University Press.

"French Outraged by Tokyo Governor." 2005. BBC News, July 13. http://news.bbc.co.uk/2/hi/europe/4678209.stm.

Fujita, Kuniko. 2003. "Neo-Industrial Tokyo: Urban Development and Globalisation in Japan's State-Centered Developmental Capitalism." *Urban Studies* 40 (2): 249–81.

Gans, Herbert J. 1962. *The Urban Villagers: Group and Class in the Life of Italian-Americans.* New York: Free Press.

Gerster, Robin. 1999. *Legless in Ginza: Orientating Japan.* Carlton South: Melbourne University Press.

Gill, Tom. 2001. *Men of Uncertainty: The Social Organization of Day Laborers in Contemporary Japan.* Albany: State University of New York Press.

Godoy, Tiffany, and Ivan Vartanian. 2007. *Style Deficit Disorder: Harajuku Street Fashion—Tokyo.* Tokyo: Goliga Books.

Gordenker, Alice. 2002. "Furigan Fears Prompt School Safety Drills." *Japan Times*, June 14.

Grazian, David. 2008. *On the Make: The Hustle of Urban Nightlife.* Chicago: University of Chicago Press.

Greenfield, Karl Taro. 1994. *Speed Tribes: Days and Nights with Japan's Next Generation.* New York: Harper Perennial.

Grunebaum, Dan. 2008. "Last Call: After 17 Years, Legendary Club Closes Its Doors." *Metropolis* 741 (June 6): 16–17.

Guillain, Robert. 1981. *I Saw Tokyo Burning: An Eyewitness Narrative from Pearl Harbor to Hiroshima.* Trans. William Byron. Garden City, N.Y.: Doubleday.

Hadfield, Phil. 2006. *Bar Wars: Contesting the Night in Contemporary British Cities.* Oxford: Oxford University Press.

Hane, M. 1982. *Peasants, Rebels and Outcastes: The Underside of Modern Japan.* New York: Pantheon Books.

Hayakawa, K., and Y. Hirayama. 1991. "The Impact of the Minkatsu Policy on Japanese Housing and Land Use." *Environment and Planning D* 9 (1): 151–64.

Hill, Peter B. E. 2003. *The Japanese Mafia: Yakuza, Law and the State.* Oxford: Oxford University Press.

Ishihara, Shintarō. 1991. *The Japan That Can Say No.* Trans. Frank Baldwin. New York: Simon and Schuster.

Ito, Teruhiko. 2003. *Roppongi roku-chome zanei.* Tokyo: Bee Books.

Japan: An Illustrated Encyclopedia. 1993. Vols. 1–2. Tokyo: Kodansha.

"Japan Threatened by China, Its Own Timidity: Ishihara." 2007. Bloomberg, February 9. http://www.bloomberg.com/apps/news?pid=newsarchive&sid=aqkKn5G.sOhk.

Jenks, Charles. 1973. *Le Corbusier and the Tragic View of Architecture.* London: Allen Lane.

Jinnai, Hidenobu. 1988. *Ethnic Tokyo.* Tokyo: Process Architecture 72.

———. 1995. *Tokyo: A Spatial Anthropology.* Berkeley: University of California Press.

Kageyama, Yuri. 2002. "Tokyo Complex Targeting Rich." *Honolulu Advertiser,* December 24. http://the.honoluluadvertiser.com/article/2002/Dec/24/bz/bz08a/html.

Kami, Ryosuke. 1992. *Tokyo Sights and Insights: Exploring the City's Back Streets.* Rutland, Vt.: Charles E. Tuttle.

Kamiya, Setsuko. 2003. "There's a Green Revolution on High." *Japan Times,* May 18.

Kamiyama, Masuo. 2005. "Japan Becoming 'Paradise' for Growing Numbers of Nigerians." *Mainichi Daily News,* December 17. http://mdn.mainichi-msn.co.jp.

Kanazawa, Mari. 2008. "Lehman Brothers Is Sacrificed of Roppongi Hills?" Watashi to Tokyo, September 30. http://smt.blogs.com/mari_diary/2008/09/lehman-brothers.html.

Kane, Tim. 2006. "Global U.S. Troop Deployment, 1950–2005." The Heritage Foundation, Center for Data Analysis Report, #06-02, May 24. http://www.heritage.org/research/nationalsecurity/cda06-02.cfm.

Kaplan, David E., and Alec Dubro. 2003. *Yakuza: Japan's Criminal Underworld.* Berkeley: University of California Press.

Kawabata, Yasunari. 2005. *The Scarlet Gang of Asakusa.* Trans. by Alisa Freedman. Berkeley: University of California Press.

Keet, Philomena, and illus. Yuri Manabe. 2007. *The Tokyo Look Book.* Tokyo: Kodansha International.

Kelling, George H., and Catherine Coles. 1996. *Fixing Broken Windows: Restoring Order and Reducing Crime in Our Communities.* New York: Martin Kessler Books.

Kern Leslie. 2007. "Reshaping the Boundaries of Public and Private Life: Gender, Condominium Development, and the Neoliberalization of Urban Living." *Urban Geography* 82 (7): 657–80.

Kerr, Alex. 1996. *Lost Japan.* Footscray, Australia: Lonely Planet.

———. 2001. *Dogs and Demons: Tales from the Dark Side of Japan.* New York: Hill and Wang.

"Kids Harvest Rice from Roppongi Hills Roof." 2005. *Japan Times,* September 20.

Kingston, Jeffrey. 2001. *Japan in Transformation: 1952–2000.* Essex: Longman/Pearson Education.

———. 2004. *Japan's Quiet Transformation: Social Change and Civil Society in the Twenty-First Century*. London: Routledge/Curzon.

Kiritani, Elizabeth. 1995. *Vanishing Japan: Traditions, Crafts and Culture*. Rutland, Vt.: Charles E. Tuttle.

Knight, Kathryn. 2007. "He Is Immoral and Appalling: Lucie Blackman's Mother Slams Her Ex-Husband." MailOnline, April 23. http://www.dailymail.co.uk/femail/ article-450018/.

Knox, Paul L., ed. 1993. *The Restless Urban Landscape*. Englewood Cliffs, N.J.: Prentice-Hall.

Kohama, Hirohisa. 2007. *Industrial Development in Postwar Japan*. London: Routledge.

Koike, A. 2005a. "Roppongi Marks 60th Anniversary of End of wwii." *Kyodo News International*, January 19.

———. 2005b. "Tokyo Olympics Sparked Changes in Roppongi." *Kyodo News International*, January 20.

Komai, Hiroshi. 2001. *Foreign Migrants in Contemporary Japan*. Melbourne: Trans Pacific Press.

Kosugi, Reiko. 2006. "Youth Employment and Japan's Economic Recovery: 'Freeters' and 'NEETs.'" *Asia-Pacific Journal: Japan Focus*, May 11. http://www.japanfocus.org/ -Kosugi-Reiko/2022.

Kumazawa, Makoto. 1996. *Portraits of the Japanese Workplace: Labor Movements, Workers, and Managers*. Boulder, Colo.: Westview Press.

Lee, C., and G. De Vos. 1983. *Koreans in Japan: Ethnic Conflict and Accommodation*. Berkeley: University of California Press.

Lewis, Leo. 2005. "Monuments to Ugliness and the Triumph of Cash over Culture." *Times Online*, December 31. http://www.timesonline.co.uk/tol/news/world/asia/ article783848.ece.

———. 2008. "Sayonara to the Western Playboys." *Times* (London), November 13, 6.

Lewis, Peirce F. 2003. *New Orleans: The Making of an Urban Landscape*. Santa Fe: Center for American Places.

Ley, David. 1974. *The Black Inner City as Frontier Outpost: Images and Behavior of a Philadelphia Neighborhood*. Washington, D.C.: Association of American Geographers.

Liddell, C. B. 2007. "Kurokawa Art Center." *Architecture Week*, April 4, D1.

Liebow, Elliot. 1967. *Tally's Corner: A Study of Negro Streetcorner Men*. Boston: Little, Brown.

Longstreet S., and E. Longstreet. 1988. *Yoshiwara: The Pleasure Quarters of Old Tokyo*. Rutland, Vt.: Yenbooks.

Machimura, Takashi. 1992. "The Urban Restructuring Process in Tokyo in the 1980s: Transforming Tokyo into a World City." *International Journal of Urban and Regional Research* 16 (1): 114–28.

———. 1994. *The Structural Change of a Global City: Urban Restructuring in Tokyo*. Tokyo: University of Tokyo Press.

———. 1997. "Building a Capital for Emperor and Enterprise: The Changing Urban Meaning of Central Tokyo." *Culture and the City in East Asia*, 151–66. Oxford: Clarendon Press.

———. 2000. "Local Settlement Pattern of Foreign Workers in Greater Tokyo: Growing Diversity and Its Consequences." In *Japan and Global Migration: Foreign Workers and the Advent of a Multicultural Society,* ed. M. Douglas and G. S. Roberts, 176–95. London: Routledge.

———. 2003. "Neo-Industrial Tokyo: Urban Development and Globalisation in Japan's State-Centered Developmental Capitalism." *Urban Studies* 40 (2): 249–81.

Macias, Patrick, and Izumi Evans. 2007. *Japanese Schoolgirl Inferno: Tokyo Teen Fashion Subculture Handbook*. San Francisco: Chronicle Books.

Malbon, Ben. 1999. *Clubbing: Dancing, Ecstasy, Vitality*. London: Routledge.

"Man Arrested after Cop Fires Warning Shot." 2009. *Daily Yomiuri*, January 1, p. 2.

"Man Cleared over Death of Lucie." 2007. BBC News, April 24. http://news.bbc.co .uk/2/hi/uk_news/6241831.stm.

Marcuse, Peter, and Ronald van Kempen, eds. 2000. *Globalizing Cities: A New Spatial Order?* Oxford: Blackwell.

Matsuba, Kazukiyo. 2004. "Roppongi Hills' International Cultural Strategy." *Visual Architecture* 40 (305; March): 32–33.

McCormack, Gavan. 1996. The Emptiness of Japanese Affluence. Armonk, N.Y.: M. E. Sharpe.

McGee, John. 2003. "Akira Yamaguchi Exhibition." *Metropolis* 480. http://metropolis .co.jp/tokyo/480/art.asp.

McLelland, Mark. 2005. *Queer Japan from the Pacific War to the Internet Age*. Lanham, Md.: Rowman and Littlefield.

———. 2006. "Japan's Original 'Gay Boom.'" In *Popular Culture, Globalization and Japan*, ed. Matthew Allen and Rumi Sakamoto, 158–73. London: Routledge.

McLelland, Mark, Katsuhiko Suganuma, and James Welker, eds. 2007. *Queer Voices from Japan: First-Person Narratives from Japan's Sexual Minorities*. Lanham, Md.: Lexington Books.

Milne, Dave. 2002. "Alcohol Consumption in Japan: Different Culture, Different Rules." *Canadian Medical Association Journal* 167 (4; August).

Minato Ward Creative Arts Council Executive Committee. 2007. *Minato Ward: A Story of My Town and I (Minato-ku: Watashi to machi no monogatari).* 2 vols. Tokyo: Sanshu-sha.

Minato Ward School Board. 2007. *Supplement: Photographs of Minato Ward 3 (Azabu District: Azabu, Roppongi . . .).* Part 3. Tokyo: Sanshu-sha.

Mishima, Yukio. 1996. *Patriotism*. Trans. G. W. Sargent. New York: New Direction Books. (Orig. pub. 1952.)

Mitsui Fudōsan Co., Ltd. 2007. *Tokyo Midtown*. Tokyo: Nobuyuki Yoshida.

Miyazaki, Manabu. 2005. *Toppamono: Outlaw. Radical. Suspect. My Life in Japan's Underworld*. Tokyo: Kotan.

Mori, Minoru (producer). 2003. *The Global City (Roppongi Hills Opening Exhibition)*. Tokyo: Mori Building Co., Ltd.

Mori, Minoru, Hiroo Yamagata, and Bruce Mau. 2001. *New Tokyo Life Style Think Zone*. Tokyo: Mori Building Co.

Mori Building Company. 2007. *Mori Building*. Tokyo: Mori Building Co.

———. 2008. "Roppongi Hills: Art and Cultural Facilities." http://www.mori.co.jp/en/ projects/roppongi/art_cultural.html.

———. n.d. "Message from the President. http://www.mori.co.jp/en/company/ about_us/message/.

Mori Building Company and Mori Art Museum. 2004. *Art, Design and the City: Roppongi Hills Public Art Project 1*. Tokyo: Mori Building Co.

Mori Living. n.d. "Roppongi Hills Residences." http://www.moriliving.com/en/ residence/66/.

Morita, Toyoko. 2003. "Iranian Immigrant Workers in Japan and Their Networks." In *Global Japan: The Experience of Japan's New Immigrant and Overseas Communities*, ed. R. Goodman, C. Peach, A. Takenaka, and P. White, 159–64. London: Routledge Curzon.

Moriyama, Tae. 1993. *Tokyo Adventures: Glimpses of the City in Bygone Eras*. Tokyo: Shufunotomo.

Murakami Wood, David Lyon, and Kiyoshi Abe. 2007. "Surveillance in Urban Japan: A Critical Introduction." *Urban Studies* 44 (3): 551–86.

Naito, Akira. 2003. *Edo: The City That Became Tokyo*. Tokyo: Kodansha.

Nakamura, Takafusa. 1995. *The Postwar Japanese Economy: Its Development and Structure, 1937–1994*. Tokyo: University of Tokyo Press.

Nanjo, Fumio, Asako Ogita, and Kayoko Machino, eds. 2004. *Art, Design and the City: Roppongi Hills Public Art Project 1*. Tokyo: Mori Art Museum.

Nibayashi, Maki. 1999. "Stop the Music." *Metropolis* 296. http://metropolis.co.jp/ tokyofeaturestoriesarchive299/296/tokyofeaturestoriesinc.htm.

Nijman, Jan. 1999. "Cultural Globalization and the Identity of Place: The Reconstruction of Amsterdam." *Ecumene* 6 (1999): 146–64.

Noblestone, Josh. 2004. "Law and Order." *Metropolis* 543. http://archive.metropolis .co.jp/tokyo/543/feature.asp.

Noguchi, Sharon. 2006. "Hard Work, Furtive Living: Illegal Immigrants in Japan." *Yale Global* (Yale Center for the Study of Globalization), March 2.

Norrie, Justin. 2007. "A Tale of Rape, Murder and a Japanese Playboy." *Age*, April 21. http://www.theage.com.au/news/world/a-tale-of-rape-murder-and-a-japanese -playboy/2007/04/20/1176697090797.html.

Olds, Kris. 1995. "Globalization and the Production of New Urban Spaces: Pacific Rim Megastructure Projects in the Late 20th Century." *Environment and Planning A* 17:1714–43.

Onishi, Norimitsu. 2005. "Japan, Easygoing till Now, Plans Sex Traffic Crackdown."

New York Times, February 16. http://www.nytimes.com/2005/02/16/international/asia/16japan.html.

Osnos, Evan. 2009. "The Promised Land: Guangzhou's Canaan Market and the Rise of an African Merchant Class." *New Yorker*, February 9 and 16, 50–55.

Otake, Tomoe. 2005. "Go! Go! Kingyo!" *Japan Times*, February 13.

Perin, Constance. 1977. *Everything in Its Place: Social Order and Land Use in America.* Princeton: Princeton University Press, 1977.

"Police, Immigration Launch Joint 'Gaijin Hostess Hunt' in Kinshichō, Ikebukuro." 2007. *Japan Today*, July 18. Available at Arudou Debito/Dave Aldwinckle's Home Page, http://archive.japantoday.com/jp/kuchikomi/475e.

Pons, Philippe. 1984. "Shinjuku, Le Kaléidoscope Babylonien." *Autrement: Des Villes Nommes Tokyo, Paris*, September, 32–39.

Popham, Peter. 1985. *Tokyo: The City at the End of the World.* Tokyo: Kodansha International.

Reichl, Alexander J. 1999. *Reconstructing Times Square: Politics and Culture in Urban Development.* Lawrence: University of Kansas Press.

Relph, E. C. 1987. *The Modern Urban Landscape.* Baltimore: Johns Hopkins University Press.

Richie, Donald. 1999. *Tokyo.* London: Reaktion Books.

———. 2003. *The Image Factory: Fads and Fashions in Japan.* London: Reaktion Books.

Roa, Richard. 2004. *American Maverick in Japan: The Rick Roa Story as Told to Tony Teora.* New York: iUniverse.

Robertson, Jennifer. 1991. *Native and Newcomer: Making and Remaking a Japanese City.* Berkeley: University of California Press.

"Roho, Hakurozan Test Positive for Marijuana." 2008. *Japan Times*, September 3. http://search.japantimes.co.jp/cgi-bin/ss20080903a1.html.

Ryang, Sonia. 2003. "The Great Kanto Earthquake and the Massacre of Koreans in 1923: Notes on Japan's Modern National Sovereignty." *Anthropological Quarterly* 76 (4): 731–48.

Sagalyn, Lynn B. 2001. *Times Square Roulette: Remaking the City Icon.* Cambridge, Mass.: MIT Press.

Schreiber, Mark. 2002. "See You at Almond: Where Roppongi's Boogie Nights Begin." *Japan Times*, June 2.

Schreiber, Mark, et al., eds. 2007. *Tabloid Tokyo 2.* Tokyo: Kodansha International.

Seidensticker, Edward. 1983. *Low City, High City: Tokyo from Edo to the Earthquake.* New York: Charles E. Tuttle.

———. 1990. *Tokyo Rising: The City since the Great Earthquake.* Tokyo: Chares E. Tuttle.

Seigle-Segawa, C. 1993. *Yoshiwara: The Glittering World of the Japanese Courtesan.* Honolulu: University of Hawaii Press.

Serenyi, Peter, ed. 1975. *Le Corbusier in Perspective.* Englewood Cliffs, N.J.: Prentice Hall.

Shillony, Ben-Ami. 1973. *Revolt in Japan: The Young Officers and the February 26, 1936 Incident*. Princeton: Princeton University Press.

Shinoyama, Kishin. 2006. *Roppongi Hills X Kishin Shinoyama*. Tokyo: Gentosha.

Silverberg, Miriam. 2006. *Erotic Grotesque Nonsense: The Mass Culture of Japanese Modern Times*. Berkeley: University of California Press.

Smith, Neil. 1996. *The New Urban Frontier: Gentrification and the Revanchist City*. New York: Routledge.

Smith, Neil, and Peter Williams, eds. 1986. *Gentrification of the City*. Boston: Allen and Unwin.

"Sommerset Roppongi, Tokyo." N.d. http://www.somerset.com/en/japan/tokyo/somerset_roppongi/gallery.html.

Sorensen, André. 2001. "Subcenters and Satellite Cities: Tokyo's 20th Century Experience of Planned Polycentrism." *International Journal of Planning Studies*, 6 (1): 9–32.

———. 2002. *The Making of Urban Japan: Cities and Planning from Edo to the Twenty-First Century*. London: Routledge.

———. 2003. "Building World City Tokyo: Globalization and Conflict over Urban Space." *Annals of Regional Science* 37 (3): 519–31.

———. 2010. "Urban Renaissance as Intensification: Building Regulation and the Rescaling of Place Governance in Tokyo's High-Rise Manshon Boom." *Urban Studies* 47 (3): 556–83.

Sorkin, Michael, ed. 1992. *Variations on a Theme Park: The New American City and the End of Public Space*. New York: Hill and Wang, 1992.

Spielvogel, Laura. 2003. *Working Out in Japan: Shaping the Body in Tokyo Fitness Clubs*. Durham, N.C.: Duke University Press.

Sugi, Ryoji. 2005. *Roppongi Suimyaku* [Roppongi Water Stratum]. Tokyo: кк Best Book.

Suttles, Gerald D. 1968. *The Social Order of the Slum: Ethnicity and Territory in the Inner City*. Chicago: University of Chicago Press.

Takahara, Kanako. 2008. "Goodwill to Liquidate Temp Agency." *Japan Times*, June 26. http://search.japantimes.co.jp/cgi-bin/nb20080626a1.html.

Takemae, Eiji. 2002. *Inside GHQ: The Allied Occupation of Japan and Its Legacy*. Trans. Robert Ricketts and Sebastian Swann. New York: Continuum.

Takenaka, Aumi, and Mary Johnson Osirim. 2010. *Global Philadelphia: Immigrant Communities Old and New*. Philadelphia: Temple University Press.

Talani, Leila Simona. 2009. *From Egypt to Europe: Globalisation and Migration across the Mediterranean*. London: I. B. Tauris.

Tanaka, Chotoku. 2004. *Chotoku X Roppongi Hills*. Tokyo: Tokyo Kirarasha.

Taylor, William R., ed. 1991. *Inventing Times Square: Commerce and Culture at the Crossroads of the World*. Baltimore: Johns Hopkins University Press.

"10,000 Descendents of Outer Space Fish Move into Tokyo's Roppongi Hills." 2003. JPubb, July 30. http://www.jpubb.com/en/press/15533/.

Till, Karen E. 2005. *The New Berlin: Memory, Politics, Place*. Minneapolis: University of Minnesota Press.

Tokyo Statistical Yearbook, 2004. 2004. Tokyo: Tokyo Statistical Association.

U.S. Department of State. N.d. "Japan: Country Specific Information." http://travel .state.gov/travel/cis_pa_tw/cis/cis_1148.html.

Van Hook, H. 1989. "Prime Time in Kabuki-Chō." *Tokyo Journal* 9 (3): 4-9, 12-17.

"Wakakirin Admits, Denies Buying Dope from a Foreigner." 2009. *Daily Yomiuri*, February 2, p. 18.

Waley, Paul. 1984. *Tokyo Then and Now: An Explorer's Guide*. New York: Weatherhill.

———. 1990. "Tokyo's Long History of Pleasure Districts." *Japan Times*, March 25, 12.

———. 2000. "Tokyo: Patterns of Familiarity and Partitions of Difference." In *Globalizing Cities: A New Spatial Order?*, ed. P. Marcuse and R. van Kempen, 127–57. Oxford: Blackwell.

———. 2002. "Moving the Margins of Tokyo." *Urban Studies*, 39 (9): 1533–50.

———. 2007. "Tokyo-as-World-City: Reassessing the Role of Capital and the State in Urban Restructuring." *Urban Studies* 44 (8): 1465–90.

Western John C. 1981. *Outcast Cape Town*. Minneapolis: University of Minnesota Press.

———. 1992. *A Passage to England: Barbadian Londoners Speak of Home*. Minneapolis: University of Minnesota Press.

Whiting, Robert. 1999. *Tokyo Underworld: The Fast Times and Hard Life of an American Gangster in Japan*. New York: Vintage, 1999.

Whyte, William F. 1943. *Street Corner Society: The Social Structure of an Italian Slum*. Chicago: University of Chicago Press, 1943.

Wijers-Hasegawa, Yumi. 2002. "Hooligan Phobia Triggers Siege Mentality." *Japan Times*, May 31.

———. 2004. "Gang-Rape Ringleader Gets 14 Years." *Japan Times*, November 3.

Wills, Jane, Kavita Datta, Yara Evans, Joanna Herbert, Jon May, and Cathy McIlwaine. 2009. *Global Cities at Work: New Migrant Division of Labor*. London: Pluto Press.

Wilson, James Q., and George L. Kelling. 1982. "Broken Windows." *Atlantic Monthly* 249 (3): 29–38.

Wilson, Thomas M., ed. 2005. *Drinking Cultures: Alcohol and Identity*. Oxford: Berg.

"Women's Work and Japan's Hostess Culture." 2009. *New York Times*, August 12.

Woronoff, Jon. 1983. *Japan's Wasted Workers*. Totowa, N.J.: Allanheld, Osmun.

Worrall, Julian, and Erez Golani Solomon. 2010. *21st Century Tokyo: A Guide to Contemporary Architecture*. Tokyo: Kodansha.

Wright, Evan Alan. 2001. "Death of a Hostess." *Time Asia* 157 (19), May 14.

Wu, Fulong. 2000. "The Global and Local Dimensions of Place-Making: Remaking Shanghai as a World City." *Urban Studies* 37:1359–77.

Yamaguchi, Akira. 2004. *The Art of Akira Yamaguchi*. Tokyo: University of Tokyo Press.

Yamawaki, Keizo. 2000. "Foreign Workers in Japan: A Historical Perspective." In *Japan and Global Migration: Foreign Workers and the Advent of a Multicultural Society*, ed. M. Douglas and G. S. Roberts, 38–51. London: Routledge.

Zhargalant, R. 2005. "Yaponi oros, orosin yapon." *Mongol News Group*, July 24. http://www.mongolnews.mn/weekend.php?n=136.

Zielenziger, Michael. 2006. *Shutting Out the Sun: How Japan Created Its Own Lost Generation*. New York: Vintage Books.

INDEX

Academy Hills, 214
Adelstein, Jake, 165
"after clubs," 90
Akasaka, 2, 62; hostess clubs in, 54; mentioned, 48, 66, 90, 92, 106
Akihabara, 188, 275n14; mentioned, 40
alcohol consumption, 16, 103, 108–9, 121, 131, 176–77, 185; abstinence from, 140
Almond (coffee shop), 6, 14, 105–6, 222, 251, 261n2, 261n4; mentioned, 254
Amagi Building, 254
American Club, Tokyo, 38, 148
Ando Tadao, 45, 240
antismoking campaign, 182
Aoyama, 36, 45
Aoyama Cemetery, 71
ARK Hills, 48, 187, 204, 208–10; mentioned, 202
"Artelligent City," 214, 261
Asakusa, 51–53, 269n6; preservation of Japanese culture in, 262
Atago Green Hills, 204–5, 210, 247; mentioned, 43
Atlas Tower Roppongi, 244
Axall Roppongi, 245–46
Azabudai, 38, 81, 149
Azabu Hills, 43
Azabu Jūban, 254–55; public bath in, 255
Azabu Police Station, 16, 83, 176, 186, 188, 190

bar buildings, 122–24
bars, 21, 107–14; "dandy," 96; by ethnic identity, 115–16; Heartland, 217, 232; by music genre, 115; raids of, by police,

176–77; in Yokohama history, 69; mentioned, 200
beautification efforts in Roppongi, 183–87
Blackman, Lucie, 134, 166–69, 253, 273n3
black markets, 87
bubble economy, 1–2, 47–48, 94–95, 99; in Ginza, 54–55
"bubble gents," 94

Casablanca (hostess club), 166
CBD. *See* central business district
CCCP Girls (members' club), 111, 271n2
cemeteries, 77–78, 149
central business district (CBD), 31, 48, 54; expansion of, 46–48; mentioned, 56, 74, 78, 81, 198
Chianti (Italian restaurant), 90
citizens' security patrols, 181–83
commuters, 30–32, 40, 47, 57, 104, 106, 130; mentioned, 74
Conder, Josiah, 46, 70–71
construction state, 266; definition of, 3–4, 9–11; mentioned, 1, 70, 73
corporate offices in Roppongi, 66
Crazy Horse (supper club), 90
crime, 2–3, 152–61, 188; in Roppongi Hills, 229–32; scams, 160–61; mentioned, 28. *See also* human trafficking; murders
crows, 103–4; new tastes of, 243

daimyō estates, 3, 43, 46, 76, 77, 78, 79, 81, 247
dance curfew, 177, 194–95, 274n8
"dandy bars," 96
decentralization in Tokyo, 31

GEOGRAPHIES OF JUSTICE AND SOCIAL TRANSFORMATION

9 780820 338323